*The New Evangelical
Social Engagement*

W9-AUK-521

The New Evangelical Social Engagement

———◦◉◦———

Edited by

BRIAN STEENSLAND

PHILIP GOFF

OXFORD
UNIVERSITY PRESS

OXFORD
UNIVERSITY PRESS

Oxford University Press is a department of the University of Oxford.
It furthers the University's objective of excellence in research, scholarship,
and education by publishing worldwide.

Oxford   New York
Auckland   Cape Town   Dar es Salaam   Hong Kong   Karachi
Kuala Lumpur   Madrid   Melbourne   Mexico City   Nairobi
New Delhi   Shanghai   Taipei   Toronto

With offices in
Argentina   Austria   Brazil   Chile   Czech Republic   France   Greece
Guatemala   Hungary   Italy   Japan   Poland   Portugal   Singapore
South Korea   Switzerland   Thailand   Turkey   Ukraine   Vietnam

Oxford is a registered trademark of Oxford University Press
in the UK and certain other countries.

Published in the United States of America by
Oxford University Press
198 Madison Avenue, New York, NY 10016

© Oxford University Press 2014

All rights reserved. No part of this publication may be reproduced, stored in a
retrieval system, or transmitted, in any form or by any means, without the prior
permission in writing of Oxford University Press, or as expressly permitted by law,
by license, or under terms agreed with the appropriate reproduction rights organization.
Inquiries concerning reproduction outside the scope of the above should be sent to the Rights
Department, Oxford University Press, at the address above.

You must not circulate this work in any other form
and you must impose this same condition on any acquirer.

CIP data is on file at the Library of Congress

978-0-19-932953-3 (hardback)
978-0-19-932954-0 (paperback)

1 3 5 7 9 8 6 4 2
Printed in the United States of America
on acid-free paper

To
Robert Wuthnow
and
George Marsden

Contents

PART TWO: *Areas of Evangelical Social Engagement*

PART THREE: *Reflections on Evangelical Social Engagement*

Acknowledgments

THIS VOLUME BEGAN as a conversation between the editors. It seemed to us that things were happening within American evangelicalism that scholars had yet to sufficiently examine. Toward this end, we organized a conference in May 2012 that brought together an interdisciplinary group of scholars to discuss some of the facets of contemporary evangelicalism that constitute what we have called the new evangelical social engagement. In organizing the conference and bringing the conference papers to publication, we owe a number of people and organizations debts of gratitude that we are happy to acknowledge.

Foremost is our gratitude to the conference participants themselves, whose insightful papers, lively exchange of ideas, and timely cooperation made everything possible. For valuable input and support as we organized the conference, we thank Nancy Ammerman, Mark Chaves, Richard Flory, Rob Robinson, Ron Sider, Corwin Smidt, Christian Smith, and Bob Wuthnow. For providing financial resources, we gratefully acknowledge John Bodnar and the Institute for Advanced Study at Indiana University, David Zaret and the College of Arts and Sciences at Indiana University, and the Center for the Study of Religion and American Culture at Indiana University–Purdue University Indianapolis. Becky Vasko at the Center gave us expert assistance with handling conference logistics. Amanda Friesen, David Gushee, Amy Reynolds, John Schmalzbauer, Christian Smith, and Lawrence Snyder gave us valuable feedback on the introductory chapter. Jennifer Kash helped assemble the final manuscript. At Oxford University Press, we thank Cynthia Read for her early support for the project and Marcela Maxfield for handling the production logistics. Our final and most fundamental debts go to our families, who generously encouraged our work even as it stole time away from family life. Brian thanks Shana and his daughters, Minna and Maxine, who were both born after the inception of the project and bring him great joy. Philip thanks Kate, Ning, and CeCe, who are willing to let him hang out at conferences with smart people because he enjoys it and then comes home ready for fun.

As we worked together on this project, we repeatedly recognized the deep influence that two of our mentors have had both on our own intellectual outlooks and in their respective fields. It is with gratitude that we dedicate this volume to Robert Wuthnow and George Marsden.

Contributors

James S. Bielo is Lecturer in the Department of Anthropology at Miami University. He is the author of *Words upon the Word: An Ethnography of Evangelical Group Bible Study* (2009) and *Emerging Evangelicals: Faith, Modernity, and the Desire for Authenticity* (2011) and editor of *The Social Life of Scriptures: Cross-Cultural Perspectives on Biblicism* (2009).

Adriane Bilous is a PhD candidate in Sociology at Fordham University. Her areas of interest include the sociology of religion, faith-based social movements, and organizational strategies among faith-based political movements. Her dissertation explores the connections between religion, gender, geographical context, and activism among millennials.

Joel Carpenter is Professor of History and Director of the Nagel Institute for the Study of World Christianity at Calvin College. His best known book is *Revive Us Again: The Reawakening of American Fundamentalism* (1997), and his most recent one is an edited work, *Walking Together: Christian Thinking and Public Affairs in South Africa* (2012).

Omri Elisha is Assistant Professor of Anthropology at Queens College of the City University of New York. He is the author of *Moral Ambition: Mobilization and Social Outreach in Evangelical Megachurches* (2011).

Michael O. Emerson is the Allyn & Gladys Cline Professor of Sociology and Co-Director of the Kinder Institute for Urban Research at Rice University. He is the author of many research articles and a dozen books, including *Divided by Faith: Evangelical Religion and the Problem of Race in America* (2000) and, his most recent, *Transcending Racial Barriers* (with George Yancey, 2011) and *Blacks and Whites in Christian America* (with Jason Shelton, 2012), winner of the 2012 C. Calvin Smith Book Award from the Southern Conference of African American Studies.

Philip Goff is Director of the Center for the Study of Religion and American Culture and Professor of Religious Studies and American Studies at Indiana

University–Purdue University Indianapolis. His most recent book is *The Blackwell Companion to Religion in America* (2010). Since 2000, he has coedited *Religion and American Culture: A Journal of Interpretation.*

John C. Green is a Distinguished Professor of Political Science at the University of Akron and a Senior Research Advisor with the Pew Forum on Religion & Public Life. Best known for his research on American politics and religion, he is the author of *The Faith Factor: How Religion Influences American Elections* (2010) and coauthor of *The Diminishing Divide: Religion's Changing Role in American Politics* (2000).

Laurel Kearns is Associate Professor of Sociology of Religion and Environmental Studies at Drew Theological School. In addition to coediting *EcoSpirit: Religions and Philosophies for the Earth* (2007), she has contributed to volumes such as *The Blackwell Companion to Modern Theology, The Wiley-Blackwell Companion to Religion and Social Justice, The Oxford Handbook on Climate Change and Society,* and *Grounding Religion.*

Gerardo Marti is L. Richardson King Associate Professor of Sociology at Davidson College. He is author of *A Mosaic of Believers* (2005), *Hollywood Faith* (2008), and *Worship across the Racial Divide* (2012).

Stephen Offutt is Assistant Professor of Development Studies at Asbury Theological Seminary. He has an MA in International Relations from The Johns Hopkins University's School of Advanced International Studies (SAIS) and a PhD in Sociology from Boston University. Prior to his doctoral studies, he worked for five years in international relief and development, living in Southern Africa and Central America.

Amy Reynolds is Assistant Professor of Sociology at Wheaton College. Before going to Wheaton, she was a Visiting Fellow at Notre Dame's Kellogg Institute for International Studies. Amy's research and teaching interests include the sociology of religion, the international political economy, and the sociology of gender.

Will Samson is a PhD candidate in Sociology at University of Kentucky and Executive Director of the Seminary Stewardship Alliance, an educational nonprofit that develops environmental curricula for seminaries. He was previously appointed to the faculty of Georgetown College. His research focuses on politics, food and the environment, and the intersection of these issues with American evangelicalism.

John Schmalzbauer holds the Blanche Gorman Strong Chair in the Religious Studies Department at Missouri State University. A sociologist of religion, he is the author of *People of Faith: Religious Conviction in American Journalism and*

Higher Education (2003). He is completing a coauthored book on the return of religion on campus. He is coinvestigator on the National Study of Campus Ministries.

Glen Harold Stassen is Smedes Professor of Christian Ethics, Fuller Theological Seminary. He is the author of *A Thicker Jesus: Incarnational Discipleship in a Secular Age* (2012), *Living the Sermon on the Mount* (2006), and, with David Gushee, *Kingdom Ethics: Following Jesus in Contemporary Context* (2003) and editor of *Just Peacemaking: The New Paradigm for the Ethics of Peace and War* (2008).

Brian Steensland is Associate Professor of Sociology at Indiana University. He is the author of the award-winning book *The Failed Welfare Revolution* (2008). His coauthored article, "The Measure of American Religion," is widely cited in the social sciences.

David R. Swartz is Assistant Professor of History at Asbury University. He is the author of *Moral Minority: The Evangelical Left in an Age of Conservatism* (2012).

R. Stephen Warner is Professor of Sociology, Emeritus, at the University of Illinois at Chicago. His book, *New Wine in Old Wineskins: Evangelicals and Liberals in a Small-Town Church* (1988), received the Distinguished Book Award of the Society for the Scientific Study of Religion in 1989. He was elected president of the Society for the Scientific Study of Religion in 2005.

Daniel K. Williams is Associate Professor of History at the University of West Georgia and the author of *God's Own Party: The Making of the Christian Right* (2010).

Introduction

THE NEW EVANGELICAL SOCIAL ENGAGEMENT

Brian Steensland and Philip Goff

CONSIDER THE FOLLOWING scenes. A young Ohio couple from a middle-class background relocates to a struggling inner-city neighborhood. They open a coffee shop, hoping to create a public space that fosters relationships between students at the nearby college campus and poor neighborhood residents. In Central America, representatives of an international nonprofit organization help local farmers strengthen their export business by supplying them with essential financial and organizational resources and by backing the formation of a strong farmer's association. In Kentucky, members of an environmental advocacy group gather to participate in a rally protesting mountaintop removal mining in the Appalachians. Around a conference table, members of a committee hammer out the details of a major public statement on matters such as human rights, pandemic disease, racism, and illiteracy.

These are examples of contemporary evangelical social engagement. Evangelical Christians, who constitute about one-quarter of the nation's population, are increasingly involved with issues ranging from the environment, urban renewal, and homelessness in the United States to economic development, human trafficking, and HIV/AIDS at the international level.[1] This expansive range of social concerns is part of the "new" evangelicalism, a label that observers use to distinguish it from mainstream evangelicalism's social priorities over the past few decades. Evangelicals themselves are aware that change is afoot. Some welcome this broadened agenda as long overdue while others see it as a misguided (or worse) expression of the Christian message.

This trend has largely gone unrecognized outside the confines of evangelical media outlets and cultural trend spotters. The popular press has given it only limited attention, and then mainly due to its potential implications for electoral politics. In the public mind, evangelicalism carries a narrow range

•

of associations. Chief among them are combating abortion and same-sex marriage, enforcing the boundaries of Christian orthodoxy, and spreading the Christian gospel and bringing people to the faith.[2] Academic scholarship on contemporary evangelicals reflects these associations as well. It typically focuses on evangelical stances toward hot-button social issues related to sexuality, reproduction, and family structure, or on the close relationship between evangelicals and the Republican Party. To be sure, there are well-founded historical and contemporary reasons for scholars and the general public to view evangelicalism along these lines, not least of which are the strategies activists have used to politically mobilize evangelicals. But given the breadth of what is happening today, this narrow view risks freezing evangelicalism in time (notably the 1980s) rather than recognizing its continuing evolution.

This book offers one of the first scholarly research efforts to document the forefront of contemporary evangelical social engagement.[3] Based on original research, scholars from a range of disciplines examine key groups, significant issues, and emerging trends. The chapters provide a description of what evangelical social engagement looks like on the ground, examine factors that help account for the changes taking place, and look prospectively toward what the future might hold. Because journalists and evangelicals themselves have already introduced the term *new evangelicalism* into the cultural lexicon, we employ this term as well, both for ease of exposition and to contribute to the growing discussion about this phenomenon. But we also use this terminology with some reluctance. Today's new evangelicals are but the most recent iteration of evangelicalism's long-standing tendency to spin off its own renewal movements. Recognizing this in no way minimizes the importance of what is happening in the contemporary moment. Today's tumult and transformation are a part of evangelicalism's essence, and the new social engagement, many would argue, is central to its mission in the world. But our perspective casts a different light on what is "new" within evangelicalism. Compared to the 1980s, recent trends mark a notable departure. Compared to the 1880s, there is as much continuity as there is change.

So what is the new evangelical social engagement? Its boundaries are not sharply defined, and there is no single issue, demographic group, or organization that defines it, but there are central tendencies that give it coherence. As the term *new evangelicalism* suggests, the recent forms of engagement are in critical dialogue with the immediate past—namely, with the strains of mainstream evangelicalism that gave rise to the Moral Majority, the suburban megachurch movement and its ethos, and the close allegiance with the Republican Party. New evangelicals are broadly united by what they have reacted against. Yet there is a positive vision that replaces the older one. Contemporary evangelicals pursue an expanded range of social concerns that in their view better reflects the comprehensive vision of the Christian gospel. This is more than a simple numerical increase in agenda items. Evangelical engagement has increasingly prioritized aiding the disadvantaged and seeking the public good. This expanded range of concerns is complemented by a multifaceted social ethic that seeks to change social structures in addition to transforming individual lives and that is growing more comfortable with the aim of seeking justice. New theological perspectives undergird this contemporary social vision.

These changes can be seen in many places—among prominent evangelical organizations and opinion leaders, in Christian publishing, in evangelical public opinion, and among grassroots movements. The National Association of Evangelicals is generally seen as taking a turn toward the new evangelicalism with the 2004 publication of its major statement, *For the Health of the Nation: An Evangelical Call to Civic Responsibility*. Books like Timothy Keller's *Generous Justice* and Richard Stearns's *The Hole in Our Gospel* present strong arguments along these lines. A generational dimension is clearly seen in the writing of younger evangelicals, such as Jonathan Merritt's *A Faith of Our Own*. Single-issue advocacy groups, such as the Evangelical Environmental Network, have grown significant enough to generate organized opposition. Umbrella organizations like the New Evangelical Partnership for the Common Good advance numerous facets of the new evangelical agenda. Recent surveys show a significant basis in evangelical public opinion for these concerns.

Two movements among lay evangelicals also exhibit manifestations of the new evangelical engagement. The Emerging Church movement has sought to introduce new theological and ecclesiastical elements into mainstream Christianity. While the movement self-consciously aims to transcend particularistic religious traditions and labels, it has had its deepest impact on evangelicals. Ideas like the notion of being "missional" have influenced how many evangelical congregations engage the world around them. The New Monasticism is a movement that places social engagement at the heart of its ministry. The movement emphasizes living in community, a commitment to place, radical hospitality, and local outreach. Based on the attention garnered by some of the movement's leaders, the ethos of the New Monasticism extends well beyond the confines of New Monastic groups themselves.

So far we have offered only a brief sketch of contemporary evangelical social engagement. Before going further, we offer some broader context with a brief tour of American evangelicalism's history of activism. We then further elaborate on recent trends in evangelical engagement and sketch out some factors that help account for the changes taking place. We close with a few implications, such as why recent trends in evangelical engagement are likely to have a limited but nonetheless meaningful impact on partisan politics and how the changes taking place raise questions about the meanings associated with the term *evangelical*.

Evangelical Social Engagement in American History

Social activism has long been part of the evangelical tradition, even though its public manifestations have waxed and waned across eras. Against the backdrop of the last thirty years, recent trends in evangelical engagement are a marked departure from a public agenda focused on issues such as abortion, homosexuality, and family structure. They also diverge from the social quietism that characterized much of mid-twentieth-century evangelicalism. Yet contemporary trends are consonant with prominent evangelical reform movements of the nineteenth century and the voices of marginalized progressive evangelicals during the 1970s.

American evangelicalism finds its roots in the transatlantic spiritual revivals that marked the eighteenth century. The same may be said of evangelical social action, at least in its nascent forms that would come to influence so many nineteenth-century reform movements. Historian David Bebbington identified four defining markers of evangelicalism: biblicism, a focus on Christ's atoning sacrifice, conversion as a requirement for salvation, and activism—that is, the understanding that the gospel's truth must be expressed in effort.[4] One can discern two models for social activism growing in the ministries of the two English ministers who most influenced religion in America. George Whitefield, the young Anglican minister whose preaching tour was the eye of the revivalist storm in colonial America, called for individual voluntary efforts to address social problems. Whitefield did not simply visit cities to induce conversions through what he understood as a more biblically based gospel; he also was raising funds for an orphanage in Savannah, Georgia, where he had been assigned as parish priest. Meanwhile, John Wesley, who saw abusive slavery firsthand during his 1737 visit to the colonies, concluded that human bondage was "the execrable sum of all villainies." He called on his fellow Methodist ministers to push for abolition of the slave trade on both sides of the ocean, writing a popular short treatise on the topic in 1774. Preferring direct action by the state over exclusively voluntary effort to address social injustice, he remained in constant contact with the Abolition Committee of Parliament during the height of England's debates on slavery. Indeed, the last letter Wesley wrote before his death in 1791 was to William Wilberforce, the famous member of Parliament who finally secured abolition. This message of the need for salvation and the Christian's responsibility to help with social problems—either through individual effort or by influencing state action—marked the message of many evangelicals by century's end.

Like their European counterparts, evangelicals in the new United States were divided by theological differences, but both the Calvinist and the Methodist wings of evangelical Protestantism encouraged social activism for American believers. Among Calvinists, many followed the writings of New England minister Samuel Hopkins, who promoted "disinterested benevolence," a distinct move away from self-love and self-absorption toward self-denying service. This New Divinity movement was a departure from more traditional forms of Calvinism, emphasizing charitable action inspired by sympathy rather than downplaying human effort. Simultaneously, the quickly expanding Methodist movement preached the idea of perfectionism. This doctrine claimed that converted Christians were morally obligated to, and theoretically capable of, living lives of spiritual and social holiness. In this pursuit, Methodists took up the cause of a number of social injustices in the new nation, including slavery and prison reform. Despite theological differences among Calvinists and Methodists, the nineteenth century began with two distinct evangelical arguments—disinterested benevolence and perfectionism—for social engagement by believers.

The main drivers of evangelical social action in the nineteenth century were many nimble and highly creative parachurch organizations that gathered believers from various Protestant denominations.[5] Each organization addressed a particular social problem, although their membership and their means (persuasion and humanitarian aid efforts) often overlapped. These evangelical voluntary reform organizations, referred to as the "benevolent empire," became the primary engine for addressing social ills in the new republic. While some were created to persuade individuals to convert and thereby change their behavior (the American Bible Society, the American Sunday School Union, the American Tract Society, the American Temperance Society), others provided more tangible and direct relief to people as the nation's cities became overcrowded, industrial, dirty, and marked by intense poverty and crime.

Still other efforts went well beyond suasion or relief to bring about social reforms. They included the founding of direct aid societies and the use of political pressure to create or change existing laws. Activists outraged by the treatment of prisoners and the insane (who were generally treated as criminals) worked to change penal laws, found humane prisons, and create asylums for the mentally ill. Others were inspired by the plight of children in the harsh world of urban America. Evangelical activists were instrumental in founding orphanages and juvenile delinquent homes for thousands of urban children, often working with local government officials, thereby beginning the bureaucratization of humanitarian assistance.[6]

Over time, several key social and intellectual crises divided evangelicals over how they should address social problems. As the Civil War approached, some argued for radical state action in the form of abolition—a move others saw as contrary to the idea of converting individuals' hearts in order to bring lasting change to society. The publication of Darwin's *The Origin of Species* in 1859, which called into question literal readings of Genesis, followed by German higher criticism of the Bible, cast doubt on biblicism altogether for many. The broad evangelical coalition that had preached the primacy of biblical truth and the need for personal salvation found itself under pressure from the learned ranks of society. Meanwhile, beginning in the 1870s, immigration, urbanization, and industrialization challenged evangelicals' earlier dreams of creating the millennial kingdom. Many grew pessimistic about the intellectual and social climate and adopted a new stance toward their ministerial roles in the world. Rather than convert individuals in an effort to change society for the better, these so-called premillennialists put more effort into revivalism for the sake of converting people before Christ's return—the only event that could save humanity from its increasing sinfulness. This attitude stood in stark contrast to the developing liberal Protestantism that accepted the science of evolution and the higher criticism of the Bible, seeking to find middle ground between the truths of science and the truths of faith. For them, progressive social reform was not only important, it was required in order to build the kingdom of God.

It is important to note that no one owned the term *evangelical* up to this point. Throughout most of the nineteenth century, it was used broadly by most Protestant Christians who shared similar beliefs and engaged the developing American society. In his mid-century classic, *Religion in America*, clergyman Robert Baird applied the term to include virtually every Christian group except Roman Catholics, Unitarians, Universalists, Shakers, Swedenborgians, and Mormons. However, with the developing division in Protestantism caused by late-nineteenth-century modernity, *evangelical*—which means "marked by the gospel"—became a contested term and remained so into the early twentieth century. During this period, there was considerable overlap between evangelism and social activist efforts. Many of those we think of as influenced by liberal Protestant theology were as concerned for evangelical, experiential conversion as they were with postmillennial social hopes. Walter Rauschenbusch, Josiah Strong, and George Herron were deeply influenced by pietistic, evangelical religious experience and built theological systems that tied social reform to individual conversion.[7] As late as 1912, Rauschenbusch was arguing for a "liberal evangelicalism." Meanwhile, alongside proponents of the Social Gospel, with their millennial urgency to create in society the kingdom of God, labored many conservative Protestants working in the streets to convert sinners and ameliorate the social effects of sin. Revivalist and faith healer A. B. Simpson founded soup kitchens and homes for prostitutes in Hell's Kitchen, the filthiest section of Manhattan during the 1880s. Other examples abound of theologically conservative Protestants who differed with the Social Gospel's liberal Protestant millennialism but worked beside them to relieve the suffering of urban America during its messiest period—William and Catherine Booth's Salvation Army, to name but one.

By the early twentieth century, the previous century's evangelical coalition in all its variety had disintegrated under the pressure of intellectual differences and social changes. Was Christianity about social and moral progress or about preserving ancient truths? The public battles among Protestants in the 1920s, epitomized by the Scopes trial in 1925, forced Christians who sought both conversion and social reform to choose sides. By the 1930s, liberal Protestantism was pitted against fundamentalism, with little talk of social activism among the latter for fear it would be confused with the work of its enemy. The result was not simply silence but active avoidance of anything beyond very local, often congregational, social action among evangelicals throughout the mid-twentieth century. This was not a period of inactivity for fundamentalists, who built an infrastructure of colleges and magazines, but it was a massive turning inward, away from the social problems they ceded to the more ecumenical mainline denominations who formed the Federal (later National) Council of Churches.

The seeds of modern engagement can be seen in the founding of the National Association of Evangelicals (NAE) during World War II. While still convinced that society is best changed by converting individuals, a group of evangelical leaders sought to distinguish themselves from separatist fundamentalists by pursuing social engagement through intellectual production, which they viewed as the other primary way to transform culture. Led by such thinkers as Carl F. H. Henry and Harold John Ockenga and such doers as J. Elwin Wright, the NAE sought to offer the world a body of Christian intellectual thought alongside popular revivals. As Joel Carpenter discusses in greater detail in his chapter, these mid-century "new evangelicals," as they came to call themselves, while still tethered to conservative Protestant reactions against unions and government programs as agents of social reform, engaged American culture with ideas in ways their more fundamentalist fathers had rejected. They produced scholarly books that sought to place orthodox Protestantism amid other philosophical discussions of the day, set up offices in Washington, D.C., to influence federal broadcasting policy on radio access (which at that time allowed free time only to Catholics, Jews, and mainline Protestants), and held national rallies to spread the word of their new cooperative ventures. While the evangelical coalition was a broad one, including Reformed Calvinists, Wesleyan holiness, and ethnic Protestants from northern Europe, it did not include African Americans. Early attempts to include black evangelicals, with whom they shared many concerns, were thwarted by neo-evangelicals' generally negative response to black civil rights activism, which gained steam just as the NAE began to flex its newfound muscles.[8]

In the 1970s, a new generation of so-called young evangelicals arose, one that turned their intellectual work toward an internal critique of evangelicalism's narrow view of social engagement.[9] Inspired by the work of evangelical historian Timothy L. Smith, whose work on the nineteenth century detailed the deep connections between revivalism and social reform, some began to call for a return to social activism.[10] Evangelical sociologist David O. Moberg took up Smith's call. In his 1972 book, *The Great Reversal: Reconciling Evangelism and Social Concern*, Moberg reopened the seemingly settled question for evangelicals over whether the gospel is primarily personal or social. Seeing the inadequacies of each view in isolation, and questioning whether either was fully scriptural, he rejected what he viewed as a false choice: "There was a time when evangelicals had a balanced position that gave proper attention to both evangelism and social concern, but a great reversal early in this century led to a lopsided emphasis upon evangelism and omission of most aspects of social involvement.... Evangelism can be a motive for social welfare ... and can play an important role in social action to change society and deal with social sin."[11]

Within a year, a group of like-minded evangelicals met in Chicago. Responding to the conservatism of mid-century neo-evangelicalism, particularly its quietism on social problems, this new generation came together ready to work in the world toward social reform.[12] The "Chicago Declaration of Evangelical Social Action" bemoaned the conditions that allowed racism, materialism, hunger, blind patriotism, and women's inequality to flourish. They called for "total discipleship," affirming that "God lays total claim upon the lives of his people. We cannot, therefore, separate our lives from the situation in which God has placed us in the United States and the world."[13] This call for social action influenced such existing institutions as InterVarsity Christian Fellowship and both political parties, where evangelicals pushed to end the war in Vietnam. The roster of those attending the Chicago conference became a veritable who's who of progressive evangelicalism, spinning a web of interconnected parachurch organizations that addressed social ills. Jim Wallis's Sojourners and Ronald Sider's Evangelicals for Social Action are but two of the more well-known and influential, both of which have served as important conduits and points of continuity between the new evangelicalism then and now. In his chapter, Carpenter argues that there is little in today's new evangelicalism that was not anticipated by Chicago Declaration–era evangelicals.

While evangelicals of this stripe faithfully advanced their agenda over the following decades, an ascendant Religious Right soon eclipsed their activities and became the face of evangelicalism in public life during the Reagan years and beyond. Pursuing a political agenda centered on ending legal abortion, combating civil rights for gays and lesbians, bolstering traditional family structure, and keeping Christian influences in public schools, the movement forged a close alliance with the Republican Party by embracing direct political activism in ways that distinguished them from their neo-evangelical forebears.[14] The legacy of this social agenda and the evangelical embrace of partisan politics serve as the immediate backdrop for the contemporary moment.

The Contemporary Evangelical Landscape

Compared to the evangelical mainstream in recent decades, today's evangelical social engagement stands apart. It extends beyond the intellectual engagement that characterized the neo-evangelicals of the 1950s and 1960s. It has clear affinities with the Chicago Declaration–era evangelicalism of the 1970s but has moved beyond the voices of an embattled minority. Compared to the era of the Religious Right's dominance, which is the most salient and immediate reference point, the new evangelical social agenda is broader and more holistic. If Moberg's "great reversal" is taken as an important turning point in evangelical social engagement a century ago, what's happened at the dawn of the twenty-first-century could be characterized as a "great return" or "great expansion." The current breadth and prominence of social concerns is more akin to the social impulses of nineteenth-century evangelicalism. Beyond this breadth, two other features characterize the new evangelicalism: an expanded vision for pursuing social change and a desire to rehabilitate the evangelical identity.

Pursuit of a broadened social agenda is percolating throughout evangelicalism, not solely among opinion leaders. But a good place to see it is at the top. The National Association of Evangelicals is the most prominent evangelical parachurch organization in the country. It represents 45,000 local churches across forty denominations and has long defined the evangelical mainstream. In 2004, the NAE released a major statement on social engagement called *For the Health of the Nation: An Evangelical Call to Civic Responsibility*.[15] The document contended that "faithful evangelical civic engagement must champion a biblically-balanced agenda."[16] It advocated active public involvement in seven broad areas: religious freedom, family life, the sanctity of life, justice and compassion for the poor and vulnerable, human rights, peace and the reduction of violence, and the environment. The statement received unanimous support from the NAE's board of directors. This support, however, did not dissuade politically conservative evangelical leaders from sharply criticizing this new set of commitments, particularly regarding environmental concern and campaigns against torture.[17] The NAE's statement was not an isolated case. In 2008, a different group released *An Evangelical Manifesto*. The drafting committee comprised leading evangelicals, such as Richard Mouw, the president of Fuller Theological Seminary, and David Neff, the editor-in-chief of *Christianity Today*, and its charter signatories included acclaimed pastors, academics, activists, and nonprofit leaders. As with the NAE's statement, the *Manifesto* recommitted to existing evangelical engagement on abortion and homosexuality. But it called for a broader and more comprehensive public vision that represented the entirety of the Christian Gospels: "We must follow the model of Jesus, the Prince of Peace, engaging the global giants of conflict, racism, corruption, poverty, pandemic diseases, illiteracy, ignorance, and spiritual emptiness, by promoting reconciliation, encouraging ethical servant leadership, assisting the poor, caring for the sick, and educating the next generation."[18]

While both of these statements came from national opinion leaders, there are grounds for support among laypeople for this expanded social agenda. John C. Green's chapter gauges evangelical attitudes toward issues that are part of the new and old social engagement. He finds substantial ideological diversity within evangelicalism. Around half of evangelicals hold attitudes that favor positions taken by new evangelicals on issues like the environment, peacemaking, and the role of government. This support comes from two different clusters within evangelicalism. Evangelicals on the political left support the new agenda while also holding more liberal attitudes on abortion and homosexuality that run at odds with the older agenda. "Populist" evangelicals, on the other hand, straddle the new and old agendas, holding attitudes that support both. This populist cluster is notable for a few reasons. It is the largest faction within evangelicalism and has recently been growing. Populists exhibit high levels of religiosity that are comparable to the levels found on the evangelical right, indicating that support for the new agenda is not associated with a weak commitment to evangelical theology or practices. And populists, unlike the evangelical left or right, have attitudes that do not fit well within the existing platforms of either major political party.

The breadth of recent evangelical engagement can be seen in a number of places. One of the most prominent, and contentious, of the new public priorities has been the environment. In her chapter, Laurel Kearns outlines the growth of environmental concern within evangelicalism since the 1970s. While engagement has spanned issues ranging from habitat conservation to human population growth, a central focus has been global warming. Under the banner of "creation care," a number of evangelical organizations brought attention to the dangers of global warming in the 1990s and 2000s, setting off controversy and contention in evangelical circles. This contention included a countermovement to downplay environmental threats and reframe the policy debate by emphasizing stewardship and human dominion.[19] Another growing priority is race relations. This includes efforts ranging from interracial alliances to address endemic inner-city problems to programs designed to foster multiculturalism and racial reconciliation within congregations.[20] In their chapter, Gerardo Marti and Michael O. Emerson discuss the rise of this attention to race relations and document some of the ironies of congregational efforts in particular. In attempting to heal the wounds of race relations, many white evangelicals downplay some of its most salient and injurious dynamics, thus ignoring the very sources of continuing racial division they seek to heal. David R. Swartz's chapter highlights the changing nature of evangelical engagement at the international level. Given their historic commitment to global missions, anticommunism, and religious liberty, internationalism itself is nothing new for evangelicals. Yet today they are increasingly turning their efforts to basic issues of economic development and to human rights concerns of all types, such as sex trafficking, slavery, and torture. Among other things, this shift reflects the influence of international evangelicals on their American counterparts.

A different way of describing what is new in evangelical engagement involves not *what* issues evangelicals seek to engage, but *how* they engage them. Greater breadth can be seen here, too. Evangelicals articulate an expanded sociological vision, one that recognizes the need for a multifaceted approach to social transformation and exhibits a greater openness to seeking social justice. Twentieth-century evangelicalism has historically been characterized by its individualistic approach to social change. As Christian Smith has described it, evangelicals subscribe to a "personal influence strategy" of social transformation. If enough people are converted to Christ, society will change for the better.[21] While an evangelical minority has seen this as theologically narrow and practically inadequate, and held a more multifaceted vision for social transformation, this broader view has moved toward the mainstream. The NAE's *For the Health of the Nation* captures this vision well: "From the Bible, experience, and social analysis, we learn that social problems arise and can be substantially corrected by both personal decisions and structural changes. On one hand, personal sinful choices contribute significantly to destructive social problems, and personal conversion through faith in Christ can transform broken persons into wholesome productive citizens. On the other hand, unjust systems can also help create social problems, and wise structural change can improve society. Thus Christian civic engagement must seek to transform both individuals and institutions."[22] The reference to "unjust systems" signals a further shift within evangelicalism: a shift toward greater emphasis on seeking social justice. The link between systemic thinking and justice is a close one, as justice often refers to whether a society fairly distributes and protects the benefits of social membership. Pursuing justice has a strong biblical basis, but one more central within mainline Protestantism and the African American church. The dominant strains of twentieth-century evangelicalism, in contrast, held that in the New Testament, love supplanted justice.[23]

A number of our chapters explore these new approaches to engagement. Amy Reynolds and Stephen Offutt discuss the steady rise of systemic thinking in evangelical efforts to combat global poverty. Concern about the poor is itself nothing new for evangelicals. What has changed is the way this concern is manifested. Nongovernmental organizations have slowly shifted their efforts from short-term relief to long-term development strategies. This reflects a transition to thinking about the features of social systems that create and perpetuate poverty. Indicating a further shift toward structural reform, policy advocacy has begun to gain a place in the international antipoverty portfolio, though these efforts remain limited so far. John Schmalzbauer looks at campus ministry and collegiate evangelicals through the lens of InterVarsity's large Urbana student missions conference. While evangelization to non-Christians remains the highest priority at InterVarsity, social justice concerns are prominent and growing. Among the most prevalent issues at the 2006 conference, for instance, were poverty, the environment, and racial reconciliation. Each is part of the new evangelical agenda, and each was viewed as a matter of social justice. Similar concerns and perspectives are seen elsewhere, such as in the list of books published by InterVarsity Press. Notable is Schmalzbauer's insight that while concerns about social justice are prominent among collegiate evangelicals and in campus ministries, "justice" is a multifaceted concept that means different things to different people. Given these differences, the resonance of justice language is even more striking for what it reveals about contemporary trends.

Evolving perspectives on social change have been attended by new emphases in theology and Christian ethics. Scholars of American evangelicalism have long noted that the withdrawal of evangelicals from social engagement in the early twentieth century coincided with the growth of premillennial dispensationalism: a biblical interpretation of the end times that sees the increasing depravity of human history ushering in the return of Christ. Based on this eschatological view, evangelical leaders emphasized the urgent nature of the saving souls and the hopelessness of social reform. Different streams of theology inform many of today's new evangelicals. Particularly prominent among those who are part of self-conscious renewal movements is "kingdom theology," which in contrast to premillennialism situates the present as a liminal yet hopeful moment in God's ultimate plan. The kingdom of God is simultaneously "already" and "not yet." In this formulation, Christians are called to work toward a better world today in ways that reflect God's immanence and prefigure the perfection to come upon Christ's return.[24] This eschatological perspective aligns with new lines of thinking in Christian ethics. In this volume, Glen Harold Stassen draws out connections between contemporary social engagement and new emphases on the teachings of Jesus. The new evangelicalism foregrounds Jesus' teaching about the kingdom of God, particularly in the Sermon on the Mount. In doing so, it situates the teachings of Jesus within the historical concerns of first-century Galilee and Israel and recognizes the influence of the Hebrew Scriptures, particularly the prophet Isaiah. Stassen also highlights a rapprochement between the Anabaptist and Calvinist traditions in some quarters that moves Jesus' views of God's kingdom to the center of activism.

Two social movements—the Emerging Church and the New Monasticism—exemplify many of the trends we have highlighted. Emerging evangelicalism began in the mid-1990s as a loose network of leaders, writings, and conferences. The movement aimed at Christian renewal through a trenchant though ultimately sympathetic critique of mainstream evangelicalism that encompassed theology, ecclesiology, liturgy, social ethic, and politics.[25] While self-conscious use of the "emerging" label has varied widely (and seems likely to wane), many evangelical congregations, especially those that attract a younger demographic, have been informed by the movement's critique of the past and its vision for the future. James S. Bielo's chapter offers an overview of the Emerging Church movement and presents a fine-grained look at an emerging community in Cincinnati, Ohio. He shows how members see social engagement as inextricably linked to spiritual formation and how this reflects a refusal to draw sharp boundaries between personal and public transformation.

The New Monasticism is a sympathetic movement, sharing much of the Emerging Church's critique of mainstream evangelicalism. What distinguishes the New Monastics is a commitment to live in intentional community with one another, abide by the "twelve marks" of New Monasticism, show hospitality to the poor and the marginalized, and engage in contemplative spiritual practices. A 2005 cover story on the movement in *Christianity Today* closed by suggesting that its cultural impact on contemporary Christianity would extend far beyond the followers actually living in New Monastic communities. Will Samson's chapter describes the broad contours of the movement, shows how the twelve marks of New Monasticism are lived out in one community in Kentucky, and highlights how the nature of the movement can be understood as a reaction to trends within American evangelicalism.

A thread that connects the Emerging Church and New Monastic movements, but that extends far beyond it, is concern with the evangelical identity and what it has come to represent. Some Christians distance themselves from the label; others want to rehabilitate it. A best-selling book by two young evangelicals addresses this directly. It begins, "Christianity has an image problem."[26] Another group of evangelicals has adopted the alternative moniker "red-letter Christians," a reference to seeking to live in accordance with the words of Jesus (printed in red ink in many Bibles).[27] The first third of the 2008 *Evangelical Manifesto* was devoted to defining evangelicalism and distinguishing its theological commitments from political ones. Even some of the contributors to a recently published "new evangelical manifesto" questioned whether to apply the evangelical label to themselves.[28] In her chapter, Adriane Bilous shows this dynamic at work among female evangelical activists in New York City. In a typical response to questions about the congregation they attend, Bilous hears "It's evangelical, but not *that* type of evangelical." These women's struggles to locate a resonant label for themselves are inextricably linked to developing a self-identity that is distinct from evangelicalism's existing associations, especially those having to do with gender-based expectations and appropriate outlets for activism.

What Accounts for the New Evangelicalism?

The new trends in evangelical social engagement beg the question of why they have arisen. This question is broader than any of the individual chapters in the book. But when the chapters are taken collectively and coupled with historical perspective, we can see three broad dynamics that help account for evangelicalism's recent trajectory.

The first is generational change within evangelicalism itself. This is not simply about the passage of time. It refers to the active response by new evangelical opinion leaders to the dominant ethos in American evangelicalism and to the more slowly changing demographic makeup of rank-and-file evangelicals. The two major waves of late-twentieth-century evangelical change were efforts to correct the perceived shortcomings of the day. The neo-evangelicals of the 1940s sought to distinguish themselves from the stridency and separatism of the so-called fundamentalists who came before them. They sought intellectual respectability and active engagement with American culture. In light of the moral crisis they saw besetting the nation in the late 1970s, the leaders of the Religious Right were not satisfied to rely on revivalism and personal conversion strategies to redeem society, so they entered more actively into public debate and electoral politics than their predecessors. Similar dynamics are at work today. Prominent within the cadre of new evangelical voices are some shared sentiments—that evangelicalism's public witness has been overly focused on a limited range of issues to the detriment of other social concerns, that American evangelicalism has become too closely tied to the politics of the Republican Party, and that evangelical theology has offered a limited vision of social engagement and the public good. New evangelicals, as part of a loose movement, have both advanced a new agenda and created space for sympathetic perspectives that were older but did not fit well in the mainstream.

There is another type of generational change happening among the laity: the shifting sociodemographic makeup of evangelicalism itself. During the rise of neo-evangelicalism in the years following World War II, evangelicals were more southern, more white, less educated, and less urban than the population at large. They were racially privileged but otherwise had the low-status characteristics often associated with the "disinherited." This demographic profile is changing. Evangelicals as a group are growing less distinct from other Americans. They are less likely to be white and southern and more likely to be better educated and urban.[29] As Michael Lindsay has documented, many have entered "the halls of power" and hold positions of influence in business, government, and entertainment.[30] These shifting demographics and professional trajectories mean new concerns and perspectives. Emblematic of this shift is Timothy Keller, head pastor of Redeemer Presbyterian Church in New York City. He has become a prominent evangelical voice by filling a growing need: ministering to evangelicals who are more urban, multiethnic, professional, and cosmopolitan in outlook.[31] That many of his books become best sellers indicates a wide audience, one that appears disposed toward many elements of the new evangelical agenda.

Beyond the changes happening within evangelicalism itself, a second factor shaping patterns of evangelical engagement is contemporary culture, which influences society at large. Historians have documented how evangelicalism has long been influenced by its cultural context.[32] In regard to contemporary evangelicalism, the focal points of the new social engagement reflect trends happening in America more broadly. While these trends are impacting the entirety of evangelicalism, one way of tracing them is to look at generational differences among evangelicals, since the younger cohort has come of age in a different cultural context than their parents and grandparents.[33] For instance, attention to environmental issues, specifically global warming, has grown in recent years. One of the clearest generational divides within evangelicalism is the younger generation's greater liberalism on environmental issues.[34] Consciousness-raising movements have heightened awareness of other issues as well, for instance, global inequalities, sex trafficking, and public health crises, such as the lack of clean water in Africa. There is a shortage of hard data on evangelical views of these types of concerns, but if they are similar to patterns of environmental attitudes, concern is more likely to be found among younger evangelicals.

At the same time that newer concerns have arisen among evangelicals, others have receded. Perhaps most significant is the rapidly increasing tolerance of homosexuality. Within the general public, for instance, rates of acceptance of same-sex marriage increased from 11 percent in 1988 to 46 percent in 2010, with pronounced differences across generations.[35] While acceptance among evangelicals is lower than among the general population at large, evangelical views have also shifted toward greater tolerance, also with significantly greater acceptance of gay marriage among the younger cohorts.[36] Robert Wuthnow correctly cautions that young evangelicals' greater willingness to extend civil liberties to gays and lesbians does not necessarily mean moral acceptance of homosexuality.[37] Nevertheless, this pronounced trend toward tolerance, if not acceptance, means that one of the central issues in evangelical activism for the past thirty years has lost its motivating force, making room for other issues to come to the fore.

While slow-moving social trends have carried many evangelicals, much like the population at large, along in their currents, key events also mark inflection points where the potential of these trends is crystallized. Perhaps most significant for the rise of a self-conscious new evangelical movement was President George W. Bush's declaration of war on Iraq in 2003. Much as the Vietnam War played a key role in galvanizing the young evangelicals of the 1970s, the Iraq War and its consequences presented a clarifying moment for many evangelicals of the contemporary generation.[38] As Will Samson points out in his chapter, the leaders and early participants in the New Monastic movement uniformly shared a strong critique of the ease with which the evangelical mainstream uncritically embraced the war. This critique extended beyond the realm of the youthful, urban counterculture. Megachurch pastor Greg Boyd lost many members of his congregation when he renounced the alliance between evangelicals and Republican foreign policy hawks and has gone on to develop a sympathetic following among new evangelicals with his writing about the public witness of evangelicalism.[39] Like many others, David Gushee, another new evangelical leader, responded with grave concerns about torture and other human rights abuses in the years following the war's onset.[40] These various responses to the war among New Monastics and other evangelicals do not mean that the new evangelical engagement is necessarily pacifist. The point is that for many evangelicals antiwar sentiments and human rights concerns played an important role in clarifying broader questions about the appropriate relationship between religion and partisan politics, and where evangelicalism's social priorities should properly be focused.

The third factor influencing recent evangelical social engagement involves changes within the American religious field—specifically the declining relevance of the boundary between evangelical Protestantism and mainline Protestantism and the influence of Roman Catholic social teaching on evangelical activism. For the last century, a core element of evangelical identity has been the distinction that evangelicals draw between themselves and mainline Protestants. This distinction has been based on theology, social ethics, and politics.[41] On the issue of social engagement specifically, this was explicit. For instance, *Christianity Today* published a major statement on evangelical social action in 1965 that drew a sustained contrast to the social reformism of the mainline churches on issues such as civil rights and antipoverty legislation. Foremost among the article's "controlling convictions" was that "the Christian Church's distinctive dynamic for social transformation is personal regeneration by the Holy Spirit" in contrast to the mainline's reliance on "political and sociological forces."[42]

Yet mainline Protestantism has been in a state of steady decline since the 1960s. The number of Americans claiming affiliation with mainline Protestant denominations declined from 27 percent in the 1972 to 14 percent in 2008.[43] The declining cultural significance of the mainline is just as pronounced.[44] Because the shape of evangelicalism has been so influenced by efforts to maintain its boundary with mainline Protestantism, the decline of the mainline holds significant implications for evangelical social engagement. Prohibitions against social action and reformism, which have long been associated with religious liberalism, lose their force without the associated threat of the mainline's abandonment of the Christian gospel. Furthermore, the expanded array of social concerns among new evangelicals fills the absence left by a diminished mainline public presence.

At the same time that the diminishing boundary between evangelical and mainline Protestantism has created space for evangelical engagement, closer relations with Catholics provide theological ballast and practical exemplars for evangelicalism's expanded public witness. By now it is well known that the relationship between evangelicals and Catholics began to warm during the 1970s, as they sought common cause on issues related to abortion, sexuality, family structure, and religious liberty.[45] Beyond constituting a mere political alliance, this relationship fostered theological dialogue and influence. For instance, as Daniel K. Williams discusses in his chapter, Catholic social teaching on the sanctity of life had a strong impact on evangelicals' evolving stance toward abortion in the decade following the passage of *Roe v. Wade.* Today we see similar patterns of borrowing and influence playing out with the new evangelical social agenda. Omri Elisha's chapter highlights the congruence between Catholic social teaching and evangelical perspectives on social welfare and discusses some of the ways Catholic influence has been transmitted within evangelical communities. Other chapters highlight similar influences in such areas as social justice and human rights.

More generally, we see three strands of Catholic social ethics in evangelical engagement today.[46] The first is the search for the common good, which has long been an express priority of Catholic public engagement. Among evangelicals, we see recognition of the importance of the public good entering the evangelical lexicon in book titles, organizational names, and programmatic public statements. Second, and closely related, is the commitment to address a comprehensive range of social issues. In practice, Catholic activism has been uneven in this regard over the years, but Catholic social teaching manifests a deep historical commitment to applying the lessons of the Christian gospel to a broad range of issues. Third is the recognition of Christianity's disestablishment within a pluralistic liberal democracy.[47] The move toward a post-Christian missional stance among evangelicals recognizes one's own society as a mission field because Christianity does not provide the foundation for the social order.

In sum, three broad factors help account for the contours of contemporary evangelical social engagement. Each is consistent with patterns throughout the history of evangelicalism, and each works in conjunction with the others. Generational change has been perennial within evangelicalism. Yet its specific characteristics at a given time vary according to the elements of contemporary culture that provide the concerns, values, and strategies that are selectively absorbed and appropriated by new waves of evangelicalism. The fact that in recent years much of the new evangelical engagement has focused on issues that were formerly the province of religious liberals is a partial consequence of the declining significance of the boundary between evangelical and mainline

Protestantism, a boundary that defined the limits of appropriate evangelical concern for most of the twentieth century.

Implications for the Public Sphere

Given the change afoot within American evangelicalism, what are some of its implications? The material covered in the chapters hold insights for politics, civic engagement, and American religion, a few of which we draw out here. Beyond these, an open question remains concerning the extent to which the new evangelicalism will endure in the absence of the types of institutionalization that have characterized past waves of evangelical transformation.

The close relationship between contemporary evangelicalism and the Republican Party is well known. By the close of the twentieth century, evangelicals had become the most important constituency in the Republican electoral coalition. Between 1980 and 2012, evangelical support for Republican presidential candidates ranged between 65 and 79 percent.[48] There was an uptick in support for the Democratic candidate, Barack Obama, in 2008. Yet according to the authors of an in-depth analysis of that election, evangelical support for Republican candidates remains steady. Given the enthusiasm for Obama among the millennial generation and the speculation at the time about the swing toward the Democrats among young evangelicals, it is especially notable that evangelicals under forty-five years old were less likely to vote for Obama than older evangelicals.[49] Four years later, evangelical support for the Republican presidential candidate, Mitt Romney, rose to its highest level in forty years.

A few of our chapters shed light on the future of evangelical politics. John C. Green highlights both the potential and challenge of transforming evangelical electoral patterns. The evangelical right is currently much better integrated into regularized politics than the evangelical center or evangelical left. This is based on some shared ideological affinities. But it is also the product of a thirty-year mobilization effort by the Religious Right. Seen in this light, new movements can potentially shift the political winds because there are also shared ideological affinities between evangelicals and the political left. In fact, the largest cluster of evangelicals—the populists—straddles the partisan divide in their social commitments and thus presents an opportunity for new mobilization. (As one indication, they shifted toward Obama in 2008.) Yet doing so requires overcoming conflicts of different types that populists could have on the left and the right. On the left, one highly salient issue in this regard is abortion. Daniel K. Williams's chapter describes the forty-year trajectory of what he calls prolife progressives: evangelicals who hold liberal-leaning views on issues relating to economics, the environment, and human rights but who also have strongly held antiabortion views. If the Democratic Party maintains its unalloyed commitment to abortion rights, evangelicals who fit this profile will struggle to find a place within the Democratic tent. Many evangelicals may not seek to engage the political parties at all. As R. Stephen Warner observes in his chapter, an important thing that separates the Chicago Declaration–era evangelicalism of the 1970s and today's new evangelicalism is the rise of the Religious Right. A lesson many evangelicals have drawn from the Religious Right era—a lesson signaled by book titles such as *Evangelical ≠ Republican . . . or Democrat* and *Jesus for President*—is the importance of maintaining a vision of the common good grounded in Christian scripture and not party platforms. A concern for observers like Warner is that partisan dealignment will lead to political disengagement altogether, a situation that would not bode well for the democratic process.

Taken together, our chapters indicate that the turn toward new forms of social engagement among many evangelicals will not translate into a realignment toward the Democratic Party. Even a realignment among a portion of evangelicals would be a longer process; the analogous shift toward political conservatism and the Republican Party predated the Reagan era by decades and involved change on the part of Republicans as well as evangelicals.[50] Instead, the groundwork for more local political engagement and case-by-case electoral choice at the national level appears to be underway. Here there is potential for partisan movement. Evangelicalism is becoming more diverse demographically and ideologically. Democrats may be able to appeal to a significant segment of evangelicals if they are attentive to the political cross-pressures many evangelicals feel on the issues and are respectful of the role faith plays in shaping their views of public policy.

These political patterns are closely related to civic engagement. On its face, there appears to be common ground for activism and advocacy between new evangelicals and religious and secular liberals. They share concerns about a range of social issues. Yet there are two potentially limiting factors on the evangelical side. First, evangelicalism has long thrived upon the distinctions evangelicals draw between themselves and "the world."[51] This trait manifests itself in civic engagement, where evangelicals have not been inclined to enter into coalition with ecumenical, interfaith, or secular civic groups, even when they share common concerns and goals. The imperative to maintain boundary distinction outweighs the value of coalition work.[52] Evangelicals instead establish their own organizations. The emphasis on seeking the common good among new evangelical leaders provides an opportunity to see if this changes. A second factor concerns evangelical views of government—specifically, how readily evangelicals may accept the government's role in addressing social problems in the future. New evangelicals appear more comfortable with social reform than evangelicals have been for the last century. Attendant with this is recognition of systemic sources of disadvantage and suffering, which means seeking to transform unjust social structures in addition to transforming spiritual lives. Among political liberals today, structural change typically implies support for governmental action of some type. Yet this is not the case for evangelicals, who are embedded in the most robust sector of civil society in contemporary America and have a reflex toward voluntaristic collective action rather than turning to government.[53] So even broad agreement among new evangelicals and potential coalition partners on the need for structural change will still require deliberation on the best balance between civic and governmental action.

While the implications of the new evangelicalism for politics and civic engagement are significant, the most direct implication concerns American religious life itself. What does *evangelicalism* mean today? This question is a hardy perennial, both within evangelicalism and for the scholars who study it, but a number of contemporary social dynamics make it more salient than ever. The decline of mainline Protestantism means that evangelicals are losing a foil against which to define themselves. Ever since the split between so-called modernists and fundamentalists during the Social Gospel era, theology and social ethics have been bundled together by the "two-party" system of white Protestantism. Theological modernism and social reformism were viewed as the province of the mainline, while theological orthodoxy, evangelization, and personal piety were evangelical terrain. This bundling meant that an impulse toward social activism was typically seen as a marker of weak commitment to orthodoxy. Today's expansion of social engagement among doctrinally conservative Protestants means that scholars and evangelicals themselves need to recognize the unbundling of theological commitment and social outlook. Doctrinal adherence can no longer be inferred from social commitments (if it ever could). Working toward social justice is no longer what only theological liberals do.

The growth of nondenominational churches pushes questions about the meaning of *evangelical* even further to the forefront. Recent studies show that around 20 percent of all Protestants attend nondenominational congregations, a number that is likely to further increase.[54] For these churches, rather than organizational affiliation—such as being part of the Presbyterian Church of America—determining whether a congregation is evangelical, other markers must. Up to this point, most all the nation's nondenominational congregations have been considered evangelical by religious observers. This has been based as much on what they are not—mainline congregations—as it has been on other characteristics. Many of today's nondenominational congregations, especially those with a younger demographic, are committed to working toward social justice in addition to spreading the faith. Will they be seen as truly evangelical? To the extent that orthodox belief continues to be inferred from social ethics, we are likely to see the energy formerly devoted to policing the boundary between evangelicalism and mainline Protestantism shift to monitoring the boundaries between different facets of evangelicalism and debating which groups fit the label.

A question that remains outstanding is the extent to which the traits associated with the new evangelicalism will endure. A striking feature of past waves of new evangelicalism is a commitment to institutionalizing the changes underway. Key ingredients included entrepreneurial leadership, new organizations, and distinctive discourses. The cast of influential leaders is familiar to people who follow recent evangelical history: Carl Henry, Billy Graham, and Harold Ockenga among the neo-evangelicals; Jerry Falwell, Pat Robertson, and Francis Schaeffer within the Religious Right. Both movements produced distinctive discourses that identified core commitments, such as the importance of religious revival or the creeping threat of secular humanism. Both movements locked in these ideas through new organizational vehicles: parachurch organizations, such as the National Association of Evangelicals and the Moral Majority; educational institutions, such as Fuller Theological Seminary and Liberty University; and intellectual outlets, such as *Christianity Today*. These organizations institutionalized change in ways that transcended the personalities of movement leaders and routinized the production and dissemination of new ideas and commitments.

Seen in this light, the new social engagement appears to be only partially institutionalized. There are intellectual and organizational entrepreneurs, such as Brian McLaren, Shane Claiborne, David Gushee, and Richard Cizik. There are distinctive discourses, such as those that emphasize the common good, biblical justice, and kingdom theology.[35] And there are single-issue and broad-based parachurch organizations, such as the Evangelical Environmental Network and the New Evangelical Partnership for the Common Good. These overlap with more established Chicago Declaration–era evangelical voices, such as Ronald Sider, Jim Wallis, and *Sojourners* magazine. We believe that aspects of the new evangelicalism are likely to have staying power in some form because the slow-moving changes we have identified in the American religious landscape, such as demographic shifts and the decreasing presence of the mainline, show little likelihood of reversing. But whether elements of the new evangelical engagement become deeply engrained in the evangelical mainstream or circulate on the periphery depends more on compelling voices, organizational infrastructure, and ideological innovations that carry these contemporary impulses into the future.

*　*　*

The chapters ahead are divided into three parts. Part I covers significant groups and trends: emerging evangelicals, campus ministry and social justice, Catholic influences, New Monastic communities, women's activism and evangelical identity, and public opinion. Part II examines specific issue areas: the environment, race relations, abortion, international human rights, and global poverty. Part III contains reflections on the new evangelical social engagement from three prominent senior scholars in the fields of history, sociology, and Christian ethics.

The new evangelical social engagement is broad and multifaceted, and the topics covered in our chapters do not capture its full range. There is engagement on issues like economic inequality, immigration reform, and peacemaking that are not reflected in our pages. We hope the exploration we present here bears fruit in further scholarly examination.

NOTES

1. On the percentage of evangelicals, which is based on denominational affiliation, see the 2008 U.S. Religious Landscape Survey conducted by the Pew Forum on Religion and Public Life (http://religions.pewforum.org/pdf/report-religious-landscape-study-full.pdf). Like the Pew survey, we follow the current scholarly practice of distinguishing between evangelical Protestant and black Protestant religious traditions, thereby defining evangelicalism as a nonblack religious tradition. We recognize that this definition is not without problems. Yet given our interest in patterns of social engagement, black Protestantism's distinctive theology, social ethic, and political history, when compared to historically white evangelical Protestantism, warrants separate treatment.

2. On public views of evangelicalism, especially among young adults, see David Kinnaman and Gabe Lyons, *Unchristian: What a New Generation Really Thinks about Christianity…and Why It Matters* (Grand Rapids, MI: Baker Books, 2007).

3. The other main scholarly study, which takes the relationship between the new evangelicalism and liberal democracy as its point of entrée, is Marcia Pally, *The New Evangelicals: Expanding the Vision of the Common Good* (Grand Rapids, MI: William B. Eerdmans, 2011). There are a number of illuminating books on the new evangelicalism written by activists themselves: for

programmatic statements, see Ronald J. Sider and Diane Knippers, eds.,
*Toward an Evangelical Public Policy: Political Strategies for the Health of the
Nation* (Grand Rapids, MI: Baker Books, 2005); David P. Gushee, ed., *The
New Evangelical Manifesto: A Kingdom Vision for the Public Good* (St. Louis,
MO: Chalice Press, 2012); Bruce Ellis Benson, Malinda Elizabeth Berry, and
Peter Goodwin Heltzel, eds., *Prophetic Evangelicals: Envisioning a Just and
Peaceable Kingdom* (Grand Rapids, MI: William B. Eerdmans, 2012). For an
argument in favor of the emerging "evangelical center," see David P. Gushee,
*The Future of Faith in American Politics: The Public Witness of the Evangelical
Center* (Waco, TX: Baylor University Press, 2008.)

4. David Bebbington, *Evangelicalism in Modern Britain: A History from the 1730s
to the 1980s* (London: Routledge, 1989).

5. Steven Mintz, *Moralists and Modernizers: America's Pre–Civil War Reformers*
(Baltimore, MD: Johns Hopkins University Press, 1995).

6. Jennifer Graber, "Social Reform," *Encyclopedia of Religion in America*, vol. 4,
ed. Charles H. Lippy and Peter W. Williams (Washington, DC: CQ Press,
2010), 2098.

7. Matthew Bowman, "Sin, Spirituality, and Primitivism: The Theologies of the
American Social Gospel, 1885–1917," *Religion and American Culture: A Journal
of Interpretation* 17:1 (Winter 2007): 99–100.

8. George M. Marsden, *Reforming Fundamentalism: Fuller Seminary and the
New Evangelicalism* (Grand Rapids, MI: William B. Eerdmans, 1987), 8; Miles
S. Mullen II, "The Quandry of African American Evangelicals," www.patheos.
com, The Anxious Bench blog, February 27, 2013.

9. On the "young evangelical" descriptor, see Richard Quebedeaux, *The Young
Evangelicals: The Story of the Emergence of a New Generation of Evangelicals* (San
Francisco: Harper and Row, 1974).

10. Timothy L. Smith, *Revivalism and Social Reform in Mid-Nineteenth Century
America* (New York: Abingdon Press, 1957).

11. David O. Moberg, *The Great Reversal: Reconciling Evangelism and Social Concern*,
reprint (Eugene, OR: Wipf and Stock, 2006), 26.

12. David R. Swartz, *Moral Minority: The Evangelical Left in an Age of Conservatism*
(Philadelphia: University of Pennsylvania Press, 2012). See also Quebedeaux,
The Young Evangelicals.

13. "Chicago Declaration of Evangelical Social Concern (1973)," Evangelicals
for Social Action website, www.evangelicalsforsocialaction.org/chicago-
declaration-of-evangelical-social-concern.

14. Daniel K. Williams, *God's Own Party: The Making of the Christian Right*
(New York: Oxford University Press, 2010).

15. For the full text of the document together with much of the background material, see Sider and Knippers, *Toward an Evangelical Public Policy*.

16. Sider and Knippers, *Toward an Evangelical Public Policy*, 336.

17. On the statement and its reception, see Gushee, *The Future of Faith in American Politics*, 95–97.
18. *An Evangelical Manifesto*, 13–14. See http://anevangelicalmanifesto.com.
19. On evangelical environmentalism, also see Katharine K. Wilkinson, *Between God and Green: How Evangelicals Are Cultivating a Middle Ground on Climate Change* (New York: Oxford University Press, 2012).
20. On evangelicals and race, also see Michael O. Emerson and Christian Smith, *Divided by Faith: Evangelical Religion and the Problem of Race in America* (New York: Oxford University Press, 2000); and Peter Goodwin Heltzel, *Jesus and Justice: Evangelicals, Race, and American Politics* (New Haven, CT: Yale University Press, 2009).
21. Christian Smith, *American Evangelicalism: Embattled and Thriving* (Chicago: University of Chicago Press, 1998), 187.
22. Sider and Knippers, *Toward an Evangelical Public Policy*, 366.
23. Nicholas Wolterstorff, *Justice: Rights and Wrongs* (Princeton, NJ: Princeton University Press, 2008).
24. On kingdom theology, see James Bielo, *Emerging Evangelicals: Faith, Modernity, and the Desire for Authenticity* (New York: New York University Press, 2011); for its roots in the 1950s-era writings of George Eldon Ladd and the reaction among evangelicals, see John A. D'Elia, *A Place at the Table: George Eldon Ladd and the Rehabilitation of Evangelical Scholarship in America* (New York: Oxford University Press, 2008).
25. On emerging evangelicals, see Bielo, *Emerging Evangelicals*; and Jason Wollschleger, "Off the Map? Locating the Emerging Church: A Comparative Case Study of Congregations in the Pacific Northwest," *Review of Religious Research* 54 (2012): 69–91.
26. Kinnaman and Lyons, *Unchristian*, 11.
27. See Tony Campolo, *Red Letter Christians: A Citizen's Guide to Faith and Politics* (Ventura, CA: Regal Books, 2008) and http://redletterchristians.org.
28. Gushee, *New Evangelical Manifesto*, xiii.
29. On demographic shifts in evangelicalism, especially rising levels of education, during the postwar years, see Robert Wuthnow, *The Restructuring of American Religion: Society and Faith since World War II* (Princeton, NJ: Princeton University Press, 1988); on more recent trends, see Jerry Z. Park and Sam Reimer, "Revisiting the Social Sources of American Christianity, 1972–1998," *Journal for the Scientific Study of Religion* 41 (2002): 733–46.
30. D. Michael Lindsay, *Faith in the Halls of Power: How Evangelicals Joined the American Elite* (New York: Oxford University Press, 2007).
31. See, for instance, Susan Wunderink, "Tim Keller Reasons with America," *Christianity Today*, June 2008. www.christianitytoday.com/ct/2008/june/23.38.html.
32. E.g., Bebbington, *Evangelicalism in Modern Britain*. Bebbington notes that evangelicals themselves began to acknowledge the influence of cultural

context on Christianity at the Lausanne Congress of 1974, where evidence from the mission field was difficult to contest.

33. Differences between generations at a given point in time can be attributed to either age effects or cohort effects, which are often challenging to disentangle. While a number of important generational differences within evangelicalism seem largely attributable to age effects, especially to features of "emerging adulthood" such as delayed family formation, the differences in views of environmentalism and homosexuality discussed here appear to be more attributable to cohort effects. On religion and emerging adulthood, see Robert Wuthnow, *After the Baby Boomers: How Twenty- and Thirty-Somethings Are Shaping the Future of American Religion* (Princeton, NJ: Princeton University Press, 2007); and Christian Smith with Patricia Snell, *Souls in Transition: The Religious and Spiritual Lives of Emerging Adults* (New York: Oxford University Press, 2009).

34. Buster Smith and Byron Johnson, "The Liberalization of Young Evangelicals: A Research Note," *Journal for the Scientific Study of Religion* 49 (2010): 351–60.

35. This data is from the General Social Survey. See www.norc.org/PDFs/2011%20 GSS%20Reports/GSS_Public%20Attitudes%20Toward%20Homosexuality_ Sept2011.pdf.

36. Justin Farrell, "The Young and the Restless? The Liberalization of Young Evangelicals," *Journal for the Scientific Study of Religion* 50 (2011): 517–32; and Wuthnow, *After the Baby Boomers*. For conflicting evidence, see Smith and Johnson, "The Liberalization of Young Evangelicals."

37. Wuthnow, *After the Baby Boomers*, 174–76.

38. On Vietnam and the new evangelical engagement of the 1970s, see Robert Booth Fowler, *A New Engagement: Evangelical Political Thought, 1966–1976* (Grand Rapids, MI: William B. Eerdmans, 1982).

39. Gregory A. Boyd, *The Myth of a Christian Nation: How the Quest for Political Power Is Destroying the Church* (Grand Rapids, MI: Zondervan, 2005).

40. See, for instance, David P. Gushee, "5 Reasons Torture Is Always Wrong," *Christianity Today*, February 2006.

41. Martin E. Marty, *Modern American Religion, Vol. 3: Under God, Indivisible, 1941–1960* (Chicago: University of Chicago Press, 1996).

42. "Evangelicals in the Social Struggle," *Christianity Today*, October 8, 1965, 11.

43. Mark Chaves, *American Religion: Contemporary Trends* (Princeton, NJ: Princeton University Press, 2011).

44. Jason S. Lantzer, *Mainline Christianity: The Past and Future of America's Majority Faith* (New York: New York University Press, 2012).

45. Wuthnow, *The Restructuring of American Religion*.

46. For an insightful discussion of Catholic influences on the public witness of the new evangelicalism, see Kristin E. Heyer, "Insights from Catholic Social Ethics and Political Participation," 101–14, in *Toward an Evangelical Public Policy: Political Strategies for the Health of the Nation*, ed. Ronald J. Sider and Diane Knippers (Grand Rapids, MI: Baker Books, 2005).

47. For instance, see *An Evangelical Manifesto*, 16.

48. For evangelical voting patterns between 1936 and 2004, see Lyman Kellstedt, John Green, Corwin Smidt, and James Guth, "Faith Transformed: Religion and American Politics from FDR to George W. Bush," 269–95, in *Religion and American Politics: From the Colonial Period to the Present*, ed. Mark A. Noll and Luke E. Harlow (New York: Oxford University Press, 2007); for 2008, see Corwin Smidt, Kevin R. den Dulk, Bryan T. Froehle, James M. Penning, Stephen V. Monsma, and Douglas L. Koopman, *The Disappearing God Gap? Religion in the 2008 Presidential Election* (New York: Oxford University Press, 2010); for 2012, see "How the Faithful Voted: 2012 Preliminary Analysis," www.pewforum. org/Politics-and-Elections/How-the-Faithful-Voted-2012-Preliminary-Exit-Po ll-Analysis.aspx.

49. Smidt et al., *Disappearing God Gap*, 191–220.

50. Williams, *God's Own Party*.

51. Smith, *American Evangelicalism*.

52. Paul Lichterman, "Religion and the Construction of Civic Identity," *American Sociological Review* 73 (2008): 83–104.

53. On the views of some of today's new evangelicals in this regard, see Pally, *New Evangelicals*, 150–164, 192–203.

54. Chaves, *American Religion*, 57.

55. For one recent articulation, see David P. Gushee, *The Sacredness of Human Life: Why an Ancient Biblical Vision Is the Key to the World's Future* (Grand Rapids, MI: William B. Eerdmans, 2013).

PART ONE

Recent Evangelical Movements and Trends

I

"FORMED"

EMERGING EVANGELICALS NAVIGATE
TWO TRANSFORMATIONS

James S. Bielo

THIS BOOK ASKS a vital question. Is there a sea change happening on the social, political, and cultural front of evangelical social engagement? And if so, just how is that sea floor shifting? These questions are important due both to the significant influence of evangelicals in American public life and to the received wisdom among academic and mainstream discourses about evangelicals' public presence. There is a familiar story at work here. American evangelicals are culture warriors, obsessed with abortion and homosexuality, who seek to elect their own into public office so they can codify religious morality.[1] They create Christian alternatives to every imaginable form of popular culture and democratic institution.[2] And they do service work with people who are socially disadvantaged and marginalized, largely from the comfortable confines of middle-class suburbia.[3]

We might read this volume as a call to take seriously the complexity and tensions within the amorphous category "evangelical." As Steensland and Goff outline in the Introduction, evangelicals have recently made waves on their own shores and those of secular media outlets for appearing in unexpected places: taking up arms in debates about sustainable development, climate change, HIV/AIDS, human trafficking, and global peacemaking. This chapter proceeds from the assumption that while platforms and agendas are indeed up for grabs, the future of evangelical social engagement will not unfold on the basis of specific public issues. It will unfold along the cultural contours that give expression and direction to evangelicals' ongoing public influence.

Any comparative analysis of a new social engagement must confront the institutional and ideological changes that evangelicals have produced and wrestled with in recent years. The diverse movement known as the Emerging Church exemplifies such changes and was the focus of my ethnographic research from October 2007 to July 2011.[4] In this chapter, I highlight one institutional invention among a small group of emerging evangelicals in Cincinnati, Ohio, to consider how views of social engagement are tethered to ideals of spiritual formation.

Emerging evangelicalism is best defined as a movement of cultural critique grounded in a desire for change. "The Emerging Church" is a label, created by movement insiders in the mid-1990s, marking a dual assumption: that contemporary evangelicalism is undergoing profound change and that the Christian church always has and always will be changing. The label itself is of increasingly little interest to adherents as a meaningful self-identifier, but the movement it was intended to capture continues to thrive. Their critique is aimed—in general and targeted fashions—at the religious culture cultivated among conservative evangelicals (though emerging evangelicals are also apt to reference the troubles of mainline Protestants and Catholics). As a movement, the Emerging Church has not developed as a tightly coordinated effort; it is equal parts improvisation and strategized maneuvering, formally institutional and informally relational, virtual and intersubjective, local and national. Their cultural critique is diverse and wide-ranging, aimed at both private and public religious life. It encompasses doctrinal theology, scriptural hermeneutics, congregational ecclesiology, liturgical ritual, social memory and relations to church history, scrutiny of dominant values such as consumerism, and, most germane to this book, the form and content of social engagement. Demographically, the emerging movement coalesced and has been primarily successful among middle-aged and younger, white, middle-class and upwardly mobile, educated, urban and suburban evangelicals. Emerging evangelicalism is undoubtedly a transnational movement in the Anglophone world; however, my research has addressed only its U.S. incarnations.[5]

This chapter emerges from nearly four years of multisited ethnography, which began in Lansing, Michigan, from October 2007 through July 2008.[6] From August 2008 through July 2011, the research was based in southwestern Ohio (primarily Cincinnati, but also in several surrounding urban and suburban locales). Data collection focused on four fieldwork activities. First, I conducted formal interviews with ninety emerging evangelicals from forty different church communities and eleven denominations. The sample consisted of sixty-eight men and twenty-two women; fifty-six were doing urban ministry, thirty-four suburban; nearly all were middle-class whites; and all were born between 1958 and 1989 (most between 1970 and 1980). Second, I conducted systematic observations of collective religious practices: from church worship to weekly small groups, informal church gatherings, national and regional conferences, workshops, and book promotional tours. Third, I engaged in several forms of collaborative ethnography, in which the researcher attempts some remove from authority by involving consultants in the design of fieldwork activities (e.g., pastors led me on guided tours of the urban neighborhoods they approached as mission fields).[7] Fourth, I collected a variety of material culture and textual items produced, used, and circulated by the individuals and congregations I worked with.

Any genealogy of the movement must follow at least five interwoven tracks.[8] First, the theological lineage is grounded in an epistemological critique. The organizing claim is that Protestant theology developed in the cultural context of philosophical modernism. As a result, certain doctrinal beliefs, models of religious selfhood, and hermeneutic methods are said to carry deeply rooted, questionable assumptions. Second, emerging evangelicalism is influenced by missiologists who focus on the challenges of evangelizing in Western societies. The base critique is that Christianity has shifted from being the default worldview among Westerners to being widely considered merely a spiritual option, irrelevant, anachronistic, or destructive. In turn, American evangelicals need to approach their own society as a foreign mission field. Third, the ecclesiological lineage works off a critique of local congregational trends, in particular, a distrust of church growth models and megachurch aspirations. The result has been a renewed focus on the spiritual and social engagement potentialities of house churches and new church plants. Fourth, the liturgical lineage is fixated on meaningfully connecting with Christian history. This desire has been neatly captured by the trope of "ancient-future," which suggests that modernity's unwelcome influence materializes as a flawed disposition toward worshiping God: too much disconnect with past Christianities, too much emphasis on the power of the spoken sermon to convince and convert, and too little integration of embodied experience with mental comprehension. Fifth, emerging evangelicalism roundly rejects any definitive political allegiance or agenda. The movement largely retains an acceptance of political activism but promotes a broader conception of moral governance.

As this genealogy suggests, reimagining evangelicalism's proper role in public life is central to emerging identity. While this chapter seeks an up-close, detailed analysis of one emerging evangelical community, we can speak in general terms about the movement's conception of social engagement. Omri Elisha provides a useful starting point—for emerging and nonemerging evangelicals alike—by defining the socially engaged as "pastors and churchgoers who draw strong associations between religiosity and social conscience, and are notably active (either professionally or as volunteers) in promoting and participating in various forms of organized benevolence."[9] In the ethnographic example that follows, I am less concerned about a specific act of engagement than I am with characterizing the religious sense of self that accompanies being socially engaged. Integral to my example here, as well as the emerging movement writ large, is the theme of localization (see chapter 4). Emerging evangelicals emphasize local action and mobilization, often articulated as being "neighborhood" or "city-focused." As a result, emerging evangelicals reliably cultivate an intricate sense of place through which familiar aims of evangelism and positive social change are sutured to developing a relationship to, or "dwelling" in, a specific locale.[10] This push to localize is grounded in a predominant theological focus among emerging evangelicals on "the kingdom of God." Nearly without exception in my fieldwork, emerging evangelicals rejected dispensationalist views of God's kingdom in favor of either an "already, but not yet" or "kingdom now" orientation.[11] Following Jon Bialecki's ethnographic work among Vineyard charismatics, kingdom theologies are not merely theologies; they provide models of temporality and agency.[12] For emerging evangelicals, the place-based emphasis on local action ensues from their kingdom-inspired commitment that while God's agency is unlimited, their own agency is most effective when sustained in an immediate social surround.

My organizing example in this chapter is a yearlong curriculum of spiritual formation created by emerging evangelicals in Cincinnati. From planning meetings that began in April 2010 to the curriculum's culmination in July 2011, the program created by this group exemplifies an organizing assumption of this book: evangelical social engagement has historically combined two transformations, personal spiritual change and public social change. Using the example of this group and their creative labor, I am interested in what evangelical social engagement looks like on the ground and the kinds of problems generated by new forms of engagement. With these frames in mind, I pursue two interests in this chapter.

First, emerging evangelicals seek to collapse any division between personal and public transformation. Individual piety and visions of the collective good are not seen as distinguishable, competing commitments, separate pursuits, or even complementary acts, but as a fused, mutually reinforcing endeavor. The group's lack of interest in disentangling the two transformations tracks with Susan Harding's recent notion of "transevangelicalism."[13] Pointing to both the emerging movement and the mass-marketed Biblezine that premiered in 2003 as examples, Harding argues that recent evangelical practices incline toward boundary refusal. These practices are marked by "their instability and their in-between-ness, neither/nor-and both/and-ness vis-à-vis the categories of 'religion' and the 'secular.'"[14] I suggest here that the same is happening with emerging evangelical social engagement, where modern distinctions are viewed with great suspicion. Binaries such as inner-outer, personal-social, and private-public are intentionally troubled to the point where they are desired to be dismissed. This interest in co-(llapsing, mbining), de-(stabilizing, constructing), and re-(fusing, integrating) projects is consistent with emerging origin stories and a self-conscious ethos that embeds critiques of modernity. Second, although emerging evangelicals hope for such boundary collapsing, they are not immediately successful—which, in this case, proves true for both program creators and participants. In particular, two tensions preoccupy their transevangelical effort. To be clear, this is a cultural argument, not a psychological one: tensions exist as competing imperatives in the production and consumption of the spiritual formation program. Tensions center on an uneasy relationship with late modern temporality and an anxiety about invoking an old fundamentalist separatism in pursuit of a changed evangelicalism.

I concentrate on a single example here, but these arguments hold up with respect to the remainder of my fieldwork and were evidenced through a wide range of practices. Emerging evangelicals pursued personal and public transformation through actions as diverse as organizing prayer walks, in which small groups of fellow congregants ambled throughout city sections praying for people and place; planting community gardens, in which small groups of congregants maintained food-bearing plots and distributed the produce to local residents; joining neighborhood associations and other forms of local governance to contribute voluntary labor and influence decision making; and entrepreneurially establishing businesses that focus on serving local neighborhoods. The example I present here is instructive, in part, because it encompasses several of these kinds of practices.

The Team

In April 2010, five emerging evangelical pastors began meeting weekly to design a yearlong spiritual formation program for use in their local communities: two house churches and two campus ministries. It all began with Kevin. He is the oldest of the five, then in his early forties, and the program originated as the final project for completing his seminary dissertation. So long as his sleeves are rolled up, Kevin's dominating feature is the large tattoo snaking up his left arm: the Latin word *Resurgam*, "I shall rise again." Since 1995, Kevin has helped pastor a house church network in the working-class neighborhood of Norwood.[15] As part of his striving to be missional and incarnational, Kevin owns an auto body shop on the neighborhood's western edge, a half mile from the communal house he and his family live in with other house church members. This kind of local, contextually oriented, holistic ministry is deemed integral to being socially engaged and reasserts the transevangelical style of boundary refusal by breaking down the modernist separation of work and home. Because the program would serve as his dissertation, Kevin often took a lead role in the group, but by no means was he a formalized leader.

The most active member was Aaron, a campus pastor at Northern Kentucky University in his late thirties, who has been friends and ministry partners with Kevin since 2003. He was rarely absent from group planning meetings and often took the lead in running them. While the program originated with Kevin, Aaron was instrumental in advancing it. He outlined an early version for a Fuller seminary course, where he was working toward a master's degree. Adam was also influential in the program's development. In his mid-thirties, he and his wife have led a house church since 2004, modeled on the communal living practiced by Kevin. The house itself is in the Clifton neighborhood, home to the University of Cincinnati and close to the independent coffee house Adam and his wife own and operate.

The remaining two members were the most marginal to the program's formation. In his early thirties, D.G. is a self-described "cultural architect," which he defines vis-à-vis religious identity: "As Christians we are called to transform the very community and culture we live in." A large tattoo of a shamrock embedded in a Celtic cross dominates his right inside forearm, and, no matter the occasion, he keeps a silver Celtic cross with the Greek letters for alpha and omega on a necklace hanging midway down his chest. The group's beginning coincided with the dismantling of D.G.'s church plant and his dismissal as an assistant pastor from a conservative United Methodist congregation in northern Kentucky. His spotty participation in the group had less to do with lacking interest than it did the competing hours from his new job at an Apple store in Cincinnati's northern suburbs. The group was both a lifeline to his heart's desire, being a missional pastor, and a reminder of what he had recently lost. Christian was the least active member and the last to join. He moved to Cincinnati in 2008 to work as a campus ministry director at the University of Cincinnati for the Church of the Nazarene. All five men are white, college-educated, and saturated in the cultural tastes and capital of middle-class life.[16]

In September 2010, Mandy and Andrea were added to the group. Mandy is a long-standing member of Kevin's house church and was brought on as a paid assistant. She handled most of the administrative responsibilities and served as scribe at weekly meetings. Immediately, though, she was also an active contributor to brainstorming and decision making. Andrea is in her late twenties and was a new addition to the whole scene. She recently began work as an interfaith campus director at Xavier University, just north of Norwood. Through informal social networks, she contacted Kevin and, after arriving in the city, moved into their communal house. She, too, played an immediately active role in the group. Both women are demographically similar to the five men.

The addition of Mandy and Andrea was not incidental or strictly pragmatic. From the very first meeting I attended, the original five talked earnestly about bringing a "female perspective" into the planning. They explicitly pitched this as a direct rejoinder to a troubling persistence in mainstream evangelicalism: a male-dominated and implicitly sexist public sphere. For them, being intentional about inviting two women to be equal contributing members was a countercultural act. The team's gendered critique of evangelicalism also indexes an important issue that appears in almost every case of evangelical social engagement. Consider the difference between individualist and structural logics for social change. In American civic life, for both faith-based and secular activists, these two orientations prevail.[17] An individualist logic concentrates on the responsibilities, motivations, and actions of individual people. The prime location of agency is the individual, and the relevance of histories, systems, and structures for determining social realities is downplayed. A structural logic combines a focus on individual agency with substantial explanatory weight given to the histories, systems, and structures that create, delimit, and constrain opportunities and actions.

Elisha, in his ethnography of socially engaged megachurch evangelicals, provides an extensive account of how individualist logics of social problems such as poverty triumph among conservative Protestants.[18] His portrayal of key consultants illustrates the point. In presenting Stacy—a mother and life-long churchgoer—he concludes: "while she recognized that uncontrollable circumstances and social structures may limit or complicate the choices people are able to make, she rarely pursued such notions very far, but rather emphasized issues of personal morality and responsibility."[19] For another, Elisha shares a revealing example from a Sunday school classroom. In teaching the class, Jim combined individualist logics with acute systemic observations: "He spoke of how Christian bookstores were full of books on topics like marriage and self-improvement but very few dealing with urban poverty and decline."[20] Yet, when his presentation shifted to group discussion, "hardly anyone took up the structural dimensions of Jim's main argument.…The discussion returned, *as if by gravitational force*, to the theme of relationships and the importance of showing God's love through direct personal influence in people's lives."[21]

Adding Mandy and Andrea to the group obviously leads to no decisive structural outcome. The evangelical public sphere remains male-dominated. However, it does mark a structural sensibility in the group's understanding of who gets heard in evangelicalism's "order of discourse."²² This interest in structural change was common in the group and marks a point of departure from conservative evangelicals. As illustrated in Elisha's ethnography and by other scholars, evangelicals return, "as if by gravitational force," to individualist explanations (a pattern that resonates with both frontier ideals of individualism and neoliberal ideals of autonomy).²³ By making structural realities and needs explicit, such as the case with gender inclusivity, emerging evangelicals prefigure their desire for cultural change within their own religious subculture.

The Curriculum

They named it FORMED. Adam first suggested this handle, and the others thought it captured well their ideal of "inviting people into a process of spiritual formation." Kevin had always thought of the program as "a curriculum for Christlikeness," a phrase he borrowed from the theologian Dallas Willard.²⁴ FORMED joins a long-standing dialogue among Christians: how to be a disciple of God. In typical emerging fashion, Kevin's initial desire to create the program and the others' desire to develop it began as a discontent. They were not satisfied with any of the vast number of discipleship resources available in the current Christian marketplace. In what came to be a predictable component of weekly planning meetings, they made sardonic reference to existing evangelical discipleship products and their shortcomings. The immensely popular (and profitable) *40 Days of Purpose*, part of Rick Warren's cottage industry, was a favorite target of derision. In particular, the group objected to the way existing products were not based on a yearlong effort, did not combine the wisdom of ancient and contemporary Christian thinkers, and did not thoroughly fuse personal spiritual transformation to public social transformation. August 2010 through July 2011 would be the beta year of FORMED, a trial run to work out kinks, and would consist of three components. It is also worth observing here that the group's decision to create FORMED rather than adopt and alter an existing program reflects their status as entrepreneurially minded, middle-class actors with the requisite social and cultural capital to imagine and complete the work of creating a new spiritual formation program.

The first component of FORMED is the use of eleven different vows to organize the program. Each month foregrounds one vow and a specific set of meanings the group attached to it (the year's final month would be a form of

Sabbath, a rest from the preceding spiritual labors). Their initial vow descriptions read as follows:

> *Soul-Keeping*, a renewed life: In a world frazzled by overcommitment, we'll take time for rest and recreation.
>
> *Simplicity*, a focused life: In a world that is frantic and overcommitted, we'll live simple, purposeful lives.
>
> *Community*, a shared life: In a world full of fractured relationships, we'll display unity through a shared life.
>
> *Prayer*, a God-centered life: In a world chasing "self-fulfillment," we'll center our lives on God through a prayerful life.
>
> *Study*, a transformed life: In a world that is force-fed by self-centered advertising and media, we'll regularly reflect on God's word and let that transform our minds.
>
> *Work*, a creative life: In a world drunk on laziness and entitlement, we'll be industrious and generous through meaningful work.
>
> *Service*, a generous life: In a world that idolizes power, individualism, and ego, we'll demonstrate Christ's way of serving through practical acts of love.
>
> *Hospitality*, a welcoming life: In a world filled with hostility, we'll be a warm, welcoming place for friends and strangers.
>
> *Justice*, an active life: In a world full of injustice, we'll work at the local grassroots level for visible social change and be a voice for justice among the world's oppressed.
>
> *Holiness*, a set apart and faithful life: In a world where anything goes, we'll live faithfully toward God, others, and ourselves.
>
> *Celebration*, a joy-filled life: In a world plagued by apathy and anxiety, we'll regularly and joyfully celebrate all that is good, true and beautiful.

There are several observations to make about this list. Most obviously, the enumeration of each vow follows a formula. A tag line (e.g., "a transformed life") is followed by a cultural critique (e.g., "In a world that is force-fed by self-centered advertising and media"), concluded by an evangelical-inflected riposte (e.g., "we'll regularly reflect on God's word and let that transform our minds"). For the prayer materials used each month (see later), the group sought to integrate the language of the vow as much as possible. Also, this particular collection of vows was intended as a revoicing of the traditional monastic vows of poverty, chastity, and obedience. Finally, note that the vows move back and forth between personal and social transformation. Most overtly, service, hospitality, and justice call forth the imperative of being socially engaged. Others—for example, simplicity, work, and holiness—refuse a separation of the two trans-formations, preferring to see them as too intertwined to distinguish.

The second component of FORMED is a monthly prayer book. The group was fond of reiterating, in public events and among themselves at weekly meetings, that this would "not *just* be a prayer book," but a guide for establish-ing an "internal spiritual rhythm." Borrowing another monastic element, the prayers are to be performed aloud daily at fixed hours in the morning and eve-ning and only in the intersubjective context of community (house churches and campus ministries, respectively). Each day's prayer follows a repeating structure in the morning (call to prayer, restatement of monthly vow, reading of vow-related scripture, reading of vow-related quote from past or present Christian author, a vow prayer prewritten by the group, reading of a Gospel text, reading of the Lord's Prayer, reading of a Psalm text, an open period of intercession to address specific prayer requests, a brief concluding prayer written by the group), afternoon (midday restatement of vow and vow prayer), and evening (call to prayer and then a repetition of the morning structure with the exception of a different Christian author quote, Gospel text, and Psalm text). Whenever possible, they aligned the Christian author quote with the liturgical calendar (for example, for October's "Simplicity," a prayer from St. Francis of Assisi was read on October 4, St. Francis Feast Day) or the fusing of personal-public transformation (for example, for January's "Study," the group assembled a diverse set of boundary-collapsing quotes, including this from St. Bernard of Clairvaux: "There are many who seek knowledge for the sake of knowledge: that is curiosity. There are others who desire to know in order that they may be known: that is vanity. Others seek knowledge in order to sell it: that is dishonorable. But there are some who seek knowledge in order to edify others: that is love").

The final component is a daylong event on the first Saturday of each month, where an invited speaker addresses the vow with FORMED participants. These events ended up following several different formats but at minimum involved a public talk followed by a shared meal. The group relied on their personal and ministry connections to arrange the speakers and eventually included both local pastors and published Christian authors living elsewhere. Their hope was that these events would satisfy several purposes: renew excite-ment for the program by beginning each month with a special event, present a learned introduction by someone who has devoted specialized attention to the monthly vow, and provide a public event where FORMED participants from the four different communities could gather. Throughout the year, these events drew anywhere from twenty to seventy people, almost all of whom were involved with a FORMED house church or campus ministry.

The monthly talks became a primary way of demonstrating the entanglement of personal and public transformation. One strategy was the symbolism of location. The event setting was a frequent topic of planning meeting discussions, as the group had two priorities: host the event in different locations throughout the city and host as many events as possible in public locations. The kind of structural sensibility the group displayed through including female contributors was also present in how they organized the meals following talks. The focus was trained on "sustainable food," and most meals were biographically introduced. For example, the February "Work" meal was prepared and introduced by Robert, a member of Kevin's house church, who maintains several community gardens in Norwood. He explained the seasonality of two different vegetarian soups, their ingredients, and when the herbs and vegetables were planted and harvested. These biographical introductions were explicitly framed as rejoinders to the spiritual damages of relying on the industrialized food system for sustenance. Finally, the subject of the monthly talks affirmed the approach to social engagement. For example, the June "Holiness" event hosted the vice president of a Cincinnati-area ministry that develops and supports anti-human-trafficking campaigns. The April event featured a widely read evangelical author on the vow of "Hospitality." Her organizing idea was "Hospitality as a dangerous practice," which she presented to the gathered group of twenty over the course of several hours in an alternating lecture and question-answer format. She introduced the vow with an autobiographical anecdote that intended to be both humorous and demonstrative of boundary-collapsing social engagement:

> Funny story, from when I was doing my dissertation. I did a Ph.D. in Ethics, but I did my dissertation on recovering the hospitality tradition. And when I would tell people that they would look at me absolutely blankly; now, mind you this was, I sort of started working on it in '88, so this was before there's been a real resurgence of interest in hospitality. But, they would look at me and say, "You're doing a dissertation on coffee and doughnuts?" [group laughs] This was really a little bit disturbing. But, then they would follow that up with, "Are you doing a real Ph.D.?" And, it was a very interesting, I mean it was actually impossible for them to fathom that somehow hospitality was connected to ethics or to issues of justice or recognition or inclusion, those kinds of questions. It was still a few years down the road before that really became even possible for people to imagine, and that really it's actually a pretty useful framework for thinking about issues of how we

negotiate difference, how we make room, find unity amidst diversity and so on, how we allow people to have voice.

In walking through the FORMED curriculum, my aim has been to illustrate how the group sought to fuse the two transformations of personal and public change. The example of FORMED is striking because it is, most overtly, a discipleship program: a "curriculum for Christlikeness," where individuals work to strengthen their individual faith. Yet, even when the design is about fostering inner spirituality, emerging evangelicals constantly import desires and material goals for social engagement. It is this striving toward inseparability, this refusal to recognize or reify distinction between the two transformations that defines the group's creative labor.

Two Tensions

The FORMED beta year concluded with no major stumbles. The prayer books were completed—quotes collected, scriptural texts selected—and distributed on time. The monthly speakers were arranged, brought in, housed, and fed with few delays, no cancellations, and no crash-and-burn performances. The planning group met nearly every week to brainstorm, make decisions, and reflect. As the summer of 2011 waned, the group exchanged congratulations and began plotting version 2.0. However, through my ethnographic observation of version 1.0, I saw two tensions become apparent in the production and consumption of FORMED, both of which incite familiar evangelical dilemmas.

The first tension ensues from an uneasy relationship with late modernity. On the one hand, the group, as with the emerging movement more broadly, is fueled by cultural critique. Something is awry with contemporary life, an insistence made clear by their vow enumerations. On the other hand, there is much about the group that is unapologetically contemporary. Their affinity for technology is an easy illustration: weekly planning meetings were replete with Facebook posts, Twitter updates, Google doc sharing, ring tones, and message alerts; Aaron released the prayer book in regular and mobile versions; at monthly gatherings, as many people were reading Bible verses from iPhones as were from printouts of the prayer book or print Bibles. In anthropological terms, this uneasiness can be framed as a matter of temporality: cultural assumptions about the nature of time and its passing. Jane Guyer argues that late modern America has witnessed an "evaporation of the near future" in favor of immediate and far distant futures.[25] Evangelical Protestants are no stranger to the power of temporality; we need look no further than the extensive impact of rapture eschatology on shaping social practice.[26] What emerging evangelicals seem to struggle with is how to square their vehement cultural critique with their relative cultural comfort. The temporality of late modernity is troubling to them because it poses opportunity and danger, benefit and cost, promise and fear.

The FORMED year launched publicly with the September speaker for the opening vow, "Soul-Keeping." They invited a trusted friend, Dave, the pastor who cofounded the Norwood house church with Kevin. This was a choice less about convenience and more about expertise: Dave regularly speaks at national conferences on sustainable faith, teaching other pastors how to "establish rhythm" and "avoid burnout." Near the beginning of his talk, Dave voiced a definitively emerging critique of contemporary life:

> I believe that we are living in a time that is unparalleled in human history. And by that I don't mean that there's some rapture that's about to occur. I just mean that where we find ourselves in the early part of the 21st century is unlike, in the Western world, is unlike anything that we have ever experienced before, both qualitatively and quantitatively. We are in what many sociologists would say is a liminal point. We are seeing the deconstruction of old ways, but we don't really know clearly what the new way looks like. And, the church is filling this.... Where before have we ever in history been inundated with marketing to the degree that we now are?... When have we ever experienced the incursions against the gift of sleep that we have experienced in our day and age? And, had the kind of inundation of noise and lights and sounds and distractions? When have we had an industrialized food system before?... When have we ever been so confused as to what is food and what is not food before? We live in a topsy-turvy society.... It's as if we're living in a perpetual hiccup and people cannot seem to find the rituals and the rhythms that give sanity to life.... And, when before in human history have we ever been so isolated as a people from one another?...[27]

Dave went on to explain how Christians can work against the grain of these in-(cursions, undations, dustrialized) pressures to foster a healthier spiritual life. The talk seemed well received, which I found not surprising, given the shared ground of cultural critique. But Aaron did surprise me at the following planning meeting. The group was discussing Dave's talk, all very positive, when Aaron added how he "wasn't crazy about the 'ain't the past great and doesn't now suck'" tone he thought dominated the presentation. Part of my surprise was that I had heard Aaron articulate this same critique numerous times. Dave had gone too far for Aaron, but how? A clear answer never materialized for me ethnographically, but the root dilemma for Aaron seems to be defining the proper relationship to "now." It is a dilemma of temporality. A brief but telling example is found in the monthly prayer books beginning with the second vow of "Simplicity," and continuing through the present month in version 2.0. On page three, the midday prayer is printed in a small, dotted-line box with the following written beneath it: "Here's a handy Midday Prayer for the month that you could cut out and pocket for days when you are on the go." I would remind you of the tag line for the "Simplicity" vow: "In a world that is frantic and overcommitted, we'll live simple, purposeful lives." I take the copresence of "frantic and overcommitted" and "pocket for days when you are on the go" not as evidence of contradiction or as FORMED accommodating late modern pressures, but as a reduplication of Aaron's dilemma. Consider two further examples.

On October 1, the last weekly meeting before the "Simplicity" talk, Adam shared a book he had just finished with Aaron and Kevin: *Starbucked*.[28] The book is part journalistic observation, part socially engaged satire that explores the infamous coffee chain's dominance. As Aaron and Kevin perused the book, I shared an anecdote. The day before, walking in downtown Cincinnati, I had seen etched on a Starbucks store door their new national campaign: "Take Comfort in Rituals." Since seeing it, I had thought of the group, both their critique of consumerism and their own investment in the power of ritual. Without my asking, as if on cue, almost scripted, Aaron and Kevin laughed and then pulled out their iPhones and retrieved photos they had each taken, separately at different Starbucks, of this same campaign etching. They, too, were struck by Starbucks' appeal to one of their most valued symbols. Again, my point is not about contradiction. My point is that late modern life is both problem and solution to the group: here was something central to their discipleship program, ritual, being presented as attractive and not archaic by the troubled vehicle of consumerism's coffee behemoth.

Two weeks later, as the group prepared for the "Community" vow presentation, Christian presented the group with a problem. He had been struggling to convince his campus ministry participants to buy into FORMED. He thought that the web page needed something specific for college students. Aaron, who was having more success with his campus ministry, agreed. So did Kevin, who extended the suggestion to tailoring unique pages for small groups, house churches, college students, and other demographics. Christian made an analogy to eating at a Mongolian barbecue, where everyone has all the same ingredients, but you should be able to combine them to fit your taste. Aaron analogized it to the modular movement in art and architecture. As they traded parallels, I could not help considering all their ideas as exercises in late modern specialization. The economic anthropologist William Roseberry argued, ironically using coffee as his prime example, that late modern life is defined by post-Fordist production regimes and niche marketing.[29] Yet, the group marshals a similar impulse toward specialization in their efforts to localize social engagement. Once again, their relationship to "now" is defined by conflicting imperatives.

Taken together, these examples illustrate the group's tension with late modern temporality. While their cultural critique of contemporary life is vital for their sense of self, they are also thoroughly late modern in many ways. This tension surrounds the two transformations FORMED seeks to collapse. The very project of tethering personal change to social engagement, in fact, draws the group into this dilemma. What parts of themselves as late modern beings and what parts of public life as late modern institutions need transformation, and which are worth retaining? Ultimately, this incites a very familiar evangelical dilemma: how to be in the world, but not of it.

The second tension ensues from an uneasy relationship with exclusion. The question that FORMED raised for many who participated was how to be a new evangelical without becoming an old fundamentalist. Consider the following example.

The invited speaker for the "Community" vow was a house church pastor from Minneapolis. Mark was not a polished presenter, far more comfortable during informal conversations and the public question-answer session. He was short and heavyset, sporting a large beard, leather Kangol hat, baggy clothes, and dark-frame glasses. Mark began by informing everyone that he was distracted. By being there, he was missing a big day for his house church. For over a year, they had been holding a weekly Saturday dinner in an abandoned neighborhood parking lot. Much like Kevin's missional life in Norwood, this type of action was taken to exemplify the lack of division between private religious community and public social engagement. Recently, local police had threatened to disrupt the dinner due to their never having obtained a city permit. Mark forcefully observed that "breaking bread" has become "civil disobedience in America." This Saturday was supposedly the day when police would intervene. So, he was distracted. He used the story to segue into his primary premise: the "American Dream" and "the Kingdom of God" are "competing stories." Their job as Christians is to "challenge the whole system." "Community," the vow he was invited to speak on, "is an act of revolution." Making ample use of references to "empire" and "imperialism," Mark invoked the familiar evangelical trope of comparing contemporary life to biblical times: in this case, the United States is Rome, and the Religious Right are Pharisees.[30] Much like the preceding and subsequent monthly events, the day proceeded favorably: engaged and curious questions were asked, and participants exited seeming edified.

One participant, Chris, was a house church pastor in suburban Cincinnati and had been close friends with Kevin for a decade. After the event ended at 2 P.M., Chris and I spent several hours debriefing at a nearby coffee shop. It was an intense interview, primarily because Chris was bothered by Mark's talk. Generally, he found the whole presentation "separatist," "exclusionary," and "narrow-minded." Since 2001, Chris has led a network of house churches where his desire has been to "live simply" amid suburban largesse, "in the belly of the beast." He teaches his house church that conspicuous consumption is a pervasive sin they can address as a community. He talked about house church members who are upwardly mobile in their companies and likened their experience to Old Testament figures like Joseph and Daniel, who had "success in foreign kingdoms. We can subvert it if we don't belong to it." Chris was critical of Mark, in part, because the extreme difficulty of avoiding "the system" went unrecognized. He offered several examples of how Mark is "implicated": he flew on a plane from Minneapolis, he used his Mac laptop to present, and he used a bank mortgage to attain their communal house. For Chris, Mark's "operating completely in absolutes" was a "sign of spiritual immaturity."

Mark and Chris are both emerging evangelicals. The dissonance separating their versions of authentic community helps bring into view the tension of inclusion-exclusion in evangelical social engagement. What does it mean to be countercultural? How do you change "the system"? From a historical vantage point, Mark and Chris appear to be reenacting a lasting twentieth-century debate between fundamentalists and neo-evangelicals. Should Christians separate themselves from their social surround or integrate physically in order to alter it ideologically? As with the tension of temporality, questions of inclusion and exclusion frame the broader project of fusing personal and public transformations. And like the case of gender inclusivity pointing to a structural sensibility, we must account for how folk theories of agency and change are operative among emerging evangelicals. For Mark, public transformation is unlikely at the macrolevel; "the empire" will destruct before it changes. Meaningful change is only truly possible at the local level and will happen when Christian communities (i.e., house churches) bridge personal and neighborhood transformation. For Chris, a similar transformative weight is placed on Christian community, but the extent of potential change is different. Through changed individuals, his Josephs and Daniels, the system can eventually be rewritten so long as the script originates locally.

In my work with emerging evangelicals, these are the questions, tensions, and internal debates fueling social engagement. One finding I consider especially revealing is the way in which the new evangelical social engagement incites familiar evangelical tropes (how to be in the world, but not of it) and dilemmas (how to manage cultural separation). FORMED is an instructive example because it resonates with the broader trend of refusing divisions such as inner-outer, personal-social, and private-public. Transevangelical projects open a space to talk of monastic vows as a strategy for social change and neighborhood transformation as an enactment of personal faith.[31] While platforms and agendas are indeed shifting—broadening to human trafficking and sustainable development, for example—the future of evangelical social engagement will not unfold according to issue. It will unfold along the kinds of contours that shaped the production and consumption of FORMED.

NOTES

1. Susan Harding, *The Book of Jerry Falwell: Fundamentalist Language and Politics* (Princeton, NJ: Princeton University Press, 2000).

2. Heather Hendershot, *Shaking the World for Jesus: Media and Conservative Evangelical Culture* (Chicago: University of Chicago Press, 2004).

3. Omri Elisha, *Moral Ambition: Mobilization and Social Outreach in Evangelical Megachurches* (Berkeley: University of California Press, 2011).

4. James S. Bielo, *Emerging Evangelicals: Faith, Modernity, and the Desire for Authenticity* (New York: New York University Press, 2011).

5. John Drane, "Editorial: The Emerging Church," *International Journal for the Study of the Christian Church* 6 (2006): 3–11.

6. George Marcus, "Ethnography in/of the World System: The Emergence of Multi-Sited Ethnography," *Annual Review of Anthropology* 24 (1995): 95–117.

7. Luke Eric Lassiter, "Collaborative Ethnography," *AnthroNotes* 25 (2004): 1–14.

8. For an elaborated explanation of these five tracks see Bielo, *Emerging Evangelicals*, 10–16.

9. Elisha, *Moral Ambition*, 7–8.

10. Keith H. Basso, "Wisdom Sits in Places: Notes on a Western Apache Landscape," 53–90, in *Senses of Place*, ed. Steven Feld and Keith H. Basso (Santa Fe, NM: School of American Research Press, 1996); James S. Bielo, "Purity, Danger, and Redemption: Notes on Urban Missional Evangelicals," *American Ethnologist* 38 (2011): 267–80.

11. For a detailed analysis of the competing kingdom theologies among emerging evangelicals, see Bielo, *Emerging Evangelicals*, 138–56. Briefly, the "already, but not yet" asserts that God's kingdom was introduced by Jesus but will remain incomplete and unfulfilled until the Second Coming. As a result,

kingdom realities like divine healing are possible but not assured. The "kingdom now" theology asserts that God's kingdom was ushered in fully with the New Testament reported event of the Jewish temple destruction in A.D. 70. "Kingdom now" is also referred to as "fulfilled eschatology" and "Preterism." I reference these competing kingdom theologies here only to make the point that they embed models of temporality and agency.

12. Jon Bialecki, "Disjuncture, Continental Philosophy's New 'Political Paul,' and the Question of Progressive Christianity in a Southern California Third Wave Church," *American Ethnologist* 36 (2009): 35–48.

13. Susan Harding, "*Revolve*, The Biblezine: A Transevangelical Text," 176–93, in *The Social Life of Scriptures: Cross-Cultural Perspectives on Biblicism*, ed. James S. Bielo (New Brunswick, NJ: Rutgers University Press, 2009).

14. Harding, "*Revolve*," 181.

15. Norwood's local economy still suffers from the 1987 closing of a General Motors automotive factory. The outward aesthetic bares this impress. Houses are run-down: crooked and broken fences, chipping paint, cracked windows, few attempts at outward beautification. Streets are uninviting: trash scattered along curbs, rusty and bent road signs, potholes and eroding asphalt. Cars are categorically tattered, modest, and older—nothing glitzy or ostentatious. Yet, Norwood is lively because it is a lived-in place. Children play on sidewalks when days are not dampened by rain. Mothers push strollers. Older men and women sit in expired lawn chairs, idling or observing. Men congregate on corner pub stoops to smoke and talk. Demographically, the neighborhood is predominantly working-poor and lower-middle-class whites, most with kinship ties to central Appalachia from successive waves of migration following the steep decline in coal-mining employment.

16. Pierre Bourdieu, *Distinction: A Social Critique of the Judgment of Taste* (Cambridge, MA: Harvard University Press, 1984 [1979]).

17. E. Paul Durrenberger, "Explorations of Class and Consciousness in the U.S.," *Journal of Anthropological Research* 57 (2001): 41–60.

18. Elisha, *Moral Ambition*.

19. Elisha, *Moral Ambition*, 104.

20. Elisha, *Moral Ambition*, 108.

21. Elisha, *Moral Ambition*, 109.

22. Michel Foucault, "The Order of Discourse," 51–77, in *Untying the Text*, ed. R. Young (London: Routledge, 1981).

23. John P. Bartkowski, *The Promise Keepers: Servants, Soldiers, and Godly Men* (New Brunswick, NJ: Rutgers University Press, 2004); Tanya Erzen, "Testimonial Politics: The Christian Right's Faith-Based Approach to Marriage and Imprisonment," *American Quarterly* 59 (2007): 991–1015; Sally K. Gallagher,

Evangelical Identity and Gendered Family Life (New Brunswick, NJ: Rutgers University Press, 2003).

24. Dallas Willard, *The Divine Conspiracy: Rediscovering Our Hidden Life in God* (New York: HarperCollins, 1998).

25. Jane Guyer, "Prophecy and the Near Future: Thoughts on Microeconomic, Evangelical, and Punctuated Time," *American Ethnologist* 34 (2007): 410.

26. Harding, *The Book of Jerry Falwell*; Amy Frykholm, *Rapture Culture: Left Behind in Evangelical America* (Oxford: Oxford University Press, 2004); Joel Robbins, "Secrecy and the Sense of an Ending: Narrative, Time, and Everyday Millenarianism in Papua New Guinea and in Christian Fundamentalism," *Comparative Studies in Society and History* 43 (2001): 525–51.

27. The several ellipses in this example mark where Dave goes off script, annotating his prepared outline. None of this improvising added substantially to or challenged anything that appears here.

28. Taylor Clark, *Starbucked: A Double Tall Tale of Caffeine, Commerce, and Culture* (New York: Little Brown, 2007).

29. William Roseberry, "The Rise of Yuppie Coffees and the Reimagination of Class in the United States," *American Anthropologist* 98 (1996): 762–75.

30. James S. Bielo, *Words upon the Word: An Ethnography of Evangelical Group Bible Study* (New York: New York University Press, 2009), 47–72.

31. Harding, "*Revolve.*"

2

Whose Social Justice? Which Evangelicalism?

SOCIAL ENGAGEMENT IN A CAMPUS MINISTRY

John Schmalzbauer

EVANGELICAL CAMPUS MINISTRIES have an ambiguous reputation in higher education. Many faculty and administrators have only a vague notion of evangelical Christianity, often associating it with the political movement of the new Christian right or the 2006 documentary *Jesus Camp*. Others think of conservative positions on abortion and homosexuality.

Much of the scholarship and journalism on evangelical campus ministries confirms these preconceptions. In *Bill Bright & Campus Crusade for Christ*, historian John G. Turner details the connections between the founder of America's largest evangelical campus ministry and the religious right.[1] Along the same lines, journalistic treatments by Lauren Sandler and Jeff Sharlet portray an evangelical youth movement that uses countercultural style to mask a deep-seated political and social conservatism.[2] Likewise, a number of evangelical campus ministries have made news because of policies barring gays and lesbians from leadership positions in their organizations.[3] All of this would suggest that evangelicalism is a conservative force on the American college campus.

Though the conservative narrative contains a good deal of truth, it does not adequately capture the theological and cultural diversity of campus evangelicalism. This ideological diversity was on display during the 2008 presidential election, when many young evangelicals declared their support for Barack Obama. A postelection survey of younger evangelicals revealed that a significant minority cast their votes for the Democratic candidate.[4] Picking up on this development, dozens of news stories have described the growing engagement of evangelicals with progressive social causes.[5] A few have mentioned the impact of evangelical campus ministries.[6]

Despite these scattered treatments of evangelical social engagement, it has received relatively little scholarly scrutiny. For starters, most observers have ignored an earlier wave of evangelical activism that crested in the 1960s and 1970s. While older works explore the leftward drift of sixties evangelicalism, more recent studies offer the first comprehensive histories of this era. Despite the availability of such works, few have connected the current state of evangelical campus life to these earlier movements.[7]

In addition, very little attention has been paid to the role of campus ministries in the evangelical rediscovery of social justice. Writing in the *Christian Education Journal*, Evan Hunter discussed the recovery of a "holistic gospel" on campus, noting the popularity of groups like International Justice Mission and the One Campaign.[8] In a similar way, journalist Francesca Jarosz detailed the "push for social change" by evangelical college students in the Chicago area.[9] Activist Lisa Sharon Harper has also written about the role of campus ministries in *Evangelical ≠ Republican ... Or Democrat*, focusing on InterVarsity Christian Fellowship and Campus Crusade for Christ (now known as Cru). Yet apart from these works, most observers have ignored the growing activism of campus evangelicals.[10]

To address this gap in our understanding, this article uses a case study of InterVarsity Christian Fellowship to explore the social engagement of evangelical students. In particular, it focuses on InterVarsity's massive Urbana student missions conference, a gathering that drew 23,000 young evangelicals to St. Louis in 2006. Drawing on ethnographic field observations of Urbana, it profiles an organization that combines evangelism with a focus on poverty, the environment, and race.

From one angle, InterVarsity belongs on the evangelical left. Though this is often the case, the reality is far more complex. While more progressive than many evangelical organizations, InterVarsity takes a traditional approach on issues of human sexuality. Its approach to racial reconciliation has been criticized for promoting a conservative view of race.[11] Although highlighting structural injustices, InterVarsity's speakers and publications sometimes employ the language of evangelical relationalism. According to Christian Smith, "relationalism is profoundly individualistic," emphasizing personal influence rather than systemic social change.[12]

In a study of evangelical social engagement, anthropologist Omri Elisha describes the "plasticity of evangelicalism as lived religion."[13] In assessing InterVarsity's social engagement, this essay highlights the plasticity of campus evangelicalism and the multivocality of its social justice rhetoric. Rather than placing InterVarsity (IV) on the Christian left, it is more helpful to highlight the tensions in evangelical discourse. While IV has collaborated with

progressive groups such as Sojourners, it has been careful not to identify with
one side of the political spectrum. Reflecting this diversity, many campus
evangelicals have embraced an alternative definition of social justice, shifting
the conversation away from progressive social causes. Focusing on human
trafficking, some have adopted a legal understanding of injustice and oppression. Still others have emphasized local and decentralized strategies for fighting poverty, rejecting state-centered approaches to public policy.

In InterVarsity and other evangelical campus ministries, social justice
means different things to different people. Though much of this rhetoric has
a progressive feel, conservative voices are also getting a hearing. Far from a
monolith, evangelical campus ministries employ multiple and conflicting
models of social engagement. While profiling the progressive strains within
InterVarsity's discourse, this chapter also discusses more conservative understandings of social justice. Concluding with a discussion of the future of evangelicalism, it begins with an overview of InterVarsity's Urbana meeting.

Observing InterVarsity

InterVarsity Christian Fellowship has long been a moderating influence in
American evangelicalism. Many attribute this fact to its British origins.
Adopting a more cerebral approach to evangelism, it has emphasized the life of
the mind.[14] More than any other evangelical campus ministry, it has embraced
the cause of social action. As David R. Swartz argues in chapter 10, this is an
outgrowth of InterVarsity's internationalism. A transatlantic group with roots
in the modern missionary movement, it has always had global aspirations.
Since 1946, the ministry has sponsored a large gathering on world missions.
From 1948 to 2003, this gathering met on the campus of the University of
Illinois at Champaign-Urbana. In 2006, it moved to St. Louis, retaining the
name Urbana.

As part of the National Study of Campus Ministries, I attended Urbana
2006. Beginning on December 27 and concluding on New Year's Eve, this
gathering had nine plenary sessions, as well as dozens of seminars and exhibits. I took field notes running to 121 single-spaced pages at plenary events, seminars, the book display, and other public events. Whenever possible, I checked
them against videos on the Urbana website.[15]

Larger than most campus ministry gatherings in America, Urbana 2006
was held in the massive Edward Jones Dome. Usually quiet and empty (except
on St. Louis Rams game days or during conventions), the blocks around the
dome became the temporary home of 23,000 young evangelicals. Attendees
were a mix of students and nonstudents. Fifty-nine percent of the students

belonged to InterVarsity, and an additional 12 percent were affiliated with other campus ministries. Five percent came from Campus Crusade.[16]

Looking over the mass of people, it was hard to miss the ethnic composition of the crowd. Only 60 percent of attendees were white. At 29 percent, Asian Americans were the next largest group, followed by African Americans (6 percent), and Latinos (3 percent).[17] These statistics reflect the growing numbers of Asian Americans in many evangelical campus ministries, as well as the underrepresentation of blacks and Hispanics.[18] The multiethnic background of participants was reflected in the makeup of the speakers, the emcees, and the band. The main emcee for the event was second-generation Chinese American Greg Jao, a graduate of Northwestern University Law School and the director of InterVarsity's New York–New Jersey section. Of the eleven speakers, only four were white males. Worship was led by African American musician Daryl Black and included such selections as "Con Mis Manos" and "Yae Su Sa Rang Hae Yo."[19]

Consistent with this mix, Urbana highlighted themes that are often missing from evangelical churches. The first night, participants saw a video produced by InterVarsity's in-house media unit. Entitled "The Church Working," it featured several men and women talking about greed, sexism, pollution, and war. Following this litany of problems, a voice announced, "There are some things about the world that just aren't right." Comparing contemporary social institutions to the ruling authorities referred to in the New Testament, the narrator noted that life is influenced by "governments, large corporations, media, apathy, and consumerism." After a montage of young people reflected on the obstacles to social change, the video concluded with a charge to carry out God's purposes here on earth.

Later in the evening, attendees heard from Terry LeBlanc, national ministries director for My People International of Canada. Wearing a Native American vest and a black shirt, he spoke passionately about pollution, global warming, the "techno-pollution" of entertainment culture, and our society's lack of solitude. Drawing on indigenous traditions of spirituality, LeBlanc said that the most fruitful times of God's direction in his life had been in moments of quiet reflection, noting that for him "the sweat lodge, a tradition of prayer and fasting, of listening and seeking for many of our peoples in Native North America, has become a most powerful time."

In the space of a few hours, the young evangelicals at Urbana were confronted by a host of social issues, as well as new forms of cultural diversity. They were also encouraged to share the gospel with the whole world. In his welcoming remarks, Urbana director Jim Tebbe emphasized the themes of evangelism and world missions, stressing the call "to serve, witness, and suffer in the world." At the conclusion of the first evening, participants sang, "Lord I want to come and discover my path, to take the next step on this road of life. Give me the courage to seek your grace and to answer my call."

By connecting vocation with evangelism, Urbana 2006 combined themes that are not always found together in American Christianity. Though evangelical proclamation was always in the foreground (receiving by far the most airtime), the meeting also gave voice to a host of social issues. Three of the most prominent were poverty and injustice, the environment, and racial reconciliation.

Poverty and Injustice

The problem of poverty and injustice was a recurring theme during Urbana 2006. On the very first night, a drama troupe performed a skit about a group of college students volunteering with Homes for the World, a fictionalized version of Habitat for Humanity. On the second evening, Kenyan evangelical Oscar Muriu predicted that "new theologies of liberation from oppression" would take center stage in world Christianity, noting that in Africa theology is being rewritten in the context "of famine, of poverty, of HIV-AIDS, of disease, of hunger, and of oppression."

One of the most passionate calls for justice came on the third evening of the convention. That night Sharon Cohn told of her work as an attorney for International Justice Mission, an organization that works on behalf of the "victims of slavery, sexual exploitation and other forms of violent oppression."[20] Founded by InterVarsity alumnus Gary Haugen, it has been praised by *New York Times* columnist Nicholas Kristof for its work with Third World sex workers.[21] At Urbana, Cohn spoke of her interest in God's "relentless concern for the poor," noting that "God reserves his strongest commentary for the offense of injustice."

Focusing on poverty in America, urban ministry specialist Ray Bakke recalled the civil rights movement's "liberation of those trapped in oppression," criticizing white evangelicals for abandoning the cities. Later in the week, a video celebrated those Christians who have worked "for the poor and oppressed," highlighting the witness of Justin Martyr, Fannie Lou Hamer, Martin Luther King Jr., and Archbishop Oscar Romero.

Emulating such role models, some evangelicals have joined forces with neomonastic organizations focused on simple living and voluntary poverty.[22] A December 29 seminar with the neomonastic group Word Made Flesh drew an overflow crowd eager to hear about the group's work with Third World children. On December 31, Urbana's book of the day was Scott Bessenecker's

The New Friars, a work that describes this movement to identify with the global poor. Under Bessenecker's direction, students in Urbana's Slum Communities of the Developing World track learned about urbanization, sex trafficking, shantytowns, and advocacy in the "halls of power." Although the students stayed in the Wyndham Mayfair Hotel, they abstained from hot showers, instead bathing each day with a bucket and a sponge. In the words of a participant, it helped her "understand the reality of what we're learning about."[23] Along with *The New Friars*, InterVarsity Press has published such titles as the *Social Justice Handbook, Welcoming Justice, Just Courage, Friendship at the Margins, Power and Poverty*, and *A Theology as Big as the City*. The Urbana bookstore carried Barbara Ehrenreich's *Nickel and Dimed*.

The culmination of the week's justice emphasis came in a surprise message from U2's Bono, appearing live via satellite. Opening with "Greetings Urbanites!" he made a heartfelt plea for the victims of HIV/AIDS, adding that the disease demanded "an urgent, comprehensive and massive" response. Citing Matthew 25, Bono declared that "God is in the slums," "God is in the cries heard under the rubble of war," and "God is with us if we are with them." He spoke of the work of the ONE Campaign, an organization dedicated to fighting global poverty. After Bono disappeared from the Jumbotrons, World Vision's Steve Haas urged students to text the ONE Campaign. All across the Edward Jones Dome, cell phones lit up, demonstrating their commitment to social justice and the persuasive powers of an Irish rock star. A grassroots advocacy group, ONE actively lobbies governments on poverty, debt cancellation, climate change, and HIV/AIDS. Though InterVarsity is far from a political organization, its involvement with ONE signals a new engagement with politics and public affairs.[24]

Environmental Stewardship

Poverty and AIDS are not the only issues on the minds of evangelical college students. Thanks to a nascent movement of green evangelicals, caring for the planet is also in the mix. This concern was made manifest in an InterVarsity video shown on the second night of Urbana. As a voice-over declared, "The earth is the Lord's and all that is in it," images of children, nature, and animals flashed on the screen. Featuring Christian environmentalists Cal DeWitt and Ed Brown, the video focused on climate change. Noting that global warming is driven by the practices of rich countries, it warned that the consequences would be felt by the poor, especially those living in floodplains and in island nations.

"Creation care" has become a priority for InterVarsity. In recent years, InterVarsity Press has published books such as *Green Revolution, The Care of*

Creation, Redeeming Creation, and *Our Father's World.* Back in 1994, InterVarsity President Steve Hayner signed "An Evangelical Declaration on the Care of Creation." A pioneering document among green evangelicals, this statement urged "individual Christians and churches to be centers of creation's care and renewal, both delighting in creation as God's gift, and enjoying it as God's provision, in ways which sustain and heal the damaged fabric of the creation which God has entrusted to us."[25]

Racial Reconciliation

The topic of racial reconciliation was also high on the agenda of Urbana 2006. On most mornings, the main speaker was Sri Lankan evangelical, Ajith Fernando. Though his main focus was on the New Testament book of Ephesians, he used the Bible to talk about race. Discussing the multiethnic character of first-century Christianity, Fernando said that today's Christians must break down barriers. Arguing that "the death of Jesus changes the way we look at people," he stressed that in Christ "race, class, caste are not a big deal."

Focusing on the same topic, a December 28 video addressed the "dividing walls" separating whites from Native Americans in British Columbia. Noting that "the First Nations People in the United States and Canada have suffered broken promises," it told of the theft of land and the forced schooling of Native American children by the Canadian government. Discussing the emotional and sexual abuse of Native American children, the video called for repentance on the part of whites. Ending on a hopeful note, it told of the budding friendship between a local church and the indigenous community.

Later that evening, Chicago's Brenda Salter-McNeil spoke on the topic of racial reconciliation. A consultant on cultural and racial issues who has blogged for *Sojourners* magazine, Salter-McNeil is part of a network of progressive African American evangelicals. At Urbana, she used the story of the Tower of Babel to talk about race and ethnicity, recalling how God forced the people to interact with diverse cultures by scattering them to the ends of the Earth. Noting that Babel is "really all of our stories," she said that we have a tendency to "segregate ourselves in our own little cultural ghettoes." Challenging her listeners, Salter-McNeil asked them to leave behind their "homogeneous comfort zones to be a part of a multicultural, multiethnic, multilingual, multinational family of God."

Perhaps the strangest discussion of race and ethnicity occurred in an afternoon seminar on "Being White." It was strange because evangelicalism has rarely problematized whiteness, often treating it as the default identity for

North American Christians. Mixing essentialism with multiculturalism, Doug Schaupp talked about his own "white culture" (including white individualism), his interracial marriage, and his experience serving as a pastor in a black church. In the early years of Urbana, such a session would have been unlikely. With the diversification of evangelical campus ministries, white Christians are on their way to becoming one group among many.

Schaupp's seminar was one of a dozen smaller gatherings on race and ethnicity. Another examined "the Korean-American community and the kingdom of God." Much more intense was a late-night worship session with Korean American and Japanese American college students. In an emotional exchange, participants in this event witnessed apologies for Japanese atrocities during World War II and forgiveness on behalf of the Korean people. According to a Japanese graduate student, "It was the greatest international God-moment I had ever experienced."[26] Along the same lines, the Urbana bookstore offered works like Cornel West's *Race Matters* and Michael Emerson and Christian Smith's *Divided by Faith*. Other recent InterVarsity Press titles include *The Heart of Racial Justice, Beyond Racial Gridlock, More Than Equals, Reconciliation Blues*, and *Being Latino in Christ*.

Making Sense of Urbana's Social Engagement

Urbana's emphasis on poverty, the environment, and racial reconciliation does not square with the public image of American evangelicalism. Far from an anomaly, Urbana reflects InterVarsity's historic ties with the evangelical non-right. In *The Worldly Evangelicals*, Richard Quebedeaux described a heightened attention to social issues in InterVarsity, noting "it now represents a diversity of positions characteristic of the evangelical left." As early as 1974, the *National Review* warned of the political apostasy of younger evangelicals, an issue that has remained a concern on the right.[27] More recently, David Swartz has examined the history of InterVarsity in *Moral Minority: The Evangelical Left in an Age of Conservatism*. In particular, Swartz portrays the 1970 Urbana meeting as a key event in the mobilization of evangelical progressives. That year African American evangelical Tom Skinner chastised American Christians for their complicity with racism, announcing that "the liberator has come!" Anabaptists Ronald Sider and John Howard Yoder were also closely identified with InterVarsity during the early years of the evangelical left.[28]

That progressive history was itself an outgrowth of InterVarsity's roots in the Student Christian Movement in Great Britain and the United States. In the early years of the twentieth century, organizations such as the YMCA combined personal evangelism with a conservative version of the social gospel.

By the 1920s, the Y was hosting socialist Norman Thomas. In *The College "Y,"* David Setran described a time when the YMCA was the dominant campus religious organization in the United States. Though the "social evangelism" of the Y gave way to secularization, it anticipated the dual focus of InterVarsity on personal faith and social justice. InterVarsity emerged out of a British context shaped by similar developments.[29]

This dual focus on social justice and evangelism was reflected in a 2006 web survey of 535 InterVarsity campus ministers. Part of the larger National Study of Campus Ministries, it was administered by a team led by Betty DeBerg and John Schmalzbauer. In the survey, 87 percent of InterVarsity campus ministers agreed that social justice was at the heart of the gospel. Likewise, 70 percent said that fostering a commitment to social justice was very important, though only 15 percent ranked it among their top three goals. By contrast, 82 percent ranked bringing students to Christ as a top three goal, an indication of the centrality of evangelism to InterVarsity's mission.[30]

In recent decades, InterVarsity has increased its emphasis on social justice. This shift reflects larger changes in the evangelical subculture, including the growth of Sojourners and the new Christian left.[31] It also reflects changes in IV's own constituency. Writing in 2004, Rebecca Kim noted that the number of Asian Americans in IV had increased by 267 percent since the 1970s.[32] Currently, racial minorities comprise 36 percent of InterVarsity's student population.[33] Responding to this diversity, the organization added "ethnic reconciliation and justice" to its list of core commitments.[34] Consistent with this vision, InterVarsity Press has published twenty-eight books by Asian and Asian American authors.[35] Many Asian evangelicals draw on African American language about social justice.[36] The resurgence of evangelical social engagement cannot be understood apart from the diversification of groups like InterVarsity.

Several years after Urbana 2006, IV has continued to focus on social change. Consistent with this trajectory, Urbana 2009 spent even more time on poverty, race, and the environment. In 2009, InterVarsity offered an Advocacy and Poverty track designed to "equip participants to act as advocates and community organizers." Plenary sessions included an entire evening devoted to the theme of the environment. Speakers included Shane Claiborne, a Christian pacifist and practitioner of communal living.[37] Picking up on the progressive agenda, several evangelical news organizations reported a shift toward social activism at Urbana 2009. Noting the emphasis on HIV/AIDS, poverty, and environmental justice, a headline in the *Mission Network News* asked, "Social Justice vs. Gospel—Is It a Battle at Urbana?"[38] Likewise, the *Christian Post* reported a "stronger emphasis on social justice."[39] Celebrating this shift, a press release from World Vision declared that this was the "first time political advocacy on poverty and social justice–related issues has been an official focus track in the 63-year history of the largest Christian student missions conference in North America."[40] Along the same lines, Urbana 2012 featured forty-eight seminars in the same track, noting that "Scriptures echo a provocative challenge to be engaged with poverty and biblical justice."[41]

Echoing Urbana, many local chapters have embraced the cause of social justice. The InterVarsity Social Justice League meets at the University of Washington. Its mission is "promoting a faith-rooted culture of social justice and compassion," as well as "saving the world from villains."[42] Focusing on human trafficking and world hunger, Michigan Tech's chapter sponsors a Social Justice Week, complete with a mock slave auction and a broken bread dinner.[43] Such initiatives are encouraged in *The InterVarsity Chapter Leaders' Handbook*, which urges leaders to "develop disciples, in light of Biblical teaching on social justice and compassionate service."[44] Like Urbana, local chapters have emphasized a wide range of issues, including poverty, AIDS, genocide, home foreclosures, microenterprise, and homelessness.[45]

In InterVarsity's literature, social justice is linked with evangelism.[46] In the judgment of a staff member, "It is unfathomable to introduce the Gospel to student activists without this dimension of social justice and reconciliation."[47] Some students even tell social justice conversion stories. According to one alumnus, "My heart for social justice started with InterVarsity, because it challenged me to engage with scripture."[48] Another attributed his vocation to the group, noting that "since becoming involved in InterVarsity, I have seen how I can live out my faith in vocations that aren't technically in the ministry, like working at a university or at an NGO fighting poverty."[49] In this way, InterVarsity has bridged the worlds of evangelicalism and social activism.

Tensions within Campus Evangelicalism: Competing Definitions of Social Justice

Some might be tempted to see InterVarsity as the Democratic Party at prayer. In reality, IV spans the ideological spectrum. In the 2006 survey of InterVarsity staff, 27 percent identified as liberal, 36 percent as moderate, and 37 percent as conservative. This compares with a breakdown of 21 percent liberal, 35 percent moderate, and 40 percent conservative in the general population. While IV is more liberal than the American public, it still attracts plenty of Republicans.[50]

A mix of conservative and liberal attitudes was evident at Urbana 2006, a meeting that combined calls for social justice with an affirmation of traditional sexual mores. Like most evangelical campus ministries, InterVarsity regards homosexuality as a sin, publishing such works as *A Parent's Guide to Preventing Homosexuality*. Not surprisingly, such positions are controversial on the American campus. InterVarsity has also courted controversy through its choice of speakers. In 2006, Urbana featured talks by Rick and Kay Warren, the latter focusing on AIDS in Africa. Since then the Reverend Warren has been embroiled in controversies over California's Proposition 8, Uganda's proposed ban on homosexuality, and abstinence-only approaches to AIDS.

InterVarsity has articulated a mixture of positions on race. In a discussion of IV, sociologist Antony Alumkal argues that evangelical racial reconciliation theology has been transformed into what he calls a "conservative racial project." He is especially critical of the tendency to treat racism as a psychological disposition, rather than a structural feature of American society.[51] Along the same lines, Rudy Busto criticizes InterVarsity for perpetuating the model minority stereotype.[52] By contrast, sociologist Elaine Howard Ecklund is more hopeful, seeing Asian American evangelicalism as the source of a new racial consciousness.[53] At Urbana 2006, racism was discussed using both psychological and structural vocabularies, suggesting that InterVarsity is beginning to learn from such critiques.

InterVarsity Press authors often use structural language. While Kevin Blue's *Practical Justice* includes forty-one references to structures and systems, Mae Elise Cannon's *Social Justice Handbook* refers to systems seventy-two times.[54] Some IV authors emphasize the topic of economic redistribution. In *Transforming Power*, Robert Linthicum writes that a "nation and culture built on relationship with God and each other requires a government that will seek justice in all it does." According to Linthicum, the ancient Hebrews used several mechanisms "to periodically redistribute wealth so that no one in that economy experiences either extreme poverty or extreme wealth."[55] Expressing a similar vision, author John Perkins argues that "God meant for equality to be expressed in terms of economics."[56] In an interview with IV Press, Perkins notes that "the third R is redistribution," acknowledging that this "sounds like communism." In his judgment, "God never gives ownership, he gives stewardship for the human good."[57] While preserving a role for government programs and affirmative action, he believes that redistribution should be carried out by the church.[58]

Reflecting the ideological diversity of the evangelical subculture, campus movements employ multiple definitions of social justice. Leading the fight against human trafficking, International Justice Mission (IJM) has close ties to InterVarsity, Campus Crusade, and the Passion Conferences. Adopting a more circumscribed definition of justice, IJM founder Gary Haugen does not address the redistribution of wealth. According to Haugen, "Trafficking is not a poverty issue. It's a law enforcement issue."[59] While IJM employs a vice president for structural transformation (a position currently held by Urbana 2006 speaker Sharon Cohn Wu), this office focuses on legal structures. A similar view of justice can be found in other IJM publications. Partnering with Campus Crusade's CruPress, the organization recently published an IJM/CCC Social Justice Bible study. Drawing on Micah, Amos, and Isaiah, it argues that "God hates injustice." While highlighting several passages on the poor and oppressed, it does not discuss inequality.[60]

Emphasizing the criminal justice system, IJM has avoided the topic of social stratification. Though the fight against human trafficking has united evangelicals and mainstream feminists (including the National Organization for Women), some have criticized the "carceral turn in feminist advocacy movements."[61] In the judgment of these critics, the anti-sex-trafficking movement "seeks social remedies through criminal justice interventions rather than through a redistributive welfare state." Though the evangelical foes of human trafficking employ the language of social justice, they tend to locate all "social harm outside the institutions of corporate capitalism, the state apparatus, and the nuclear family." For some feminist scholars, that is not enough. Critiquing the neoliberal assumptions of the antitrafficking movement, they call for a more radical approach.[62]

In spite of such criticism, the movement has sometimes united the left and the right. In January 2012, the Atlanta-based Passion Conference addressed the problem of human trafficking. Drawing 42,000 college students to the Georgia Dome, Passion 2012 raised $3.1 million for groups like IJM.[63] Short films told the stories of men and women rescued from prostitution and forced labor through the intervention of faith-based organizations, exhorting viewers "to rise up for freedom."[64] Illustrating the broad appeal of this issue, *Sojourners* commended Passion 2012 for its efforts.[65] One month later, President Barack Obama praised Passion 2012 in a speech at the National Prayer Breakfast, noting "it was inspiring to see thousands of young Christians filling the Georgia Dome at the Passion Conference, to worship the God who sets the captives free and work to end modern slavery."[66]

More conservative definitions of social justice are also circulating among campus evangelicals. In 2010, the Heritage Foundation released *Seek Social Justice*, a six-segment small group study and DVD on the "complex problems of poverty, addiction, and homelessness." Published by the Southern Baptist LifeWay Christian Resources, it is available free at www.seeksocialjustice. com.[67] As Heritage's Ryan Messmore told Focus on the Family's *CitizenLink*, "We've really found a welcome audience for our material among young people, college campuses, professors, churches and small groups."[68] Endorsed by Gary Haugen of IJM, the video includes interviews with Albert Mohler and the late Charles Colson. Discussing both spiritual and material poverty, *Seek Social Justice* focuses on broken relationships and family breakdown. In place of federal programs, it shows how churches, families, and nonprofit organizations minister to poor neighborhoods. According to the study's website, "Churches and ministries can offer a comprehensive set of resources to help cultivate and restore all the foundational relationships of human life." Government exists to "sustain an environment of safety, freedom, order and peace." Though aimed at a general audience, *Seek Social Justice* features several prominent evangelical scholars, including journalism professor Marvin Olasky (the father of compassionate conservatism) and public policy expert Amy Sherman.[69]

One segment highlights the activities of Trevecca Nazarene University's J. V. Morsch Center for Social Justice, where Sherman serves as a consultant. According to the center's director, James Casler, "We draw our definition of social justice from the Scripture, not so much from the secular terminology."[70] Emphasizing microfinance and local outreach, Casler rejects the notion that government "administers the redistribution of basic resources." In his view, a biblical view of redistribution can be found in Acts 4:32–35, where the early church gave to "those in need in reflection of Christ's love, grace, and mercy."[71] Currently, the center's projects include a community garden and a neighborhood empowerment program.[72]

Rather than abandoning the term *social justice*, some evangelicals have tried to redefine its meaning.[73] This process has its origins among conservative Catholics. In lectures to the Heritage Foundation and the American Enterprise Institute (AEI), Michael Novak traced the term back to the nineteenth-century Italian Jesuit Luigi Taparelli D'Azeglio and Pope Leo XIII's *Rerum Novarum*.[74] Arguing that progressives have misused the word, he articulated a nonstatist conception of social justice, focusing on the "virtue of cooperation and association."[75] Ten years earlier, he addressed this topic in the conservative magazine *First Things*, invoking the work of Austrian economist Friedrich A. Hayek.[76] The same article appeared on the web page of Campus Crusade's Leadership University and in the recommended readings for the Heritage Foundation's *Seek Social Justice* study.[77] In 2005, Heritage sponsored the First International Conservative Conference on Social Justice. The speakers included evangelical public policy expert Don Eberly and Senator Dan Coats. Senator Rick Santorum gave the keynote address.[78]

More recently, the American Enterprise Institute sponsored several campus debates between Sojourners founder Jim Wallis and AEI president Arthur Brooks, a passionate defender of free enterprise. In 2010, Brooks and

Wallis appeared at Wheaton College. Since then, they have visited Gordon and Messiah Colleges.[79] Other debates have featured microfinance advocate Peter Greer and Neo-Anabaptist Shane Claiborne. Concerned that evangelical young people are "increasingly attracted to leftist arguments for 'social justice' and its resulting dependencies," the Kern Family Foundation has funded several of these events. The goal is to help college students "see the connections between following God and serving others in a free marketplace."[80] Part of the same initiative, AEI's Common Sense Concepts project has published works such as *Wealth and Justice* and *Mere Environmentalism.*[81]

Advancing a similar view of social justice, the Acton Institute has addressed an ecumenical audience of Catholics, Protestants, and Eastern Orthodox Christians. Founded by Father Robert Sirico, it focuses on religion and economics. Like Novak, Sirico has been influenced by Ludwig von Mises and Friedrich A. Hayek, seeing a connection between Austrian economics and the personalism of John Paul II.[82] Combining free market approaches with Catholic social thought, Sirico argues that "there is no 'social justice' without economic freedom."[83] Instead of "a vast impersonal welfare state," social justice is "about people fulfilling *their* responsibilities in justice to their neighbor."[84] With the support of the Kern Family Foundation, Acton has sponsored curricular initiatives at thirteen evangelical seminaries.[85] It has also provided minigrants to faculty at evangelical colleges.[86] A 2013 Acton Institute conference focused on "clergy, church, and parachurch workers." Assessing "the idea of social justice," it questioned "calls for the reduction of personal liberty and a concomitant increase in state power to distribute material goods and the resources of private enterprise in common."[87]

Such initiatives have complicated the meaning of social justice among Catholics and evangelicals. Responding to Novak and Sirico, many liberal Catholics have criticized the synthesis of free market thought and Catholic social teaching. Noting Hayek's distaste for the church's doctrine on social justice, they have rejected the "libertarian heresies" of the Austrian school.[88] Their critiques have elicited vigorous rejoinders from conservatives and libertarians.[89] Among campus evangelicals, the conversation has been less polarized. Though some have blasted the use of social justice rhetoric at evangelical colleges, most have remained relatively civil.[90] Commenting on the Sojourners-AEI debate at Wheaton College, one blogger noted "how similar [Jim] Wallis and [Arthur] Brooks sounded throughout the night."[91] A more heated debate broke out on the Facebook page of InterVarsity's Emerging Scholars Network after a postdoc criticized the Acton Institute. In the spirit of dialogue, InterVarsity posted an interview with Acton research fellow Jordan Ballor on its Emerging Scholars blog.[92]

Some evangelicals have tried to bridge the divide between left and right. In *Generous Justice*, Timothy Keller drew on conservative and liberal approaches to social justice. Using Amy Sherman and Robert Linthicum to illustrate the two sides, he recommended them both. According to Keller, "The divergent theories of justice in our society are very powerful, and Christian authors are usually influenced by one of them or the other. Some of these books will assume a more conservative, individualistic theory of justice and others the view that poverty is almost completely the result of unjust social systems." In his view, "it should be possible to glean great ideas from all kinds of sources." An alumnus of InterVarsity, Keller exemplifies the tensions in evangelical discourse.[93]

Conclusion: The Future of Evangelical Social Engagement on Campus

What does InterVarsity's social engagement mean for the future of evangelicalism? Across the nation, campus ministries have embraced the issues of racial reconciliation, poverty, and the environment. After witnessing IV's embrace of social justice, some have concluded that evangelicals are moving to the left. While there is an element of truth in such observations, the larger picture is far more complex.

Far from a representative slice of campus evangelicalism, InterVarsity's students and staff are a socially conscious subset. While 87 percent of InterVarsity staff believe social justice is at the heart of the gospel, such views are not widely shared by students at evangelical colleges. Reporting on a 1996 survey of undergraduates at nine conservative Protestant institutions, Corwin Smidt and James Penning note that "evangelical college students are inclined to assert that the church should focus more on personal morality (54 percent) than on social justice (12 percent)."[94] Likewise, a 2010 survey found that students "favored a more individualist social theology instead of a communitarian or structuralist one, though a plurality still believed that the solution lies in an addressing both individual hearts and changing social institutions equally."[95] Surveys of evangelical clergy have revealed a similar pattern.[96]

Even within InterVarsity, there is considerable diversity. As noted earlier, social justice is a multivocal term. Though some campus evangelicals employ structural metaphors, many avoid the language of inequality. In particular, opponents of human trafficking have invoked a narrower understanding of justice. Focusing on legal and criminal justice, they have steered clear of social and economic factors. Still others have advanced a small-government definition of social justice.

In the mid-1960s, sociologist Phillip Hammond described the "segmentation of radicalism" among mainline Protestant campus ministers, noting the tendency of radical clergy to end up in higher education.[97] When it comes to InterVarsity, it might be more accurate to speak of *segmented moderatism.* Describing Urbana's focus on social justice and multiethnicity, blogger Nick Liao called InterVarsity "a curious minority report in North American evangelicalism."[98] Far from inconsequential, this minority has influenced the evangelical subculture. Despite this influence, it shows no signs of taking over.

What does InterVarsity's social engagement mean for colleges and universities? For starters, it shows that campus evangelicals cannot be lumped together with the new Christian right. It also reveals that groups like InterVarsity promote a mixture of conservative and progressive social positions. Finally, it suggests the potential for common ground between campus progressives and some evangelicals. Though such coalitions may frustrate those on either end of the political spectrum, they offer the best chance of enlisting evangelical young people in grassroots movements for social change.

NOTES

1. An earlier version of this essay was published as John Schmalzbauer, "Social Engagement in an Evangelical Campus Ministry: The Case of Urbana 2006," *Journal of College and Character* 11:1 (2010). This essay is available at http://www.degruyter.com/view/j/jcc.2010.11.1/jcc.2010.11.1.1247/jcc.2010.11.1.1247.xml. The publisher was De Gruyter. Missouri State University graduate students Steve Fouse and Michael Bohlen provided valuable research assistance on this article. John G. Turner, *Bill Bright & Campus Crusade for Christ: The Renewal of Evangelicalism in Postwar America* (Chapel Hill: University of North Carolina Press, 2008).

2. Lauren Sandler, *Righteous: Dispatches from the Evangelical Youth Movement* (New York: Viking, 2006); Jeff Sharlet, "Teenage Holy War," *Rolling Stone*, April 19, 2007.

3. Richard Ostling, "Strict Tenets Put Fellowship at Odds with Universities," *Deseret News*, January 18, 2003.

4. In 2008, 32 percent of white evangelicals between 18 and 29 voted for Barack Obama, double the percentage that backed John Kerry in 2004. See Laurie Goodstein, "Obama Made Gains Among Younger Evangelicals," *New York Times*, November 7, 2008.

5. Francis Fitzgerald, "The New Evangelicals: This Election, a Growing Movement Presents a Challenge to the Religious Right," *New Yorker*, June 30, 2008; Samuel Freedman, "Evangelical, and Young, and Active in New

Area," *New York Times*, November 28, 2009; Nicholas Kristof, "Evangelicals a Liberal Can Love," *New York Times*, February 3, 2008; Jon Ward and Ralph Hallow, "Obama Attracts Young Evangelicals: Move Worries Older Pro-Lifers," *Washington Times*, August 15, 2008.

6. Evan Hunter, "'Converted to the Kingdom': Social Action among College Students Today," *Christian Education Journal*, 5:1 (2008): 88–100; C. L. Lopez, "A More Social Gospel," *Christianity Today*, December 18, 2009.

7. Robert Booth Fowler, *A New Engagement: Evangelical Political Thought, 1966–1976* (Grand Rapids, MI: Eerdmans, 1982); Richard Quebedeaux, *The Worldly Evangelicals* (New York: Harper & Row, 1978); Richard Quebedeaux, *The Young Evangelicals* (New York: Harper & Row, 1974); Preston Shires, *Hippies of the Religious Right* (Waco, TX: Baylor University Press, 2007); David Swartz, *Left Behind: The Evangelical Left and the Limits of Evangelical Politics, 1965–1988*, unpublished doctoral dissertation, University of Notre Dame, 2008, http://etd. nd.edu/ETD-db/theses/available/etd-07082008-105512/; David Swartz, *Moral Minority: The Evangelical Left in an Age of Conservatism* (Philadelphia: University of Pennsylvania Press, 2012); Turner, *Bill Bright & Campus Crusade for Christ*; Timothy Tseng and Janet Furness, "The Reawakening of Evangelical Social Consciousness," 114–125, in *The Social Gospel Today*, ed. Christopher H. Evans (Louisville, KY: Westminster/John Knox, 2001).

8. Evan Hunter, "'Converted to the Kingdom.'"

9. Francesca Jarosz, "Evangelicals Push for Social Change," *Daily Northwestern*, April 25, 2007, http://dailynorthwestern.com/2007/04/24/archive-manual/ evangelicals-push-for-social-change/.

10. Lisa Sharon Harper, *Evangelical ≠ Republican...or Democrat* (New York: New Press, 2008).

11. Antony Alumkal, "American Evangelicalism in the Post–Civil Rights Era: A Racial Formation Theory Analysis," *Sociology of Religion*, 65:3 (2004): 195–213.

12. Christian Smith, *American Evangelicalism: Embattled and Thriving* (Chicago: University of Chicago Press, 1998), 189.

13. Omri Elisha, *Moral Ambition: Mobilization and Social Outreach in Evangelical Megachurches* (Berkeley: University of California Press, 2011), 221.

14. Mark Noll, *The Scandal of the Evangelical Mind* (Grand Rapids, MI: Eerdmans, 1996).

15. Videos of Urbana were retrieved from InterVarsity Christian Fellowship, Urbana 06 Webcast, at www.urbana.org/archives/2006/webcast. Though this website no longer exists, an archived copy can be accessed at http://web. archive.org/web/*/www.urbana.org/archives/2006/webcast. Unfortunately, the videos are no longer available.

16. Darin Miller, "Urbana 06 Breaks Registration Record," *Urbana Today*, December 28, 2006, 1, http://web.archive.org/web/20071028012356/http:// www.urbana.org/pdf/Urbana06_Urbana_Today_Dec28.pdf.

17. Miller, "Urbana 06 Breaks Registration Record."

18. Rebecca Y. Kim, "Asian Americans for Jesus: Changing the Face of Campus Evangelicalism," Social Science Research Council web forum on "The Religious Engagements of American Undergraduates," February 6, 2007, http://religion.ssrc.org/reforum/Kim.pdf; Rebecca Y. Kim, "Second-Generation Korean American Evangelicals: Ethnic, Multiethnic, or White Campus Ministries," *Sociology of Religion* 65:1 (2004): 21.

19. As Gerardo Marti and Michael O. Emerson argue in chapter 8, evangelicalism often takes an essentialist approach to diversity. This was sometimes the case at Urbana 2006. In a session on "Being White," the speaker attributed several character traits to Anglo-American culture. In the worship times, certain songs represented particular cultures. For example, the website for Urbana 2006 called "Con Mis Manos" a "new arrangement of 'an old school jam for Latinos.'"

20. International Justice Mission, "About Us." Retrieved from www.ijm.org/?gclid=CNeypY7zjZ8CFcx25QodggfohQ.

21. Nicholas Kristof, "Sex Slaves? Lock Up the Pimps," *New York Times*, January 29, 2005. Retrieved from www.nytimes.com/2005/01/29/opinion/29kristof.html?_r=1.

22. Molly Worthen, "The Unexpected Monks," *Boston Globe*, February 3, 2008, www.boston.com/bostonglobe/ideas/articles/2008/02/03/the_unexpected_monks/.

23. John Wagner, "Students Learn about Poverty in Experiment," *Urbana 06 Today*, December 29, 2006, http://web.archive.org/web/20071028012254/http://www.urbana.org/pdf/Urbana06_Urbana_Today_Dec29.pdf.

24. Nonpartisan in orientation, ONE has employed both Republicans and Democrats. In 2010, former Bush speechwriter Michael Gerson began a year-long fellowship with ONE. A prominent evangelical, Gerson is a columnist for the *Washington Post*. Former Arkansas Governor Mike Huckabee is also a strong supporter of ONE.

25. Evangelical Environmental Network, "On the Care of Creation: An Evangelical Declaration on the Care of Creation," 1994. Retrieved from http://www.creationcare.org/blank.php?id=39.

26. Ingrina Shieh, "Japanese and Koreans Seek Reconciliation," *Urbana Today*, December 31, 2006, 14, http://web.archive.org/web/20071028012236/http://www.urbana.org/pdf/Urbana06_Urbana_Today_Dec31.pdf.

27. Quebedeaux, *The Worldly Evangelicals*, 103; Harold O. J. Brown, "Restive Evangelicals," *National Review*, February 15, 1974, 192–94; Russ Jones and Becky Yeh, "Young Evangelicals High on Social Issues, but Lean toward Socialism," *OneNewsNow*, March 8, 2011, http://web.archive.org/web/20120806153346/http://www.onenewsnow.com/Culture/Default.aspx?id=1307868.

28. Swartz, *Moral Minority*, 35.

29. David P. Setran, *The College "Y": Student Religion in the Era of Secularization* (New York: Palgrave Macmillan, 2007); Keith and Gladys Hunt, *The Story of*

InterVarsity Christian Fellowship, 1940–1990 (Downers Grove, IL: InterVarsity Press, 1991); A Donald MacLeod, *C. Stacey Woods and the Evangelical Rediscovery of the University* (Downers Grove, IL: InterVarsity Press, 2007).

30. The survey was administered between May 2006 and September 2006. In all, 3,788 invitations to complete the survey were sent. With 1,659 individuals responding, we achieved an overall response rate of 44 percent. The response rate for InterVarsity was 60 percent. For more information, visit www.campus-ministrystudy.org/.

31. Fitzgerald, "The New Evangelicals."

32. Kim, "Second-Generation Korean American Evangelicals," 21.

33. Data on InterVarsity's racial/ethnic composition is taken from www.intervar-sity.org/about/our/vital-statistics.

34. Kathleen Garces-Foley, *Crossing the Ethnic Divide: The Multiethnic Church on a Mission* (New York: Oxford University Press, 2007).

35. Figure on books published taken from InterVarsity's Asian American Ministries website, http://mem.intervarsity.org/aam/our-mission/vital-stats.

36. Elaine Howard Ecklund, *Korean American Evangelicals: New Models for Civic Life* (New York: Oxford University Press, 2006).

37. Information taken from InterVarsity's Urbana 09 website. Retrieved from http://www.urbana09.org/home.main.cfm. Unfortunately, this site is no longer available.

38. Mission Network News, "Social Justice vs. Gospel—Is It a Battle at Urbana?" *Mission Network News*, December 30, 2009, www.mnnonline.org/article/13684.

39. Victor Anderson, "Urbana 09 Kicks Off with Challenge to Reach Neighbors," *Christian Post*, December 28, 2009, www.christianpost.com/article/20091228/17-000-youth-gather-for-urbana-09/.

40. "Political Activism on Poverty and Justice Issues Gains Focus at Christian Student Conference," World Vision, December 21, 2009, www.worldvision.org/content.nsf/about/20091221-urbana.

41. See the website for Urbana 2012: https://urbana.org/urbana-12/seminars.

42. The website of the InterVarsity Social Justice League is available at http://ivjusticeleague.wordpress.com/about/.

43. Binghamton InterVarsity Christian Fellowship, "Social Justice Week Re-Cap," November 18, 2010\, http://binghamtonivcf.blogspot.com/2010/11/social-justice-week-re-cap.html.

44. InterVarsity Christian Fellowship, *InterVarsity Chapter Leaders' Handbook* (Madison, WI: InterVarsity Christian Fellowship, 1990), www.intervarsity.org/sites/default/files/uploaded/handbooks/ChapterLeadersHandbook.pdf.

45. Accounts of local chapters and issue advocacy can be found at www.intervarsity.org.

46. InterVarsity Christian Fellowship, *InterVarsity Chapter Leaders' Handbook*.

47. Yu-Shuan Sho, "Activism with an Edge," InterVarsity Christian Fellowship, June 14, 2005, www.intervarsity.org/news/activism-with-an-edge.

48. Kaitlin Ho, "Northeastern Transformations," InterVarsity Christian Fellowship, May 7, 2010, www.intervarsity.org/news/northeastern-transformation-stories.

49. Gordon Govier, "Anxious to Change the World," InterVarsity Christian Fellowship, May 23, 2008, www.intervarsity.org/news/anxious-to-change-the-world.

50. Lydia Saad, "Conservatives Remain the Largest Ideological Group," Gallup Politics, January 12, 2012, www.gallup.com/poll/152021/Conservatives-Remain-Largest-Ideological-Group.aspx.

51. Alumkal, "American Evangelicalism in the Post–Civil Rights Era," 195.

52. Rudy Busto, "The Gospel According to the Model Minority? Hazarding an Interpretation of Asian American Evangelical College Students, *Amerasia Journal* 22:1 (1996): 133–47.

53. Ecklund, *Korean American Evangelicals.*

54. Kevin Blue, *Practical Justice: Living Off-Center in a Self-Centered World* (Downers Grove, IL: InterVarsity Press, 2006); Mae Elise Cannon, *Social Justice Handbook: Small Steps for a Better World* (Downers Grove, IL: InterVarsity Press). Word searches were conducted using Amazon.com.

55. Robert Linthicum, *Transforming Power: Biblical Strategies for Making a Difference in Your Community* (Downers Grove, IL: InterVarsity Press, 2003), 31, 56.

56. John Perkins in John Perkins and Charles Marsh, *Welcoming Justice: God's Movement toward Beloved Community* (Downers Grove, IL: InterVarsity Press, 2009), 29.

57. InterVarsity Press, "Q & A Author Interview: An Interview with John Perkins and Charles Marsh," www.ivpress.com/title/ata/3453-q.pdf.

58. Perkins and Marsh, *Welcoming Justice*; Michael Barkey, "Models of Effective Compassion: Dr. John M. Perkins and the 'Three R's' of Community Development," *Acton Commentary*, June 28, 2000, www.acton.org/pub/commentary/2000/06/29/models-effective-compassion-dr-john-m-perkins-and-three-rs-community-development.

59. Haugen quoted in Elizabeth Bernstein, "The Sexual Politics of the 'New Abolitionism,'" *Differences: A Journal of Feminist Cultural Studies* 18:3 (2007): 137.

60. For more information on IJM's view of structural transformation, see Wu's web page at http://web.archive.org/web/20130119032507/http://ijm.org/staff/sharon-cohn-wu. The quotation is from International Justice Mission, *The World as We Know It: Cru/Justice Study 1* (Orlando, FL: CruPress, 2012), 2. See http://crupressgreen.com/ijmccc-social-justice-bible-studies/Revised.pdf.

61. Elizabeth Bernstein, "Carceral Politics as Gender Justice? The 'Traffic in Women' and Neoliberal Circuits of Crime, Sex, and Rights," *Theory and Society* 41:3 (2012): 233.

62. Elizabeth Bernstein and Janet R. Jakobsen, "Sex, Secularism, and Religious Influence in U.S. Politics," *Third World Quarterly* 31:6 (2010): 1032, 1034.

63. Mark Hensch, "Passion 2012 Closes with Spiritual Call to Arms for College Youths," *Christian Post*, January 5, 2012, www.christianpost.com/news/passion-2012-closes-with-call-to-arms-for-college-youths-66525/.

64. Passion Conferences, "Freedom Video: Episode 1," Passion 2012, www.youtube.com/watch?v=20ybCN8W6To.

65. Matthew Santoro, "Passion 2012 Calls Us to Rise Up against Modern-Day Slavery," *Sojourners* God's Politics Blog, January 9, 2012, http://sojo.net/blogs/2012/01/09/passion-2012-calls-us-rise-against-modern-day-slavery.

66. Barack Obama, Remarks by the President at the National Prayer Breakfast, February 2, 2012, http://www.whitehouse.gov/the-press-office/2012/02/02/remarks-president-national-prayer-breakfast. President Obama later asked Passion Conferences founder Louis Giglio to give the benediction at his second inauguration. Though Giglio initially accepted, he opted not to participate after a firestorm of criticism over a 1990s sermon against homosexuality. See Lesley Clark, "Pastor Louie Giglio Withdraws from Inauguration after Criticism of '90s Anti-Gay Comments," *Miami Herald*, January 10, 2013, www.miamiherald.com/2013/01/10/3176612/pastor-louie-giglio-withdraws.html.

67. Heritage Foundation, *Seek Social Justice: Transforming Lives in Need* (Nashville, TN: LifeWay, 2010). See www.seeksocialjustice.com. The quotation is from www.lifeway.com/Product/seek-social-justice-transforming-lives-in-need-dvd-leader-kit-P005271226.

68. Ryan Messmore is quoted in Catherine Snow, "Friday Five: Heritage's Ryan Messmore on Seeking Social Justice," *CitizenLink*, November 19, 2010, www.citizenlink.com/2010/11/19/friday-five-heritage%E2%80%99s-ryan-messmore-on-seeking-social-justice/. A Google search on January 12, 2013, yielded 306,000 hits for "Seek Social Justice."

69. Quotations are from www.seeksocialjustice.com.

70. James Casler quoted in Elizabeth Waibel, "Redefining 'Social Justice,'" *World*, June 18, 2011, www.worldmag.com/articles/18140.

71. James Casler, "Q&A: What is Biblical Social Justice?" *Engage*, December 21, 2011, http://engagemagazine.com/content/qa-what-biblical-social-justice.

72. Waibel, "Redefining Social Justice."

73. Waibel, "Redefining Social Justice."

74. Michael Novak, "Social Justice: Not What You Think It Is." Lecture delivered at the Heritage Foundation on December 29, 2009, www.heritage.org/research/lecture/social-justice-not-what-you-think-it-is; Michael Novak, "Social Justice Isn't What You Think It Is." Lecture delivered at the American Enterprise Institute on May 9, 2011, www.aei.org/files/2011/05/09/Transcript%20-%20Bradley%20Lecture%20by%20Michael%20Novak.pdf.

75. Novak, "Social Justice: Not What You Think It Is."

76. Michael Novak, "Defining Social Justice," *First Things*, December 2000, www.firstthings.com/article/2007/01/defining-social-justice-29.

77. Part of Campus Crusade's faculty ministry, the Leadership University site includes ten references to Hayek. Most appear in articles from *First Things*. The Novak article is available at www.leaderu.com/ftissues/ft0012/opinion/novak.html.

78. For more on the First International Conservative Conference on Social Justice, see www.heritage.org/events/2005/09/the-first-international-conservative-conference-on-social-justice; Rick Santorum, "The Conservative Future: Compassion." Address delivered at the First International Conservative Conference on Social Justice, Washington, D.C., September 27, 2005. Available at http://src.senate.gov/public/_files/graphics/RJSConservativeCompassion.pdf. While focusing on civil society, Santorum urged conservatives "to stop treating government as if its elimination were the highest good that could come to humankind." He also discussed the drawbacks of libertarianism.

79. American Enterprise Institute, "Does Capitalism Have a Soul?" Values & Capitalism Blog, December 10, 2010, www.valuesandcapitalism.com/dialogue/economics/does-capitalism-have-soul.

80. Evan Sparks, "Intellectual Capital," *Philanthropy Roundtable*, Spring 2011, www.philanthropyroundtable.org/topic/excellence_in_philanthropy/intellectual_capital.

81. Arthur Brooks and Peter Wehner, *Wealth and Justice: The Morality of Democratic Capitalism* (Washington, DC: AEI Press, 2010); Steven F. Hayward, *Mere Environmentalism: A Biblical Perspective on Humans and the Natural World* (Washington, DC: AEI Press, 2010).

82. Robert Sirico, "The Late-Scholastic and Austrian Link to Modern Catholic Economic Thought," *Journal of Markets and Morality* 1:2 (1998): 122–29.

83. Robert Sirico, "There is No 'Social Justice' without Economic Freedom," FOX News, May 25, 2012, www.foxnews.com/opinion/2012/05/25/there-is-no-ocial-justice-without-economic-freedom/.

84. Sirico quoted in Joseph E. Gorra, "What If 'Social Justice' Demands Small Government? Interview with Robert Sirico," Patheos, June 24, 2012, www.patheos.com/Evangelical/Social-Justice-Demands-Small-Government-Joseph-Gorra-06-22-2012.html.

85. Sparks, "Intellectual Capital."

86. Council for Christian Colleges and Universities, "CCCU Announces Recipients of Mini-Grants for the Study and Teaching of Free Market Economics," June 12, 2012, www.cccu.org/news/articles/2012/CCCU-Announces-Recipients-of-Mini-Grants-for-the-Study-and-Teaching-of-Free-Market-Economics.

87. For more information on this event, see www.acton.org/event/2013/evaluating-idea-social-justice.

88. Peter Steinfels, "Michael Novak & His Ultrasuperdemocraticaptialism," *Commonweal* 14 (January 1983): 11–16; Angus Sibley, "The Cult of Capitalism: Hayek, Novak & the Limits of Laissez Faire," *Commonweal*, April 25, 2008, 18–21; Daniel K. Finn, "Nine Libertarian Heresies Tempting Neoconservative Catholics to Stray from Catholic Social Thought," *Journal of Morality and Markets* 14:2 (2011): 487–503.

89. Anthony E. Santelli II, "'Nine Libertarian Heresies': A Response to Daniel Finn," *Journal of Morality and Markets* 14:2 (2011): 505–17; John D. Mueller, "Finn's 'Nine Libertarian Heresies' and Mueller's First Lemma," *Journal of Morality and Markets* 14:2 (2011): 519–33.

90. For a critique of social justice rhetoric among campus evangelicals, see Julie Roys, "'Social Justice' at Wheaton College," *Multiply Justice*, February 23, 2010, http://multiplyjustice.net/what-justice-isnt/.

91. Matthew Lee Anderson, "Wallis vs. Brooks: The Debate That Wasn't," *Mere Orthodoxy*, October 31, 2010, www.mereorthodoxy.com/wallis-vs-brooks-the-debate-that-wasnt/.

92. Jordan Ballor, "Evangelicals, Scholarship, and the Acton Institute," Acton Institute PowerBlog, September 7, 2011, http://blog.acton.org/archive s/26036-evangelicals-scholarship-and-the-acton-institute.html; Michael Hickerson, "Q&A with Acton Institute's Jordan Ballor," InterVarsity Emerging Scholars Blog, September 7, 2011, http://blog.emergingscholars.org/2011/09/qa-with-acton-institutes-jordan-ballor-and-a-free-subscription/.

93. Timothy Keller, *Generous Justice: How God's Grace Makes Us Just* (New York: Dutton, 2010), 213–14. Both Sherman and Linthicum are InterVarsity Press authors.

94. Corwin Smidt and James Penning, *Evangelicalism: The Next Generation* (Grand Rapids, MI: Baker Academic, 2002), 101.

95. Matthew Kuchem, Micah Watson, and Sean Evan, "Forecasting the Future: The Politics of Evangelical College Students," April 21, 2011, 28. Unpublished paper presented at the 2011 Western Political Science Association, San Antonio, Texas, http://papers.ssrn.com/sol3/Delivery.cfm/SSRN_ID1813284_code1321409.pdf?abstractid=1767165&mirid=1. Unlike the Smidt and Penning survey, the 2010 study was conducted at a single institution. It is based on a survey of 224 Union University students.

96. James Guth, John Green, Corwin Smidt, Lyman Kellstedt, and Margaret Poloma, *The Bully Pulpit: The Politics of Protestant Clergy* (Lawrence: University Press of Kansas, 1997).

97. Phillip E. Hammond, "Segmentation of Radicalism: The Case of the Protestant Campus Minister," *American Journal of Sociology* 71:2 (1965): 133–43.

98. Nick Liao, "Radical Evangelicalism," Call & Response Blog, January 7, 2010, http://faithandleadership.com/blog/01-07-2010/nick-liao-radical-evangelicalism.

3

All Catholics Now?

SPECTERS OF CATHOLICISM IN EVANGELICAL
SOCIAL ENGAGEMENT

Omri Elisha

ADDRESSING AN AUDIENCE of conservative leaders and lobbyists in February
2012, evangelical pundit and former governor Mike Huckabee boldly
announced, "*We are all Catholics now.*" The surprising rallying cry, coming
from an ordained Southern Baptist pastor, was in response to a controversy
over an Obama administration proposal to require private employers, including religious organizations, to provide insurance coverage for contraception.
Catholic bishops came out vigorously opposing the measure, and Huckabee's
show of solidarity, in the name of religious liberty and defeating President
Obama, was adopted by a variety of high-profile conservatives, including evangelicals as well as other non-Catholics. In July, in what was heralded as an
unprecedented move, evangelical flagship Wheaton College joined Catholic
University of America in a lawsuit against the federal mandate.

Such politics of affinity may seem counterintuitive, but they make sense
in the context of an election year when two GOP contenders (Newt Gingrich
and Rick Santorum) and the party's vice presidential nominee (Paul Ryan)
were Roman Catholics with strong support among conservative evangelicals.
Indeed, evangelicals and Roman Catholics have found ways to get along for
decades, demonstrating repeated, albeit cautious, willingness to forge meaningful partnerships despite stark doctrinal differences and mutual recrimi-
nations. From the ecumenism of the Billy Graham crusades to the abortion
activism of the religious right, to interfaith dialogue groups like Catholics and
Evangelicals for the Common Good (spearheaded by veteran bridge-builders
like Ron Sider), evangelicals and Catholics routinely find common cause
around moral, political, and social issues. In recent years, leaders and intellectuals of both traditions have come together to form coalitions and working

groups, issuing influential (and controversial) manifestos such as the land-mark "Evangelicals and Catholics Together" document of 1994 and the Manhattan Declaration of 2009. The charismatic renewal movement opened up multiple lines of communication and joint worship that continue to influence adherents in both camps. And as is evident in this book, especially in chapters 2, 9, and 10, politically and socially engaged evangelicals have been borrowing conceptual tools and mobilization strategies from Catholic activists for many years.

Aside from formal partnerships and dialogues, there are subtle and implicit resonances between contemporary evangelical and Catholic sensi-bilities that are less conspicuous but worth investigating as well. This chapter is an attempt to think about notable features and cultural characteristics of evangelicalism's new social engagement that recall or resonate with Roman Catholic theology and practice, with an emphasis on shared motivational themes especially as applied to ministries of social welfare. While the fact that evangelicals and Catholics are able to come together around certain social and political issues is significant, issue agreement is only one marker of elective affinity. By framing my discussion in terms of resonance (intentional or other-wise) rather than collaboration, I point to underlying affinities between these two traditions, and, more important, I highlight the ways that divergent tradi-tions separated by centuries of theology and ritual practice may find them-selves drawn into closer alignments in their modalities of religious and social action, resulting from gradual shifts in public consciousness. The possible ways in which uniquely evangelical influences make their way into Catholic ministries and services merit exploration as well, but this is not within the purview of my discussion here.

Three themes in particular are brought into focus in the foregoing analy-sis. First, I explore the theme of suffering, rendered in both humanitarian and theological terms, which has achieved new relevance and symbolic import in evangelical social engagement. Second, I discuss the sacramentalist under-currents in the ministries of socially engaged evangelicals, especially when it comes to benevolence and charitable giving. Third, I turn to the question of social justice, a consistently controversial theme in American evangelicalism and one that is being played out on stages of public discourse where the influ-ence of Catholic social teaching can hardly be ignored.

My discussion is based on what I perceive as a noteworthy and growing tendency among socially engaged evangelicals to embrace concepts with Catholic undertones somewhat more readily than other evangelicals and a greater willingness on their part to recognize or even collaborate with Catholic social teachings and ministries.[1] Despite the fact that the socially engaged evangelicals I have studied in Knoxville, Tennessee, were generally keen to distinguish their "faith-based" orientation from what they dismiss as the "performance-based" theology of Catholic ministry, I was often struck by how religious motifs and references normally associated with Catholicism found their way into the discourse and practice of local outreach and social engagement, at times explicitly (although this was not especially common). I believe that this trend is likely to continue, perhaps even accelerate, as the field of Christian social engagement in the United States continues to evolve and expand in the postwelfare era.

I am not arguing that evangelical social engagement in the twenty-first century is fundamentally (or even incidentally) Catholic, nor am I suggesting that it is inevitably becoming Catholic in style or structure. I do not maintain that evangelical social ministries are something entirely other than what they claim to be. However, religious and social movements are never static, nor are they completely immune from wider cultural influences, including some that their members might not normally account for. In identifying resonances and symbolic parallels, I am interested to situate evangelical engagement within a religious and social field that is broader than evangelicalism itself, making it possible to contemplate different thematic adaptations, variations, and shifts in emphasis that may be either inspired by external cultural sources or at least gesturing toward them. The prospects of socially engaged evangelicalism, in the increasingly diverse and competitive realm of civil society, should be imagined in light of the social realities of religious pluralism.

Though based on empirical observations, the thrust of my argument is perhaps more speculative and forward-looking than deconstructive, more prognosis than genealogy. When appropriate, I trace direct and explicit paths of Catholic influence that have informed elements of evangelical social engagement, but my analysis is not primarily about cause and effect. Rather, I bring together a set of observations that illustrate, on the one hand, some of the ways that Catholicism informs certain aspects of evangelical social engagement both nationally and locally, and on the other hand, the mutual resonances that have become more pronounced in recent decades as American evangelicals have sought to reclaim and renew their collective commitments to social and humanitarian concerns.

Apart from the fact that evangelicals and Catholics share common biblical foundations and roots in historical Christianity, there are additional reasons that, in the contemporary moment, it is useful to highlight Catholic resonances and parallels in evangelical social engagement (or any aspect of evangelicalism for that matter). For one thing, the U.S. evangelical population includes Catholic converts in its ranks. According to one recent survey, roughly 11 percent of evangelical churchgoers were raised Roman Catholic.[2] This is not a large minority by any means but a presence nonetheless, and some of these converts—including a sizable number of Latinos—undoubtedly carry with them ideas and symbolic associations from their former faith, whether or not they acknowledge them as such. In addition, evangelicals are known to convert to Catholicism, a faith migration that provokes all manner of internal consternation but suggests that even though evangelicals routinely criticize Catholic doctrine (especially regarding the pope), there are those who are sufficiently drawn to elements of Catholic tradition that they "cross the Tiber," while others may seek to modify and reproduce those elements in their religious lives without risking apostasy.

We might also note that educated evangelicals are voracious and often broadly curious readers. Pastors, ministry leaders, and activists, especially those with seminary training, are inclined to read books by nonevangelicals from time to time, including devotional works by well-known Catholics such as Pope John Paul II, Mother Teresa, Thomas Merton, and Henri Nouwen. Moreover, as figures like John Paul II and Mother Teresa are venerated by large segments of the American public, many evangelicals openly recognize them as cultural icons as well as ethical role models.

Finally, although American religiosity is widely characterized as bending to the hegemonic pull of Protestant tradition—consider Alan Wolfe's quip, a decade before Huckabee, that "we are all evangelicals now"[3] —Catholicism has certainly made its mark in society, not just demographically but through its many influences in fields such as higher education, academic scholarship, political organizing, social activism, popular culture, and theology. The ideological arsenal of the religious right has always relied heavily on Catholic thought, for example, on "sanctity of life" issues and theories of natural law, much as liberals draw inspiration from modern Catholic traditions when it comes to social justice, human rights, and antiwar activism.

On social welfare, it is important to stress the differences between Catholic and conservative Protestant approaches to faith-based activism. Catholic and evangelical charity organizations, for example, are quite unlike each other in terms of administration, and they rely on very different theologies of salvation and ethics of care in their work.[4] Catholic agencies also tend to be far more socially progressive than their evangelical counterparts, emphasizing justice-oriented principles in contrast to the evangelical focus on personal evangelism and discipleship. At the congregational level, Catholic churches are by and large more involved in social services and civic bridge-building activities, and their congregants are more likely to be politically active.[5] This may be attributed to the working-class immigrant roots of many Catholic parishes in the United States, their long-standing links to labor unions and community organizing, and the role of prominent influences from social encyclicals to the Catholic Worker movement and liberation theology.

And yet, as the scope of this volume attests, the social conscience of American evangelicals is experiencing notable shifts that, I argue, herald new points of confluence. Churches are increasingly attuned to social issues and participating in a variety of welfare-related services, partnerships, and collaborations previously associated mainly with liberal Protestant, Jewish, and Roman Catholic congregations. This is therefore a historic development that should be studied on its own terms and also in relation to the established cultural field to which evangelicals now commit themselves. The new social engagement is a multifaceted evolution, one composed of diverse inheritances and heralding multiple possible trajectories. In my attention to the presence of Catholic resonances, I explore but one facet of this evolution and ask whether, and to what extent, this particular facet will make a difference in future directions of evangelical social engagement.

Boundaries and Assemblages

According to Christian Smith's theory of subcultural identity, the "religious strength" of American evangelicalism in the modern era lies in its ability "to create both clear distinction from and significant engagement and tension with other relevant groups."[6] In other words, evangelicals benefit collectively from cultural pluralism because it allows them to confront the points of contact between evangelical and nonevangelical traditions, and between orthodox and secular values, in ways that actually reinforce group identity. To this we should add that there are considerable lines of difference even *within* the boundaries of evangelicalism. The subcultural world of evangelicals is pluralistic in its own right and frequently defined by internal fluctuations, attitudinal shifts, and tensions (for example, on issues such as race, gender, and doctrine), some of which spark public controversy while others simmer over time.

While doing ethnographic fieldwork in megachurches and faith-based organizations in Knoxville, Tennessee, I discovered that socially engaged evangelicals—whom, for the purposes of my study, I defined as individuals with a more than casual commitment to social outreach and charitable voluntarism—tend to occupy ambiguous and uneasy roles in predominantly conservative congregations. On the one hand, they represent and promote religious virtues that are regularly valorized, such as selfless compassion, radical generosity, a "heart" to serve the poor and needy, and missionary zeal when it comes to championing biblical orthodoxy in the public sphere. On the other hand, their efforts to mobilize support and cooperation are frequently met with reluctance, evasion, skepticism, and even antipathy. Pastors and church-goers alike worry about whether getting too involved in welfare initiatives will make them vulnerable to the influence of liberal activists and social progres-sives. As a result, socially engaged evangelicals end up feeling overextended, frustrated, and cynically inclined to criticize their faith communities for put-ting all their support behind foreign missions while failing to carry the gospel tangibly into the lives of poor and distressed people at home.

My book *Moral Ambition* detailed the challenges and paradoxes that pre-occupy evangelicals in matters of social engagement, including this tension between the general impulse to valorize and at the same time marginalize social ministries, and how it is inflected by issues of race and class, the politics of welfare, and conflicted ideas of kingdom theology as a blueprint for moral action.[7] Central to my analysis was an understanding of evangelicalism as an internally diverse religious milieu, where different styles, sensibilities, and political inclinations come together and sometimes collide. While being an evangelical is predicated on a commitment to an absolutist, unwavering ortho-doxy, the everyday lived religion of evangelicals is driven by what often seem like multiple, often competing, and at times disparate social ethics, influenced by a range of legacies from the social gospel to the new Christian right. This is especially true in megachurches and large urban-suburban communities. Socially engaged evangelicals struggle continuously with the implications of evangelicalism's expansive and contested boundaries. To become socially engaged is to embody areas of ministry infused with new paths of conviction and discovery, as well as possibilities for discord.

The point in relation to this chapter is that evangelical social engage-ment is, and has always been, what anthropologist Jarett Zigon has called an "assemblage" of intersecting currents and streams, "a plurality of institutional moralities," rather than a singular or uniform body of discourse and practice.[8] The conflicted history of evangelical engagement is not so much a neat linear narrative as a series of oscillations, shifting continuously between programs of reform and renunciation, between revivalist optimism and fundamentalist rancor. This dialectical (and often fraught) movement of ideological variations and counterpositions has meant that many evangelicals today internalize worldviews that are informed by a more diverse range of religious disposi-tions than they necessarily realize. While my previous work examined the efforts of evangelical outreach workers to reconcile different moral attitudes and approaches to ministry and evangelism within their own religious circles, my discussion in this chapter is an attempt to broaden that frame with an exploration of underlying themes and motivational concepts that may have been absorbed from Catholic influences, or at least resonate with Catholic sensibilities in such a way that might potentially enable novel developments and innovations in social engagement, as evangelicals become more deeply committed and embedded in newly reconstituted arenas of civic voluntarism, social welfare, and interreligious cooperation.

Suffering Others, Suffering Self

In his discussion of *For the Health of the Nation*, the National Association of Evangelicals' (NAE) public policy statement from 2004, Peter Goodwin Heltzel notes the rather prominent inclusion of "suffering" as a theological leitmotif.[9] He interprets this as a discursive move that was part of larger efforts of NAE representatives to counter the religious right's narrow focus on the "traditional institutions of society (family, government, and church)" in favor of a broad policy agenda covering a wider range of social institutions and problems. Noting the direct influence of Roman Catholic social teaching, Heltzel proposes that reinvigorated notions of suffering in the discourse of evangelical social engagement have contributed to broader, more holistic visions of social transformation, as well as reassertions of a Christological outlook in which the suffering of others and the suffering of Jesus emerge as linked concepts, combining radical concern for the poor and prophetic ideas of justice.[10]

For socially engaged evangelicals at the heart of my research in Knoxville, suffering entered into the ministry imagination through the subject of compassion, a topic of foremost intellectual and emotional interest among local volunteers and activists. The word *compassion* means literally "to suffer with," and this aspect was rarely lost on evangelicals who spent time thinking about how to deepen their spirituality and discipleship by serving others in need. Following centuries of church teaching and scriptural interpretation, as well as the political and cultural climate of the times, outreach pastors, ministry leaders, and volunteers I interviewed repeatedly described "active compassion" as a moral imperative of paramount importance in the life of the devoted Christian. For local faith-based and outreach ministries in communities across the United States, compassion frequently serves as a cornerstone concept for purposes of mobilization because it reinforces crucial biblical notions of grace and mercy, while it additionally evokes neo-Tocquevillian civic virtues of citizenship, voluntary association, and community service that have gained tremendous currency in the era of faith-based initiatives and welfare privatization. But compassion is also valued among evangelicals precisely because of its linguistic and theological associations with suffering, especially the sympathetic and redemptive suffering of Christ, whom all evangelicals constantly seek and struggle to emulate in their daily lives.

Of the various devotional works and Bible commentaries that evangelicals in Knoxville turned to in their efforts to understand Christian compassion as a form of sympathetic suffering, one particularly influential source was Catholic priest and author Henri Nouwen.[11] A number of my informants admitted to having been greatly inspired by Nouwen's eloquent and poignant musings on the subject, so much so that his work became an integral part of a mobilization discourse that several outreach pastors regularly drew on, including some who remained unfamiliar with the original source. When I asked one prominent organizer, who was especially fond of Nouwen's perspective, whether he saw any problem in advocating the views of a Catholic priest, especially one associated with liberal positions as well as spiritual practices that many evangelicals find distasteful, he casually shrugged his shoulders and said, "He was a man who loved Jesus, just like me."[12] In fact, it is not just the love of Jesus that validates Nouwen's devotions among some evangelicals; it is his emphasis on suffering and "brokenness" as fundamental conditions of human existence, as well as vehicles for redemption. For evangelicals today, especially those in relatively affluent or comfortable social positions, the idea of simultaneously relieving human suffering and *embodying* suffering in the model of Christ is tremendously appealing.

References to Henri Nouwen provide but one illustration of the fact that discourses on suffering are well-worn paths of Catholic contemplation that inquisitive evangelicals may draw on for spiritual guidance or edification. Of course, Catholics don't have a monopoly on suffering. For Protestants and Catholics alike, manifestations of suffering—physical, emotional, catastrophic—are linked to the presence of sin and evil in the world, as a consequence of the fall in Genesis, and they figure centrally in prophetic renditions of human history and millennial redemption. Rhetorics of suffering appear throughout the history of Protestant revivalism, especially in connection with renewalist churches such as the Holiness movement, where theologies of sanctification are often linked to aspirations of pious and obedient suffering. Nonetheless, there is little doubt that suffering is and has long been a far more prominent and elaborated theme in Catholic theology and devotional practice. On a most basic level, the alleviation of human suffering is vital to the Church's universal mission, as the Catholic catechism clearly establishes. For centuries, Catholic orders and charities have been dedicated to "doing God's work" among the world's poor, sick, and vulnerable, who possess moral worth as objects of pity, regardless of original sin. The rationale for this is primarily theological and metaphysical rather than ethical: the Church does not merely

represent the Body of Christ; it *is* the Body of Christ. The Church is therefore mandated and empowered to heal all manner of temporal suffering while
simultaneously administering the means of eternal salvation.

On another level, Catholicism idealizes suffering. As graphic depictions of
Jesus crucified and the trials of saints and martyrs affirm, the suffering of the
righteous serves a positive purpose when it increases sanctification, advances
God's will, and promotes religious virtue. This is referred to in Catholic teaching as *redemptive suffering*, and a plethora of Bible passages are mustered in
support of it. With the Passion of Christ as the prime example, redemptive
suffering is an ideal that invites believers not only to patiently endure hard-
ships and afflictions but also to actively seek out, embrace, and even rejoice
in occasions to "take up the cross" or suffer faithfully in God's name.[13] In this
theological vein, suffering is less a consequence of sin than a quality associated with the incarnation, persecution, and atoning sacrifice of Jesus Christ.
Any opportunity to achieve humility and spiritual insight through experiences
of direct, sympathetic, or mimetic suffering brings sinners closer to holiness.

Thus we see several corresponding ideas of suffering at work in the
Catholic imagination, including recognition of the abject state of humanity,
the need for mercy and intervention in response to worldly afflictions, and a
supernaturalist elevation of virtuous suffering as a medium of divine embodi-
ment. None of this is absent from Protestant tradition, but, as noted earlier,
narratives and images of suffering are integral to elementary conceptions of
what it means to be a Christian in the Roman Catholic tradition. Modern evangelical Protestants typically place their strongest emphases on biblical authority, evangelism, justification by faith, and spiritual rebirth. While evangelical
ministries that help people in distress have always been part of the landscape,
evangelical interventionism has tended to focus less on suffering itself as
an object or virtue and more on the imperative to spread the Word of God,
bring new confessing converts into the fold, and save as many souls as possible before the end times.[14] For evangelicals, suffering represents the fate of
the temporal world; it is a reality understood chiefly in theodical rather than
devotional terms.

In recent decades, however, evangelical charities, relief missions, and nongovernmental organizations (NGOs) have become prominent on the world
stage, giving renewed voice to a conservative Protestant emphasis on the suffering of others, especially in the developing world. Humanitarian groups
like Samaritan's Purse and World Vision promote poverty relief and development initiatives through symbolically loaded representations of misery and
destitution, particularly images of needy children. Such evocations, common
throughout the aid world, are meant to trigger compassionate responses—one

must not merely witness the suffering of others, but suffer with them, and for them. Evangelicals push the logic even further in that compassionate responses are understood to facilitate spiritually transformative experiences for believers and beneficiaries alike. In another vein, evangelical advocacy groups like Voice of the Martyrs bring attention to the persecution of Christians by drawing symbolic connections between three poles of heroic suffering: the global "persecuted church," the agony of the persecuted Savior, and the sympathetic agony of the compassionate Western self. By recognizing and valorizing the resilience of Christians who are oppressed, imprisoned, and tortured around the world, American churchgoers learn to equate suffering with radical faith, perseverance, and political action.

In American communities, middle-class evangelicals who become involved in social outreach ministries and urban community development projects regard their participation as a form of active compassion, inspired by nearby realities of suffering and need. Many of my informants in Knoxville spoke of their desire to volunteer or become socially engaged in the inner city, which they described in terms of "spaces of hurt" and "pockets of despair." In regions where the spatialization of need is mapped closely along urban-suburban divides, and where well-to-do evangelicals yearn to discover avenues of radical piety, serving impoverished inner-city communities evokes incarnational virtues. In the discourse of outreach, churchgoers are instructed to see themselves as agents of healing with a missionary imperative to occupy (and in some cases empower) places of anguish, where "the least of these" await their intervention. For some, this might mean going as far as relocating to poor, crime-ridden neighborhoods where needs can be served more directly. For others, it is enough to support and intermittently participate in ministries that remind them that there are hurting people in their nearby communities and that hurting people benefit materially and spiritually from the sacrifices of those who feel their pain.

In short, whereas the public rhetoric of evangelical preachers and revivalists has traditionally emphasized spiritual regeneration through repentance of personal sins, socially engaged evangelicals have become increasingly focused on calibrating their conceptual frameworks to highlight suffering, compassion, and healing. This shift marks, among other things, a renewed affinity toward notions of redemptive suffering and other religious themes that have traditionally been the purview of the Catholic Church. In practice, this shift also influences on-the-ground approaches to social outreach and makes it possible for new generations of socially engaged evangelicals to think about the work of outreach in ways that do not strictly reduce the relational dynamics between givers and receivers to a simple dichotomy of "saved versus unsaved," although such lines of differentiation remain salient nonetheless.

The Spirit of Sacramentalism

One of the more intriguing developments in American evangelicalism in recent years is the growing popularity of sacramentalist symbols and practices, which is actively taking place in new and emerging congregations and in older, more established churches as well. This is an interesting development in light of the fact that evangelical theology, since the time of the Reformation, has emphasized the immateriality of the sacred and the interiority of born-again faith, principles that typically entail strong ideological biases against material mediations such as the ecclesial rites and ordinances of Roman Catholicism. In doctrinal terms, the "priesthood of all believers" amounts to a full-scale rejection of the Church's historical claim to administer salvation and channel supernatural grace exclusively. For the most part, evangelicals observe only two of the traditional sacraments—baptism and the Lord's Supper—and even then, such rites tend to be regarded as chiefly symbolic acts. In the contemporary moment, however, sacraments appear to be enjoying something of a renaissance among Protestants. More important, the logic of sacramentalism—the idea of divine grace directly mediated through persons, objects, and experiences—is increasingly prevalent throughout evangelical communities.

Many evangelical groups and denominations today have been known to experiment with aspects of ritual sacramentalism, from Lenten observances to the Stations of the Cross and even elements of Catholic mysticism. James Bielo has documented how members of the Emerging Church movement adapt liturgical and monastic practices in order to reconnect with sensory, spiritual, and intellectual traditions they believe will strengthen evangelicalism's claims to "authentic" Christianity.[15] Even high-profile figures like Rick and Kay Warren have stirred the ire of doctrinal purists by going public with their interest in the works of Catholic mystics such as Brother Lawrence, Henri Nouwen, Madame Guyon, and, in the case of Kay, the seventeenth-century Quietist Francois Fenelon.[16] While the fact of evangelical Protestants experimenting with the boundaries of their spirituality is hardly unprecedented,[17] the renewed interest in sacraments and monasticism suggests that evangelicals are hungry for diverse approaches to mediating the sacred. And the fact that some are turning to Catholic devotions suggests that negative perceptions of Catholic tradition are changing.

With regard to social engagement, though I do not recall instances when sacramentalism was directly invoked during my fieldwork, I did observe that some of the most committed actors in social outreach ministries often described the significance of their work by expressing an idiom of grace that was curiously sacramentalistic in tone. They spoke as though they believed that concrete spiritual outcomes could take effect, or were taking effect, as an immediate or direct result of the benevolent services and acts of compassion they performed. To be sure, many volunteers understood charitable gifts and works on behalf of the poor to be mainly demonstrative, setting the stage, as it were, for God's grace but not necessarily generating miraculous powers in and of themselves.[18] However, and perhaps paradoxically, charitable gifts and works were also frequently idealized as literal *embodiments* of grace and thus, in turn, opportunities to transmit grace from one individual to another. This is not surprising, given how keen outreach ministry workers and volunteers generally are to maintain a strong connection between social outreach and evangelism.

Consider the following passage from a motivational guide addressed to local churches and volunteers in Knoxville and published by a group of local faith-based activists dedicated to interdenominational outreach mobilization: "When people who love Jesus come face to face with suffering and injustice, God Himself comes face to face with the same. Not that we bring Him there, because He is already there. But we bring Him there in the sense that He becomes tangible, touchable. He has our 'skin' on.... The simple fact is that people see and meet God through us. And when that occurs, life is forever changed for them. In this encounter, purpose, significance, and even eternal life follow." Such sentiments support an emphasis on missional strategies of social outreach that require direct and intimate interactions with individuals in need, the kinds of hands-on interactions that are assumed to be effective in summoning, and mediating, the transformative presence of the Holy Spirit.

In justifying the potential for outreach to promote relational evangelism, engaged evangelicals portray altruistic acts not simply as acts of goodwill but rather as events that effectively promote sacred encounters and virtues. Believing that one's concern for the poor and needy is inspired by the Holy Spirit in the first place, through the "gift of mercy," their motivation for helping others is thus understood to originate essentially from a source above and beyond human volition, which increases the sense of moral and spiritual potency attached to their actions.[19] As evangelicals externalize gifts of the Spirit in the form of generosity (described as uncommon, risky, and sacrificial), they hope to channel divine inspiration, establish new lines of interpersonal connectivity, and harness the power of the Spirit to modify behavior, giving hope to the distressed and producing changed hearts that are drawn irresistibly to God. I have even observed outreach volunteers and charitable givers draw an invisible sign of a cross with their fingers on material donations or monetary gifts, or lay hands on gift objects in prayer before offering them to the intended recipients, as if to reinforce or augment the power of the Spirit by converting everyday objects into silent vessels of spiritual mediation.

The tendency to put a supernaturalist gloss on social engagement can create challenging ambiguities with regard to exactly what it is evangelical actors believe they are doing, especially when it comes to charity and benevolence. Many of the ministry workers and outreach volunteers I have encountered would agree that a theology of grace is essential for helping people in need, because it reinforces an egalitarian model of social relations that guards the giver against arrogance, prejudice, or a sense of superiority. Once you realize the extent of your own spiritual poverty and the role of God's extraordinary mercy and generosity in your life, the logic goes, it is easier to see the poor and destitute as equally deserving (and undeserving) of that grace, which you then share and reproduce through compassionate action. This dynamic, in which human relationships are conceived horizontally, is consistently cited as the most important ingredient for effective social ministry, and it is this that is said to distinguish faith-based from secular and nonevangelical welfare models.

However, by the same token, acts of generosity and presumptions of need can reproduce paternalistic attitudes, in which grace—like material wealth and status—becomes something possessed by some more than others, that is, something of value to be dispensed from positions of moral or spiritual authority. Relational power dynamics between affluent individuals, on the one hand, and needy individuals who are expected to receive the substance and Spirit of their gifts, on the other hand, are thus to a large extent conceived vertically, though not often explicitly. The ensuing interpersonal and theological tensions are of great concern to socially engaged evangelicals as they seek to implement strategies for demonstrating grace without acting as though it is their priestly prerogative to dictate when and how grace is distributed.

I am not arguing that there is something characteristically Catholic in how evangelicals think about their interactions with the recipients of faith-based services, especially since, as I mentioned before, the differences between Catholic and evangelical ministries are stark. I also do not suggest that an emphasis on grace as an embodied gift that circulates through human exchanges and relationships is uniquely Catholic. Contemporary evangelical fascinations with the corporeal and experiential dimensions of faith have drawn considerable inspiration from neo-Pentecostal and charismatic influences since the 1960s.[20] I do propose, however, that as increasing numbers of evangelicals come to see social ministries as opportunities to channel God's grace and not merely as lesser alternatives to preaching the gospel, they allow the theological significance attributed to nonproselytic acts of mediation to be intensified.

And as more evangelicals come to embrace holistic ministries that promote social engagement as an integral element of evangelism, rather than insist that they remain separate and differentiated, they come into closer alignment with historically Catholic sensibilities, even if only at an abstract level.

The problem is that for most hard-line conservative evangelicals, no such alignment, however abstract, can really be tolerated. Indeed, one of the objections that conservative evangelicals express in their opposition to those who would privilege social ministries is that they will end up like Catholics, that is, doing good for the sake of *being* good rather than the sake of Christ-centered proclamation evangelism. According to this viewpoint, Catholic charities and social services lack total validity because they lack spiritual power. The Spirit, they say, cannot be present when actors' intentions are fundamentally misguided. Nonetheless, from the perspective of socially engaged evangelicals—many of whom share this skeptical disregard for Catholic charity—much of the perceived effectiveness of Spirit-filled social ministries stems from their confidence in what I would call sacramental modes of intervention. These may not directly resemble patterns of Catholic social action, but they are reminiscent of certain aspects of Catholic ritual, especially with regard to the legitimation of religious authority through ritualized channels of exchange. Ironically, the determination of hard-liners to keep their churches from acting like Catholics may be motivated less by convictions about how Catholics and evangelicals are different than by an unconscious recognition of just how much their traditions overlap.

Social Justice and the Common Good

The issue of social justice is a perennial lightning rod in American evangelicalism, galvanizing opinions, igniting passions, and inviting all manner of criticism, including self-critique and that of outsider observers. Generally, evangelicals agree that justice is central to the message of the Bible and a foundational principle for any godly society. Those who invoke justice rely heavily on scripture and invoke the works of Protestant luminaries, from Martin Luther to Martin Luther King Jr. Yet few can agree on the immediate social implications of the concept, and controversies over the politics of justice make it particularly hard for socially engaged evangelicals to advance the concept in explicit, programmatic terms. This is partly due to the fact that it has so many potential referents, religious and secular. It is also because the critical differences between one meaning of justice and another reflect politicized struggles in which church communities have long been implicated, reinforcing seemingly irreconcilable divisions along lines of ideology as well as race.[21]

For all the difficulties, socially engaged evangelicals are leading efforts to develop ministries that promote social justice without alienating majority evangelicals (especially white conservatives) who may be disinclined to embrace notions of structural sin.[22] The trick for them is to maintain a safe discursive distance from anything that smacks of liberal Protestantism. While many evangelicals would like to see their churches be more proactive on social issues and readily identify with evangelical reform movements of the nineteenth century, such as abolitionism, there is an even stronger impulse to avoid direct or even implied associations with the social activism of the Protestant mainline. At the same time, socially engaged evangelicals are keen to enact broader visions of social transformation than those currently embraced within evangelicalism writ large. In my fieldwork, I found that socially engaged evangelicals were typically more likely than less engaged churchgoers to reconcile, or at least try to reconcile, the differences between structural and individualist views on justice, but this required conscious effort and did not erase uncertainty. Perhaps it is not surprising that, given such challenges, some evangelicals have turned to Catholic social teachings (in addition to other Protestant sources) for insights or inspiration.[23] It is also not inconceivable that such Catholic insights, both progressive and conservative ones, will continue to resonate for socially engaged evangelicals in the future.

Since Pope Leo XIII's landmark 1891 encyclical, *Rerum Novarum*, the Catholic Church assumed a prominent role in promoting social ethics that helped define political and social movements over the course of a century. *Rerum Novarum* and later social encyclicals (especially in the 1960s and 1970s) provided doctrinal guidelines for social responsibility and specifically addressed the detrimental effects of industrial capitalism. While defending the moral and economic validity of the free market, Catholic social teachings counseled caution and offered criticism about economic practices that reproduce structural sins and threaten human dignity, including labor exploitation and unbridled consumerism. Of particular importance were the Church's positions on safeguarding worker's rights, including fair wages and the right to unionize, and the legitimacy of state intervention for the sake of preventing economic abuses and protecting private property.

Catholic social teaching inspired an array of left-leaning movements in the twentieth century, including the Catholic Workers, liberation theology, and antiwar activism. Officially, the Church did not advance an anticapitalist rhetoric like that of the social gospel, but it offered correctives in the form of coherent doctrines that lent support to policies of redistributive justice. However, as postwar Catholicism became aligned with anticommunism and the Church hierarchy became more politically conservative, especially under

Pope John Paul II, Catholic social teaching shifted as well. While still advocating justice for the poor and oppressed and warning against the excesses of the market, John Paul II spoke out against the welfare state and presented a more limited view of government with regard to social justice. Following his lead, Catholic leaders placed renewed emphasis on subsidiarity—the principle that governments are meant to support and empower local communities and institutions—which has been used to advance conservative positions on reduced government and welfare privatization.

Interestingly, the diverse ways that Catholic social teaching has resonated or been absorbed in evangelical discourse reflect the range of liberal and conservative positions that are associated with it historically. For example, on the evangelical left, Reverend Jim Wallis of *Sojourners* and Call to Renewal cites Catholic social teaching, especially Dorothy Day's Catholic Worker movement, as having had a major influence in his own approach to serving the poor while remaining politically engaged.[24] Wallis's particular brand of intellectual and ethical ecumenism does not sit entirely well with most white evangelicals, many of whom gravitate more readily toward his counterparts on the political right. The late Chuck Colson, for example, was unrivaled in his public role as an evangelical interpreter of Catholic theology and ethics, as a result of decades of dialogue and collaboration with Catholic figures such as Fr. Richard John Neuhaus, Michael Novak, and Fr. Robert Sirico. Indeed, Colson's views on social justice coalesced with and were partially inspired by the conservative and libertarian views of his Catholic interlocutors. Instead of challenging large-scale structures of poverty and oppression, Colson generally argued in favor of traditional moral values as a framework for promoting the sanctity of life, human rights, and the importance of the free market and civil society. Echoing, often explicitly, Catholic principles of *imago Dei* and subsidiarity among others, Colson advocated an ideological agenda that facilitated the rise of compassionate conservatism in the late 1990s, which remains popular in evangelical circles.

In the years since federal welfare reform and faith-based initiatives came into the national spotlight, evangelicals have renewed their commitments to social responsibility and social entrepreneurship. In a cultural climate favorable to the politics of "the third way," conservative evangelicals have opened up considerably in their support of local ministries and initiatives that help people in need while advancing some form of redistributive justice, as long as they do not contradict the tenets of evangelical theology. Though evangelism and personal accountability remain primary concerns, evangelical churches and denominations have become more forward in their embrace of urban policy reforms, programs of racial reconciliation, and community development projects that promise to redress the perceived failures of the welfare state to ensure equal opportunity, stimulate economic growth, and restore civic virtues.

Critics may (and do) suggest that evangelical overtures toward social justice come nowhere near even an approximation of the rich and elaborated legacy of the Catholic tradition. There is good reason for skepticism, to be sure, as relationalist ethics privileging individual over structural accountability continue to be dominant, particularly in white evangelical churches.[25] Indeed, the austere morality of compassionate conservatism and the episodic, pragmatic, and often narrow style of personalized charity that middle-class evangelicals are known to perform may not seem like grounds for asserting that justice is rolling down like water on the hardened fields of evangelical consciousness. And yet, as indicated before, the chorus of voices within evangelicalism calling churches and faith communities to task for their deficiencies in this area has only become louder and more confident in recent years. In addition, the conceptual tools employed by key proponents of renewed social engagement are increasingly resonant with collectivist and covenantal social imaginaries that, while by no means unique to Catholicism, suggest growing affinities and potential avenues of convergence.

For example, one interesting recent trend in the discourse of social engagement is a reliance on the language of "common good," a concept the religious articulations of which owe much to Catholic influences in modern thought. Evangelicals have tended to place greater emphasis on biblical orthodoxy, personal piety, and evangelism in the last century, not necessarily to the exclusion of the social but in ways that privilege personal responsibility and private morality as focuses of public concern. Lately, however, evangelicals at the organizational and intellectual vanguard of the new social engagement—such as Richard Cizik and David Gushee, founders of New Evangelical Partnership for the Common Good—have pushed for wider commitments to the common good broadly conceived. The phrase even found its way into a string of public declarations of evangelical identity and social concern, including the Evangelical Manifesto (2008), the Manhattan Declaration (2009), and NAE's *For the Health of the Nation* (2004). The fact that these statements make repeated references to "the common good" or "common welfare" is significant in light of the relative scarcity or absence of such terms in earlier documents of the same kind.

This shift entails more than semantics. It is being borne out in practice through new models of faith-based social and economic action. The latest generation of engaged evangelicals is eagerly drawn to ambitious holistic initiatives regarding social welfare, economic uplift, and environmental sustainability, broadly conceived.[26] These include entrepreneurial ventures such as micro-financing programs, development projects, and profit-sharing arrangements guided by common good principles as opposed to strictly profit-driven market principles.[27] Moreover, my own research shows that recent evangelical forays into the field of urban renewal reveal a tendency to rely on certain utopianist ideals and millennialist notions that straddle the line between competing notions of kingdom now and kingdom come, thereby allowing visions of imminent social reformation to coexist alongside long-term visions of ultimate reward. As Heyer observes, Catholic social teaching highlights continuities rather than ruptures between this world and the kingdom of God, and it furthermore calls on would-be disciples to embody "faithful citizenship" through public as well as private action, and with concern toward institutional structures as well as pious devotions.[28] This is a model of engagement that evangelicals are undoubtedly drawing nearer toward, in both principle and practice.

Conclusion

Theology matters, and rarely as acutely as when it comes to evangelical Protestants distinguishing themselves from Roman Catholics. Thus we can well imagine the lengths that publicly and socially engaged evangelicals will go to (including those with a penchant for building bridges across communities of faith) in order to avoid the stigmas of Catholic imprimatur and to affirm their commitments to evangelical doctrines and tenets. David Gushee, a moderate evangelical who was raised Roman Catholic, confesses to be among those who "often draw on the profound resources of the magisterial Roman Catholic social-teaching tradition," including its "determined tradition of public engagement," its "theological sturdiness," and "the richness of the sacramental vision of life." Yet he is quick to counsel caution, adding that "there are significant differences in approach between Protestant and Roman Catholic ethics," and therefore "we evangelicals need to develop our own social teaching-tradition that more aptly reflects our particular theological, ecclesial, and moral commitments."[29]

Such caveats notwithstanding, the areas of past, present, and future confluence are worth taking into account, even if they appear to exist on levels of abstraction (which are nonetheless consequential). Studying faith in action requires that we remain attentive to cultural trends and sensibilities that complicate the usual boundaries that are meant to distinguish one religious group from another. In the preceding analysis, I have sought to identify emerging themes of the new evangelical social engagement that resonate with those that have more stable moorings in Roman Catholicism, thus demonstrating points of mutual affinity while drawing attention to the intrinsic multidimensionality of this engagement, which should not be seen as a narrowly defined field but one that is constituted by, and oriented toward, larger cultural, theological, and institutional assemblages. In other words, by exploring symbols and patterns that evoke Roman Catholic ideals, independent of whether they do so deliberately, I hope to open new paths of inquiry that do not take evangelicalism itself as the beginning and end point of analysis, but rather acknowledge a wider range of influences and possibilities that are likely to shape the field of potential and conceivable action.

Evangelical social engagement, like other social movements, relies on the coherence of group identity, that is, the distinction between the group that engages and the larger world with which it engages. Acts of engagement can challenge such distinctions, however. As evangelicals become committed volunteers, social workers, activists, and advocates, they enter into a realm of new partners and interlocutors, and occasionally strange bedfellows. This chapter has explored inter-Christian affinities of a mostly thematic nature with regard to social welfare, with less attention to actual partnerships, collaborations, and explicit talking points between evangelicals and Catholics. We can proceed further by asking how these affinities will evolve over time, especially in terms of (1) evangelical commitments to holistic ministry and corresponding changes in how evangelicals define and practice evangelism; (2) evangelical attitudes toward issues of poverty, social justice, and the politics of welfare; and (3) evangelical openness to new strategies of ecumenical cooperation and outreach, including bridge-building efforts with Catholic charities and nonprofits. Such inquiries will need to be assessed over time. For the time being, I propose that as we evaluate the new evangelical social engagement, we do well to recognize that while it is not entirely new, historically speaking, it also is not strictly defined by the boundaries of evangelicalism alone.

NOTES

1. In 2009, for example, a group of nearly seventy public evangelicals released a statement commending Pope Benedict XVI's social encyclical entitled *Caritas in Veritae* and encouraging fellow evangelicals to engage with the document. The list included Richard Cizik, Richard Mouw, David Neff, Ronald Sider, and Jim Wallis.

2. *U.S. Religious Landscape Survey*, "Religious Affiliation: Diverse and Dynamic" (Pew Forum on Religion and Public Life, 2008).

3. Alan Wolfe, *The Transformation of American Religion: How We Actually Live Our Faith* (New York: Free Press, 2003), 36.

4. Rebecca Allahyari, *Visions of Charity: Volunteer Workers and Moral Community* (Berkeley: University of California Press, 2000).

5. Nancy T. Ammerman, *Pillars of Faith: American Congregations and Their Partners* (Berkeley: University of California Press, 2005); Mark Chaves, *Congregations in America* (Cambridge, MA: Harvard University Press, 2004).

6. Christian Smith, *American Evangelicalism: Embattled and Thriving* (Chicago: Chicago University Press, 1998), 118.

7. Omri Elisha, *Moral Ambition: Mobilization and Social Outreach in Evangelical Megachurches* (Berkeley: University of California Press, 2011).

8. Jarett Zigon, *"HIV Is God's Blessing": Rehabilitating Morality in Neoliberal Russia* (Berkeley: University of California Press, 2011), 67.

9. Peter G. Heltzel, *Jesus & Justice: Evangelicals, Race & American Politics* (New Haven, CT: Yale University Press, 2009), 133.

10. Heltzel, *Jesus & Justice*; see also Kristen E. Heyer, "Insights from Catholic Social Ethics and Political Participation," 101-14, in *Toward an Evangelical Public Policy: Political Strategies for the Health of the Nation*, ed. Ronald J. Sider and Diane Knippers (Grand Rapids, MI: Baker Books, 2005).

11. Henri Nouwen, *Compassion: A Reflection on the Christian Life* (New York: Doubleday, 1982).

12. Elisha, *Moral Ambition*, 166.

13. For an interesting discussion of how ideas of suffering have been applied by American Catholics with regard to bodily afflictions and disabilities, see Robert A. Orsi, *Thank You, St. Jude: Women's Devotion to the Patron Saint of Hopeless Causes* (New Haven, CT: Yale University Press, 1996).

14. I do not mean to downplay evangelicals' historical sensitivity to human suffering, nor to ignore the fact that Catholic missions have always had evangelistic as well as humanitarian dimensions. My point pertains to differences in doctrine and symbolic emphasis, differences that correlate with other cultural distinctions between evangelicals and Catholics.

15. James S. Bielo, *Emerging Evangelicals: Faith, Modernity, and the Desire for Authenticity* (New York: New York University Press, 2011).

16. Anthony M. Petro, "After the Wrath of God: American Christian Sentiment and the Biopolitics of AIDS," unpublished paper.

17. Leigh Eric Schmidt, *Restless Souls: The Making of American Spirituality* (New York: HarperCollins, 2005); Patricia A. Ward, *Experimental Theology in America: Madame Guyon, Fenelon, and Their Readers* (Waco, TX: Baylor University Press, 2009).

18. See Timothy J. Keller, *Ministries of Mercy: The Call of the Jericho Road* (Phillipsburg, NJ: P&R, 1997); and Steve Sjogren, *Conspiracy of Kindness: A Refreshing New Approach to Sharing the Love of Jesus with Others* (Ann Arbor, MI: Vine Books, 1993).

19. Omri Elisha, "Faith beyond Belief: Evangelical Protestant Conceptions of Faith and the Resonance of Anti-Humanism," *Social Analysis* 52 (2008): 56–78.

20. Donald E. Miller, *Reinventing American Protestantism: Christianity in the New Millennium* (Berkeley: University of California Press, 1997).

21. See Michael O. Emerson and Christian Smith, *Divided by Faith: Evangelical Religion and the Problem of Race in America* (New York: Oxford University Press, 2000).

22. Ronald J. Sider, *The Scandal of the Evangelical Conscience* (Grand Rapids, MI: Baker Books, 2005); Timothy J. Keller, *Generous Justice: How God's Grace Makes Us Just* (New York: Dutton, 2010).

23. For example, Heyer, "Insights from Catholic Social Ethics and Political Participation"; and David P. Gushee, *The Future of Faith in American Politics: The Public Witness of the Evangelical Center* (Waco, TX: Baylor University Press, 2008), 219.

24. Jim Wallis, *Faith Works: How Faith-Based Organizations Are Changing Lives, Neighborhoods, and America* (New York: Random House, 2001); and see Heltzel, *Jesus & Justice*.

25. Emerson and Smith, *Divided by Faith*, 77.

26. Marcia Pally, *The New Evangelicals: Expanding the Vision of the Common Good* (Grand Rapids, MI: Eerdmans, 2011).

27. On this particular distinction, see Marcia Pally's essay "Entrepreneurial Evangelicals for Economic Justice," posted February 2012 at www.telospress.com.

28. Heyer, "Insights from Catholic Social Ethics and Political Participation," 102.

29. Gushee, *Future of Faith*, 219–20.

4

The New Monasticism

Will Samson

NO MUSIC MINISTER stands and gathers up the emotions of the congregation into a state called worship. No assistant pastor reads the announcements or gives a short lesson to the children before they file out of the sanctuary. A senior pastor never walks on a stage and presides over an audience sitting in parallel pews, Bibles open in their laps, ready with a pen and notepad. After the sermon, nobody disassembles a stack of brass plates, distributes them to deacons or elders, and passes the communion elements to the same group sitting in lines.

This is a gathering in a New Monastic community. The worship happens when a guitar or a banjo is pulled out, an original song is shared, or someone just leads the group in "There Is a Balm in Gilead." Every community member is a pastor, and the announcements could range anywhere from who has kitchen duty to when the bus leaves for a demonstration against mountaintop removal mining. Bibles are sometimes open, usually to read a portion of the lectionary reading that had been assigned for the week. Perhaps someone will share an insight. But the sermons are lived each day of the week, not just on Sunday, and the experiences are collected here in a circle of mismatched chairs, the smell of the potluck offerings making its way into the gathering room. Members share how they saw God in the eyes of the schizophrenic woman who yells at people by the library, how a refugee experienced a miraculous turnaround in the hospital. Miracles, still performed by a Savior who helps the homeless and the heartsick, don't just happen in the pages of scripture.

So they come, and they feast, and they worship, and nobody quite knows which is which.

* * *

Scholars and commentators perpetually predict the decline of American evangelicalism. In the 1980s, James Davison Hunter argued that evangelicalism would falter against the "quandary of modernity."[1] Recently, the *Christian Science Monitor* suggested there was a "coming evangelical collapse."[2] And as one young evangelical put it, "Our pastors might not like it, but the world is changing, and we are changing with it. Unless the evangelical church in America can adapt and evolve, it might not survive in a postmodern world."[3] Yet despite the prognostications and attention-grabbing headlines about changes and challenges within evangelicalism, the reality is that it thrives in an embattled state and has done so for the past century.

What is the source of this constant state, this embattlement, and this continued vigor? Christian Smith argues that cultural distinction is at the core of evangelicalism: "American evangelicalism, we contend, is strong not because it is shielded against, but because it is—or at least perceives itself to be—embattled with forces that seem to oppose or threaten it. Indeed, evangelicalism, we suggest, thrives on distinction, engagement, tension, conflict and threat."[4] Evangelicals, in other words, feel compelled to live in opposition to the culture.[5] Yet evangelicals also seek to share their vision of Christianity in a way that resonates and gains adherents. This motivates a quest for cultural accommodation within the movement. So as a frame from which to understand today's evangelicals, there is an ongoing dialogue within the movement between accommodation and distinction and a dialectical relationship between embattlement and thriving.

But if distinction from the dominant culture is deeply embedded in the DNA of American evangelicalism, what happens when evangelicalism becomes deeply embedded in American culture? As Michael Lindsay points out, American evangelicals, after spending much of their movement living on the outs with the dominant culture, have moved well into the "halls of power" in business, government, and other critical sectors of American society. A logical question follows: What if today's younger evangelicals are simply following the established evangelical pattern and turning against mainstream evangelicalism itself? If, as Lindsay has suggested, evangelicalism has become a dominant part of the culture in America, what if younger evangelicals, as they seek to create distinction against the reigning culture, are creating distinction against the previous generation of evangelicals who "now wield power in just about every segment of American society?"[6]

This chapter addresses these dynamics by exploring three interrelated questions about a significant movement within contemporary evangelicalism: the New Monastic movement. What does the New Monastic movement look like on the ground? In what ways do the New Monastics seek to differentiate themselves from the previous generation of evangelicals in terms of beliefs and social engagement? And how might the New Monasticism affect the future of evangelical social engagement? The examination that follows is based on research I conducted in a number of New Monastic communities, including interviews with over forty New Monastic leaders and community members.

The New Monasticism

In the midst of sweeping changes taking place within American Christianity and within evangelical Protestantism in particular, there is a growing movement of young evangelicals who are not satisfied with the current state of the Christian church. They are particularly disappointed by the politicization of religion. Consider the following from Jonathan Wilson-Hartgrove: "One side says our moral fabric has worn thin and we have to defend the family. The other side says we're drunk on war and need to defend the poor. Both camps circle the wagons and insist that their concerns are most important. Either way there isn't much hope the world will know we are Christians by our love for one another. Often we can't even agree that we are all Christians." Wilson-Hartgrove is one of the leaders of a new social movement happening largely within American Protestantism known as New Monasticism. Wilson-Hartgrove, Shane Claiborne, and Chris Haw, three of the more prominent movement actors, have been featured in media ranging from the *Boston Globe* to CNN and have written about the subject in such books as *New Monasticism, Jesus for President,* and *The Irresistible Revolution.*[7]

So what exactly is New Monasticism? Perhaps a good place to start is by defining old monasticism, which will then provide points of comparison. Early Christianity struggled with many definitional issues, including what it meant to be a follower of a religion that was banned by the Roman Empire. However, when Christianity was legalized under Constantine, the questions changed. A new set of issues emerged for religious adherents that concerned the struggle to embrace a government and its militarism that had previously oppressed them. Many individuals, particularly clergy, found that they could not embrace the empire. Instead, they chose to establish alternative communities that served as "acts of renunciation" against the mixing of the state and the church.[8] While these communities had some early influence on both the church and the government, their influence was nonetheless limited. All that changed when Benedict of Nursia began his monastic life in the sixth century. While his work was still rooted in the renunciation of the world, his was the first monastic order to establish a firm disciplinary rule. This rule was modified because of earlier failures, but the power of a structured counter-resistance formed a movement of monastic orders that spread throughout the world within two hundred years.[9]

Like the ancient monastics before them, the New Monastics also see themselves as creating a community that serves as an alternative to the contemporary
American church and its strong connection to the state. It grew out of a sense
of social justice that many young evangelicals increasingly embraced. They
actively sought to live among the poor and those in need. A signal moment
in this movement happened in Philadelphia in 1997. Shane Claiborne and
a group of students from Eastern College in St. David's, Pennsylvania, were
working and living in the Kensington area of Philadelphia, an area plagued by
crime and poverty. What began as a movement without a plan quickly took on
a revolutionary feel when the city of Philadelphia and the local Catholic arch-
diocese threatened to move a group of homeless people out of an abandoned
Catholic church. Claiborne and the other students stood in solidarity with the
homeless and eventually prevailed over both the city and the church. Out of
this social action was born the community known as the Simple Way.

Claiborne went on to influence two other students, Jonathan
Wilson-Hartgrove and Chris Haw. Wilson-Hartgrove subsequently traveled
with Claiborne to Iraq to serve with a Christian Peacemakers Team prior to
the U.S. invasion of that country in 2003. Haw traveled to Belize to spend a
semester studying Christian views of the environment. Both men, inspired
by Claiborne and radicalized by what they had seen themselves, began their
own monastic communities. Haw settled across the river from Claiborne in
Camden, New Jersey, founding the Camden House, and Wilson-Hartgrove
settled in the Durham, North Carolina area, founding Rutba House.

Many communities have followed. The Community of Communities, a
website for New Monastics, lists over two hundred communities in the United
States that identify themselves as New Monastic.[10] Some of these are new communities; others are existing communities that find resonance in the notions
of New Monasticism.

The Twelve Marks of a New Monasticism

Traditional monasticism formed orders that were designed to serve as a
renunciation of the outside world. But Dietrich Bonhoeffer recast the notion
of a monastic community that could serve as a renunciation to the empire's
captivation of the church in 1935. He wrote the following to his brother
Karl-Friedrick: "...the restoration of the church will surely come only from
a new type of monasticism which has nothing in common with the old but
a complete lack of compromise in a life lived in accordance with the Sermon
on the Mount in the discipleship of Christ. I think it is time to gather people
together to do this..."[11] Bonhoeffer was referring specifically to the captivity

of the German church by Hitler. But this theme of "a new monasticism" was resounded by Jonathan Wilson in 1997[12] and then picked up again by Wilson's son-in-law, Jonathan Wilson-Hartgrove. In 2004, Wilson-Hartgrove convened a group of twelve communities to think through what rule of life could govern New Monastic communities. He wrote: "In an age when 'Christian' America is the 'last remaining superpower' in an all-out 'war on terror,' we've begun to think that once again it is time for a new monasticism. Indeed, this is how we see the Spirit moving in North America today."[13]

Out of that conference of Christian communities came "The 12 Marks of the New Monasticism." They are:

1. Relocation to the abandoned places of empire.
2. Sharing economic resources with fellow community members and the needy among us.
3. Hospitality to the stranger.
4. Lament for racial divisions within the church and our communities combined with the active pursuit of a just reconciliation.
5. Humble submission to Christ's body, the church.
6. Intentional formation in the way of Christ and the rule of the community along the lines of the old novitiate.
7. Nurturing common life among members of intentional community.
8. Support for celibate singles alongside monogamous married couples and their children.
9. Geographical proximity to community members who share a common rule of life.
10. Care for the plot of God's earth given to us along with support of our local economies.
11. Peacemaking in the midst of violence and conflict resolution within communities along the lines of Matthew 18.
12. Commitment to a disciplined contemplative life.

The Twelve Marks in Practice

Communality is an example of a New Monastic community in action. Founded in 2000 with six original members, it has grown to over fifty and receded back to the low teens in membership. With its early founding relative to the birth of New Monasticism, it represents one of the older communities in the movement. Like the Simple Way, Communality was birthed out of a connection to the poor, in this case, those living in downtown Lexington, Kentucky.

Geoff and Sherry describe themselves as urban missionaries. They met while studying at Asbury Seminary in the school of missions. Geoff is from Australia but considers himself home in Kentucky, the place where he believes God has led them to minister. Sherry is a Georgia native but shares the sense of place with Geoff in their location as a white family within a predominantly African American neighborhood. In this sense, they typify relocation to abandoned places of empire. Their home is not just where they live. Rather, it is the place to which they have purposely relocated to serve as a witness to the need for reconciliation and a sense of rootedness. They recently purchased the lot next to their house, turned it into an urban farm, and now provide their neighbors with eggs from their chickens.

This illustrates how the group sees its resources as a means to bless the community. Even the group's gatherings are evaluated through that lens. Consider the following explanation of their weekly meetings from one member: "We gather regularly as a wider community to affirm our unity and to be encouraged in the work that we do the other days of the week, and that our commitment is to seek the welfare of the city, and that's equal to anything we do to care for one another." This ethic pervades the remaining members of the community, with most members residing in downtown Lexington's racially mixed areas. They share economic resources with fellow community members and the needy by gardening and sharing that food.

In keeping with these decisions, many of the members of the community are involved in their neighborhood associations, often as the only white members of that group. Similar to the other New Monastic communities, Communality is exclusively white. Yet the "lament for racial divisions within the Church and our communities combined with the active pursuit of a just reconciliation" is an area where this community has done sustained work. For instance, Communality helped sponsor a garden near a burial ground that sought to bring a historically African American Episcopal congregation together with the predominantly white cathedral. The garden was named for the only African American buried in that cemetery.

Geographical proximity to community members who share a common rule of life remained a struggle for the group. Only one house in the community is more than six blocks from another. Almost every family had someone outside the family living with them. However, as the community aged and members have had children, residential proximity is increasingly hard to maintain. Given the lack of a firm binding disciplinary rule, this mark remains frustratingly elusive.

Ryan and Jodie were church shopping when they came upon Communality. They were looking for a more genuine experience. Quoting from Jodie: "I felt like all the evangelical churches that I had been in, they all seemed like a fake. Like a show. And I didn't want it to be a show. I wanted it to be 'This is what we come here and do and there are no bells and whistles.'" Nurturing common life among members of an intentional community is an area where Communality shines. In addition to the Sunday gatherings, there are various groups that meet during the week. Most of the community is involved in some form of common gardening practices. And until recently, most of the community worked together on refugee resettlement issues in conjunction with Kentucky Refugee Ministries. Ryan and Jodie also typify the way in which community members have made deliberate employment choices that allow them time to be involved in their neighborhood. Jodie is the director of an after-school kids program called Kids Café and Ryan is the director of Seedleaf, a community gardening initiative.

Other monastic marks are clearly discernible. Care for the plot of God's Earth, along with support of local economies, is an ethos to which the members of Communality connect deeply. At the time of this writing, every household in the community had their own garden. Most raised chickens in the backyard for egg production. And the community helped birth Seedleaf, which has become the dominant community gardening organization in the city. Submission to the church is a mark that may look different, depending on one's ecclesial perspective. Most of the members consider Communality their primary church home. However, it should be noted that the community was founded, at least in small part, with funds from the Christian and Missionary Alliance denomination church-planting group, and, until very recently, the community maintained informal ties with that group. Regarding peacemaking in the midst of violence and conflict resolution along the lines of Matthew 18, this community has been at the forefront of various racial reconciliation movements in the city. In that same vein, Communality has been a leader in the fight against mountaintop removal mining, particularly with regard to efforts at community building among those affected by the practice.[14]

If Communality were to be evaluated against the twelve marks, there would be weaknesses as well as strengths. The formation of a novitiate for this community would be by far the weakest element, as it would for every other New Monastic community. Many of the members of these communities were drawn to the New Monasticism because they did not connect with the institutional church in America. Accordingly, convincing people to commit to a rule of life is a challenge. Support for celibate singles alongside monogamous married couples and their children is not a strength of this group. Although there is a wide age range, from one to sixty, most in the community are young married couples. Additionally, the community, like most of the New Monastic communities, has not yet addressed the question of what to do with homo-sexual relationships.

New Monasticism as a Theopolitical Response to American Evangelicalism

To understand the theological and political motivations of the New Monastics, one must first understand that, for this group, these are not separate questions. Motivated by writers like John Howard Yoder and William Cavanaugh, the leaders of the New Monastic movement would contend that is precisely the false dichotomy of these two spheres that has gotten the church into trouble.[15] Consider the following from Claiborne and Haw's *Jesus for President*: "We in the church are schizophrenic: we want to be good Christians, but deep down we trust that only the power of the state and its militaries and markets can really make a difference in the world. And so we're hardly able to distinguish between what's American and what's Christian. As a result, power corrupts the church and its goals and practices."[16]

Three theopolitical frameworks are apparent in New Monastic writing and my qualitative interviews. The first is that of an *alternative politic*, which is suggested by the title of the book *Jesus for President*. For virtually all of the New Monastics I interviewed, both leaders and community members, there is a sense that the politics of man fails, but the politics of God provides an alternative that is different than simply a third way between the political parties.[17] This alternative politic is captured well in an ABC interview from 2010 with a leading young evangelical, Gabe Lyons, the head of the Q Project: "What we're seeing is the church start to flourish as Christians embrace that, you know, the way to be Christian isn't just to vote a certain way or to align yourself with a certain political persuasion or a party, but it's to be thoughtful about all the issues confronting us and the world and to choose how we're going to engage in those thoughtfully."[18]

The second theopolitical framework with which to analyze evangelical social engagement in general and the New Monasticism in particular is that of a *communal politic*. This is telegraphed by a chapter title in Wilson-Hartgrove's book *New Monasticism*, which discussed "God's plan to save the world through a people." In that chapter, he argues for the importance of learning to read the "you" in the Bible as "y'all"; in other words, for the New Monastics, "salvation and sanctification depend on finding my true home with God's people."[19] This has implications for evangelical social engagement. Collective centers of moral authority are more typically found within with Orthodox and Catholic traditions, which have also historically been more engaged in collective civic behavior.[20] Many of the New Monastic communities are deeply engaged in neighborhood associations, community-based social justice organizations, and other forms of collective social engagement.

The third theopolitical framework with which to interpret the social engagement of the New Monastics is that of a *narratival politic*. There is an interesting tension that exists in the writings of New Monastic leaders between a rootedness in a vision of the past and a sense of the prophetic nature of these communities focused on change in the future. In multiple articles and books, Wilson-Hartgrove speaks of New Monasticism as having a "vision so old it's new." In that sense, he is seeking to connect today's evangelicals with the long history of the church and, in particular, with communities that renounce the intrusion of the empire into the church.

However, Wilson-Hartgrove also speaks of New Monasticism as pointing to something new. That something, he suggests, will look like the past, such as like the church's work on civil rights for black Americans and Dorothy Day's work for the poor. But, he writes, "as we begin to share our stories with one another, they begin blending into a wonderful gift: the sketch of a new monastic movement in which all of us agreed the Holy Spirit was at work." Thus, for Wilson-Hartgrove, it is the narrative that ties together the past and the future. This is similar to sentiments expressed by a New Monastic community member in an interview: "I spent so much time in my childhood learning to defend whether the Bible was *right*. These days I am far more concerned with whether the *story* is right. That's not to say that I don't believe in the Bible anymore, but I realize now that we don't have to start from scratch—people have already dealt with some version of the issues that we face today.... And we make the future together, in community, as we tell the story of God. And that has to be in community."

New Monasticism as a Countermovement to American Evangelicalism

Three specific themes mark areas where the New Monasticism is distinguishing itself from mainstream evangelicalism: militaristic moralism, therapeutism, and placelessness. The first theme is the reaction to the militaristic moralism of the Religious Right. In simplest terms, the New Monasticism should be seen as a countermovement to evangelical dominance in the political sphere since the years leading up the election of Ronald Reagan. In an interview with Claiborne, he offered the following:

What seems clear to me is that thirty years ago there was this growing movement of the Moral Majority and the Religious Right and all that, and that became increasingly a disconnect for a lot of Christians, especially young Christians, that felt like, wow, where did this come from and why is it so specialized in its hot button issues that Jesus spoke very little about.

To unpack this broader theme, there were a few subthemes that emerged to explain the concern over militaristic moralism. The first is that of *America as aggressor*. This was clearly the most dominant subtheme. Interestingly, every interviewee mentioned the attacks of September 11 and the subsequent invasion of Iraq as motivating them to seek an alternative ecclesiology and body politic. Most interviewees mentioned concern over the reaction to these events from both the left and the right as a motivating reason for their involvement with the New Monasticism. One community member listed it as the foremost reason:

> I heard Jerry Falwell say that God is pro-war and I thought, which God is he talking about? The God I know preached sacrificial peace. Anyway, it just got to the point where I got sick and tired of the pro-American agenda coming from the pulpit and I had to get out. That's the start of the story of how I got here [to a New Monastic community].

A second subtheme that emerged from the research is concern over the dominance of *the politics of personal piety*. While a perhaps surprising number of New Monastic community members hold conservative positions on social issues, particularly on the issue of abortion, there was an overwhelming consensus that abortion and gay marriage should not dominate the conversation within the church in the way they have for the past generation. One quote from a community member illustrates this widespread view: "The gay issue and the abortion issue, they're just not in the Bible, at least not the way they are lived out today. So you've got people pushing these agendas and then you've got us [younger Christians] who really want to read our Bible and do what it says but we're like—dude, where were those verses about gay marriage again?"

A third subtheme that emerged is the concern over the belief of *America as a Christian nation*. Consider the following quote from Claiborne: "But what happened after September 11th broke my heart. Conservative Christians rallied around the drums of war. Liberal Christians took to the streets. The cross was smothered by the flag and trampled under the feet of angry protestors. The church community was lost, so the many hungry seekers found community in the civic religion of American patriotism."[21]

So how then do these communities work against this militaristic moralism? One way is through a radical commitment to peace work. Rather than rely on reading a Daniel Berrigan book (although most had books by Berrigan, John Dear, and other peace activists on the community bookshelf), many in these communities were involved with Christian Peacemaker Teams. Many had been arrested for protesting at the School of the Americas, a military base that trains Latin American military personnel. At one Family Reunion, an annual gathering of New Monastic communities, one individual was reporting to jail the following week for protest activities. The speaker, Chris Haw from the Camden House, asked for all who had been arrested for protest work to come up on the stage and lay hands on the person headed to jail. Half of the audience of more than fifty people headed to the stage.

Another practice of New Monastic communities that seek to work against the militaristic moralism of the Religious Right is that of radical hospitality. Although the communities are mostly white and middle-class, every community in my study had one or more individuals who did not fit the dominant type. Several communities had folks coming off the streets and dealing with mental illness. Several had folks working through their sexuality or struggling to stay in the church after coming out sexually.

The second theme is the reaction to the therapeutism that has dominated American evangelicalism in modern times. Wilson-Hartgrove critiques a religion that only required that people "make a simple choice for Jesus from the comfort of their homes," one where "all their listeners needed to do was believe."[22] In his *Triumph of the Therapeutic*, Rieff speaks of the effect of therapeutism in creating a culture where each person is given "permission to live an experimental life." And further, "Psychological man, in his independence from all gods, can feel free to use all god-terms; I imagine he will be a hedger against his own bets, a user of any faith that lends itself to therapeutic use."[23] Fast-forward forty years, and in a quintessential statement of therapeutic evangelicalism, Joel Osteen states: "God wants to make your life easier. He wants to assist you, to promote you, to give you advantages. He wants you to have preferential treatment."[24]

G. K. Chesterton once said, "Christianity has not been tried and found wanting. It has been found difficult and left untried." The data suggest that the opposite is true for those drawn to New Monastic communities. Specifically, community members are looking for creeds that hold a greater claim on their lives than the therapeutic deism that pervades American evangelicalism. In terms of practices, New Monastics are increasingly turning to more ancient and communal practices such as *lectio divina* and reading scripture guided by the church calendar. This offers a stark contrast with the individualistic, entertainment-based mentality of the megachurches.

It's striking that the therapeutism against which many of the New Monastic community members are reacting was a product of the megachurches that were designed for their parents. Preston Shires speaks of this generational dynamic when he observes that the baby boomers grew weary of their parents' church and created the more experiential, more individually oriented style of church found in the megachurch movement.[25] A generation later, it is this individualistic and therapeutic style of church that is driving younger evangelicals to New Monastic lifestyles and away from the ecclesiastical models of the baby boomers.

The practices by which New Monastics combat therapeutism are fairly self-evident. Even the choices themselves—to seek to live in community, to seek to live among the poor, and often to seek to grow at least some of your own food—put community members in a different place than other evangelicals, even compared to those among the younger generation. The question remains, though, whether the New Monastic lifestyle is qualitatively different than their megachurch forebears. Although many choose to live among the poor, few New Monastics are more than a phone call away from prosperity. Many choose to grow their own food, but few would struggle to pay for basic needs at the grocery store. An open question is whether the New Monastics are simply choosing an aesthetic that makes them distinct.

The final theme concerns the idea of placelessness, a disconnection from physical space. Among both scholars and laypeople, there is a growing awareness of "the importance of local context in constituting social worlds."[26] Wilson-Hartgrove addresses this issue in his book *The Wisdom of Stability: Rooting Faith in a Mobile Culture*: "In a culture that is characterized by unprecedented mobility and speed, I am convinced that the most important thing most of us can do to grow spiritually is to stay in the place where we are."[27] Or consider the following from a respondent:

That our lives are always worked out somewhere—geography, location, site—is always a part of who we're meant to be as the people of God. And so place, now I would say, is much broader than a group of people doing some kind of ministry project. Place is the city where we're located and where we live and where we work and where we carry out our lives.

To see evidence of the importance of place in the New Monastic movement, one need only look at the first mark of the New Monasticism, "relocation to the abandoned places of empire." New Monastics believe that certain places need to be reclaimed, and they take that admonition seriously. Place also relates directly to context. In an interview, Wilson-Hartgrove talked about the importance of his neighborhood and what he was learning by committing to stay put in a place where he was not the majority race. Place also has a strong relationship with hermeneutics and approach to the text. The following quote from Doug Pagitt is suggestive: "...there is a shift in the seat of authority. It isn't in the wisdom of the village leaders or the deep pockets of the factory owners or the knowledge of the corporate executives. Authority is found in the way our experiences come together and create reality. It is found in relationships. We tend to be suspicious of objectivity, uncertain if it is possible or even desirable. Authority—as much as anything else in the Inventive Age—is user generated."[28]

Looking to the Future

The New Monasticism has been one of the most high-profile evangelical movements in recent years. Its leaders have garnered significant attention for their ideals, and these ideals have inspired adherents to reorder their lives in accordance with monastic rules such as the twelve marks and to live in intentional Christian community. Countless other evangelicals have sought to incorporate insights from the New Monasticism—concerning geographical stability, spiritual practice, local community, and radical hospitality—into their daily lives. What does the New Monasticism, especially its broader ethos, suggest about the future of evangelical social engagement?

First, the New Monastics are inclined to think locally and act locally. Their emphasis on immediate context and place makes the national political scene appear less relevant. This suggests that evangelicals informed by the New Monastic ethos are more likely to work with local nonprofits on issues that affect their proximate surroundings rather than on national issues or political campaigns. Second, the future of evangelicalism, to reference Pagitt, is likely to be more "user generated." Whereas in the past, national parachurch organizations played a strong top-down role in shaping the direction of evangelicalism, the future may more be in the hands of numerous local communities than in those of organizations such as the National Association of Evangelicals. Third, today's evangelicals are less likely than the generation before them to be politically committed to either major political party. If the New Monastics portend the future, rather than moving to the political center or left, younger evangelicals may disengage from the political process altogether.

NOTES

1. James Davison Hunter, *American Evangelicalism: Conservative Religion and the Quandary of Modernity* (New Brunswick, NJ: Rutgers University Press, 1983).

2. M. Spencer, "The Coming Evangelical Collapse," *Christian Science Monitor*, 2009 101 (71): 9.

3. R. H. Evans, "The Evolution of a Christian Creationist," *Washington Post*, August 6, 2010.

4. Christian Smith, *American Evangelicalism: Embattled and Thriving* (Chicago: University of Chicago Press, 1998).

5. George M. Marsden, *Understanding Fundamentalism and Evangelicalism* (Grand Rapids, MI: W. B. Eerdmans, 1991); Smith, *American Evangelicalism*; J. M. Penning and C. E. Smidt, *Evangelicalism: The Next Generation* (Grand Rapids, MI: Baker Academic, 2002).

6. Michael Lindsay, *Faith in the Halls of Power: How Evangelicals Joined the American Elite* (New York: Oxford University Press, 2007).

7. Jonathon Wilson-Hartgrove, *New Monasticism: What It Has to Say to Today's Church* (Grand Rapids, MI: Brazos Press, 2008); Shane Claiborne and Chris Haw, *Jesus for President: Politics for Ordinary Radicals* (Grand Rapids, MI: Zondervan, 2008); Shane Claiborne, *The Irresistible Revolution: Living as an Ordinary Radical* (Grand Rapids, MI: Zondervan, 2006).

8. H. B. Workman, *The Evolution of the Monastic Ideal: From the Earliest Times Down to the Coming of the Friars* (London: C. H. Kelly, 1913).

9. W. A. Meeks, *The Origins of Christian Morality: The First Two Centuries* (New Haven, CT: Yale University Press, 1993).

10. See www.communityofcommunities.info.

11. Dietrich Bonhoeffer, Geffrey B. Kelly, and F. Burton Nelson. *A Testament to Freedom : The Essential Writings of Dietrich Bonhoeffer*. Rev. ed. [San Francisco, Calif.]: HarperSanFrancisco, 1995, 424.

12. J. R. Wilson, *Living Faithfully in a Fragmented World: Lessons for the Church from MacIntyre's "After Virtue"* (Harrisburg, PA: Trinity Press International, 1997).

13. The Rutba House, *School(s) for Conversion: 12 Marks of a New Monasticism* (Eugene, OR: Wipf & Stock, 2005), ix–x.

14. See chapter 8 of W. Samson and L. Samson, *Justice in the Burbs: Being the Hands of Jesus Wherever You Live* (Grand Rapids, MI: Baker Books, 2007).

15. Cavanaugh employed the term *theopolitical* in his work: W. T. Cavanaugh, *Theopolitical Imagination* (New York: T & T Clark, 2002). This has been influential in the New Monastic movement.

16. Shane Claiborne and Chris Haw. *Jesus for President: Politics for Ordinary Radicals*. Grand Rapids, Mich.: Zondervan, 2008, 20.

17. For more on this topic, see J. Ellul, *The Politics of God and the Politics of Man* (Grand Rapids, MI: Eerdmans, 1972).

18. Quoted on http://abcnews.go.com/US/video/face-american-evangelicalism-10744135.

19. Wilson-Hartgrove, *New Monasticism*.

20. Fred Kniss and Paul Numrich, *Sacred Assemblies and Civic Engagement: How Religion Matters for America's Newest Immigrants* (New Brunswick, NJ: Rutgers University Press, 2007).

21. Claiborne, *The Irresistible Revolution*, 151.

22. Wilson-Hartgrove, *New Monasticism*, 11.

23. Philip Rieff, *The Triumph of the Therapeutic; Uses of Faith after Freud.* [1st ed.] (New York: Harper & Row, 1966), 27.

24. Joel Osteen, *Your Best Life Now: 7 Steps to Living at Your Full Potential.* 1st Warner Faith ed. (New York: Warner Books, 2004), 38.

25. P. Shires, *Hippies of the Religious Right* (Waco, TX: Baylor University Press, 2007).

26. G. A. Fine, "The Sociology of the Local: Action and Its Publics," *Sociological Theory* 28:4 (2010): 355–76.

27. Wilson-Hartgrove, *The Wisdom of Stability: Rooting Faith in a Mobile Culture*, 1.

28. Doug Pagitt, *Church in the Inventive Age* (Minneapolis, MN: Sparkhouse Press, 2010), 32.

5

"We Need a Revival"

YOUNG EVANGELICAL WOMEN REDEFINE
ACTIVISM IN NEW YORK CITY

Adriane Bilous

WHETHER IT IS reading about how to strengthen governmental control over pornography or watching evangelical pundits argue over the need to eradicate sex education programs from public schools, we have long been fascinated by evangelical civic engagement.[1] Recently, evangelical millennials (those between the ages of eighteen and twenty-nine) have captured our attention, due in part to a decline in their political activism.[2] This decline has left some to question the strength of a shared evangelical view on civic engagement with Christian Right activists and may be merely the tip of an iceberg portending greater changes to come. In the November 6, 2008, edition of the *New York Times*, David P. Gushee clarifies the current predicament within American evangelicalism: "there is definitely a generational division...young evangelicals are attracted to a broader agenda beyond abortion and homosexuality, [including] the environment, poverty, human rights and [ending] torture."[3] Further tension surfaces as more young evangelicals join socially conscious organizations devoted to these causes—causes not often associated with Christian Right activism but with "left-leaning" activism. These shifts in concerns and subsequent intergenerational divisions have resulted in a veritable new evangelical, one who pursues different causes and redefines what it means to be evangelical.[4]

While it has been noted that activism among evangelical millennials appears to be in transition, the experiences of young evangelical women remain largely unexamined. Media coverage and academic research do not tease out their unique experiences, and much of the existing research indicates that there exists tension between generations of evangelical activists and evangelical women in particular. For example, Judith Stacey and Susan

Elizabeth Gerard reveal how evangelical women engage the permeation of feminist ideas into evangelical definitions of womanhood.[5] In "Where Are the Antifeminist Evangelicals?" Sally K. Gallagher highlights the gender identity negotiations that occur among evangelical women, specifically showing that these negotiations are not merely a reaction to contemporary feminism but an incorporation of many potentially divisive factors, including "local subcultures and affiliation with specific denominational subgroups."[6] Works such as these highlight the need to extend our knowledge and explore the experiences of millennial evangelical women *activists* in light of the emerging data on new evangelical identities and interests.[7]

After a brief contextual discussion, I present four analytical sections that deepen our understanding of these young new evangelical women activists. These sections are inspired by the following questions: What sources do these women draw on to legitimize activist pursuits? How do these women resolve potential intergenerational tensions resulting from these new activist causes? How are their identities as activists shaped by their evangelical identities? To answer these questions, I use a blend of interview and ethnographic data collected from 2010 to 2012 in the metropolitan New York City area. My interview data include roughly fifty interviews with young evangelical women activists between the ages of eighteen and twenty-nine, of which thirty-one are white non-Latinas. The average age of respondents is twenty-six, and, notably, all women in the sample hold a minimum of a bachelor's degree, with sixteen women holding a master's degree or higher. These women are involved in a variety of activist organizations, ranging from large nongovernmental organizations (NGOs) to local community service projects, including Hope for New York, Father's Heart, and World Vision. Respondents attend a variety of churches, ranging from Acts 29 Network church plants to Tim Keller's Redeemer Presbyterian Church and its New York City church plants. Congregation sizes range from a few hundred up to a thousand attendees at each Sunday service, with some churches offering multiple Sunday services.

Recent developments in evangelical activism seem to show a generational disconnect between millennial and older evangelicals. In this chapter, I examine ways in which young evangelical women resolve intergenerational tensions resulting from new activist interests by disregarding the label "evangelical" and instead using a narrative identity I call "I'm evangelical but not *that* type of evangelical." Moreover, while these young women stand firm in their ties to the evangelical institution, they strive to carve out a niche within the evangelical tradition by engaging head-on the legacy of evangelical women's submission and female empowerment with a second narrative identity I call the "servant activist." In sum, I argue that shifts in young evangelicals' value systems and their lives as emerging evangelical adults directly affect their civic engagement, making a considerable impact on future activism.[8]

Evangelical Activism in Context

Beginning in the 1970s, Jerry Falwell's Moral Majority, along with other such prominent groups as the Christian Voice and Concerned Women for America, rose to prominence as the "Christian Right."[9] Members stood together on many issues, notably against abortion, pornography, and the Equal Rights Amendment. These groups were not embraced wholeheartedly by all their GOP brethren, with many long-standing GOP evangelicals disagreeing partic- ularly with Falwell's views on maintaining subminimum wages and disman- tling the welfare system.[10] In truth, as Robert Wuthnow argues, a more serious consequence of the pull to the political left in the late 1960s was the "opening up of a potentially serious cultural gap between the evangelical left on the one hand and fundamentalist politically conservative evangelicals on the other."[11] Antagonism among evangelicals increased as this political movement was impacted further by an impressive influx of younger evangelicals.[12] Despite such divisions, Falwell's strong support for the GOP's political goals helped cement a strong position within the GOP for Christian Right activists. Though the Moral Majority was not able to sustain itself beyond the 1980s, Falwell con- tinued to focus on the desired image he wanted for a new, younger, stronger Christian Right.[13] Like Falwell, Pat Robertson also made similar efforts to build bridges with younger evangelical members of the GOP, including the creation of Regent University in 1978 to ensure the education of future generations of evangelical political activists.

The current cohort of younger evangelicals stands apart from cohorts of evangelicals like those in the 1970s for more reasons than one. Today's evan- gelical millennials, socialized into a culture of political activism by parents and church leaders, might know of the Christian Right's history but find that their own values and beliefs are not mirrored in Christian Right ideologies. These young adults reject their elders' activism and are somewhat disillusioned with the politically flavored religious culture in which they grew up.[14] The result is distaste not only for joining Christian Right activist groups but also for being associated with the movement at all.

With an acute awareness of how evangelical activists have been perceived by outsiders, young evangelical women construct identities that show a deep desire to separate from the political activism of older generations while still incorporating traditional evangelical values taught by these same older cohorts. Indeed, young evangelical women have grown up in the shadows of some memorable activists—both male and female. When learning about their predecessors, these young women internalize not only evangelical views on civic engagement but also views on gender roles as well. They also learn how previous generations of evangelical activists externalized these combined activist-gender ideals to combat feminists, career-focused women, and those who denounced evangelical women as mere captives in their own faith.

"I'm Evangelical but Not *That* Type of Evangelical"

Young evangelical women use a distinct language as they work to reduce inter-generational anxiety and confront ideas of "Christian womanhood." While I was interviewing women, one story in particular emerged repeatedly—a narrative I call "I'm evangelical but not *that* type of evangelical." Many women hesitated before talking about evangelicalism while others emphatically refused to be associated with the term altogether. For example, Elise and I discussed how young evangelicals differed in many respects from older evangelicals. She specifically addressed the label of "evangelical" itself and how many young people refuse to be labeled "that way." Using the words "those people" or "that way" highlights a generational divide and a desire to stand apart from older evangelical counterparts. Elise paused when asked about using the term *evangelical* to describe herself. She was concerned about how the label was used—claiming that "it's different for those who are insiders." She continued: "I don't use that word if I can help it. . . . I usually just say I'm Christian if someone asks." Elise cringed when I used the word *evangelical*, saying, "When I hear 'evangelical,' I go [makes face] because it reminds me of all the judgment. One thing is . . . sin is sin. It's [sin] period." For Elise, all sins, from white lies to abortion, should be judged equally—no sin is worse than any other in her opinion. With all sins being equal, she saw no need to judge others as more or less sinful. In her opinion, Christians are not meant to judge and isolate each other since everyone is equally sinful. For example, when asked about dissension from church-held views on abortion, Elise felt that abortion was wrong, something she learned from her pastor and mother, but she chose not to abandon a friend who chose abortion. In a similar vein, she described her friendship with a lesbian couple—again, she firmly believes that homosexuality is wrong but characterized her actions in terms of love rather than condemnation as taught by her pastor and church elders.

With this focus on redefining evangelicalism in mind, these women not only use the "I'm not *that* type of evangelical" narrative to carefully describe themselves but also use it to carefully define their congregations. Indeed, many women described their desire to join churches they saw as welcoming communities focused on social justice and equality, though not necessarily evangelical. Lynne chose to become a member of her church not because of its denomination but upon hearing one sermon in particular:

> A sermon that hit home recently [concerned scripture] where it talks about all creation is groaning for the Redemption. There is this perception that injustice should grind at us because this is the intention of that. This isn't how things should be. I'm like this is just awful and how could people possibly be living like this. So that's often a scripture that is powerful to me. I guess in general we should be for social justice.

When asked whether or not they would consider their congregations evangelical, the answers revealed another layer to their struggle with the term *evangelical*. For example, when asked whether her congregation is evangelical, Lynne continued:

> No, I wouldn't in terms of what I consider evangelical. I just think [of evangelical as] very radical. More like what I said about the signs and Bibles and damnation kind of thing. So I wouldn't consider [my church] evangelical but maybe in a different way.

In other interview, Anna suggests that her use of *evangelical* to describe her congregation is situation and person specific:

> Depends. Evangelicals have been using their energy to stand out against abortion and gay rights. Those are the two main issues. I think that they realize a shift in energy too. [I say] Let's work at least towards social change and social justice and so we can work together instead of butting heads....

When pressed, these women confirm that their congregations are evangelical by definition,[15] but are also very different from the "evangelical" presented in the media and used by outsiders. Many respondents suggested that current depictions of evangelicals in the media also led to their efforts to make a distinction between their own religious identities and their congregations. Many wished to distance themselves from criticisms launched against known evangelical congregations of which they were members, often using a derivative of the evangelical narrative—"people see my congregation as evangelical, but I'm not *that* type of evangelical."

The narrative "I'm evangelical but not *that* kind of evangelical" has two purposes. First, it represents both an attempt to reduce cognitive dissonance felt between the religious values these women have come to hold and their activist interests. Women are able to quickly and effectively handle negative comments from outsiders, especially those comments from what are considered biased media sources. Moreover, the use of this narrative opens up the conversation between disparate parties, allowing these young women to inform others about evangelicalism. Second, the narrative reduces the tension felt between generations of evangelical women activists. Since these women are often thrust into leadership roles in their services projects, community service, and/or NGO work, defining themselves as new evangelicals allows them to bridge the gap between themselves and their elders. These young women are honoring their elders but just not in the same ways as previous generations. For them, the evolution of evangelicalism in these new activist ways is not wrong, just different than the experiences of their elders.

Coming of Age: The Past Meets the Future

Today's young evangelical women must grapple with locating themselves within the institution of American evangelicalism, as well as the stress of separating themselves from some of the traditions of their elders. Looking back at some formidable American evangelical women activists and their work, we find that the tensions experienced today by younger generations are not new. Starting as early as the 1960s, several key events created conflict within the nascent Christian Right, including disagreements over America's role in the Vietnam War, increased concerns over racial desegregation stemming from the civil rights movement and the ERA, and the rise of second-wave feminism.[16]

Activist groups like Concerned Women for America (CWA), formed in 1979, led the way in tackling many issues raised by second-wave feminists. Looking back, Janice Crouse, a senior fellow at CWA's Beverly LaHaye Institute, reflects on Betty Friedan and second-wave feminism:

> By devaluing home and hearth, far too many women have found their window for opportunity for marriage and family closed.... By eschewing marriage, single mothers have ended up both rocking the baby and paying the rent. The children of single mothers are paying an even higher price—one third of U.S children are born out of wedlock, the majority of whom will grow up in poverty and at-risk in every outcome category.... Certainly, women want the freedom to be all that they can

be and they want to be treated with dignity and respect—but most aren't willing for their ambition to harm their relationships or damage their children.[17]

To fully understand the impact these issues had on female evangelical identity, there are two main ideas that must be addressed from these comments. First, one notes the focus on the protection of children. Crouse's rhetoric suggests the role of woman as mother involves the protection of children against poverty and other risk categories. This argument presented the opportunity for diverse generations of women to come together with a common set of goals— raising and protecting the family and children - while carving out their place in a sea of much larger social change.[18] Second, one notes the affirmation of the mother role, the idea that there is freedom in the role of mother and wife. For these women, known as traditionalist evangelicals, a woman's freedom is achieved through her role of mother and wife.[19] Yet many evangelical women found themselves questioning the notion of "a woman's submission." These women, known as evangelical feminists,[20] argued that both men and women are to be mutually submissive in the home. Both husbands and wives are called to be submissive to Jesus Christ and submissive to each other—forming a triangle of submission with Jesus at the top.[21]

Today, most evangelical millennial women may be too young to grasp the impact these activists had on American evangelicalism and the country as a whole, but the church can provide the context to bridge the old and the new. Within many evangelical communities, a woman's identity is positively affirmed if she is an "ideal Christian woman" (a woman who wholeheartedly embraces her role as mother and wife) who strives to maintain the time-honored biblical traditions of womanhood. It is critical to remember what these young women are learning in church in order to draw connections to their current activism and activist identities.

Young evangelical women are socialized into these roles from an early age and continue to learn their roles well into adulthood before even considering themselves as activists. In New York City, women's groups often meet once a week at churches across the city and watch educational videos on dating, marriage, and emotionally healthy relationships with men. For example, one New York City women's group in particular spent a number of months working through the series *Love and Respect* led by Emerson Eggerichs. Each week, women learned how to best speak to, listen to, and motivate their husbands, even though many in the group were single. Watching Eggerichs's DVD, they learned how they should act as Christian women, the Christian roles they should seek in their relationships with men, and how good Christian women and men should relate to each other in healthy Christian marriages. The discussions and subsequent workshops usually corresponded to some sort of social norm, as in how to fight fair, for example, and in this case, the arguments were made by a religious authority figure using a Christian lens to understand the issue. From this series, the young women could be seen internalizing these values while working through how to determine their own identity based on these images of the ideal Christian woman. Through the use of powerful rhetoric and heavenly authority, a woman can empower herself through her role as wife, mother, and helper as her destiny and God-given identity.[22] Below the surface, a woman rationalizes her identity within this ideal Christian image and makes great efforts to mold her own identity to fit this ideal. These negotiations are not without conflict, as many women struggled with Eggerich's argument that, in a relationship, women respond best to love while men respond best to respect.

For the most part, women accept these gender roles for a number of reasons, including, according to Gallagher, "individual embeddedness in conservative local religious subcultures, belief in a husband's [or male authority figure's] headship and authority, affiliation with religious subcultures and communities that help to locate the sources that create, reinforce and sustain more negative views towards feminism."[23] The integrative process represents a gendered identity formation that is also evident in the study of women's submission and lived religion. For example, McGuire argues that "because modern religion often involves groups of people committing to developing 'new selves,'"[24] men and women are actively "living" their spirituality through the expressly submissive position of women and men's institutionally defined role as the authority in the household. Speaking of women's submission, Victoria summed up the reason why she accepted the submission argument among young women perfectly when she said: "It's a pick your battle situation. I know there is a history of [power] being abused and lots of dissension over that topic." In the following comments, two women elaborate on their interpretations of submission from Ephesians 5:21–32. Quinn and Victoria, respectively, explain:

It's almost like there [are] two [opinions]...not that it's split down the middle...half of the women in the group are very much like..."Yeah, submission. I don't have a problem with that. The word is totally fine for me across all areas and across marriage, across my job." And then the other half, they can't even look at the word. They just freak out. And they're like, "No, sorry. The connotations of the word *submit* is just not...." It's like...I mean not like pro-feminism, but it just feels like back in the old days....I would say I'm somewhere in the middle....In my opinion, I think I'm going to be the healthy view of what it means to submit and what it also means to be your own person.

I think I'm fine with it, and the sad thing is it doesn't matter if I'm fine with it or not, if God wants it a certain way then He knows best, interactions are intended to be how we've been designed to interact [sic]. Anyway, if all parties are doing what God has described, I can see how that works out well. It's just we've been given different roles; everyone's intended to be treating one another, fully in love and fully with respect.

Note the expressions of profound honesty and how they work through the cognitive dissonance in order to incorporate these values into their lives. These two comments emphasize a reality whereby many evangelical women find themselves trying to live according to a set of religious values that they know are often misinterpreted by outsiders. So young women reaffirm these gender roles through an interactive process whereby their actions and words are interpreted positively through an evangelical lens. Perhaps more important, they change the very institution of evangelical activism with shifts in rhetoric and action—for their views on a woman's place in society are imperative to how they see their own activism.

Servant-Activist Identities: Political Activism versus Service

For the past few years, media accounts have suggested that support from young evangelicals (typically ages eighteen to twenty-nine) for Christian Right groups and the Republican Party is slipping.[25] In a report from the Pew Forum on Religion and Public Life, John P. Avlon finds that the percentage of young white evangelicals age eighteen to twenty-nine identifying as Republican dropped from 55 percent to 40 percent between 2005 and 2007.[26] Similarly, 33 percent of evangelicals in Missouri and Tennessee and 43 percent in Ohio voted Democratic in the 2008 primaries. Avlon summarizes where many young evangelicals now find themselves politically: "It's not a re-alignment as much as a *dealignment*—two-thirds of those ex-Republicans now describe themselves as Independent."[27] Dan Cox further clarifies these data by arguing that although there is a transition, these young adults are not necessarily less conservative; in fact, they remain more conservative on such issues as the war in Iraq, abortion, and capital punishment.[28]

What these data don't express is that many of these young evangelicals are not only leaving the Republican Party but also disengaging from politics in general. Although immersed in a unique geographical area, young evangelical women in New York City exemplify this political *dis*engagement. They have cast aside many evangelical political causes and created new avenues of activism grounded in service and their local communities—avenues that are totally disengaged from politics and political issues. The gradual emergence of a *new* young evangelical activist identity can be seen in the general shift away from political activism and issues toward a servant-activist identity focused on solving social injustices.

These shifts away from political activism are due to a number of important factors. First, young evangelicals are wary of past forms of activism—namely, the outspoken evangelical activists who pervaded the political scene with fear and hate mongering, Today's young female believers attempt to create a space within American evangelicalism focused on activism through service rather than carve out a space within the activist platforms of older generations. In his work on emergent Christians, Tony Jones clarifies this position:

> Emergent [youth] have grown up in the dire shadow of the Moral Majority and the Christian Coalition, who too closely allied with the Republicans in the 1980s and 1990s. From the emergent perspective, this partnership was a match made in hell, a marriage in which one partner [Republican Party] inevitably corrupt[ed] the other [Christian Right]....Thus many emergents have expressed to me great hesitation about building momentum of leftward or progressive groups. Their fear is that these groups will make the same mistakes that their conservative brethren did 30 years ago—lose their independence by aligning with a political party. [29]

Many young evangelical women share the views of these emergents, namely, a weariness of political associations. Thus, in defining who they are, these women must decide what they consider to be righteous types of activism (volunteering, philanthropy versus lobbying, and so on) and which social ills should be corrected. The formation of a new evangelical activist identity outside the political sphere is inevitably affected by the hesitations Jones mentions and any attempts to distinguish between insiders versus outsiders and youth versus elders.

Second, throughout the 1980s and 1990s, evangelicals were too often associated with political activism. As well, although some young evangelicals may have grown up during the height of Christian Right activism, many were too young at the time so are somewhat disengaged from this history. Now we find that these assumed associations might have had a detrimental effect on current recruitment to political activist causes,[30] although perhaps not to the religious movement.[31] Young evangelical women struggle to work through a current reality in which the individual evangelical identities they've come to accept potentially conflict with what many would describe as leftist concerns, including social welfare, poverty, and social class disparities. One young woman summed up the sentiments felt by her cohort: "Pat Robertson? Jerry Falwell? Beverly LaHaye? I've never heard of those guys." Indeed, these women have little connection to political institutions and to the political activism of the past. In fact, many don't follow politics unless it is discussed by Jon Stewart or Stephen Colbert. Importantly, while these women are somewhat disconnected from politics, they are by no means more liberal in terms of social values.

The servant-activist identity narrative highlights one way in which women reconcile traditional gender roles with the desire to address new social injustices outside political activism. The call to activism is described as a call to *service*. For instance, one young woman described her activism as grounded in "service" and "community" rather than "lobbying, rallies and politics." Pinky's and Nina's views on their own activism clarify the servant-activist identity narrative and its connection to gender identity:

> I do think that women are more nurturing and more service oriented in a different way [than men]. I'm not saying that women are more service-oriented, but I think that women are, just naturally, more emotionally caring.
>
> I believe that it's our calling to serve others.... We're here to serve God and serving God is serving others. And that's, like, our calling in life and so that's why I do it. [I]f I didn't believe that then I probably would have a job that just made lots of money so that I could go have fun and go to cool places and do all these fun things. But I just can't do that because I don't think that's what we're called to do, you know, why we're actually here.

The servant-activist identity narrative reduces tension by borrowing from the learned gender role ideologies. It combines time-honored gender roles emphasized in church with a desire to increase community presence.

With an emphasis on women's ability to serve, console, and help through activism, women embrace their roles as activists within the boundaries of work defined as fulfilling for women. When asked what activism meant to her, Quinn said she was not an activist in the "traditional sense" because, in her mind, "activists were men." She continued by arguing that men were the more active sex and thus it was more acceptable for them to be activists. Her comments echo similar findings from Amy Blackstone, who studied women volunteering for the Susan G. Komen Foundation. Blackstone notes that these women are performing activism by definition but do not define themselves as activists—thus they are what she calls "border activists."[32] Indeed, the young evangelical women in this study performed a variety of different activists' tasks, including "common" government lobbying, raising money for local charities, helping homeless families find shelter, and traveling abroad to work with formerly trafficked women. Yet the majority of these women do not define themselves as activists. Similar to Blackstone's sample, these young evangelical women reject the activist identity label because of the masculine gendered meaning. At the same time, they find that their activism itself is also gendered, as it is labeled by outsiders not as "activism" but as "volunteering" or "community service." Many young evangelical women see their projects as fitting logically within a woman's duty to serve, help, and take care of others—whether they are defined as activism or service. The combined rejection of the activist identity and of others' gendered definition of their work often creates an unreceptive environment within which to pursue their work. To clarify, many of these women are project leaders but are not defined as such, or they find themselves having to negotiate their identities in several male-dominated activist fields. Along these lines, the use of the servant-activist identity is an effective (and strategic) way to pursue their interests while negotiating time-honored evangelical gender roles and male-dominated congregations.

The servant-activist identity narrative also creates an identity more acceptable to older generations. Many respondents spoke of tension with older members in both their current and childhood congregations—especially those elders who were politically active. This tension often stemmed from the fact that many young women were more concerned with being visible in and serving their communities than with arguing over politics and political issues. Young evangelical women are constructing a new set of experiences and identities that provide new ways of acting outside politics while acknowledging many traditions having to do with gender roles (and not political engagement) in order to maintain their ties and relationships in the congregations that remain at the center of their lives.

By using several narratives (including the "I'm not *that* type of evangelical" narrative mentioned previously), the servant-activist identity narrative allows these women to gain respect and be recognized for their nonpolitical activism, although intergenerational tensions do not totally disappear. Religious identity plays a large role in determining an individual's participation in activist groups, as we have historically seen in the evangelical contingent within the

Christian Right movement.[33] Young evangelical women are concerned with a number of issues, including poverty, the environment, women's health and safety, and homelessness. Based on these interests, parents and youth are divided, even though they have been socialized by their church into a set of similar religious values. Speaking about intergenerational tensions, Anna and Elise argue:

> The two issues that I have a problem with [when talking with my parents] are their [views of] homosexuality and also...just the idea that they think it's Christ-like to give tax breaks to the rich. They can't explain it. I have said that so many times. At this point, you could say something completely logical and you could prove it...and they are still...older people stuck in their ways....They can't explain it.
>
> It's sad because we believe in the same God. It's just different versions of Scripture that I don't agree with. We're the same...but a completely different generation. [My uncle who is seventy] made a comment that we shouldn't go into other countries and help other countries. [He said] they need to fend for themselves. And here I am...someone [who sponsors] a child in Rwanda. And I send [money] and I do other things for other countries. [Helping] makes sense to me.

Many young evangelical women expressed similar feelings of frustration with their elders. Despite these often upsetting battles over issues of social justice and social class, these young women remain faithful to their church and to certain theological teachings about gender—even staying within church networks when they move to new neighborhoods, boroughs, or cities. For example, many women used networks like Acts 29 to locate a congregation when they moved to New York. What we find is that in order to reduce these intergenerational tensions, young evangelical women have begun replacing older ideologies with new narratives that allow them to reinterpret evangelicalism as a nondiscriminatory faith, fulfilling their desire to serve without having to leave their faith.

Servant-Activism in the Church: Plugging in and Helping Out in New York City

Young evangelical women attend their churches to socialize, learn, and make important connections. Through conversation and connection, these young women work to minimize potential tensions that exist between their evangelical upbringings and their current interests in activism. In the city, these women find themselves bombarded by the demands of jobs, friends, and special interest groups, both secular and religious, and have reinterpreted their faith to make these negotiations easier. Churches that are able to reduce these multilayered tensions by combining messages and practices are thriving.

For young women who spend what little free time they have attempting to feel plugged in, the church successfully provides instant connections, premade social groups, and, most important, serving opportunities. Vicky offered the following:

> I feel like, as we get more and more people, there's still that push and we actually [have] been holding servant-leader meetings which are all the servant-leaders and anybody else is also invited in our congregation but it's mainly the people who are leaders in the church who've been talking a lot about how can we get more welcoming [sic], how can we encourage members and other participants in our congregation to be more involved not only in church but also outside of church and getting people plugged in.

Many of these young women have become critical of their childhood congregations and look to find congregations in New York City that might match their new activist interests. In Kacy's opinion:

> Social awareness should be on every Christian's mind and where I came from in the South it wasn't. You go to church every Sunday [and] you are good for the next week. So go, commit all the sins and come back and you will be washed clean. What I feel now is that Christianity is not self-serving. All I want to do is be out there with the people and help with problems.

Although many women begin with churches within the same denominational families, they search out churches embodying specific values toward helping those in need and what many call "authenticity." When looking, many women spoke of authenticity as not "pretending to be perfect," without judgment of anyone's faults (especially those in need), and being in a community that didn't shy away from imperfection. In sum, Wuthnow calls this process a "new spirituality of seeking,"[34] though many young women described this process as "church shopping." Individuals seek new forms of religious practices that enable them to construct activist identities (communities that emphasize care and compassion for others) that fit their personal needs (being at peace with imperfection and individual weakness).

Several evangelical pastors have made great attempts to revamp their worship practices and emphasize social justice. Many pastors strive to follow a more current philosophy, arguing that "Christianity must be about serving the world, easing suffering, and making the world a better place for everyone...and if it means adopting a liberal stance (including pro-environment, pro universal health care) 'so be it.'"[35] In my sample, a third of the women in the sample moved to New York City from the South, mostly for work or graduate school. Many of these young women came from Baptist traditions and congregations that emphasized evangelism over social justice—enhancing the tensions between generations. Elisha finds similar evidence in his study of Southern white evangelicals: "Many conservative evangelicals, especially white Southerners, remain fixated on the potential difficulties and drawbacks associated with charitable social outreach."[36] In New York City, pastors must tread lightly if they are to keep older members in their pews. Tanya agrees:

> [My church] actually, I think is really careful about their word choices
> because, they're very aware, especially in New York City, just, it's smart
> to be aware, otherwise you really close the door.

To help ease congregational tensions, sustained efforts are made to create or renew existing relationships with local charities, businesses, and community services while assuring fellow community members that they are not there to "just pass out Bibles and leave," as one young woman argued. Young evangelical women show an intense desire to increase their congregation's presence in the surrounding community, which is often highly racially and economically diverse. These women are very concerned about poverty and homelessness in their own communities. Olivia argued: "I think people get caught up in the glamour of working internationally and I get that and I know that mission trips can turn into tourism." Tanya echoes Olivia's sentiments: "The thing about the environmental movement is that it's not about, like, going to Africa and doing this huge mission trip, it's about little habits that we all have to change." Many young evangelical women support projects that focus on building community relations locally rather than supporting more traditional mission trips, which people sometimes criticize for helping and leaving without providing sustainable assistance to those in need. When asked to describe her take on her church's relationship with the New York community, Mary stated:

> New York City culture feeds into that [idea of self-centeredness]. We
> are aware so much is going on. People think it's normal to work that
> much and be busy. So the craziness of life has to do with the culture

of New York. That's something I want us to overcome; you don't have
to adapt to the frantic way of living. [I wonder] what's it like to live in
a slower way of life even within the crazy city? You don't have to be so
busy and give and serve more...but it takes time to adjust to the city.

Indeed, it was these themes of compassion through community presence and
a keen awareness of social inequalities that rang true to these women. For these
women, evangelical identity construction represents a blend of old and new
religious practices and a blurring of the boundaries between these practices.
In other words, the processes by which these young women learned about the
poor and needy from their elders evolve into something completely different
as they engage with their new communities in New York City. Similarly, with
the inclusion of a spiritual instruction that emphasizes self-fulfillment taught
by their pastors, the ways women define their own womanhood and engage
social problems are transformed. Coming to terms with individual weaknesses and the conceptual changes in woman's roles have resulted in a different view on poverty and need. These themes stood out as different from what
many women had heard in childhood churches and represented, to them, the
fulfillment of an authentic Christian womanhood.

   Still, some young women face resistance from elders when older generations resist helping those suffering, thereby exacerbating the generational
divide between evangelical activists. Pauline describes the tension between her
and her parents when they talk about her work with an anti-human-trafficking
NGO in New York City:

> [My mom] in particular, is in support of it. She was a little iffy on it for a
> while...My dad is a little more, I guess, not as much towards social jus-
> tice. He thinks that the church shouldn't be involved in that so much.
> He's a little more separatist if you will. [For him], the trouble is that
> we're doing all these good things but not saving anyone...[I]t becomes
> a problem for him and he sees social justice as doing all these things
> that don't have any eternal effects.

Interestingly, women who moved to New York City from the South had more
experience dealing with these tensions. In their experiences, fellow church
members often argued over whether it was more important to save an individual or to ease their suffering. In these conversations, these two actions were
almost always mutually exclusive. Younger members worried about their legitimacy as activists if they focused on conversion, while older members were
more concerned with salvation rather than solving earthly woes.

In *A New Kind of Christianity*, Brian McLaren, a spokesperson for the emerging church movement, argues that pastors have lost touch with their congregants—spending more time preaching to the choir and involving themselves in institutional maintenance rather than reaching out to the needy.[37] Critical of the neoconservative political ideology ("traditional family values") of Protestant leaders, McLaren calls for a renewed vision of a "post-liberal, post-conservative, post-sectarian, and post-modern" Christian faith.[38] Many young evangelicals are heralding McLaren's work as revolutionary and sparking a need for change and social renewal. For these individuals, McLaren proposes a reevaluation of the evangelical faith to address issues and ideals that have isolated evangelicals from the larger Christian faith. These issues include heteronormativity, a biblical literalism that delegitimizes non-Christian faiths, claims of an exclusionary access to the truth, and, most important, a challenge to older evangelicals to stop isolating themselves in their congregations and get out into their communities.[39] For evangelicals, McLaren's work demands a radical change of mind and practice. For young evangelical women in New York, McLaren's work does more than that because his work focuses their attention on the current struggles in evangelical congregations around the country—how to redefine the role of evangelicals outside church walls and promote a more inclusionary activist ethos.

Understanding identity within the context of activism is affected by many factors, including but not limited to gender, history, and life stages. To the detriment of future generations of evangelical activists, identity construction among older generations has resulted in an exaggerated set of stereotypes, thereby negatively influencing younger generations. Evangelicals, especially women, have been stereotyped by outsiders as "sexually uptight individuals who are suspicious of all forms of merrymaking...they walk as stiffly as people just released from a straightjacket."[40] The gender identity work managed by young evangelical women is meaningful to their subsequent engagement in social activism. That is, how they work to define what it means to be an evangelical and an evangelical woman has redefined how they seek to solve social injustices and identify those they wish to help.

Further work is needed to clarify the process whereby *women* create unique evangelical identities that better fit their current interests in addressing injustices while dealing with the potential tensions these identities create outside their religious communities. For example, how does participation in U.S. secular culture shape the types of causes young evangelical women choose to support and the roles they assume as Christian women activists? How do activists and their causes change as a result of activists' participation in secular institutions? And since gender and gender identity are still potential divisive factors in how evangelical women define themselves as activists, how do young evangelical women play out these tensions in their pursuit of social justice? These questions will draw much needed attention to how young new evangelical women create unique evangelical identities. Religious practice informs individual identity as much as individuals inform religious traditions through this identity work. Evangelical women recognize that their faith requires them to address injustices that threaten people's rights to freedom from such things as poverty, abuse, and domestic violence. Combined with an ever-changing public sphere, these realities transform the way young evangelicals define themselves while transforming their ties to institutional religions.

NOTES

1. Robert Wuthnow and John H. Evans, eds., *The Quiet Hand of God: Faith-Based Activism and the Public Role of Mainline Protestantism* (Berkeley: University of California Press, 2002).

2. John P. Avlon, "The Rise of the Evangelical Center," *Politico*, August 18, 2008, accessed November 7, 2008, www.politico.com/news/stories/0808/12569. html.

3. Laurie Goodstein, "Obama Made Gains among Younger Evangelical Voters, Data Show," *New York Times*, November 6, 2008, accessed November 7, 2008, www.nytimes.com/2008/11/07/us/politics/07religion.html.

4. Frances FitzGerald, "The New Evangelicals," *New Yorker*, June 30, 2008, accessed June 30, 2008, www.newyorker.com/reporting/2008/06/30/080630fa_fact_fitzgerald.

5. Judith Stacey and Susan Elizabeth Gerard, "We Are Not Doormats: The Influence of Feminism on Contemporary Evangelicals in the United States," 98–117, in *Uncertain Terms: Negotiating Gender in American Culture*, ed. Faye Ginsburg and Anna Lowenhaupt Tsing (Boston: Beacon Press, 1992).

6. Sally K. Gallagher, "Where Are the Antifeminist Evangelicals? Evangelical Identity, Subcultural Location, and Attitudes toward Feminism," *Gender and Society* 18 (2004): 451.

7. Robert D. Putnam, *American Grace: How Religion Divides and Unites Us* (New York: Simon & Schuster, 2010).

8. Christian Smith and Patricia Snell, *Souls in Transition: The Religious and Spiritual Lives of Emerging Adults* (New York: Oxford University Press, 2009).

9. Justin Farrell, "The Young and the Restless? The Liberalization of Young Evangelicals," *Journal for the Scientific Study of Religion* 50 (2010): 517–32.

10. Mary E. Bendyna et al., "Uneasy Alliance: Conservative Catholics and the Christian Right," *Sociology of Religion* 62 (2001): 51–64.

11. Robert Wuthnow, *After Heaven: Spirituality in America since the 1950s* (Berkeley: University of California Press, 1998), 189.

12. Wuthnow, *After Heaven*.

13. Mary E. Bendyna and Clyde Wilcox, "The Christian Right Old and New: A Comparison of the Moral Majority and the Christian Coalition," in *Sojourners in the Wilderness: The Christian Right in the Comparative Perspective,* ed. Corwin E. Smidt and James M. Penning (Lanham, MD: Rowman & Littlefield, 1997) 41–56.

14. Christian Smith and Melina Lundquist Denton, *Soul Searching: The Religious and Spiritual Lives of American Teenagers* (New York: Oxford University Press, 2009). See also: Christian Smith with Patricia Snell, *Souls in Transition: The Religious and Spiritual Lives of Emerging Adults* (New York: Oxford University Press, 2009); Robert D. Putnam and David E. Campbell, *American Grace: How Religion Divides and Unites Us* (New York: Simon and Schuster, 2012), Barbara Ehrenreich, *Bright-Sided: How the Relentless Promotion of Positive Thinking Has Undermined America* (New York: Metropolitan Books, 2009); Susan D. Moeller, *Compassion Fatigue: How the Media Sell Disease, Famine, War and Death* (New York: Routledge, 1999).

15. The term *evangelical* can also be defined in a number of ways, and, again, for my purposes, I use a common definition in which evangelicals are Protestants who share certain religious beliefs (such as the conviction that personal acceptance of Jesus Christ is the only way to salvation, the inspired Word of God), practices (such as an emphasis on bringing other people to the faith and being born again), and origins (by defining themselves against established religious institutions). In contrast, churches in the mainline Protestant tradition share other doctrines (a less exclusionary view of salvation), practices (a strong emphasis on moral reform stemming from an engagement in the culture war) and origins (adherence to and identification with long-established religious institutions). For more details, see Alison Pond et al., *Religion among the Millennials* (Washington, DC: Pew Forum on Religion and Public Life, 2010).

16. Wuthnow, *After Heaven.*

17. Quoted in R. Claire Snyder, "The Allure of Authoritarianism: Bush Administration Ideology and the Reconsolidation of Patriarchy,", in W Stands for Women: How the George W. Bush Presidency Shaped a New Politics of Gender, ed. Michaele L. Ferguson and Lori Jo Marso (Durham: Duke University Press, 2007), 19.

18. Sally K. Gallagher, *Evangelical Identity and Gendered Family Life* (New Brunswick, NJ: Rutgers University Press, 2003).

19. John P. Bartkowski and Jen'nan Ghazal Read, "Veiled Submission: Gender, Power, and Identity among Evangelical and Muslim Women in the United States," *Qualitative Sociology* 26 (2003): 71–92.

20. Letha Dawson Scanzoni and Nancy A. Hardesty, *All We're Meant to Be: Biblical Feminism for Today* (Grand Rapids, MI: Eerdmans, 1992).

21. Bartkowski and Read, "Veiled Submission."

22. R. Marie Griffith, *God's Daughters: Evangelical Women and the Power of Submission* (Berkeley: University of California Press, 2000).

23. Sally K. Gallagher, "Where Are the Antifeminist Evangelicals? Evangelical Identity, Subcultural Location, and Attitudes toward Feminism," *Gender and Society* 18 (2004): 451.

24. Meredith McGuire, *Lived Religion: Faith and Practice in Everyday Life* (New York: Oxford University Press, 2008), 173.

25. Fitzgerald, "The New Evangelicals."

26. Avlon, "The Rise of the Evangelical Center."

27. Avlon, "The Rise of the Evangelical Center."

28. Dan Cox, *Young White Evangelicals: Less Republican, Still Conservative* (Washington, DC: Pew Research Center on Religion and Public Life, 2007).

29. Tony Jones, *The New Christians: Dispatches from the Emergent Frontier* (San Francisco: Jossey-Bass, 2008).

30. Mark Sayers, *The Trouble with Paris: Following Jesus in a World of Plastic Promises* (Nashville, TN: Thomas Nelson, 2008).

31. Smith and Snell, *Souls in Transition.*

32. Amy Blackstone, "It's Just about Being Fair": Activism and the Politics of Volunteering in the Breast Cancer Movement," *Gender and Society* 18 (2004): 360.

33. Kenneth Wald, *Religion and Politics in the United States* (Lanham, MD: Rowman & Littlefield, 2004).

34. Wuthnow, *After Heaven*, 3.

35. Brian McCracken, *Hipster Christianity: When Church and Cool Collide* (Grand Rapids, MI: Baker Books, 2010), 158.

36. Omri Elisha, "Moral Ambitions of Grace: The Paradox of Compassion and Accountability in Evangelical Faith-Based Activism," *Cultural Anthropology* 23 (2008): 156.

37. Brian D. McLaren, *A New Kind of Christianity: Ten Questions That Are Changing the Faith* (San Francisco: Jossey-Bass, 2010), 4.

38. McLaren, *A New Kind of Christianity*, 11. See also Brian D. McLaren, *A New Kind of Christian: A Tale of Two Friends on a Spiritual Journey* (San Francisco: Jossey-Bass, 2001).

39. Nancy T. Ammerman and Carl S. Dudley, *Congregations in Transition* (San Francisco: Jossey Bass, 2002).

40. R. Laurence Moore, *Touchdown Jesus: The Making of Sacred and Secular in American History* (Louisville, KY: John Knox Press, 2003), 33.

6

New and Old Evangelical Public Engagement

A VIEW FROM THE POLLS

John C. Green

THE FIRST DECADE of the twenty-first century was a time of expanded public engagement among American evangelical Protestants. Most noticed was a new flowering of progressive activism by the new evangelicals on the environment, foreign policy, and social welfare.[1] At the same time, there was an upswing in conservative activism, continuing the efforts of the once new Christian Right on same-sex marriage and abortion.[2] These progressive and conservative activists often opposed each other, especially on issue priorities.[3] But they shared a commitment to faith-based politics and frustration with the two-party system. For many evangelical activists, bringing their faith to bear on public policy was often an agonizing experience, forcing them to choose between justice and virtue.

What about the views of the evangelical public? How much support was there for the issues associated with this new and old activism? How did these attitudes cluster together? And what were the religious, demographic, and political characteristics associated with these opinion clusters? The answers to these questions help reveal the depth and breadth of evangelical public engagement and, in turn, its potential impact on public policy.

This chapter addresses these questions with survey data between 1999 and 2012. It finds support for both the new and old issues and thus considerable attitudinal diversity in the evangelical public. In this regard, there are four distinctive clusters of opinion: an evangelical left, center, and right, plus populist evangelicals. The first three clusters reflect the broader polarization of American politics on the new and old issues. On the one hand, the evangelical left is consistently liberal, less traditionally religious, with mixed social status, and opposed to faith-based politics. And on the other hand, the evangelical right is consistently conservative, traditionally religious, with high social status, and also skeptical of faith-based politics. The center lies between these poles. The fourth cluster, the populist evangelicals, is the largest group and the most intriguing, simultaneously holding progressive views on the new issues and conservative views on the old issues. They are traditionally religious, with low social status, and are supportive of faith-based activism. Taken together, this evidence reveals a popular basis for expanded public engagement by evangelicals. This pattern is likely to allow evangelicals many avenues for influencing public policy, but it also forecasts continued agony in seeking an appropriate place in American public life.

Evangelicals and Movement Politics

Evangelical Protestants have been "seeking a place" in American public life for more than a century.[4] During this long search, they have employed three major strategies: movement politics, regularized politics, and political quiescence. The best known strategy is movement politics, seeking to mobilize like-minded coreligionists on behalf of major shifts in government policy. The imperatives of movement politics often clash with the compromises of regularized politics (working through the major political parties for incremental change in government policy) but also with slow pace of political quiescence (seeking to change societal values that underlie government policy).

The recent participation of the new evangelicals in progressive movements attracted considerable attention, but antecedents to this engagement extend back to the 1960s, if not before. Broadly stated, such movements have given priority to the biblical requirement for justice at home and abroad. This perspective was well summarized in the 2008 "Evangelical Manifesto,"[5] which highlighted the need for the federal government to protect the natural environment, foster peace among nations, and fight poverty.[6] In contrast, the participation of evangelicals in the Christian Right has become a staple of contemporary politics, dating back to the 1980s and before. Broadly stated, such movements have given priority to the biblical requirement for personal and social virtue. This perspective is well summarized by the 2012 "Manhattan Declaration,"[7] which highlighted the need for the federal government to protect unborn children, traditional marriage, and sexual morality.[8]

Because movement politics is fundamentally about mobilizing citizens to foster major shifts in government policy, the views of rank-and-file evangelicals on the new and old issues are important, both overall and among internal clusters of opinion. Here Maddox and Lilie[9] offer a useful heuristic for

	OLD ISSUES	
NEW ISSUES	*less government intervention*	*more government intervention*
more government intervention	"left"	"populist"
less government intervention	"center"	"right"

FIGURE 6.1 Evangelical Public: Clusters of New and Old Issues
Source: See text and notes for details.

identifying such relevant subgroups in the public at large. Based on government intervention on economic and cultural issues, this approach identifies four opinion clusters in the American public: "liberals" (intervention on the economic issues but less on cultural issues), "conservatives" (intervention on cultural issues but less on economic issues), "libertarians" (no intervention on either), and "populists" (intervention on both).

Figure 6.1 adapts this heuristic to the evangelical public, with the vertical dimension representing more or less government intervention on the new issues (environment, foreign policy, social welfare) and the horizontal dimension the same options on the old issues. In recognition of the ethos of evangelical Protestantism, which is both individualistic and moralistic, the subgroups are labeled "left" (more intervention on the new issues and less on the old issues), "right" (more intervention on the old issues and less on the new issues), and "center" (less intervention on both), and then a fourth category, "populist" (more intervention on both).

Of course, how well evangelical public opinion actually fits these categories is an empirical question, a matter to be addressed presently. But first it is worth reviewing the characteristics likely to be associated with the clusters—and thus the potential targets of movement politics—in terms of religiosity, demography, and politics.

Evangelicals active in progressive and conservative movements find religious warrants for government intervention on the new and old issues.[10] These arguments highlight the importance of traditional religiosity. For example, biblical teachings on stewardship, war, and benevolence may lead traditionally religious evangelicals to favor more government intervention on the environment, foreign policy, and social welfare. Likewise, biblical teachings on sexual behavior, gender roles, and family life may also lead traditionally religious evangelicals to favor more government intervention on abortion, same-sex marriage, and other aspects of morality. By this logic, less traditionally religious evangelicals would be less supportive of government intervention on *all* such issues.

Another possibility is that other aspects of religiosity provide warrants for government intervention on the new issues. For example, spiritual experiences or an accommodation of religion and society may lead evangelicals to support government intervention on the environment, foreign affairs, and social welfare, but not on sexual issues.[11] These alternatives may—or may not—represent departures from traditional religiosity.

The progressive focus on justice may appeal to evangelicals with low social status. But here there are at least two ways to think about this connection.[12] On materialist issues, the relative deprivation experienced by low-status evangelicals would generate support for government intervention on economic issues. So, for example, less affluent and less educated evangelicals would support expanded social welfare programs. Other measures of lower social status could show a similar pattern as well, with female, younger, nonwhite, urban, and Southern evangelicals backing such government intervention. Sexual morality and foreign policy can also be thought of as materialist issues, and here the experience of personal insecurity would lead low-status evangelicals to support more government intervention.[13] By this logic, high-status evangelicals should be less supportive of government intervention on all kinds of materialist issues.

However, on postmaterialist issues, the relative abundance experienced by high-status evangelicals may generate support for more government intervention to secure justice in areas other than the economy. So, for example, more affluent and better educated evangelicals would favor more environmental protection. Likewise, other measures of higher social status may show this pattern, with male, older, white, nonurban, and non-Southern evangelicals supporting this kind of government intervention. Sexual issues and foreign policies could also be seen as postmaterial, and here the personal security of high-status evangelicals would generate support for government intervention. In contrast, low-status evangelicals would be less supportive of intervention on all kinds of postmaterialist issues.

A key question for evangelical activism of all kinds is the efficacy of faith-based politics, a subject that has been hotly debated among evangelicals.[14] A related question is the level of attention to public affairs by the evangelical public. The expanded public engagement of the early twenty-first century suggests rank-and-file evangelicals are supportive of a positive role for religion in public life and attentive to public affairs. But there may be variations within the evangelical public, with some evangelicals more politically quiescent than others. A central goal of movement politics is to mobilize faith-based engagement in public affairs.

Of course, evangelical movement activists are part of the broader political environment, including the increased political polarization of recent decades.[15] Thus for political reasons alone, liberal and Democratic evangelicals may be more supportive of government intervention on the new issues and not the old ones, while conservative and Republican evangelicals may hold the opposite views. But here, too, there may be variation within the evangelical community, with some evangelicals less engaged in regularized politics than others. Movement politics can offer an alternative to regularized politics.

Assessing Evangelical Public Opinion

A good place to begin is with a general assessment of the attitudes of the evangelical public on the new and old issues, before turning to internal clusters of opinion. For these purposes, an invaluable study is the Religious Landscape Survey (RLS), conducted by the Pew Forum on Religion & Public Life in 2007. Although limited to a single year, it has the advantages of a large sample size (some 36,000 total cases and 9,600 evangelicals) and very detailed measures of religious affiliation, belief, and practice. These data allow for a more precise measure of the evangelical Protestant religious tradition, including nonwhites who belong to historically white evangelical denominations.[16] By this measure, the RLS finds that evangelicals made up 26.3 percent of the adult population in 2007. These data allow for extensive analysis of differences within the evangelical community.

To put these 2007 data in temporal context, other surveys are helpful, the especially those conducted by the Pew Research Center (PRC) between 1999 and 2011.[17] These studies have the advantage of asking the same issue questions as the RLS over time. But there are two downsides to these studies: not all the issue questions were asked in every survey, and they contain few religion measures. At best, the evangelical tradition can be identified as "white born-again Protestant/Christian," a less precise measure.[18]

The difficulties are remedied in part by the National Survey of Religion and Politics (NSRP), conducted at the University of Akron between 1992 and 2012. These surveys allow for the precise measure of the evangelical tradition found in the RLS and also asked a consistent set of issue questions over time—but the issue questions are not worded identically to RLS and PRC surveys. Using these three sources of survey data helps ameliorate the deficiencies of each.[19]

New Issues and the Evangelical Public

Table 6.1 reports evangelical public opinion on three new issues (environment, foreign policy, and government services) from the RLS in 2007.[20] The environment question asked respondents to choose between two statements, "*Stricter environmental regulations are worth the cost*" or "*Stricter environmental regulations cost too many jobs and hurt the economy.*" A majority of evangelicals chose the first statement (54.5 percent) over the second (35.4 percent). Thus there was almost a twenty-percentage-point advantage for government intervention to protect the environment. However, evangelicals were slightly less favorable toward environmental regulation than the public at large (54.5 percent versus 60.7 percent).

This particular question is a broad measure of support for environmental protection that references the cost of regulation. But evidence on topics as diverse as climate change and energy development reveals similar support among evangelicals (but also at a level below the public at large).[21] As shown in figure 6.2, opinion on this environment question was stable between 2000

Table 6.1 New Issues: Evangelical Public, 2007

	All Evangelicals	Entire Public
Environmental Regulation		
Stricter environmental regulations are worth the cost	54.5%	60.7%
Stricter environmental regulations cost too many jobs and hurt the economy	35.4%	30.4%
No opinion	10.1%	8.9%
Total	100.0%	100.0%
Ensuring Peace		
Good diplomacy is the best way to ensure peace	45.7%	58.7%
The best way to ensure peace is through military strength	38.1%	27.9%
No opinion	16.2%	13.4%
Total	100.0%	100.0%
Size of Government		
A bigger government providing more services	41.0%	46.3%
A smaller government providing fewer services	48.3%	42.7%
No opinion	10.7%	11.0%
Total	100.0%	100.0%

Source: Religious Landscape Survey, 2007.

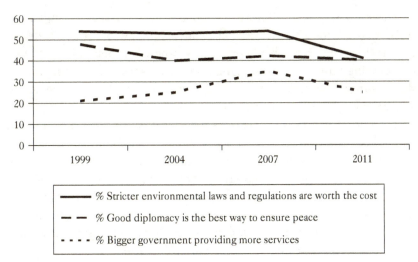

FIGURE 6.2 Evangelicals and New Issues, 1999–2011
Source: See text and notes for details.

and 2007, with a majority of the evangelical public taking the proenvironmental position. But by 2012, the proenvironmental position declined sharply to just two-fifths. This decline may reflect the effects of the 2008 recession.[22]

The long-term stability of these proenvironmental attitudes may seem counterintuitive, given the well-publicized discussion of the issue among progressive evangelical activists. However, it is important not to confuse the salience of an issue among evangelical activists with evangelical public opinion. After all, one goal of such activism is to mobilize evangelicals with proenvironmental views to political action. In this regard, progressive activists, such as the Evangelical Environmental Network, faced strong competition from conservative opponents, such as the Cornwall Alliance, on how best to protect the environment.[23] If nothing else, these patterns reveal more attitudinal diversity in the evangelical public than commonly assumed.

The second new issue in Table 6.1 concerns foreign policy. Respondents were asked to choose between "*Good diplomacy is the best way to ensure peace*" or "*The best way to ensure peace is through military strength.*" A plurality of evangelicals chose the first statement (45.7 percent) over the second (38.1 percent). Thus there was a modest seven-percentage-point advantage among evangelicals for a particular kind of government intervention—diplomatic rather than military action abroad. But evangelicals were markedly less supportive of the diplomatic approach than the public as a whole (45.7 percent versus 58.7 percent).

This question is a good measure of cooperative internationalism,[24] a perspective consistent with the focus of many progressive activists. This viewpoint is closely linked to other foreign policy issues, from opposition to torture to protecting human rights to fighting the AIDS epidemic.[25] As figure 6.2 shows, support for diplomacy declined from 2000 to 2011, with the largest drop coming after the 9/11 terrorist attacks in 2001.[26]

The third new issue in Table 6.1 is the size of government. Respondents were asked if they preferred "*A bigger government providing more services*" or "*A smaller government providing fewer services.*" About two-fifths of the evangelical public chose the larger government option (41.0 percent), while almost a majority chose the smaller government option (48.3 percent). Thus, there was a seven-percentage-point disadvantage in support for more government services. Evangelicals were also less supportive of more government services than the general public (41.0 percent versus 46.3 percent).

The size of government is related to progressive activism as it pertains to helping the disadvantaged. Here, too, there is evidence of the similar pattern on related issues. For example, in the RLS data, a majority of evangelicals favored increased efforts by the federal government to "help needy Americans" (56.9 percent), but still less than the public as a whole (61.8 percent). The pattern of evangelical opinion on these two questions suggests a desire to help the needy but also skepticism about government efforts for this purpose.[27] As figure 6.2 shows, support for more government services increased among evangelicals between 2000 and 2007, but then declined sharply by 2011.[28] This change may also reflect the effects of the 2008 recession.

Old Issues and the Evangelical Public

Table 6.2 turns to three old issues (abortion, homosexuality, and government involvement with morality) also drawn from the RLS in 2007.[29] On abortion, respondents were asked a four-part question on the legality of abortion. One-third of evangelicals said that abortion should be legal in "all or most cases" (33.1 percent) and three-fifths that abortion should be illegal in "most or all cases" (61.1 percent). Thus, there was a twenty-eight percentage-point advantage in favor of government intervention to restrict abortion. Here evangelicals differ sharply from the public at large, where a majority holds pro-choice views (33.1 percent versus 51.8 percent). It is worth noting, however, that only about one-sixth of evangelicals believed that abortion should be illegal in "all cases" (15.8 percent). So here, too, there is more diversity of opinion among evangelicals than often supposed.

Table 6.2 Old Issues: Evangelical Public, 2007

	All Evangelicals	Entire Public
Views on Abortion		
Abortion legal in all or most cases	33.1%	51.2%
Abortion illegal in most or all cases	61.1%	42.4%
No opinion	5.8%	6.4%
Total	100.0%	100.0%
Views on Homosexuality		
Homosexuality is a way of life that should be accepted by society	26.4%	50.0%
Homosexuality is a way of life that should be discouraged by society	64.2%	39.5%
No opinion	9.4%	10.5%
Total	100.0%	100.0%
View on Morality		
I worry the government is getting too involved in the issue of morality	41.1%	51.7%
The government should do more to protect morality in society	49.7%	39.8%
No opinion	9.2%	8.5%
Total	100.0%	100.0%

Source: Religious Landscape Survey, 2007.

As shown in figure 6.3, the proportion of evangelicals with prochoice views declined between 2000 and 2007, but then increased modestly in 2011.[30] Much of the recent abortion policy debate has been about modest restrictions on the availability of abortion, such as banning late-term abortions, parental notification, and mandatory waiting periods. Evangelicals tend to support these kinds of restrictions.[31]

The second old issue in table 6.2 is views of homosexuality. Respondents were asked to choose between "*Homosexuality is a way of life that should be accepted by society*" or "*Homosexuality is a way of life that should be discouraged by society.*" Nearly two-thirds of evangelicals favored discouraging homosexuality (64.2 percent) and about one-quarter favored accepting homosexuality (26.4 percent). Thus opposition to homosexuality had a nearly forty-percentage-point advantage over acceptance. Evangelicals differ from the

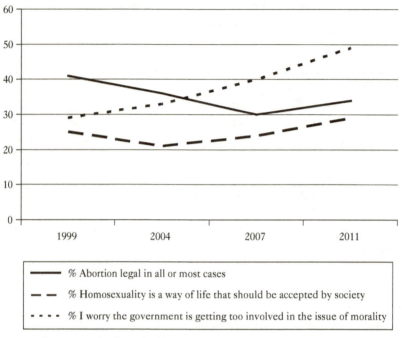

FIGURE **6.3** Evangelicals and Old Issues
Source: See text and notes for details.

public at large on this question, with half of the public agreeing that homo-sexuality should be accepted (26.4 percent versus 50.0 percent).

This particular question differs from the other items in table 6.2 because it does not directly reference government policy. However, one reason for pro-tecting the rights of gays and lesbians is to limit the kind and level of soci-etal "discouragement" of homosexuality. A key focus of this debate has been the issue of same-sex marriage, on which evangelicals have been strongly opposed.[32] As figure 6.3 reveals, acceptance of homosexuality declined among evangelicals between 2000 and 2004—right as same-sex marriage came on the political agenda. But since 2004, acceptance of homosexuality increased.[33]

The third old issue in table 6.2 is government involvement with moral-ity. Respondents were asked to choose between "*I worry the government is getting too involved in the issue of morality*" or "*The government should do more to protect morality in society.*" About half of evangelicals favored greater gov-ernment protection of morality (49.7 percent) and two-fifths expressed con-cern about government involved in morality (41.1 percent). Thus there was an eight-percentage-point advantage for government involvement in moral-ity over concern with too much involvement. Evangelicals were also more supportive of such involvement than the public at large, with about half of the public expressing concern about too much government involvement with morality (41.1 percent versus 51.7 percent).

Thus a generalized protection of morality is less popular among evangelicals than opposition to abortion or homosexuality. As figure 6.3 shows, concern about government involvement in morality has risen steadily among evangelicals since 2004.[34] Of course, the term *morality* can mean more than traditional sexual behavior, and some evangelicals may be concerned about the enforcement of other kinds of moral standards. For instance, arguments for marriage equality or the possible recognition of Sharia law by American courts may reflect such concerns. When added to views on the size of government, these data suggest skepticism toward government that may reflect the individualism of the evangelical tradition.

Issue Clusters in the Evangelical Public

How do views on the new and old issues cluster together in the evangelical public? Table 6.3 presents four combinations of these issue positions—an evangelical left, center, populist, and right. The table lists the relative size of each group as a percentage of the evangelical public in 2007 and then describes net opinion on each of the six issues. (A positive number indicates that the group has on balance progressive opinion on the issue and a negative number indicates that the group has on balance conservative opinion.)[35] These clusters fit fairly well—but not perfectly—with the categories identified in table 6.1.

In 2007, the evangelical left accounted for about one-fifth of evangelical public (21.7 percent) and had progressive views on all six issues. On balance, this cluster strongly favored environmental regulation (63 percent) and a cooperative foreign policy (72 percent), and it favored more government services but by a much smaller margin (16 percent, although a majority also believed that the federal government should do more to help the needy). The left also held progressive positions on the old issues, including prochoice on abortion (58 percent; a plurality backed legal abortion in most but not in all cases), acceptance of homosexuality (65 percent), and concern with government involvement on morality (58 percent).

The evangelical center made up a little less than one-fifth of the evangelical public in 2007 (18.3 percent). This cluster fits the table 6.1 heuristic least well. It was evenly divided on the new issues of environmental regulation and size of government (with a net score of 0 in each case, although a majority also says that the federal government should do more to help the needy). On balance, the

Table 6.3 Evangelical Issue Clusters, 2007

Net Opinion: + progressive; –conservative	Left	Center	Populists	Right
All Evangelicals (=100%)	21.7	18.3	35.6	24.4
NEW ISSUES (net opinion)				
More environmental regulation	63	0	56	–59
Good diplomacy for peace	72	–24	21	–45
More government services	16	0	27	–83
OLD ISSUES (net opinion)				
Prochoice abortion	58	93	–96	–95
Accept homosexuality	65	–52	–69	–73
Concerned about government and morality	58	–20	–60	15

Source: Religious Landscape Survey, 2007.

evangelical center held conservative views on the issue of diplomacy (–24 percent), and the old issues of government protection of morality (–20 percent) and discouragement of homosexuality (–52 percent). But a defining feature of this group is its strong progressive position on abortion (93 percent; although a majority said abortion should be legal in most but not all cases). So there is something of a libertarian cast to these centrists on abortion.

In 2007, the populist evangelicals were the largest of the groups, with more than one-third of the evangelical public (35.6 percent). This group was on balance progressive on the new issues, including environmental regulation (56 percent), where it nearly matches the left, but also on foreign policy (21 percent) and size of government (27 percent; a majority believes that the federal government should do more to help the needy). It is worth noting that the populists are on balance more progressive on government services but are far less progressive on diplomacy. The populists are conservative on all the old issues, such as abortion (–96 percent; more than half of the populists say abortion should be illegal in most but not all cases), homosexuality (–69 percent), and government protecting morality (–60 percent). On this last issue, this group is the most conservative.

The evangelical right made up about one-quarter of the evangelical public (24.5 percent) in 2007. This group held conservative views on all the new issues, including environmental regulation (–59 percent), foreign policy

(–45 percent), and especially the size of government (–82 percent; a majority opposed the federal government doing more to help the needy). The evangelical right also had strongly conservative views on two of the old issues, abortion (–95 percent, although a majority said that abortion should be illegal in most but not all cases), and homosexuality (–73 percent). But this group on balance held a progressive position on government protection of morality (15 percent). So there is also something of a libertarian cast to these conservatives on government services and involvement with morality.

If nothing else, the four clusters reveal the diversity of the evangelical public on the new and old issues. On the one hand, 57 percent of evangelicals belong to clusters characterized by progressive views on the new issues (the left and populists). But on the other hand, 59 percent belong to clusters characterized by traditional views on the old issues (the right and populists). It is worth noting that the evangelical left and right are both skeptical about government involvement with morality.

Figure 6.4 offers an estimate of the size of these clusters between 2000 and 2012 using the NSRP.[36] In 2000, the evangelical right was the largest of the clusters (about one-third of the evangelical public), but by 2012 this group had fallen to second place (at about one-quarter of the total). The largest decline occurred after 2008. Over this period, the evangelical populists had the reverse pattern, so that in 2012 they were the largest group (at about 35 percent). The evangelical left also grew by 2012 (making up almost one-quarter of the evangelical public). Although the evangelical center showed more variation

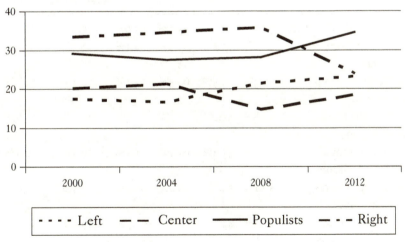

FIGURE 6.4 Evangelical Cluster Size, 2000–2012
Source: National Surveys of Religion and Politics, 2000–2012.

over the period, it remained at about one-fifth of all evangelicals. These data suggest that the evangelical left and right had roughly equal numbers by the end of the period under review.

Profiling the Issue Clusters

Tables 6.4, 6.5, and 6.6 profile the religiosity, demography, and politics of the four issues clusters in 2007. In each case, the far right-hand columns provide comparable figures for the entire evangelical public and the American public as a whole, respectively. Then table 6.7 offers a summary of the independent impact of all these variables on cluster membership. In these regards, each of the clusters had a distinctive profile.

Table 6.4 reports the religiosity of the four clusters. On all these measures, the entire evangelical public is more traditionally religious than the public as a whole and usually by large margins. On most of these measures, the evangelical right and populists are more traditionally religious than the evangelical public as a whole.

The typical pattern is for the evangelical left to score lowest and the evangelical right to score highest on these religion measures. A good example is respondents' report of being a "born-again Christian," a distinctive feature of

Table 6.4 Evangelical Issue Clusters and Religiosity, 2007

	Left	Center	Populists	Right	All Evangelicals	Entire Public
% Born-again Christian	65.0%	72.2%	85.6%	87.6%	79.2%	34.4%
% Religion "very important"	61.2%	70.8%	87.2%	87.1%	78.5%	56.5%
% Weekly worship attendance	36.4%	45.5%	69.4%	71.1%	58.3%	39.5%
% Bible the literal word of God	37.8%	54.0%	70.8%	71.4%	60.8%	34.7%
% Church should preserve traditions	38.3%	55.3%	65.7%	71.5%	59.3%	36.7%
% Monthly feel deep sense of wonder	58.1%	53.8%	56.0%	61.9%	57.5%	52.6%
% Inherent conflict religion and society	40.2%	44.7%	54.2%	52.7%	49.1%	39.5%

Source: Religious Landscape Survey, 2007.

evangelicalism: 65.0 percent for the evangelical left chose this identity compared to 87.6 percent of the evangelical right—more than a twenty-percentage-point difference. Even sharper differences occur on the importance of religion to the respondent, biblical literalism, preservation of tradition, and weekly worship attendance. Two additional patterns are worth noting in this table. First, the evangelical left often resembles the public as a whole in religious terms, suggesting that progressive views on some issues may be linked to the absence of traditional religiosity. But second, there is a strong link between traditional religiosity and new issue progressivism among the populists.

The final two religious measures in table 6.4 may reflect other forms of religiosity. One such measure was reported spiritual experiences: respondents were asked how often they feel a "deep sense of wonder about the universe." Almost three-fifths of the evangelical left said they had such an experience once a month or more often (58.1 percent), about the same proportion as the right (61.9 percent), with the center and populists scoring modestly lower. The other measure was the accommodation of religion and society: respondents were asked if there was "a natural conflict between a devout religious person and modern society." Only about two-fifths of the evangelical left (40.2 percent) and center (44.7 percent) agreed with this statement, compared to a small majority of the evangelical right (52.7 percent) and populists (54.2 percent).

Table 6.5 describes the demography of the four clusters. On many measures, evangelicals closely resembled the broader public, but exceptions include the facts that evangelicals are less affluent and have fewer nonwhites and non-Southern and urban residents than the public as a whole. The evangelical left and center had a mix of high- and low-status members. In contrast, the evangelical right is of uniformly high status, and the populists are of uniformly low status.

The clusters show important differences on income and education. The evangelical left and right were both more affluent (with, respectively, 47.3 percent and 43.0 percent with annual incomes below $50,000) and better educated (52.1 percent and 49.9 percent with less than a college degree) than the center and populists (with 51.4 percent and 52.1 percent below $50,000 a year and 62.2 percent and 59.3 percent without a college degree).

But the other measures of low social status show a different pattern. Both the evangelical left (58.1 percent) and populists (59.4 percent) had a majority of women, the most members under thirty years of age (19.3 and 21.2 percent), and the most nonwhites (23.3 percent and 22.7 percent). And the evangelical center and right had fewer women (48.5 percent and 42.2 percent), fewer members under thirty (12.6 percent and 9.5 percent), and fewer nonwhites (19.4 and 9.2 percent). The figures for younger evangelicals show diversity among the

Table 6.5 Evangelical Issue Clusters and Demography, 2007

	Left	Center	Populists	Right	All Evangelicals	Entire Public
% Annual Income under $50,000	47.3%	51.4%	52.1%	42.0%	48.4%	57.5%
% Less than college degree	52.1%	62.2%	59.3%	49.9%	56.0%	53.8%
% Female	58.1%	48.5%	59.4%	42.2%	52.9%	51.8%
% Under 30 years	19.3%	12.6%	21.2%	9.5%	16.4%	16.5%
% Nonwhite	23.3%	19.4%	22.7%	9.2%	18.9%	28.3%
% Urban residence	29.8%	25.5%	24.3%	20.3%	24.7%	32.2%
% Southern residence	45.0%	53.0%	53.7%	48.0%	50.4%	36.1%

Source: Religious Landscape Survey, 2007.

coming generation on most issues, with environmental protection being the strongest point of generational commonality, as found by Smith and Johnson.[37]

There were also important differences by geography. The evangelical left was the most urban (29.8 percent), a figure that declines across the clusters so that the evangelical right was the least so (20.3 percent). Meanwhile, a majority of the evangelical center and populists lived in the South compared to slightly less than a majority of the evangelical left and right.

Table 6.6 describes basic political attitudes of the issue clusters. On all these measures, the entire evangelical public differs systematically from the rest of the nation: it is more supportive of faith-based political activism and more conservative and Republican. But the level of attention to public affairs is about the same as the public as a whole.

Among the clusters, there are important differences over the efficacy of faith-based politics. When asked to choose between churches "staying out of politics" or "expressing views on social/political questions," the evangelical left was almost evenly divided (46.4 and 49.5 percent, respectively). But a majority of the center (55.8 percent), right (69.9 percent), and populists (72.4 percent) said churches should express their views. Interestingly, the evangelical right was the most attentive to public affairs, with 64.4 percent claiming to pay attention "most of the time." The populists were the least attentive (44.4 percent), with the left (50.0 percent) and center (50.6 percent) a bit more so.

As one might expect, the evangelical left is the most likely to self-identify as "very liberal" or "liberal" (22.1 percent) politically and least likely to identity

Table 6.6 Evangelical Issue Clusters and Politics, 2007

	Left	Center	Populists	Right	All Evangelicals	Entire Public
Faith-Based Activism						
% Churches should keep out of political matters	46.4%	39.5%	23.1%	26.4%	31.9%	45.6%
% Churches express views on social/political questions	49.5%	55.8%	72.4%	69.9%	63.8%	49.8%
Attentive to Public Affairs						
% Follow "most of the time"	50.0%	50.6%	44.4%	64.4%	51.7%	50.1%
Ideology						
% Very liberal/liberal	22.1%	11.5%	8.0%	4.8%	10.9%	20.1%
% Moderate	52.2%	43.5%	34.7%	20.7%	36.7%	43.3%
% Very conservative/ conservative	25.7%	45.0%	57.3%	74.5%	52.4%	36.6%
	100.0%	100.0%	100.0%	100.0%	100.0%	100.0%
Partisanship						
% Democratic/lean Democratic	57.4%	38.8%	31.7%	15.1%	34.4%	46.9%
% Independent	17.2%	17.8%	16.5%	10.5%	15.5%	17.8%
% Republican/lean Republican	25.4%	43.4%	51.8%	74.4%	50.1%	35.3%
	100.0%	100.0%	100.0%	100.0%	100.0%	100.0%

Source: Religious Landscape Survey, 2007.

as "very conservative" or "conservative" (25.7 percent). But note that a majority said they were "moderate" (52.2 percent). And very few members of the evangelical right identify as liberal (4.8 percent) and a large majority as conservative (74.5 percent); about one-fifth said they were "moderate" (20.7 percent).

A more polarized pattern held for the left and right on self-identified partisanship. Almost three-fifths of the evangelical left were Democrats or lean Democratic (57.4 percent), one-quarter are Republicans or lean Republican (25.4 percent), and less than one-fifth independents (17.2 percent). And one-sixth of the evangelical right are Democrats (15.1 percent), three-quarters Republicans (74.4 percent), and about one-tenth independents (10.5 percent).

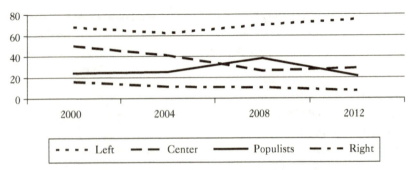

FIGURE 6.5 Evangelical Clusters and % Democratic Vote 2000–2012
Source: National Surveys of Religion and Politics, 2000–2012.

On ideology and partisanship, the evangelical center and populists fell in between the left and the right. About two-fifths of the center were conservative (45.0 percent) and Republicans (43.4 percent), while a majority of populists were conservatives (57.3 percent) and Republicans (51.8 percent).

How did the evangelical issue clusters vote in recent presidential elections? Figure 6.5 shows the reported Democratic presidential vote in the 2000, 2004, 2008, and 2012 presidential elections using the NSRP.[38] The evangelical left voted the most Democratic of the clusters over the period, and after a slight decline in 2004, it has become steadily more Democratic, with three-quarters voting for Obama in 2012. The evangelical right moved in the opposite direction, starting as the lowest Democratic vote and declining further, with less than one-tenth voting for Obama in 2012. The two remaining clusters had opposite patterns. First, the center voted steadily less Democratic until 2008, with a slight revival in 2012 (a little more than one-quarter voting for Obama in 2012). Meanwhile, the populists voted steadily more Democratic until 2008 and then shifted away in 2012 (about one-fifth voted for Obama in 2012).

Taken together, these data suggest that the evangelical right is more fully integrated into regularized politics, being both strongly Republican and strongly conservative (both at 74 percent). The other clusters do not show this level of political congruence, especially the evangelical left, where more identify as Democrats (57 percent) than as liberals (22 percent). This pattern may reflect the long-term impact of the Christian Right. From this perspective, the progressive movements may eventually have a similar effect. However, the frustration with regularized politics may be revealed in the skepticism toward government involvement with morality on the right and left and the low levels of attention to public affairs among populists, center, and left.

Table 6.7 reports the independent impact of religiosity, demography, and politics in distinguishing each cluster from the rest of the evangelical public

Table 6.7 Evangelical Issue Clusters: Multivariate Analysis

	Left	Center	Populists	Right
Religiosity				
Low worship attendance	3.14	1.62	−0.65	−0.65
Low religious importance	1.10	0.66	−0.81	−0.53
Low view of Bible	2.30	ns	−0.69	−0.11
Low traditionalism	2.65	ns	−0.36	−0.63
Low spiritual experience	−0.39	0.28	0.80	ns
Low religious conflict	0.34	ns	−0.27	ns
Demography				
Lower income	−0.35	ns	0.96	−0.49
Less education	−0.35	0.59	0.50	−0.39
Female	0.74	−0.29	0.34	−0.48
Younger age	0.35	−0.47	2.22	−0.66
Nonwhite	0.37	0.13	0.27	−0.57
Urban	0.53	ns	0.17	−0.65
Southern	−0.25	0.24	0.23	−0.25
Politics				
Religion out of politics	0.65	0.29	−0.44	−0.15
Liberal ideology	4.00	0.30	−0.38	−0.95
R-squared	0.32	0.10	0.21	0.25

See text for description of coefficients.

Ns—not statistically significant.

Source: Religious Landscape Survey, 2007.

in 2007. [39] The coefficients reported in the table are difficult to compare, but within each cluster, they reveal the magnitude of each variable's impact on cluster membership (the larger the coefficient, the more the independent effect, controlling for the effect of the other variables). The coefficients also show the direction of the impact (positive signs indicate that less traditional religiosity, lower-status demography, and liberal politics predict cluster membership, while negative signs denote that traditional religiosity, higher-status demography, and conservative politics predict cluster membership).

The evangelical left is distinguished from the rest of the evangelical public by its liberal ideology and, to a lesser extent, by the absence of traditional religiosity (especially worship attendance). It has mixed social status: more female, urban, nonwhite, and younger but also more affluent, better educated, and non-Southern. This mixed demography suggests that both the new and old issues may be perceived in postmaterial terms. The left is also characterized by more spiritual experiences, less perceived conflict between religion and society, and opposition to faith-based politics.

The evangelical center is the least distinctive of the clusters, but with religion playing the largest role (especially worship attendance). Like the left, it also has mixed social status: less educated, but also older, male, Southern, and nonwhite. This pattern suggests that this group perceives the new and old issues in both materialist and postmaterialist terms. In politics, the center is skeptical of faith-based politics and leans liberal.

The evangelical populists are distinguished from the evangelical public by uniformly low status, especially being younger and less affluent. These patterns suggest that the populists may interpret at least some of the new issues in materialist terms—with relative depravation leading to support for progressive government intervention. The populists also have uniformly traditional religiosity (especially the importance of religion), suggesting that they may also see many of the old issues in materialist terms—with personal insecurity leading to support for conservative government intervention. This group is characterized by fewer spiritual experiences, more perceived conflict between religion and society, and support for faith-based politics. The populists lean conservative politically.

The evangelical right is distinguished by its uniformly high social status. This pattern suggests that this group may also interpret at least some new issues in materialist terms—with relative affluence leading to opposition to progressive government intervention. The uniformly traditional religiosity of the right helps explain positions on the old issues—but these may not be thought of in materialist terms. It is also distinguished by conservative ideology but to a lesser extent than the liberalism of the left. However, in terms of attitudes at least, the right expresses some skepticism about faith-based politics.

Expanded Public Engagement

The foregoing survey evidence reveals a popular basis for expanded public engagement by evangelicals. This engagement includes the new issues, such as the environment, but also old issues, such as abortion. And there is considerable attitudinal diversity within the evangelical public, as demonstrated by the four opinion clusters. Each of these groups has a distinctive profile in terms of religiosity, demography, and politics.

The evangelical left provides a strong constituency for activism by the new evangelicals and progressive movements. Its diverse religiosity, mixed demography, and liberal politics may allow this group to cooperate with other progressives in regularized politics. But note that the evangelical left is opposed to faith-based politics, poorly integrated to political alignments, and not especially attentive to public affairs. Although this cluster has increased in size in recent times, it is far from fully mobilized.

In a similar fashion, the evangelical right offers a strong constituency for activism of the Christian Right and conservative movements. Its traditional religiosity, high-status demography, and conservative politics may allow this group to cooperate with other conservatives in regularized politics. But note that the right is skeptical of government involvement in morality. Although this cluster has decreased in size in recent times, it is much more fully mobilized.

It could be that in the near future, the evangelical left and right will compete in even terms outside and within the evangelical public. On the first count, both groups may add ballast to progressive and conservative policies on new and old issues. But because of the complexities of regularized politics, this influence is likely to be incremental and thus frustrating to movement activists. Even for these clusters, the temptation to political quiescence may be strong. Indeed, these data provide hints of this temptation, such as concern for government involvement with morality.

On the second count, the left and right have opportunities to influence the evangelical center and populists. The right has enjoyed some political advantages with these clusters, but these patterns may not persist in the future. The evangelical center may be more open to blandishments from the left and the right on particular new and old issues. But because of its moderation and smaller size, opportunities for permanent gains may be elusive and modest.

The large opportunity lies with the populists. The populists are the most intriguing because they hold progressive views on the new issues, especially environmental protection, and conservative views on the old issues, especially abortion. They are also the largest and fastest growing of the clusters. However, the populists have strong impediments to cooperating with the right and the left in regularized politics. They may have status conflicts with the right and religious conflicts with the left. And they are the most supportive of government involvement with morality and faith-based politics—but the least attentive to public affairs.

These data suggest that the agony experienced by evangelical activists is likely to be concentrated among the populists and those who would appeal to populists. Evangelicals who seek to follow biblical imperatives for justice and virtue are simultaneously at odds with the dominant forces in the Democratic and Republican Party coalitions. Faced with this agonizing choice, many populists may be especially tempted to become politically quiescent. It is the fate of the populists that is most likely to determine the place of evangelicals in American public affairs.

NOTES

1. Marcia Pally, *The New Evangelicals: Expanding the Vision of the Common Good* (Grand Rapids: MI: Eerdmans, 2011).

2. Clyde Wilcox and Carin Robinson, *Onward Christian Soldiers? The Religious Right in American Politics*, 4th ed. (Boulder, CO: Westview Press, 2011).

3. For the priorities of progressive and conservative religious activists in 2008, see "Faithful, Engaged, and Divergent: A Comparative Portrait of Conservative and Progressive Religious Activists in the 2008 Election and Beyond," http://publicreligion.org/research/2009/09/conservative-progressive-religious-activists-surveys/, accessed December 2012.

4. John C. Green, "Seeking a Place: Evangelical Protestants and Public Engagement in the 20th Century," 15–34, in *Toward an Evangelical Public Policy*, ed. Ronald Sider and Diane Knipper (Grand Rapids, MI: Baker Press 2011).

5. For more on the "Evangelical Manifesto," including a copy of the text and the signatories, see http://www.anevangelicalmanifesto.com/index.php, accessed December 2012.

6. David P. Gushee, *A New Evangelical Manifesto: A Kingdom Vision for the Common Good* (St. Louis, MO: Chalice Press, 2012).

7. For more on the "Manhattan Declaration," including a copy of the text and the signatories, see http://www.manhattandeclaration.org/#0, accessed December 2012.

8. Tobin Grant, "What Does the Manhattan Declaration Really Mean?" *Christianity Today*, November 24, 2009. www.christianitytoday.com/ct/2009/novemberweb-only/147-21.0.html, accessed December 2012.

9. William S. Maddox and Stuart A. Lilie, *Beyond Liberal and Conservative: Reassessing the Political Spectrum* (Washington, DC: Cato Institute, 1984).

10. Ronald Sider and Diane Knipper, eds., *Toward an Evangelical Public Policy* (Grand Rapids, MI: Baker Press, 2005). Also see Robert D. Putnam and David E. Campbell, *American Grace* (New York: Simon & Schuster, 2010).

11. Brian McLaren, "The Church in America Today," 2–9, in *A New Evangelical Manifesto*, ed. David P. Gushee (St. Louis, MO: Chalice Press, 2012); and also Margaret M. Poloma and John C. Green, *The Assemblies of God: Godly Love and the Revitalization of American Pentecostalism* (New York: New York University Press, 2010).

12. Ronald Inglehart, *Culture Shift* (Princeton, NJ: Princeton University Press, 1990).

13. Pippin Norris and Ronald Inglehart, *Sacred and Secular* (Cambridge: Cambridge University Press, 2005).

14. John C. Green, "Evangelical Protestants and Civic Engagement: An Overview," 11–30, in *A Public Faith: Evangelicals and Civic Engagement*, ed. Michael Cromartie (Lanham, MD: Rowman & Littlefield, 2003).

15. Geoffrey C. Layman, Thomas M. Casey, John C. Green, Richard Herrera, and Rosalyn Cooperman, "Activists and Conflict Extension in American Party Politics," *American Political Science Review* 104 (2010): 324–46.

16. Evangelical denominations were coded as recommended in Brian Steensland, Jerry Z. Park, Mark D. Regnerus, Lynn D. Robinson, W. Bradford Wilcox, and Robert D. Woodberry, The Measure of American Religion: Toward Improving the State of the Art," *Social Forces* 79 (2000): 291–318; also see John C. Green, *The Faith Factor: How Religion Influences the Vote* (Westport, CT: Praeger Press, 2007). For the coding details in the Religious Landscape Survey, see http://religions.pewforum.org/, accessed December 2012.

17. The following Pew Research Center data sets were used: typology surveys in 1999 ($N = 3,973$), 2000 ($N = 2,799$), 2004 ($N = 2,000$), and 2011 ($N = 2,029$). Details of these surveys can be found at www.people-press.org/typology/. Other data sets employed for particular questions included: ABC News/*Washington Post* Poll # 2004-971 (2004; $N = 1,004$); ABC News/*Washington Post* Poll # 14376 (2000; $N = 1,228$); CBS News Poll # 2003-11A (2003; $N = 1,177$); and Kaiser Family Foundation/Harvard/NPR Poll (2000; $N = 1,557$). Details on these surveys can be found at www.ropercenter.uconn.edu/, accessed December 2012.

18. The 2007 RLS allows for a comparison of the more and less precise measures of evangelicals, suggesting that the latter produces somewhat more conservative responses on most issue questions. By this measure, the RLS finds that evangelicals made up 20.7 percent of the adult population in 2007.

19. The National Surveys of Religion and Politics is an ongoing research project, and the data sets have not yet been released. These surveys were conducted before and after the presidential elections between 1992 and 2012 (before 2012, $N = 4000$; in 2012, $N = 2,000$). Details on the studies can be found at John C. Green, Lyman A. Kellstedt, Corwin E. Smidt, and James L. Guth, "How the Faithful Voted: Religious Communities and the Presidential Vote," 15–36, in *A Matter of Faith: Religion in the 2004 Presidential Election*, ed. David E. Campbell (Washington DC: Brookings Institution Press, 2007).

20. In the 2007 RLS, factor analysis showed that all three issues were part of a single "new issue" dimension of opinion in the evangelical public.

21. For example, see www.pewforum.org/Science-and-Bioethics/Religious-Groups-Views-on-Global-Warming.aspx, accessed December 2012.

22. In figure 6.2, the environment question data come from the PRC 2000 campaign typology survey, the PRC 2004 typology survey, the RLS 2007 survey, and PRC 2011 typology survey. In all cases, evangelicals were measured as white born-again Protestants.

23. For the Evangelical Environmental Network, see http://creationcare.org/; for the Cornwall Alliance, see www.cornwallalliance.org/, accessed December 2012.

24. James L. Guth, John C. Green, Lyman A. Kellstedt, and Corwin E. Smidt, "Faith and Foreign Policy: A View from the Pews," *Review of Faith & International Affairs* 3 (2005): 3–10.

25. James L. Guth, 2009. "Religion and Public Opinion: Foreign Policy Issues," 243–265, in *The Oxford Handbook of Religion and American Politics*, ed. Corwin E. Smidt, Lyman A. Kellstedt, and James L. Guth (New York: Oxford University Press).

26. In Figure 6.2, the diplomacy question data came from the PRC 1999 typology survey, the PRC 2004 typology survey, the RLS 2007, and PRC 2011 typology survey. In all cases, evangelicals were measured as white born-again Protestants.

27. See for example, "More Americans Question Religious' Role in Politics, Section 4: Faith Based –Aid -Favored-With-Reservations.www.pewforum.org/PublicationPage.aspx?id=1103, accessed December 2012.

28. In Figure 6.2, the size of government question data came from the ABC 2000 survey, the CBS 2003 survey, the RLS 2007 survey, and the PRC 2011 typology survey. In 2007 and 2011, evangelicals were measured as white born-again Protestants; in 2000 and 2003, the surveys had somewhat different religion data that came from the ABC 2000 survey, the CBS 2003 survey, the RLS 2007 survey, and PRC 2011 typology survey. In 2007 and 2011, evangelicals were measured as white born-again Protestants; in 2000 and 2003 evangelicals were estimated using religious salience and membership in the "religious right" in place of the born again question.

29. In the 2007 RLS survey, factor analysis revealed that all three of these issues were part of a single "old issue" dimension of opinion in the evangelical public.

30. In Figure 6.3, abortion question data come from the ABC 2000 and 2004 surveys, the RLS 2007 survey, and the PRC 2011 typology survey. In 2007 and 2011, evangelicals were measured as white born-again Protestants; in 2000 and 2004, the surveys had somewhat different religion measures.

31. See, for example, www.pewforum.org/Abortion/Abortion-Plays-Small-Role-in-Health-Reform-Opposition.aspx, accessed December 2012.

32. See, for example, www.pewforum.org/Gay-Marriage-and-Homosexuality/Public-Opinion-Trends-on-Gay-Marriage.aspx, accessed December 2012.

33. In Figure 6.3, the homosexuality question data come from the PRC 2000 campaign typology survey, the PRC 2004 typology survey, the RLS 2007 survey, and the PRC 2011 typology survey. In all cases, evangelicals were measured as white born-again Protestants.

34. In Figure 6.3, the government and morality question data come from the Kaiser/NOR 2000 survey, the PRC 2004 typology survey, the RLS 2007 survey, and PRC 2011 typology survey. In all cases, evangelicals were measured as white born-again Protestants.

35. These categories were created with K means cluster analysis using the six issue questions from the 2007 RLS, coded as in Tables 1 and 2. Missing data were assigned a middle position for each measure.

36. These categories were created by K means cluster analysis in the 2000, 2004, 2008, and 2012 NSRP using five common questions: environmental regulation, active foreign policy, size of government, gay rights, and abortion. Except for the abortion question (a four-point item very similar to the RLS), the items were five-point Likert scale items. The questions wording differed from the RLS, but the substantive content was similar.

37. Buster G. Smith and Byron Johnson, "The Liberalization of Young Evangelicals: A Research Note," *Journal for the Scientific Study of Religion* 49 (2010): 351–60.

38. These data come from the postelection modules of the NSRP in 2000, 2004, 2008, and 2012.

39. This analysis was conducted by means of binary logistic regression, with a separate analysis for each cluster, comparing each one to the rest of the evangelical public. All the independent variables coded between 0 and 1; variables that were not statistically significant for any of the clusters are not reported. The coefficients are log odds with –1 subtracted to give the coefficients direction.

PART TWO

Areas of Evangelical Social Engagement

7

Green Evangelicals

Laurel Kearns

The hippies of the 1960s did understand something...they were right in the fact that the plastic culture—modern man, the mechanistic worldview in university textbooks and in practice, the total threat of the machine, the establishment technology, the bourgeois upper middle class—is poor in its sensitivity to nature....The counterculture understands something very real...the poverty of modern man's concept of nature and the way the machine is eating up nature on every side.

—FRANCIS SCHAEFFER, 1970[1]

WHEN GREEN EVANGELICALISM first started capturing the news headlines in the 1990s, whether it was for the 1994 Evangelical Declaration on the Care of Creation and the work of the Evangelical Environmental Network or for Calvin DeWitt and the Noah Alliance bringing a panther to the US Capitol for a press conference regarding the threatened 1996 reauthorization of the Endangered Species Act, few remembered that this was not a new topic for evangelicals, but rather a long-standing one. With a publication date of 1970, Francis Schaeffer's *Pollution and the Death of Man* was among the earliest responses to Lynn White's infamous 1967 thesis that "Christianity bears a huge burden of guilt for the ecologic crisis."[2] Indeed, the White essay was reprinted in the back of Schaeffer's book. That same year, the National Association of Evangelicals (NAE) passed a resolution, stating: "Today those who thoughtlessly destroy a God-ordained balance of nature are guilty of sin against God's creation."[3]

Schaeffer's engagement with environmental issues foretold the complicated nature of evangelical engagement with environmental concerns that now spans the range from the Christian Right to the progressive evangelical left. Schaeffer is considered by many to be a founding figure of the Christian

Right, and opposing abortion became a pivotal concern for him. His ideological heirs on the Christian Right, however, did not follow his admonitions and are now some of the chief opponents of creation-care evangelicals, and the two ideological camps within green evangelicalism offer different understandings of what a prolife ethic encompasses. Beyond the definition of *prolife*, many of the same tensions that generate contention about evangelical social engagement writ large are present among green evangelicals. This reflects the "elastic orthodoxy" that Michael Lindsay describes as characterizing evangelicals in the United States.[4] These differences are explored here through the history of campaigns by two organizations that represent the range among green evangelicals: the Evangelical Environmental Network (EEN) and the Cornwall Alliance for the Stewardship of Creation. Both have their roots in the 1990s, the period of growing religious ecological concern.

In recognition of the deep ideological differences within evangelical environmental activism, I refer to those akin to the EEN as "creation-care evangelicals," after their major declaration on creation care. Their environmental concerns are more similar to the majority of religious and secular environmental groups—species extinction, conservation, pollution, land, water and ecosystem degradation, waste, mountaintop removal, energy use and climate change. The EEN, which in part grew out of Evangelicals for Social Action and is now two decades old, is the most prominent, advocating personal actions and reform, as well as government action and regulations. There are far more creation-care organizations in the United States than just EEN, such as the even older Au Sable Institute, Blessed Earth, Flourish, Restoring Eden, and Christians for the Mountains, which I will not discuss in as much detail.[5] I term those associated with the Cornwall Alliance for the Stewardship of Creation "wise-use stewards" to reflect their own use of the term *stewardship* and their close association with the proponents of the wise use movement and its emphasis on private property rights and its antigovernment regulation stance.[6] While voicing concern for the environment, they are vociferous climate skeptics or deniers, and the majority of their activity seems to be attacking mainstream secular and religious environmentalism. In addition to Cornwall, their work is closely related to the Acton Institute for Religion and Liberty, the Heartland Institute, and the Committee for a Constructive Tomorrow (CFACT), although none focuses as exclusively on the environment as Cornwall. They are often allied with such staples of the Christian Right as the Family Research Council, the Institute for Religion and Democracy, and creationism advocates.[7]

Complete dismissal of concern often comes from those whose apocalyptic focus on the "end times" seems to predict environmental degradation. In their view, the apocalyptic scenario is "welcomed" and "interpreted as harbingers of the second coming of Christ and the rapture."[8] Within the world of Pentecostalism, often a proponent of such apocalypticism, however, that, too, is changing (see Bishop Blake pronouncement below).[9] For instance, several Vineyard (referred to as neopentecostal or neocharismatic) church leaders, such as Tri Robinson, have a wide impact in promoting creation care.

Despite their desire that it be otherwise, white evangelicals make up the majority of actors of the US religious environmental efforts I describe.[10] This is not to say that black Protestants, who tend to be evangelical in theology but often eschew the term, do not participate in the range of religious environmental activism. Many, such as Jesus People Against Pollution and other environmental justice groups, are deeply motivated by their faith,[11] and black Protestants are more likely than any other Christian group to have heard an environmental reference from the pulpit.[12] Gerald Durley, a Baptist and one of Martin Luther King Jr.'s close associates, issued a challenge to Atlanta's black churches in 2009 to preach fifty sermons on the topic of the environment on Earth Day.[13] In a 2007 Apostolic Missive, Bishop Charles Blake[14] of the Church of God in Christ (a Pentecostal denomination which is very oriented toward personal holiness) included environmental threats among those "ill-conceived" social trends that needed increased church attention.[15]

Latino/a involvement is also changing.[16] The Evangelical Environmental Network has announced initiatives with the National Hispanic Christian Leadership Conference (the NHCLC, which lists stewardship as one of its seven directives), the Congress on Racial Equality, and the National Latino Evangelical Coalition to raise awareness of environmental issues and to work toward affordable energy.[17] Like other segments of evangelicalism, environmental concern among Latino/a and Asian American evangelicals[18] is more prevalent among the younger generations and the groups in which they are involved, such as Intervarsity, the New Monasticism, and Emerging Church movements—all covered elsewhere in this volume.[19] At the "Envision 08: The Gospel, Politics and Future" gathering of hundreds of mainly young and racially diverse socially engaged evangelicals, dozens of evangelical leaders such as Brian McLaren, Jim Wallis, and Richard Cizik signed a declaration calling for "God's work to eradicate poverty, create peace, and build just communities and right relationships with the earth."[20]

For some analysts of conservative Christianity, the environment and climate change has become a fault line that is cracking the perceived monolithic Republican voting block of predominantly white evangelicals, estimated to be near 100 million strong in the United States, partly along generational lines.[21]

I now turn to the development of this breadth of green evangelicalism in the United States, before turning to analyze the tensions present in this fault line.

The Rise of Green Evangelicals

There were and are many hurdles to developing an evangelical approach to environmentalism, and Schaeffer identified a chief one: its association with the liberal movements of the 1960s and 1970s. Hence one of the first tasks of greening evangelicalism was to ground environmental concern in the scriptures and sound science, and much of the early work was dedicated to this task. In 1977–78, Calvin College's Center for Christian Scholarship hosted a yearlong conversation among five scholars with backgrounds in economics, biology, theology/philosophy, physics, and literature. The end result was a book, *Earthkeeping* (taken from the reinterpretation of Genesis 2:15 to mean "to till and keep the earth"), that tried to outline what its subtitle described as "Christian stewardship of natural resources."[22] While a great deal of attention was paid to the necessary reinterpreting of scripture and theology, particularly the "dominion" and "subdue" passages of Genesis, what is also significant to note in the conversation at Calvin was that it was equally grounded in science. Indeed, Calvin DeWitt, the biologist who had taken on the post of executive director of the newly established Au Sable Institute for Environmental Studies at about the same time, helped move Au Sable from an outdoor camp into a full-fledged biological field studies station serving over sixty Christian colleges, an important task in a creationist-influenced atmosphere dismissive of science. DeWitt, still a key leader, likes to call evangelicals who are uninterested in understanding the workings of creation through science "creationless creationists."

Momentum from several avenues began to build in the 1980s. For instance, evangelicals and their allies, such as Dewitt and Fred Krueger, played a key role in the founding of the North American Conference on Christianity and Ecology (NACCE), an attempt to engage ecologically concerned Christians across the theological spectrum. The NACCE's 1987 conference in Indiana drew over 500 people and helped launch a range of Christian environmental organizations that reflected the theological differences among the attendees—differences that became apparent in the attempt to write a conference document. An acrimonious split developed between those more focused on the pan-faith work of "geologian" Thomas Berry and those more focused on a specifically Christian approach. It also raised the awareness of the need for an evangelical organization, and many of the evangelical participants, such as DeWitt, with international backing, would go on in 1993 to cofound EEN, which has been a leader in the US ever since with a strong track record of educational and advocacy efforts.

In 1994, creation-care evangelicals outlined their core principles in the "Evangelical Declaration on the Care of Creation."[23] In its first line, it affirms the "full authority of Scriptures." Evangelicals have always sought a strong foundation in the scriptural authority of the Bible, so by linking concern over environmental degradation to the divine assertion of the integrity and worth of all creation in the very beginning of Genesis, and God's care for all of creation seen in the Noahic covenant in Genesis 9:12, creation-care evangelicals could establish a clear and unambiguous authority, a biblical mandate, to speak on the issue. This biblical mandate provides clear moral authority to address what others view as purely scientific matters.

The document also addressed central ideological obstacles for evangelical creation care—the interpretation of Genesis 1:28 as granting humans dominion over the earth and the distrust of science stemming from the rejection of evolutionary theory. It also indirectly addressed the association of environmentalism with the new age or liberals and accusations of worshiping the creation and not the creator, themes that have continued to frame the evangelical opposition to environmentalism. As the Calvin seminar had recognized with their inclusion of an economist, the declaration addressed competing understandings of the economy.

From its founding, the EEN has been part of an interfaith coalition, the National Partnership for the Environment (NRPE), a coalition of four constituent groups.[24] Such interfaith efforts, or even the Christian ecumenism that was attempted among the founders and attendees of NACCE, provoke tension that is always present for some green evangelicals between the common concern over the fate of their one shared planet (that for many trumps a range of theological and/or ideological differences) versus possibly diluting the articulation of a specifically Christian approach and grounding and thus distracting from the work of evangelism.

As part of the early work of the NRPE in the mid-1990s, each constituent group prepared a start-up packet providing scriptural and theological foundations, practical ideas, and education plans specifically tailored for their constituency. The EEN mailed packets to over 36,000 evangelical congregations, a significant outreach effort. Beyond this awareness-raising work, tensions existed over what environmental concerns should be the coalition's central focus. Species depletion and habitat conservation were issues that fit well for the emerging evangelical environmental movement's emphasis on the implications of Genesis and the Noahic covenant in their successful work to protect the Endangered Species Act. Yet such a focus could be seen as avoiding the more complex human justice issues of an ecojustice perspective. Issues of overpopulation were anathema to the evangelical and Catholic partners, and overconsumption had too many overtones of a critique of capitalism. The one issue that clearly emerged as an NRPE focal point was global warming. Addressing climate change was clearly relevant to the evangelical focus on caring for all of creation, yet it would prove to be a difficult issue and an ongoing source of dispute and opposition to their efforts.

The clear, unjust consequences of global warming and environmental degradation are central to creation-care activists. They base their response on the scriptural admonition to care for the "least of these" who will be the most affected—the poor, the more-than-human world, and the future generations who will "inherit the earth."[25] This emphasis fits other emerging evangelical concerns about injustices and demonstrates the reason that environmentalism has been an obvious addition to the concerns of the new evangelicalism outlined in this book. Under Jim Ball's leadership, EEN linked global warming and pollution concerns with a "love your neighbor as yourself" (Matthew 22:36–40) ethic in its 2002 "What Would Jesus Drive?" (WWJD) campaign, as part of the NRPE's campaign to focus on the need to cut automobile emissions that contribute to pollution and global warming. These two biblical mandates are also evident in the recent EEN campaign to regulate mercury pollution standards, with a particular emphasis on the impact on the unborn. They are also present in the 2004 NAE broad-ranging position paper, "For the Health of the Nation: An Evangelical Call to Civic Responsibility," which called for environmental stewardship and argued that environmental health was central to community health, and in the EEN's "Healthy Families, Healthy Environment" initiative.

Based as they are in part on individual moral responsibility to love one's neighbor or care for the least, these appeals balance the more traditional evangelical approach of personal moral response and lifestyle choices with policy advocacy. So an ad related to the WWJD campaign focused on consumer choices—"if we bring God to the movies, why do we leave God behind at the auto mall?" The Declaration of the Care of Creation promotes "lifestyle choices that express humility, forbearance, self-restraint, and frugality."[26] Blessed Earth's work continues this focus on personal and lifestyle transformation, shying away from all policy issues. Christians for the Mountains and EEN have sought to connect mountaintop removal coal production for the production of electricity, which is distant for many, to personal energy consumption. In addition to this standard evangelical emphasis, these groups have focused on providing resources for congregational activity, education, and commitment.

Creation care was not just a concern of American evangelicals, however. DeWitt narrates the efforts of Au Sable and the World Evangelical Fellowship in the founding of the International EEN in 1992, from which the U.S. EEN derived.[27] A 2002 gathering of international evangelicals and scientists in Oxford on climate change led to an encounter between the very influential Richard Cizik, vice president for governmental affairs of the NAE, and Sir John Houghton, the Welsh evangelical climate scientist who cochaired the Nobel Peace Prize–winning Intergovernmental Panel on Climate Change (IPCC). Cizik credits a long walk with Houghton for his "conversion" to the importance of combating global warming that would lead to his spearheading the Evangelical Climate Initiative (ECI) and its "Call to Action on Climate Change" statement in 2006.[28] It has been signed by over three hundred evangelical leaders, including well-known pastors Joel Hunter and Rick Warren; the heads of key evangelical seminaries such as Fuller, North Park, and Gordon Conwell; and several writers from *Christianity Today*, which has supported the inclusion of environmental issues since at least 1980. The high-profile nature of this campaign, with significant media attention, heightened the tensions between the two groups and between the NAE and the Christian Right more broadly.

It was clear that creation-care evangelical environmentalism had made significant inroads when the Christian Right chose to oppose environmental concern, not as part of religious faith, but by claiming such environmental concern was directed to the wrong issues and solutions, particularly global warming and climate change. This was the motivation in the formation of the Cornwall Alliance at a gathering of religious leaders who issued the Cornwall Declaration in 2000 in response to the earlier 1994 EEN Declaration.[29] Initially it was known as the Interfaith Council on Environmental Stewardship, an affiliate of the Acton Institute for the Study of Religion and Liberty. Beginning in the 1990s, the Acton Institute has published books and produced radio spots promoting climate change skepticism and on understanding environmental issues from a free-market perspective, as well as blogs that attacked religious environmentalism as radical. Calvin Beisner, whose doctorate is in Scottish history, is the key figure behind Cornwall, which calls itself "the world's leading evangelical voice promoting environmental stewardship." Through Cornwall, Christian wise-use stewards started to articulate a different green evangelicalism, emphasizing that humans as stewards have dominion and that creation was put here for human betterment. As such, it should be cared for and managed wisely, but it does not have intrinsic worth. Their primary work is to educate others about their view of religious environmentalism through statements, publications, media and lectures.

Certainly, there has been opposition to any environmentalism from within the wide range of evangelicalism, and Cornwall has been adept at bridging and drawing on those concerns. They reiterate the Christian Right's charges against the majority of Christian environmentalism that it focuses on creation to the detriment of worshiping the Creator and saving souls. The key focus should be on God and not human relations to the rest of creation. The Cornwall Declaration reinforces the secular wise-use movement's emphases on the continuing improvement of the environment through human technology and on the abundance of resources, seen as God's gift to humanity, put here for human utility. Beisner has recently said that the environmental movement is "deadly to the gospel of Jesus Christ" and that it is insulting to God to believe in climate change and to not utilize the "abundant, inexpensive and effective [fossil] fuel sources" provided by God. He elaborated: "God buried those treasures there because he loves to see us find them and put them to use."[30] The charge of insulting God reflects a central theological difference in the understanding of God's sovereignty, as wise-use stewards believe that God's omnipotence would not allow ecological crises such as global warming.

Despite this opposition, the ECI was very successful, and poll numbers showed a shift. So threatened were James Dobson, Tony Perkins, Chuck Colson, and other old-guard Christian Right leaders that even though they are not members of the NAE, they sought, unsuccessfully, in 2006 to force Richard Cizik to resign his leadership of it. They succeeded in having his signature removed from the ECI Call to Action and, later, in demanding his resignation from the NAE in 2008.[31] To Cornwall's delight, the NAE then issued a statement that it did not have a position on global warming.

Dimensions of Ideological Tension

The work of Matthew Nisbet on framing environmental issues is particularly helpful in showing the tensions between wise-use stewardship and creation-care evangelicals. Nisbet presents seven main frames that shape science-related policy debates. Within each frame, of course, there are variations, and frames themselves are neutral but may be employed in a way that is pro, neutral, or against. He further explains that "frames are interpretive storylines that set a specific train of thought in motion, communicating why an issue might be a problem, who or what might be responsible for it, and what should be done about it."[32] Thus frames provide shorthand that counts on the reader or listener to make associations that can be left unsaid.[33]

Central to Nisbet's argument is that a Morality and Justice frame is needed in scientific debates but often overlooked (and this is what religious environmentalists bring to the task). The concern for justice can also be seen in the frame of Social Progress. Just as crucial are the frames of Scientific Certainty/Uncertainty or invocations of a Pandora's Box of catastrophes. Three other frames, Economic Competitiveness, Public Accountability and Governance, and the portrayal of Battling Elites or ideologues, are also helpful in understanding the conflicted world of evangelical environmental activism. While all of these frames can illuminate differences between the two approaches, they can be grouped around three that are key: justice, science, and economics.

Part of the strength of creation-care evangelicalism is its combination of scriptural, moral, and scientific authority, as discussed earlier in their invocation of caring for the least of these, thus reflecting Nisbet's point that a moral frame is needed. In good evangelical fashion, the Care of Creation Declaration early on admits moral failure: "we repent of the way we have polluted, distorted or destroyed so much of the Creator's work," lamenting that "we continue to degrade that creation" in ways such as "1) land degradation; 2) deforestation; 3) species extinction; 4) water degradation; 5) global toxification; 6) the alteration of atmosphere; and 7) human and cultural degradation."[34] After laying out the biblical and theological foundations for creation care, deftly negotiating all the theological hurdles, it calls Christians "to work vigorously to protect and heal that creation for the honor and glory of the Creator." The Cornwall Declaration, after stating that "the moral necessity of ecological stewardship has become increasingly clear," spends the first half of the document critiquing others, such as environmentalists, for "unfounded or undue concerns [that] include fears of destructive manmade global warming, overpopulation, and rampant species loss."[35] A continued Cornwall practice is to denounce the religious and secular environmental movement for embracing what they call "faulty science" and a gloom-and-doom approach. They call "climate alarmism," their term for advocating action on climate change, a mass delusion, thus revealing their dependency on the framing of scientific uncertainty, whereas for creation-care evangelicals, the framing of justice is central.

Despite such repeated invocations of scientific uncertainty from climate skeptics and deniers, there is an unusually strong scientific agreement, really a vast majority scientific consensus, on climate change. This means that evangelical scientists play a particularly important role on either side.[36] DeWitt, a scientist himself, has always focused on the importance of teaching sound scientific knowledge, and the Au Sable Institute has been dedicated to that goal through teaching students, and annually gathering evangelical scientists. Jim Ball, the former executive director of EEN, while not a scientist, previously worked for the Union of Concerned Scientists. More recently, Katharine

Hayhoe, associate professor of atmospheric sciences at Texas Tech University, and her pastor husband, both evangelicals, garnered a lot of attention with their book, *A Climate for Change: Global Warming Facts for Faith-Based Decisions*, for which she received death threats.[37] Harvard scientists Eric Chivian and E. O Wilson have made it a point to work with evangelicals to reach their base. Scientists such as these were key to the Evangelical Climate Initiative's statement that "many of us have required considerable convincing before becoming persuaded that climate change is a real problem and that it ought to matter to us as Christians. But now we have seen and heard enough." The first claim of the ECI's Call to Action, grounded in the work of the IPCC, with particular mention of evangelical Sir John Houghton, is that "Human Induced Climate Change is Real."[38]

The framing of scientific certainty-uncertainty is aided by the practice of the U.S. media to present two sides to every issue, often in a he said, she said format.[39] As Nisbet comments, "By giving equal weight to contrarian views on climate science, journalists presented the false impression that there was limited expert agreement on the causes of climate change."[40] Wise-use stewards have particularly benefited from this and frequently refer to the thousands of scientists that have signed the Oregon petition[41] that challenges the consensus on global warming or the similar "Manhattan Declaration on Climate Change" for which full-page ads in the *New York Timesr* were bought.[42] The media report this opposition with little investigation into the credentials of the scientists[43]. My own limited investigation, and that of the Union of Concerned Scientists, indicates that the vast majority of signers, if they are even scientists, are not in climate science fields and often are geologists and others who work for extractive industries or teach high school biology.[44] This illustrates one of the contradictions present in the religious climate-skeptic movement: despite drawing upon a general suspicion and distrust of science, played up through references to creationism and evolution, science is still used to support the frame of uncertainty; that is, they quote scientists who are challenging other scientists, indicating that science still has some master authority status.

The practice of referring to the "religion" or "theology" of global warming, as if the science was something one could choose to believe or not believe (a point that creationists like to make), is another way to emphasize the scientific uncertainty frame.[45] Further, evangelical climate skeptics like to invoke the "theory" of global warming, suggesting that theories are hypotheses, rather than explanations of scientifically observed facts which is the scientific use of the term theory, as in the "theory of gravity." Thus, the scientific uncertainty frame evokes a large and defining discourse in conservative Christianity, allowing followers to fill in the blanks about the authority of science.

Environmentalism and Economics

Although the frame of scientific certainly-uncertainty has been crucial in the contrast between the differing camps of green evangelicals, it is the economic framing that is the real battleground. As seen earlier, the framing of justice for the least of these is a central point for creation-care evangelicals. While this can be seen in the ECI Call to Action—"The Consequences of Climate Change Will Be Significant, and Will Hit the Poor the Hardest"—it is even more clearly evident in the NAE 2011 report—"Loving the Least of These: Addressing a Changing Environment."[46] But Cornwall tries to flip the assertion, painting creation-care environmentalism as a threat to the economic system and social progress, arguing that "a clean environment is a costly good; consequently, growing affluence, technological innovation, are integral to environmental improvement.... The tendency among some to oppose economic progress in the name of environmental stewardship is often sadly self-defeating."[47] The ECI Call to Action recognizes how powerful the economic and social progress frame can be, stating in the opening preamble that they seek to respond to climate change "in a way that creates jobs, cleans up our environment, and enhances national security by reducing our dependence on foreign oil, thereby creating a safe and healthy future for our children."[48]

Nisbet reports just why scientific uncertainty and economic framing is so central for wise use stewards. He points out the work of a top Republican consultant, Frank Luntz, who had, "during the 1990s, based on focus groups and polling,...helped shape the climate skeptic playbook, recommending in a strategy memo to lobbyists and Republican members of Congress that the issue be framed as scientifically uncertain, using opinions of contrarian scientists as evidence." Luntz also wrote that the "emotional home run" would be an emphasis on the dire economic consequences of action that would result in an "unfair burden" on Americans.[49] These frames have been well played and have played well, as Luntz suggested.

Cornwall's initial response to the ECI Call to Action, the "We Get It" campaign, linked the threat to economic competitiveness with several others frames—moral ethics, social progress, conflict-elitism—and revealed a new part of the climate denial playbook: a battle over who cares the most for the poor.[50] Cornwall's more recent 2009 Evangelical Declaration on Global Warming (causing confusion to anyone not well versed in the distinctions among green evangelicals), succinctly sums up their stance in its opening lines: "Proposed policies would destroy jobs and impose trillions of dollars in costs to achieve no net benefits. They could be implemented only by enormous and dangerous expansion of government control over private life. Worst of all, by raising energy prices and hindering economic development, they would slow or stop the rise of the world's poor out of poverty and so condemn millions to premature death."[51]

Cornwall ramped up its attack on religious environmentalism with a series of thirty-minute videos called "Resisting the Green Dragon." Deftly aimed at younger evangelicals with its focus on images to convey their message, it contains segments on "Going Green Impoverishes You, Your Church, and Your Society" and "Ravaging the World's Poor," while linking opposition to environmentalism to patriotism.[52] The threat to capitalism and the U.S. economic system has been a very powerful frame throughout political conservatism, transferring the energies of anticommunism after the Soviet Union disbanded. Protecting capitalism from "socialist" environmentalism is linked with the trope that capitalism promotes democracy, and thus protecting it is an issue of freedom and liberty, as clearly seen in Beisner's segment "Threats to Liberty and the Move toward a Global Government." Beisner, like many evangelicals views capitalism as the economic expression of Christianity, so if environmentalism is a threat to capitalism, it is a threat to Christianity and America. The persuasive strength of the invocation of threats to the economic and political system reveals a strong reason for the growth of religious climate skepticism during the economic downturn falsely attributed to President Obama, whom the secular and religious Right constantly and erroneously call a socialist.

"Resisting the Green Dragon" invokes the conspiracy theories that lurked on the right-wing fringes of Christian paranoia, implying that environmentalism is power hungry, with a "lust for political power that extends to the highest levels." James Tonkowich of the Cornwall Alliance asserts in the preview trailer that environmental "fearmongering" is about obtaining power, for "whoever controls the environmental regulations, controls the economy, controls the population." Beisner warns that environmentalists want to greatly reduce the population, invoking abortion, and desire a global government. In the few opening seconds of the introduction, viewers are told that radical environmentalism, "the greatest deception of our time," is trying to put America under its "destructive control." In its lust for power, it is "seducing" people (particularly children) into pantheism through popular culture, using such movies as *Avatar* and the *Lord of the Rings* trilogy, as well as various Disney productions. The images that accompany this narrative tell far more: the fierce gold eye of a dragon, a Greenpeace sign, a Communist hammer and sickle, UN flags, and a person hugging a tree. "The time is now" to resist the "green dragon," written in a font that invokes the sense of end times, is authoritatively spoken by one of the few women in the whole series, as a large clock ticks. These images and tropes of the threat of evil conjure up other familiar themes to right-wing Christians, as Yates and Hunter point out in their discussion of this "religio-political ideology" that draws on a "deep symbolic reserve" that pulls listeners into an epic tale of "dragon slayers" against the "green dragon" that threatens to bring down the world.[53] Mythic symbols, drawn directly from the book of the Revelation, are used to tell a story of what is happening in the here and now, right under unsuspecting viewers' noses. Yates and Hunter point out that the Christian Right is good at

> the striking of a collective nerve among particular people.... Fundamentalist narratives are exceedingly evocative and compelling because they "package" the religious mythos, scriptural idealism, and frames together in such a way as to place their hearers within a story, which they in turn must either endorse or reject. If they endorse the story, filled as it is with cosmic significance, subscribers are also endorsing their special place within that story, and accepting its attendant moral duties and religious obligations. If hearers reject the story, they reject their role in the Divine Plan and risk the coming judgment.[54]

In other words, they draw on emotional responses to make sure the viewer desires to be on their side and aware of the imminent danger. This emotional evocation illustrates the assertion that "there is no such thing as unframed information."[55]

Wise-use stewards have succeeded because they engage all the frames of environmental debates in such a way that listeners do not need to know anything about the actual environmental issues because more familiar tropes of economic competitiveness, liberty, and concern for the poor come across louder. These major tropes then become the frames that creation-care evangelicals have to counter. They are lumped with scientists, liberals, people of color, environmentalists, gays, and prochoice women into what the series calls "The Green Face of the Pro-Death Agenda" in an amazing American amalgamation promoted by talk show pundits like Glenn Beck, Rush Limbaugh, and Fox News, always on the lookout for the next enemy. When communism "died" as a rallying call, environmentalists were the target, until 9/11 and the demonization of Islam. Now that such demonization has become less acceptable and the economic downturn continues to cloud the futures of many, environmentalism as the cause of all evils has once again been resurrected by religious and political conservatives.

Like other Cornwall campaigns, funded in part by those with oil and mining interests such as Exxon Mobil and Koch industries, the stakes are framed as cosmic matters of the future of the world, which, indeed, for those funders, they are.[56] Such framing, as Nisbet points out, works: these images reach viewers far more effectively than all the pages that Beisner and others have written, and they reach younger viewers through fast-paced YouTube clips, viewers who might ignore a wordy statement. It also draws attention away from the vested economic interests behind the campaign.

Conclusion

In this chapter, I have focused primarily on classic environmental concerns, particularly climate change, as articulated by evangelical policy and social movement organizations, and on the range of issues that shape, in very different ways, what it means to be environmentally concerned and evangelical. Evangelicals are socially engaged with issues of environmentalism, but it is the tensions within evangelicalism—manifest in a whole range of issues discussed in this book—that shape that engagement. Nisbet's analysis of environmental discourse illuminates the complex world of green and not-so-green evangelicalism and the many dimensions of the climate change debate, not just within that Christian subculture, but in the larger society. Focusing on the world of creation-care evangelicalism is important for understanding the key role it plays in combating the larger political currents of environmental opposition and climate change scepticism and denial in the United States, as well as the hurdles faced by any religious group advocating action to counter climate change. Even as the issue of climate change has created deep fissures within evangelicalism, including within the Southern Baptist Convention,[57] it has also created fissures within green evangelicalism, with some creation-care evangelicals starting to shy away from it as too political for their liking, thus leading to a new group established by former EEN staff members, Flourish, that proclaims: "We think that environmental 'issues' are primarily heart issues, not political issues."[58] Others, recognizing a generational shift in approaches, formed Young Evangelicals for Climate Action, with the support of the EEN, who have held prayer vigils outside the campaign offices of 2012 presidential candidate Mitt Romney and one 2012 presidential debate site. Still others, like Cornwall, focus on climate skepticism and denial.

To illustrate these tensions, I have focused on social movement organizations such as EEN and their Cornwall opponents, to the neglect of the significant efforts of individual evangelical churches, such as Joel Hunter's 15,000-member Northland Church in Orlando, whose congregants undertook to make a film on creation care to convince Christians more to their right.[59] Many of the U.S. Environmental Protection Agency's (EPA) Energy

Star congregations are large evangelical churches (such as First Baptist Church of Orlando, which saved $792,000 for an estimated annual savings of nearly $373,000), whose success demonstrates what the EPA's Energy Star website proclaims: "Most congregations can cut energy costs by up to 30 percent by investing strategically in efficient equipment."[60] The write-up on the EPA website estimates that these energy efficiencies represent savings of more than 4.4 million kWh per year and "a reduction in greenhouse gas emissions equivalent to the CO_2 emissions from the annual electricity use of over 300 homes."[61] Savings such as these can reflect a purely business decision that overrides theological hesitancy, but First Baptist is clear that saving energy costs is only one part of the picture. Of equal importance was their theology. "Jesus' command to his disciples in John 6:12 is '…let nothing be wasted,'" says Jim Hughes, energy educator and manager for the congregation. "We understood our role in protecting the environment and that this is a Biblically-rooted task from God."[62] Churches and organizations can focus on energy usage and savings, while sidestepping climate change, and energy concerns continue to bring evangelicals into the environmental conversation. Polls indicate that the emboldened climate change denial movement, strengthened by the wise-use movement's success under President George W. Bush, has indeed eroded some of the success of the EEN and ECI in convincing evangelicals, but all polls indicate that the idea of caring for creation in some manner is now widespread among evangelicals.[63]

While I have focused on climate change, evangelical efforts are much broader. The efforts of EEN, Au Sable, and others have borne fruit. Today, there is a wide array of evangelical creation-care organizations, ranging from tips for personal practices and congregational greening, to transforming theology and new biblical understandings, to equipping missionaries with sustainability education, to more advocacy-oriented groups on issues such as mountaintop removal, fracking, alternative energy, endangered species and habitat conservation, air pollution and hazardous wastes. Focusing on alternative energy and energy efficiency is key for those working on the unjust nature of mountaintop removal, such as Christians for the Mountains and Restoring Eden, as they urge fellow evangelicals to move away from coal-based energy. The traditional evangelical work on disaster relief can bring a heightened environmental awareness to some, whether it is the aftermath of severe storms and flooding, such as Hurricane Sandy, or the rapidly increasing desertification and resultant crop loss and malnutrition, as was the case for megachurch pastors Rick Warren and Bill Hybels. Peter Harris, cofounder of the international Christian conservation organization A Rocha, advocates the central role of eco-educated missionaries. Cizik's post-NAE work is leading the New

Evangelical Partnership, cofounded with David Gushee, which focuses on nuclear disarmament, human rights, creation care, and fighting Islamophobia through Muslim-Christian dialogue, indicating the more socially engaged and global focus that has long been part of creation-care evangelicalism.

Other areas are now emerging as new avenues for connecting evangelicals to environmental concerns. The first is the treatment of animals. Many churches start out with pet care issues, providing veterinary care, pet food banks, and the like as a form of evangelism and outreach, realizing the close bond people have with their companion animals. But interestingly, this easily leads to broader concerns over the treatment of farm animals and species preservation. The Faith Outreach arm of the Humane Society of the United States (HSUS) reports strong evangelical support and has distributed over 35,000 copies of their DVD "Eating Mercifully." This attention to the conditions of industrial agriculture fits well with a complementary movement focused on food, the well-being of the land, and the poisoning of the "sacred" gifts of the earth through pesticide- and herbicide-intensive farming. Once thought to be the realm of granola-crunching hippies, the food movement now has deep resonance across the spectrum, with community gardens a common project. Another successful, although highly controversial, move has been to link concern for unborn children with their exposure to environmental toxins, such as mercury, for an expanded notion of prolife. In 2012, EEN sponsored billboards making this connection, which infuriated many in the prolife movement, as well as the Cornwall Alliance.

These movements illustrate the range of green evangelicals, as well as the challenges. In addition to avoiding politics and policy, the individualistic focus of much of evangelicalism means that environmental concern often sells best when focused on individual actions. This helps explain the success of focusing on individual relationships with animals or food choices; environmental concern is a much harder sell when it involves policy or structural changes. Another tension is that the more structural, policy-related concerns might be the concerns of evangelical elites, as Michael Lindsay describes them in *Faith in the Halls of Power*, but not concerns of the everyday evangelical. Katharine Wilkinson, in *God and Green*, reports that the results of her focus group interviews at evangelical churches in the South seem to confirm this.[64] At the same time, however, pretty much everyone in the focus groups agreed that there is a biblical mandate to be good stewards, a minority viewpoint when EEN started their work in the 1990s. But what that meant in terms of specific actions is not clear. In other words, the sentiment was there, but it was not a high-ranking concern if it was a concern at all. The lack of priority and the gap between belief and action haunts not just evangelical efforts, but the work of most Christian environmental activists. Still, the success of evangelical environmentalism is clear, and there are competing visions seeking to define it. Indeed, Francis Schaeffer's book has been reissued for a new generation of readers.

NOTES

1. Francis A. Schaeffer, *Pollution and the Death of Man* (Wheaton, IL: Tyndale House, 1970), 76.
2. Although White is infamous for this phrase, he did not write off Christianity and, indeed, spent the next twenty years articulating the potential within Christianity, as well as nuancing his thesis. See Matthew T. Riley, "A Spiritual Democracy of All God's Creatures: Ecotheology and Lynn White's Animals," in *Divinanimality: Animal Theory, Creaturely Theology*, ed. Stephen Moore (New York: Fordham Press, forthcoming).
3. "Ecology 1970," accessed December 18, 2012, www.nae.net/government-relations/policy-resolutions/132-ecology-1970.
4. Michael Lindsay, *Faith in the Halls of Power: How Evangelicals Joined the American Elite* (New York: Oxford, 2008).
5. Blessed Earth is associated with Matthew Sleeth, whose story of conversion has captured the hearts of many, as told in *Serve God, Save the Planet* (Grand Rapids, MI: Zondervan, 2007). See Dwight Billings and Will Samson, "Evangelical Christians and the Environment: Christians for the Mountains and the Appalachian Movement against Mountaintop Removal Coal Mining," *Worldviews* 16 (2012): 1–29.
6. Laurel Kearns, "Wise Use Movement," 1755–1757, in *The Encyclopedia of Religion and Nature*, ed. B. Taylor (New York: Thoemmes Continuum, 2008).
7. Some think humans have not done enough to subdue the earth, such as the Institute for Creation Research and its interpretation of the dominion mandate: "As far as subduing the earth is concerned, a number of nations have made contributions in terms of science, technology, commerce....In spite of all this advance in science and technology, however, mankind is still a long way from subduing the earth. We have not been able to control the weather or make the great deserts fertile and habitable...." This quotation also demonstrates that creationists are not antiscience. Henry Morris, "God's Dominion Mandate and the Nations Today," accessed May 10, 2012, www.icr.org/article/501/319.
8. Steven Studebaker, "Creation Care as Keeping in Step with the Spirit," in *A Liberating Spirit: Pentecostals and Social Action in North America*, ed. Michael Wilkinson and Steven M. Studebaker (Eugene, OR: Wipf and Stock, 2010), 255. The Public Religion Research Institute reports that 65 percent of white

evangelicals attribute recent severe weather to evidence of the end times: accessed December 14, 2012, www.publicreligion.org/research/2012/12/prri-rns-december-2012-survey/.

9. A. J. Swoboda, in "Looking the Wrong Way: Salvation and the Spirit in Pentecostal Eco-Theology," credits Jean-Jacque Suurmond with the first Pentecostal publication on ecotheology and calls Harold Hunter's article "Pentecostal Healing for God's Sick Creation" a breakthrough. See Wilkinson and Studebaker, *A Liberating Spirit*, 232–233.

10. For a relevant discussion, see the last chapter "Evangelical Politics in a Shade of Blue Green," in Peter Heltzel, *Jesus and Justice: Evangelicals, Race and Politics* (New Haven, CT: Yale University Press, 2009), 203-18,

11. Matthew Immergut and Laurel Kearns, "When Nature Is Rats and Roaches: Religious Eco-Justice Activism in Newark, NJ," *Journal for the Study of Religion, Nature and Culture*, 6:2 (2012): 178-197.

12. www.pewforum.org/politics-and-elections/few-say-religion-shapes-immigration-environment-views.aspx#2, accessed December 13, 2012.

13. Durley states, "I could not make the connections initially between my community and polar bears, so I began to read about it.... I saw the land as being all of us, as one. If God can create a climate where animals and plants and human beings work together, we have a responsibility to try to maintain that balance. That's when the 'conversion' really hit me." Anne Marie Roderick, "Reverend Gerald Durley," *Sojourners*, June 2012, accessed December 18, 2012, www.sojo.net/magazine/2012/06/rev-gerald-l-durley.

14. Bishop Blake, the well-known AME pastor Rev. Floyd Flake, and several other prominent black religious leaders signed the Evangelical Climate Initiative, as did Hispanic leaders like the Rev. Jesse Miranda, president of AMEN in Costa Mesa, California. The Pew Center reported that black Protestants were the most likely of the religious groups to believe global warming is occurring (85 percent). Accessed January 15, 2012, www.pewresearch.org/pubs/1194/global-warming-belief-by-religion.

15. There is not, however, widespread acceptance among more conservative black Protestants. Well-known Bishop Harry Jackson, founder of the International Communion of Evangelical Churches, went with Richard Cizik and other evangelicals and scientists on a trip to Alaska to see the evidence of global warming, featured in Bill Moyers's series "God Is Green." This did not "convert" him, however, to the perspective of creation-care evangelicals. Jackson is featured in Cornwall's "Resisting the Green Dragon."

16. In 2006, the Pew Hispanic Center estimated that only fifteen percent of U.S. Hispanics consider themselves evangelical. Accessed December 12, 2012, www.pewhispanic.org/2007/04/25/changing-faiths-latinos-and-the-transformation-of-american-religion/.

17. It is hard to discern the NHCLC stance. Samuel Rodriguez is a climate skeptic and, along with Harry Jackson, represents the American Power Alliance, an industry-affiliated group. This group opposes mercury pollution regulation, but Rodriguez also signed the EEN's "Evangelical Call to Stop Mercury Poisoning of the Unborn," which called for regulation. The description of progressive Latino/a evangelicals by Gabriel Salguero of the NLEC shows the complexity: "We think that poverty, economic inequality, and the environment are just as important moral issues as abortion, stem cell research, and same-sex marriage." Accessed October 13, 2012, www.blog.beliefnet.com/godspolitics/2007/04/rev-gabriel-salguero-my-living-paradox.html.

18. While there is clear evidence of environmental concern among Asian Americans, it is harder to document Asian American evangelical concerns. See Ngoc Nguyen, "Asian Americans Strong Environmentalists, Poll Finds," reprinted in the *National Catholic Reporter* 45:16 (May 29, 2009), accessed July 16, 2013, http://www.ncronline.org/news/asian-americans-strong-environmentalists-p oll-findsncronline.org/news/asian-americans-strong-environmentalists-p oll-finds.

19. Lisa Sharon Harper and D. C. Innes's *Left, Right & Christ* (Boise, ID: Russell Media, 2011) represents this next generation of evangelicals and includes a chapter on the environment. Lisa describes herself as of Puerto Rican, African, and Native American descent.

20. www.christianpost.com/news/envision-08-charts-future-of-faith-in-politics-32817/, accessed January 15, 2013.

21. For example, David Gushee, *The Future of Faith in American Politics: The Public Witness of the Evangelical Center* (Waco, TX: Baylor University Press, 2008). See also Rod Dreher, *The New Conservative Counter Culture and Its Return to Roots* (New York: Three Rivers Press, 2006); and Buster Smith and Byron Johnson, "The Liberalization of Young Evangelicals: A Research Note," *Journal for the Scientific Study of Religion* 49 (2010): 351–60.

22. Loren Wilkinson, ed., *Earthkeeping* (Grand Rapids, MI: Wm. B. Eerdman, 1980). Wilkinson wrote the initial draft of the EEN Declaration.

23. "Evangelical Declaration of Creation Care," in *The Care of Creation: Focusing Concern and Action*, ed. R. J. "Sam" Berry (Downers Grove, IL: InterVarsity Press, 2000). Quotes are from www.creationcare.org/blank.php?id=39, accessed December 19, 2012.

24. In addition to EEN, it includes the Eco-Justice Program of the National Council of Churches of Christ (NCC), which represents mainline and liberal Protestants, Orthodox, historic African American and Living Peace churches; the Environmental Justice Program of the United States Catholic Conference of Bishops (USCCB); and the Coalition on the Environment and Jewish Life (COEJL).

25. The NAE released a 2011 report "Loving the Least of These: Addressing a Changing Environment," accessed January 15, 2013, www.nae.net/lovingtheleastofthese.

26. "Evangelical Declaration."

27. Calvin B. DeWitt, "The Place of Creation in Today's Missionary Discourse: Evangelical Environmentalism in America," 174-204 in *Missiology and the Environment*, ed. Lukas Vischer (Geneva: John Knox Centre, 2007).

28. http://christiansandclimate.org/statement/, accessed July 17, 2013.

29. "The Cornwall Declaration on Environmental Stewardship" xi-xv in *Environmental Stewardship in the Judeo-Christian Tradition*, ed. Michael Barkey (Grand Rapids, MI: Acton Institute, 2007). Quotes are from: www.cornwallalliance. org/articles/read/the-cornwall-declaration-on-environmental-stewardship/, accessed December 19, 2012. The website claims over 1500 signatures, but these include a wide range of people, and anyone can sign via a link on the webpage. This is not true of the EEN Declaration or ECI Climate Change Call to Action statements.

30. Daniel Bailey and Jonathan Borwein, "Is Believing in Climate Change 'an Insult to God'?" *Huffington Post*, December 7, 2012, accessed December 14, 2012, www.huffingtonpost.com/david-h-bailey/climate-change-religion_b_2254016. html.

31. Regarding their 2006 demand that Cizik resign, Interim NAE President Leith Anderson commented, somewhat ironically, that the NAE would listen to its constituency on the subject, highlighting the fact that the majority of the signers were not members of the NAE. Anderson later gave into the pressure and fired Cizik over remarks he made on the NPR radio program *Fresh Air*. See Cizik's own narrative of these events at "My Journey Towards the 'New Evangelicalism,'" Religion and Politics Blog, September 2012, accessed December 15, 2012, www.religionandpolitics.org/2012/09/13/ my-journey-toward-the-new-evangelicalism/.

32. Michael Nisbet, "Communicating Climate Change: Why Frames Matter for Public Engagement," in *Environment* (March–April, 2009), accessed December 19, 2012, www.environmentmagazine.org/Archives/Back%20Issues/March-April%202009/Nisbet-full.html.

33. David Snow and Robert Benford, "Clarifying the Relationship between Framing and Ideology," *Mobilization* 5 (2008): 55–60.

34. Care of Creation Declaration.

35. Cornwall Declaration.

36. On July 10, 2013, 200 evangelical scientists sent a letter to Congress pleading for action on climate change.

37. Katharine Hayhoe and Andrew Farley, *A Climate for Change* (New York: Faith Words, 2009).

38. www.christiansandclimate.org/statement accessed July 17, 2013.

39. A study by Dominique Brossard and Dietram A. Scheufele ("Science, Media and the Public," in *Science* 339 (January 4, 2013): 40-41) provides further clues, as they report on the influence of search engines in reinforcing what a user has already indicated they are interested in. With the majority of people now getting their science information from blogs and non-traditional sources, this influences what kind of information they get.

40. Nisbet, "Communicating Climate Change."

41. Organized by the Oregon Institute of Science and Medicine in opposition to the Kyoto Treaty. Now just called the "Global Warming Petition Project," accessed December 13, 2012, www.petitionproject.org/index.php.

42. A similar project by the Heartland Institute: accessed December 13, 2012, www.heartland.org/press-releases/2008/03/04/new-york-global -warming-conference-considers-manhattan-declaration. The Heartland Institute is a major climate denial group, funded by oil interests (www. independent.co.uk/environment/climate-change/tobacco-and-oil- pay-for-climate-conference-790474.html). They gained notoriety for run- ning billboards that compared climate scientists to the Unabomber Ted Kaczynski.

43. NAE, ibid.

44. In its 1999–2001 version, signatories included Dr. B. J. Honeycutt and Benjamin Franklin Pierce, otherwise known as Hawkeye, from the TV show *M.A.S.H.*, indicating how loose the guidelines were for signing.

45. See Laurel Kearns, "Cooking the Truth: Faith, Science, the Market, and Global Warming," 108–116, in *EcoSpirit: Religions and Philosophies for the Earth*, ed. Laurel Kearns and Catherine Keller (New York: Fordham Press, 2007), for a longer discussion of this.

46. NAE, "Loving the Least of These."

47. Cornwall Declaration and "An Evangelical Declaration on Global Warming," accessed July 16, 2013, www.cornwallalliance.org/articles/read/ an-evangelical-declaration-on-global-warming,.

48. ECI, Call to Action, accessed July 17, 2013, www.christiansandclimate.org/ statement.

49. Nisbet, ibid. For an example of this at work, Accessed April 24, 2012 www. we-get-it.org.

50. www.we-get-it.org/information/, accessed April 24, 2012.

51. www.cornwallalliance.org/articles/read/an-evangelical- declaration-on-global-warming,/ accessed January 15, 2013.

52. www.resistingthegreendragon.com, accessed December 13, 2012. There is a book by the same name, see James Walniss, *Resisting the Green Dragon: Dominion, Not Death* (Burke, VA: The Cornwall Alliance, 2011).

53. Joshua Yates and James Hunter, "Fundamentalism: When History Goes Awry" in *Stories of Change: Narratives and Social Movements*, ed. Joseph E. Davis (Albany, NY: State University of New York Press, 2002), 126.

54. ibid, 128.

55. Nisbet, "Communicating Climate Change."

56. Lee Feng, "The Oily Operators behind the Religious Climate Change Denial Front Group, Cornwall Alliance," June 15, 2010, *Think Progress*, accessed December 19, 2012, www:thinkprogress.org/green/2010/06/15/174718/cornwall-alliance-frontgroup/.

57. "A Southern Baptist Declaration on the Environment and Climate Change," accessed January 15, 2012, www.baptistcreationcare.org/node/1.

58. www.flourishonline.org/get-involved/, accessed March 25 2011.

59. Hunter was attacked in the campaign against evangelical social engagement and forced to resign as newly appointed president of the Christian Coalition because his expanded focus on poverty, justice, and environmental concern might alienate a base mobilized around abortion and homosexuality.

60. www.energystar.gov/index.cfm?c=small_business.sb_congregations, accessed March 20, 2011.

61. www.energystar.gov/index.cfm?c=sb_success.congregations_winners, accessed December 19, 2012.

62. www.energystar.gov/index.cfm?c=sb_success.congregations2010_first_baptist_orlando, accessed December 19, 2012.

63. The Pew studies cited above report that about one-third of white evangelicals believe global warming is human induced. Without this human-induced qualification, the numbers are higher. For a sophisticated recent assessment, see Nicholas Smith and Anthony Leiserowitz, "American Evangelicals and Global Warming," Global Environmental Change 2013. http://dx.doi.org/10.1016/j.gloenvcha.2013.04.001. In my survey of the polls, it is clear that the results depend in part on question wording. For instance, the survey results reported in Chapter 6 are based on a question that measures environmental attitudes on the basis of willingness to incur costs. One could be environmentally concerned, but not in favor of regulations that incur costs, which is the Cornwall Alliance position.

64. Lindsay, *Faith in the Halls of Power (already cited)*. Katharine Wilkinson, *Between God & Green: How Evangelicals Are Cultivating a Middle Ground on Climate Change* (New York: Oxford University Press, 2012).

8

The Rise of the Diversity Expert

HOW AMERICAN EVANGELICALS SIMULTANEOUSLY ACCENTUATE AND IGNORE RACE

Gerardo Marti and Michael O. Emerson

AMERICAN EVANGELICALS CARE about "race." More white evangelicals are moving into nonwhite urban contexts to serve local populations; many evangelical denominations, parachurch organizations, and church leaders have "repented" of past racial discrimination; evangelicals of color are increasingly likely to be in formerly all-white congregations; and a growing number of evangelical congregations have adopted proactive intentions to racially diversify their churches. Yet, despite anecdotes and stories lauding such race-conscious activities, all of these initiatives taken together still fall short in making significant headway in resolving the tensions and stigmas among racial groups in America. Even those initiatives that appear most progressive, most inspiring, and most commendable may actually be hurting progress in race relations because of the specifically racialized orientations brought to such schemes.

We are witnessing the rise of evangelical "diversity experts," individuals who claim a specialized expertise in solving the problem of racial segregation in American churches. In our observation, we find that these passionate advocates for racial reconciliation orient themselves around the notion of bringing different racial groups together and achieving a common religious belonging as members of a shared congregation. Evangelicals believe in the divine power of the local church, so the focus of their social engagement for achieving racial reconciliation is most often on changing the demographic profile of their local congregations. A 2010 national survey of evangelical Protestant congregations indicates that 69 percent of evangelical churches agree or strongly agree that their congregation "wants to be racially and ethnically diverse."[1] Such overwhelming sentiment for diversity, of course, is not matched by its reality; only 13.7 percent of Protestant churches have any significant degree of diversity.[2] Although the proportion of diverse congregations is small, their influence is quite large. Leaders and members of diverse congregations are entreated for their expertise on the problem of race and its solution. Many are urged to lead how-to workshops and seminars; others write books published by Christian publishers. Even when a successfully diverse congregation lacks a strong, self-conscious agenda for resolving "the problem of race," leaders and attenders of diverse congregations end up speaking out on these issues, are pressed for experiences and formulas, and in the process express great hope in the possibility of congregational communities becoming the strategic spiritual lever for healing racial relations. Some even take on the role of diversity expert as a full-time job.

Being a member of a multiracial congregation provides a powerful platform for the performance of progressive race relations. And expertise on achieving diversity is inevitably based on the few demographically diverse congregations that currently exist. Yet, are diverse congregations on the path to "solving" the problem of race? Is the optimism of diversity experts warranted? More important, does the expert discourse emerging from racially integrated congregations provide evidence of the successful navigation of American race relations? The purpose of this chapter is to assess these central questions. To do so, we must first understand why evangelicals increasingly care about congregational diversity.

Sources of the Imperative for Integration

As detailed in the work of Michael Emerson and Christian Smith and discussed in other books such as those written by Lisa Sharon Harper, Peter Heltzel, Charles Marsh, and Soong-Chan Rah, several steps occurred between societal changes of the 1960s and the growing imperative of congregational diversification in the twenty-first century.[3] The Civil Rights movement—especially with its successes in the 1960s—ushered in substantial shifts in the legal structure of racial hierarchy. It also brought perhaps the nation's most concentrated and extended focus on racial issues and the need for reform. Its leaders became internationally known, and they remain forces in contemporary U.S. society. And since sincerely devoted Christians and poetically eloquent clergy were at the center of the movement, the modern church was infused with inspiring religious language on the evils of segregation, the love of neighbor, and the equality of races before God.

The Civil Rights movement indirectly helped bring about another important change—the 1965 Hart-Cellar Act, a law that would come to fundamentally transform the racial and ethnic composition of the United States. This new law replaced the Immigration Act of 1924, which both gave strong prefer-ence to northern and western Europeans and excluded Asians and Africans. The Hart-Cellar Act simply allocated equal numbers of visas per country out-side the Western Hemisphere. Combined with other global factors encour-aging people of developing nations to emigrate, the 1965 immigration act rapidly increased the nonwhite populations of the United States. In 1960, nearly 90 percent of the U.S. population was non-Hispanic white, and most of the remaining population was African American. By the 2010 census, the non-Hispanic white population was reduced to less than two-thirds, while Asian and Hispanic population proportions had more than quadrupled. And even these figures understate the growth of diversity. The nation's metropoli-tan areas are substantially more diverse than the nation as a whole, and many currently have minority Anglo populations. The change in immigration law is now being felt full force as the nation is no longer overwhelmingly just black and white. It has become substantially more diverse, with peoples from every-where in the world.

In short, the Civil Rights movement and the overhaul of immigration law are the two major streams serving as the sources for the imperative for racially and ethnically diverse congregations sweeping evangelicalism in con-temporary times. Out of the Civil Rights movement came a flow of Christians dedicated to what these proponents called racial reconciliation. These racial reconciliation advocates shared some common characteristics. They were African American, they were well versed in the racialized nature of the United States, they were willing to be called evangelical or to associate with white evangelicals, they were influenced by Martin Luther King Jr., and they were sold on the idea that reconciliation was at the very core of Christian gospel. These early leaders developed four major steps to racial reconciliation: (1) pri-mary relationships across race must be developed; (2) social structures of inequality must be recognized and, using new primary relationships, must be resisted together by Christians of all backgrounds; (3) accordingly, whites must repent of the personal, historical, and social sins; and (4) blacks and other Christians of color must forgive, individually and corporately.[4]

The early advocates of racial reconciliation worked tirelessly to bring this message of racial reconciliation to the white evangelical church. Through sev-eral decades and much struggle, a movement grew, impacting many black and white leaders. When Michael Emerson and Christian Smith assessed the racial reconciliation leaders of the 1990s, fully half were nonblack, a dramatic change from the roots of the movement in the 1960s.[5] What is more, the mas-sive evangelical men's movement of the 1990s—Promise Keepers—adopted racial reconciliation as one of its seven core principles. Doing so further served to bring awareness to the imperative of addressing racial division. But it was not entirely clear how to address racial division, at least as whites understood the issue. And the astounding growth of both Hispanic and Asian populations in the United States resulting from the Hart-Cellar Act further complicated the imperative—and sometimes the motive—for diversity.

Beginning about the year 2000, the message of the growing ethnic diversity and of racial reconciliation began to both become couched in and be expanded to mean—via theological and sociological arguments—a need to worship within diverse congregations. Indeed, as a 2003 book declared, "Christian congregations, when possible, should be multiracial."[6] A flow of important books were published on multiethnic congregations.[7] Internet sites sprang up focusing on helping practitioners create and sustain multicultural congregations; blogs, Facebook pages, and tweets on multiethnic ministry were made, and regional and national conferences were held. Enough change occurred that from 1998 to 2007 the percentage of evangelical congregations of 1,000 or more members that were racially diverse (at least 20 percent of the congregants not of the church's dominate racial group) quadrupled (from 6 percent to 25 percent).[8] During this time, several parachurch organizations (InterVarsity Christian Fellowship, The Leadership Network), denominational bodies (Southern Baptists, Christian Reformed Church, Evangelical Covenant, Evangelical Free Church), and various congregational networks (Mosaic Alliance, Mosaix Global Network) explicitly committed themselves to the imperative of diversity, further encouraging pastors and congregations to actualize successful integration. Popular culture took notice. In 2010, *Time* magazine's cover headline read, "How Megachurches Are Helping Bridge America's Racial Divide," focused on the growth of racially diverse large evangelical congregations.[9] In but a short generation, evangelicals have gone from hardly thinking about race (except to argue that church growth is fastest when congregations are homogeneous) to seemingly the majority desiring to grow in congregational diversity.

Folk Theories of Successful Diversification

The growth of diverse churches and the greater acceptance of the value of integrated congregations triggered expansive discussions about how diversity happens. This chapter therefore does not discuss how racial diversity occurs, nor does it isolate the mechanisms that allow for racial integration within congregations.[10] Instead, this chapter focuses on the rhetoric and practices intended to affect racial integration found among members of successfully diverse evangelical congregations. Those who are involved in diverse congregations are not themselves necessarily aware of the mechanisms that actually contribute to the diversification of their churches. Beliefs regarding diversification are not tested; indeed, our observation suggests leaders and members of diverse congregations are not motivated to test their speculative folk theories of diversification; after all, the ongoing existence of diversity in their own congregations provides continual reinforcement that their theories are true. Evidence of support for their beliefs is manifest every week. Their ideas remain unexamined, and scholars (like us) appear obtuse and unnecessarily complicated.

In examining the rhetoric and practices of evangelical diversity experts, our research confirms a recurring dynamic of social life: institutions such as racially diverse congregations can perpetuate themselves without understanding themselves. They are not necessarily sustained by the conscious intentions of their members. At the same time, we acknowledge that ideas and notions are important. By adopting a perspective on the explanation of social structures that allows a nuanced relationship between agency and structure, we assert that the racialized beliefs of participants in evangelical multiracial churches do not explain their churches but that their racialized beliefs are part of the ongoing structure of their congregations.[11] For participants in a successfully multiracial church, the ability to point to successful diversity becomes a symbolic leverage point among other evangelical churches. Phrased more strongly, we find that the *badge of diversity* is a form of *status* that conveys prestige and influence. However, in promoting their views, successful churches tout explanations for diversity that are themselves racialized, often perpetuating stereotypes and stigmas that reinforce rather than eliminate racial hierarchies.[12]

Evangelical discourse involves a complex of assumptions regarding agency and structure that underlie their religiosity. Evangelicals see change as personal and individual; conversion and repentance are generic tools for transformation that are believed to be able to conquer all forms of social ills. The local church is the site in which personal transformation occurs. It would be difficult to overstate this miracle motif: Social change comes from individual conversion, prompted by the ministry of the church, one heart at a time. According to Michael Emerson and Christian Smith's book *Divided by Faith*, American evangelicals are severely curtailed in their ability to address the issues of race relations due to such ideological constraints. Evangelicals emphasize *relationalism*, an emphasis on people from different backgrounds and lifestyles learning to get along as believers. Rodney King, whose police beating became the stimulus for the Los Angeles riots in 1992, famously said, "Can't we all just get along?" Evangelicals ask the same question and base their answers on the assertion that commonality of religious commitment provides the basis for creating community.

Here is it useful to note that in contrast to other theological schemas, the theological framework of white evangelicalism does not include an orientation for race.[13] Historically, this is because evangelicalism abstracted an anthropology of human beings that universalized both their sinful condition and their potential sanctification. The trinitarian God is a single deity with relationships to a singularly fallen humanity who are all descended from common ancestors—Adam and Eve (Romans 5:17). While the appropriation of salvation must be individualized, the radical individualization of repentance and conversion reduces systematic differences based on ethnic or racial groups.[14] The gospel within evangelicalism can be summarized as the bringing together of individuals reconciled to God who become a united body of believers known as the church. New Testament writings reinforce the formation and building of the church through the removal of ethnic differences in a resolution of ethnic conflict (Acts 7, 15) and through positive statements of common solidarity in Christ (Roman 12:5; Galatians 3:28; Colossians 3:11).

Given this individualized reconciliation and joining together, we can understand and anticipate that the language given to race relations from evangelical theology will emphasize that individuals should be joined together regardless of their ancestral background, that believers should approach fellow believers with a love of God that expresses spiritual kinship (brothers and sisters in Christ), and that Christians should approach strangers with a welcoming kindness and hospitality that opens the door to deeper interactions.

However, the pervasive focus on individualism, free will, and personal relationships renders racial injustices invisible and thereby perpetuates racial inequality. Despite such lack of conceptual language for addressing issues of race, some evangelical churches do successfully diversify. Insufficient resources for coping with macrolevel issues of race may be hindering the integration of congregations, yet many evangelicals have the satisfaction of seeing diversity happen while seemingly governed by an evangelical ideological framework. We believe what is most interesting is that *the same evangelical framework criticized by scholars for its inability to address race relations is the same framework used by diversity experts to describe their successes.* That is, successfully diverse evangelical congregations access their individualist and personalist theological language to explain their successes. Using theological language and religious imperatives, members of these congregations impose a value-laden sociology of interracial relationships.

Racial differences are not addressed directly in the New Testament, and the history of cross-racial encounters in recent memory is governed more by narratives of missionary encounters than by the diversity of schools and neighborhoods. Because evangelicalism does not contain within it the substance of what differences may need to be reconciled, evangelicals rely on their own socialization and cultural framing inherited from beyond their congregations for navigating differences with others. Their understandings of race draw on framings of race available in the culture. And this means that various stereotypes and stigmas will be adopted unless explicitly challenged.

(Non) Talking about Race: Evangelicals Both Accentuate and Ignore Race

What is the nature of the expertise evident among churches seeking to address issues of race through diversification? Through our observations of multiracial churches, we find intriguing ironies in their rhetoric and practices. Using the platform of successfully diverse congregations and guided by presumptions about how such congregations operate, we find that American evangelicals simultaneously (1) *accentuate* race yet (2) seek to wholly *ignore* race.

Notions of Racial Complementarity

The successful integration of racial groups in diverse churches is viewed as affirming the best aspects of the Christian faith. Rather than accentuating the challenges of integrating various cultural expectations and subgroup practices, the discourse of leaders and members of multiracial congregations tends to accentuate the positive things brought into Christian fellowship from different racial and ethnic groups. While acknowledging racial or ethnic differences, such differences are often seen as working together for a valued result. Even when ethnic tensions arise, they are spoken of in religious terms that affirm valued aspects of the Christian faith, like "mutual sacrifice," "learning to love one another," or "preferring others more than ourselves." Kathleen Garces-Foley's *Crossing the Ethnic Divide* especially points out the framework of Evergreen in Los Angeles as oriented around a "theology of discomfort."[15] Being willing to be uncomfortable for the faith is viewed as mirroring the loving sacrifice of Jesus himself. However, such differences are stressed as ultimately being mutually beneficial.

The most compelling set of conversations in multiracial churches regarding race relations stress the importance of racial groups complementing each other. While such language is newly discovered in these congregations, what is surprising is the continuity in the expressions of racial complementarity found throughout American religious history. Notions of racial complementarity consistently push the idea that racial groups are different, yet each group offers strengths that are not only useful but also spiritually needed by other groups. Congregations are made stronger through racial and ethnic groups complementing one another in community. Such talk consistently posits an understanding of clearly delineated racial or ethnic groups and racial differences or ethnic differences (sometimes coded as "culture" and "cultural differences") as necessary for the cultivation of diverse congregations. Notions of beneficial complementarity are especially prominent in the discourse surrounding music and worship.

Devout Christians share a conviction of the transformational force of worship and believe it to be a powerful force for accomplishing racial unity. One popular book, *The Heart of Racial Justice*, states that by being in the presence of "the God of all creation—the One who made all ethnic groups, tribes and nations and who pours out his presence wherever people are gathered together in his name—all the boundaries and distinctions that keep up separated from each other are worn down, and authentic community and reconciliation result."[16] Leaders of multiracial churches often express this belief, saying the experience of diversity worship "helps to strengthen our belief and faith in the Lord." Even more, "When you get to be around other people you get to see how they worship the Lord and that will build you up." Despite such conviction, church leaders quickly find that the ideal of worship that produces racial unity in their all-too-earthly ministries is difficult to put into practice. Spiritual unity is threatened by what Carol Doran and Thomas H. Troeger label "liturgical homelands," the supposed differences groups have toward musical genre and style.[17] Interviews with members of diverse churches show that they tend to associate rap and hip-hop with blacks, techno and trance with Asians, pop and alternative with whites, and Tejano music, salsa, and merengue with Hispanics.[18] Church leaders call on and enact these stereotypes and try implementing different kinds of music into worship. The advice to stylistically change and cater to such differences is central to some of the most prominent advice books published, including George Yancey's *One Body, One Spirit* and Pedrito Maynard-Reid's *Diverse Worship*.[19] Similarly, the recently organized International Council of Ethnodoxologists insists that every "cultural group" uses "its unique and diverse artistic expressions" to worship the God in different ways.[20] Stylistic changes happen from song to song in church services because different forms of music are assumed to resonate with different ethnic and racial groups.

Despite such complications, members of multiracial churches believe that the promotion of particular forms of music in church provides a strategic point of intervention for performing racial complementarity. For example, African Americans in multiracial churches are often called upon to perform "black music," forms of soul, funk, or gospel, as an attempt to broaden the cultural diversity of the congregation. Gerardo Martí's *Worship across the Racial Divide* demonstrates how blacks in America are universally held to be superior worshipers.[21] The word *soul* or *soulful* is consistently used as a euphemism for *black* or *African American*. Blacks are believed to have a deep capacity for intimate connection to the spirit of God, and their music is valued as a counterpoint for the solid Bible teaching and administrative organization of formerly white or Asian congregations. In short, blacks are valuable symbolic commodities within evangelical congregations, and their value is couched in a framework of what they uniquely contribute to the public ministry of the congregation.

The construction of black superiority in worship as complementing whites in worship has a long and tangled history. In *The Burden of Black Religion*, historian Curtis Evans documents religious notions that attached to African Americans, specifically how blacks and whites were considered to be religiously distinct.[22] Scholars and church leaders of the mid-nineteenth and early-twentieth centuries made a clear distinction and separation between the "religion" of blacks and whites, supported by strenuous arguments and vigorous research efforts. Racialized religious stigmas attached to African Americans in the nineteenth century were far from complimentary. Blacks were characterized by emotionalism, and whites were known for intellectualism. In 1903, Kelly Miller, dean of Howard University, characterized blacks as possessing a "deeply religious nature" and having "emotional and spiritual susceptibilities." Miller continued with notions of racial complementarity by asserting that blacks and whites each possessed virtues that the others lacked. From whites, blacks could gain a higher standard of "concrete morality" that would enable them to have more "rational modes" of worship and "orderly habits of life." From blacks, whites could learn meekness, humility, and forgiveness. These assertions were not original; rather, Miller expressed popular beliefs at the time and accentuated them in an attempt to give African Americans a viable role in American religious life.

While the language of racial complementarity is newly discovered in these congregations, what is surprising is the continuity in the expressions of racial complementarity found throughout American religious history. Racially essentialist ideas of black religiosity are rooted in nineteenth-century race theory and emphasize all sorts of traits and temperaments inherited biologically along racial lines.[23] While differences were considered to be balanced such that these two races could complement each other, the naive opposition between black and white religious sensibilities had dangerous implications. In 1910, Howard Odum claimed that the "function of the negro church is to give expression and satisfaction to religious emotions," not "to direct moral conduct."[24] Odum was among many who were deeply critical of black religion. For Odum and others, religion for blacks was primarily "pleasurable excitement" and failed to properly restrain the primitive emotionalism among blacks. Emotions ran amok while proper conduct was left unchecked. As Odum described it, "Black religion lacks practical application or moral content" and possessed a "scarcity of thoughtfulness and will-power." Their religion did not elevate their moral standing but rather debased it. It was not until the 1920s that black emotionalism and spontaneity were seen as authentic expressions of primal human urges and a necessary corrective to white urban culture. In a 1925 essay, Albert Barnes transformed belief in blacks' fundamental emotionalism from a threat to civilization to its antidote by virtue of the black race's large emotional endowment, sensitivity to nature, excellent oratory, sublime music, childlike spontaneity, infinite patience, fine humor, and what Barnes labeled a "peculiar depth of religious life."[25] For Barnes and others, worship manifests the "essence of the Negro soul." Scholars and church leaders soon became so impressed with the quality of African American worship that they believed whites could not "compete with the Negro in spiritual endowment."[26] Between emancipation and the Depression, the perception of African Americans shifted from being an "uncivilized" people who could not fit into mainstream American society to African Americans becoming highly regarded for the quality of their worship in American culture.[27] The emotionality of black religion would be absorbed into conceptions of gospel music.

In the mid-twentieth century, gospel music became known as the African American style of worship and portrayed as the epitome of true spiritual worship. A white worship director was among many leaders who created special occasions for the performance of black gospel in his church. He said, "We brought in this African American guy, and we did this old gospel song—I mean, he took us to church, you know, just how you would expect." A white member in another church said, "They are not afraid to show their praise or afraid to say 'Amen' or 'Praise God' or a 'Yes, Lord' or raise their hands or say 'Alleluia,' it just comes naturally." Another white church member simply concluded, "Black people are very spiritual. They are more spiritual than we are." Yet another white member of a diverse church said, "You have to accept a man [referring to blacks] and assume part of their worship outdoes ours and it's mainly in the music."

The emotional and racially complementary notions of African American gospel music pervade the conversation among evangelicals and their attempt to enact a positive and affirming form of race relations today. Black worship in this framework is as much distinct as it is necessary. One must be black to sing gospel—this is a fundamental belief even for nonblack church musicians who enjoy singing gospel or actively participate in a gospel choir. A white female church attender in another church said, "If you are going to have the gospelish style, if you are not black, you don't feel that you can pull it off." The racialized musical contribution of African Americans, especially in the use of gospel choirs, is now absorbed into initiatives directed toward accomplishing congregational diversity.[28] Asked if their church was doing anything in the service to attract African Americans, one worship director said, "Musically, yeah. By incorporating a little more gospel songs." Many churches have a gospel or inspiration choir because they consistently offer church leaders the opportunity to consciously promote the visible diversity of the congregation. In one pan-Asian congregation, the creation of a gospel choir ministry came from a deep sense that diversity must be created intentionally. The worship director said, "It's intentional. You have to be intentional about it. As awkward as it is and as weird as it is." Incorporating black gospel music into the service in this church and others is a strategy to create a liturgy that boldly proclaims, "We welcome blacks here."

The application of assumed expertise in promoting African Americans to be conspicuously diverse in music and worship is one example of how race is continually accentuated among diversity expert evangelicals in their project of racial integration. Overall, the use of gospel choirs and Spanish coritos, among other elements, consistently introduces the strengths of different racial and ethnic groups, who in turn benefit from the programs and teaching already found in white-dominant congregations committed to diversity. However, the accentuation of race found in these successfully diverse churches reinforces old stereotypes and achieves an ironic positive stigma that reinforces racial hierarchies.

Let's Just Not Talk about It

Another common aspect of expertise in the discussion of multiracial congregations—congregations that demographically bring diverse peoples together—is to downplay or completely ignore racial realities. Limited by their biblical understanding and cultural tools, many multiracial congregations (which most often are formerly white congregations still dominated by whites, though not always) simply avoid racial issues altogether, apart from thinking about music in racially essentializing terms. Since leaders of such congregations perceive the overriding goal to be demographically mixed and to promote unity—importantly defined as the absence of conflict—race as a reality impacting human beings' lives is completely ignored. Leaders preach and teach while avoiding racial talk, and not talking about race is a standard form of discourse among evangelicals publicly proclaiming strategies for diversification.

For example, Edward Lee in his study of multiracial congregations sought to understand what motivated church leaders to have multiracial congregations.[29] Pastor Lee, a Chinese American, leads a multiracial congregation with the direct purpose of racial reconciliation. He thought this would be the dominant reason other congregations were multiracial. He was wrong. He found this to be the minority perspective. More common were appeals to "world missions" or "reaching the neighborhood for Christ."

Typically, Lee found, pastors thought issues of racial inequality and reconciliation were not the purview of their multiracial church ministry. The pastoral role, instead, was cast as expanding the kingdom for Christ and creating unity by having people of different backgrounds worship together. In other words, many leaders of multiracial congregations simply cast their vision in the classic evangelical lingo of cross-cultural mission and, as a consequence, avoid direct (often difficult) discussion about racial inequality. Racial inequality was not addressed; even the notion of race seldom entered the conversation. Instead, a seemingly grander vision of world evangelization subverts what may be seen as more parochial, domestic issues to promote what is seen as a more noble goal of outreach across international borders.

So even in multiracial congregations—especially but not exclusively those led by white pastors—the present-day realities of race, addressing issues of racial inequities, or even talking about possible racial conflicts that might arise in the church were off limits, deemed unimportant to the true work of the church or too potentially explosive.

Our own research reveals this happens even in multiracial congregations founded and led by pastors of color. As one African American pastor of a multiracial congregation, who founded the church with the vision of being multiracial and who requested anonymity, told us, "Racial inequality is real, deep, and impacts our lives daily. But I cannot talk directly about it in my congregation, or we run the risk of blowing up this church." He continued: "Whites especially will get upset, some will leave without even saying goodbye. So I try to address racial divisions not by talking about them, but by creating a common life together. My hope is that over time we are indirectly addressing racial inequities."

Even Pastor Lee, whose entire reason for starting his multiracial congregation was for racial reconciliation, sees the difficulties in doing so. He runs monthly film sessions in which congregational members watch films addressing racial issues, and then he holds focused discussions on the meaning of the films for racial realities. He also preaches on the topic, runs Bible studies on the topics, holds seminars, and attempts to have the congregation focus on directly addressing racial inequalities through their community involvement and even political activities. But he says his direct focus has come at much cost. "I have many a person tell me that we talk too much about race in this church, and that I should focus on the gospel, not worldly issues. Too often they tell me this when they come to tell me they are leaving the church." He then adds, with bewilderment, "What I don't understand is that I do not hide what this church is about. They know from their first day here, but it still costs us. We stay small, and find it difficult to grow. Even the Chinese members tell me I should stop talking about race, because it upsets our white members, and because they are uncomfortable talking directly about such issues."

Beyond individual congregations, an analysis of the main organizations and websites advocating for church diversity reveals another common way of avoiding race talk: using the word *ethnicity* instead. In most evangelical-led parachurch organizations and networks, what they are advocating is diversifying ethnically, not racially. For example, the Mosaix Global Network says it is a "relational network of leaders in pursuit of a multi-ethnic church for the sake of the gospel"[30] The ReNew Partnerships organization, a trailblazer in helping leaders diversify their congregations, says its purpose is "to empower Christians to build and sustain multi-ethnic churches and organizations that can transform their communities and the world with the love of Christ."[31] Most multiracial congregations also use the word *ethnicity* or *culture* instead of *race*, as revealed in their mission statements. The mission of River City Community Church in Chicago is "to become a multi-ethnic community of Jesus-followers." The mission of Bridgeway Community Church in Maryland is "to be a multicultural army of fully-devoted followers of Christ." The mission of the Evergreen Baptist network of the western United States is "being a culturally diverse people who are one in Christ." The mission of one of the fastest growing congregations in the United States, Transformation Church in the Charlotte, North Carolina, area, is "to be a multi-ethnic, multi-generational, mission-shaped community that loves."

Although the concept of race has existed for several hundred years, the concept of ethnicity did not come into common usage in the American lexicon until the 1940s.[32] And in the way the terms have been used, there is a reason that ethnicity came into more popular parlance. Although both concepts appeal to origins, race is a social construction typically referring to physiological differences, whereas ethnicity is a social construction typically referring to cultural differences. Race has meant stratification and inequality; it is always hierarchical and reflects power differentials. Ethnicity is seen as more flexible and about celebrating culture; it is concerned with differences in human cultures rather than how people groups are ranked. In the study of these concepts, scholars of race focus on power differentials and racial inequality. Scholars who study ethnicity, however, focus on assimilation and mobility of groups.[33]

We suspect the conceptual distinction between *race* and *ethnicity* is the very reason evangelicals use terms such as *ethnicity* and *culture* and avoid *race*. They are neither talking about nor concerned with group inequality, stratification, or power differentials; instead, they are focused on bringing together all people to faith, regardless of their backgrounds. Using ethnicity and culture signifies their interest in all people, and avoiding talk about race smooths the path toward their goals

The end result of avoiding the hard conversations about race and racial inequality is that whatever simplified stereotypes people have of other groups when they enter often survive. Unless they get to know people of other racial groups in a deep, close way, they can hold on to gross oversimplifications, even while attending a multiracial congregation. In addition, the avoidance of discussing race in favor of focusing on culture effectively minimizes entrenched institutional inequalities in favor of focusing on conversation-friendly topics such as types of food, styles of dress, or interesting places to travel. Members of churches are allowed to find a base for being cosmopolitan in their exposure to other countries, and exoticism effectively idealizes and distances the stark realities of racial injustices. Thus, as Korie Edwards hypothesizes, even multiracial congregations can be sites for buttressing racial inequality.[34]

Diversity Experts and Valid Solutions to the Problem of Race

Advice that accentuates race yet ignores racial dynamics is found not only in discussion with members of congregations but also in the materials they write, teach, and access. The rise of seminars, conferences, and books on multiracial ministries geared toward church leaders since the early 2000s involves an ambitious attempt to build a comprehensive expert system on racial and ethnic diversity. Beliefs about when to accentuate versus when to ignore race are built into this growing expert system of racial diversity within American evangelicalism. The skillful application of expertise is supposed to allow churches to socially engineer racial relations through their worship services. In short, diversity experts seek to build a repository of technical knowledge that leaders can use in a wide range of actual contexts. Congregational leaders are expected to understand such issues regardless of specific context and to be able to achieve significant diversity even in spite of context.[35]

The assumed decontextualization of processes of diversity is inherent to being an expert. Indeed, we found pastors and worship leaders in our research who were hired away from other church ministries (sometimes moving between vast geographic distances and clashing denominational backgrounds) with the assumption that they possessed expertise in congregational diversity. Knowing that some level of diversity expertise is required to operate in many urban and suburban ministries, prospective church leaders read a few books or attend a few seminars to get up to speed on the issues. With the proliferation of experts on diversity among evangelicals, we are seeing a radical institutionalization of a form of knowledge that overly determines the proper look of diversification and how it is to be achieved, creating a narrow form of legitimacy for diversification that is accepted and even seen as proper.

When evangelicals operate as diversity experts, they act as social planners who have mastered "social laws as forms of constraint" and consequently promote expectations of what should work reliably in any environment.[36] Their folk theories are not tested, as the assurance of their efficacy is in the evidence of their own congregations, and they conform to commonsense understandings of how race works. Such confidence affirms Charles Tilly's findings in *Durable Inequality* when he wrote, "People ordinarily join (1) moral judgments, (2) conceptions of what is possible, (3) ideas of what is desirable within the realm of possibility, and (4) causal accounts of social life."[37] Among evangelicals, moral judgments about racial inequality (prejudice is wrong, discrimination is bad, etc.) are consciously intertwined with beliefs about what is achievable (more diverse people in our congregations), an ideal of what is desirable (visibly diverse church membership), and explanations for how they come together (highlighting ethnic and racial gifts yet not making a fuss about diversity issues).

What is important in this chapter is not that we wish to disprove the experts; it is to reveal that the growing system of expert knowledge is based on unexamined cultural stereotypes about what white people or black people or Asians or Latinos are really like. For example, as noted before, today music remains a primary means by which blacks are affirmed among white audiences. Against the backdrop of the development of racialized notions of black religiosity, white evangelicals view worship and liturgy as strategic entry points for manipulating racial proportions. Pastors, consultants, and denominational leaders urge congregations to adopt black styles of music and even include a gospel choir. Stories convey an inspiring and theologically rich picture of the ideal diversity that stimulates staff and lay leaders to scramble to construct weekly vehicles to actualize their vision. And more and more, a shared picture of conspicuous diversity is becoming normative. An imagined outcome is constructed out of a series of conjectures.

The ability to talk about diversity as an expert relies on the ability to construct imaginary worlds that connect supposed causes with assumed effects. John Levi Martin describes "the social planner" as one who is "able to reassure his audience scientifically that he can make sure statements about a world that does not exist, or else he is unlikely to be entrusted with the weighty responsibility of building this world."[38] The problem with the imaginary world built by social planners is that it "requires that others—the planned—be predictable and constrained."[39] For initiatives of racial complementarity to work, ethnic and racial groups must be willing to conform to the expectations set out. For nontalk of race to be acceptable, ethnic and racial groups must be willing to reassemble their self-understanding of their ancestral heritages and the approach toward racial and ethnic diversity as merely cultural differences traced back to idealized countries of origin, differences that are overcome through common identification with Christ. Even if members of diverse congregations conform to racialized expectations, this does not mean that broader, societal issues of race are effectively being addressed.

The assumptions of churches that seek to diversify depend on notions regarding the authenticity of different racial and ethnic groups and the willingness of members to play to those notions in the construction of culturally sensitive services. Concurrently, those same unexamined notions are lacking the sophistication of understanding the real inequalities, the true differences that structure the experience of different racial and ethnic groups. Since differences are ultimately not supposed to matter, pastors and dedicated lay leaders turn away from seeing those dynamics that truly affect the life circumstances of people both in their congregation and beyond.

Race Matters and Race Doesn't Matter

Among evangelicals, race matters, and race doesn't matter. Yet knowing when race *should* matter and when it *shouldn't* is tricky and demands justification. We find that evangelicals remain committed to the individualist, relational orientation informed by a theology that simultaneously adopts a cross-cultural, missional imperative. Alternating between deep inscriptions of racial differences (African Americans sing gospel music) and dismissive approaches to cross-cultural differences (reaching the neighborhood for Christ), evangelicals have taken steps toward highlighting or engaging racial and ethnic groups with the imperative of inclusion while unknowingly reinforcing pervasive stigmas and leaving institutional mechanisms for inequality unchallenged. While other examples of accentuation and ignoring could be cited, here we only wish to draw out an overall assessment.

The presence of visible, conspicuous diversity in demographically multi-racial churches provides a platform for leaders and members of these congregations to talk about their success. Drawing on theologically informed and culturally dependent commonsense knowledge, evangelicals possess intersubjectively valid expectations of what should happen in diverse congregations. Since human beings rarely question different types of causes and effects, it is not altogether surprising that evangelicals assume appropriate linkages between racial problems and religious solutions. On the one hand, liturgical initiatives like including conspicuously different worship performers are framed as solutions within racialized lenses that have been institutionalized in their understandings without their conscious knowledge. On the other hand, discussion of race is seen as disruptive and conflictual, so topics of race are avoided and topics of mission and cross-cultural outreach substituted. This allows race to be ironically highlighted and ignored in ways that reinforce stigmas and leave larger structures unchanged.

Ultimately, we see that evangelical multiracial churches, to this point at least, largely remain narrowly evangelical. By that we mean they continue to operate within the framework of an evangelical worldview, shaped by the imperatives to draw people to Christ, create cohesion among members, and train their members to share their faith. Racial injustice and stratification are simply not important in this worldview, and evangelical congregations are poorly placed to address such issues. What they can do with their current cultural tools and practices is to increasingly draw racially diverse people to their congregations on an interpersonal level, emphasize their commonalities, and encourage one another through caring relationships.

What could be done to alter such results? Religiously based cultural toolkits are constructed, which means they can be expanded. Seminaries should require that at least one course on race and racial inequality be taken for a divinity degree. If such seminaries are affiliated with a university, they could require that such a course be taken from a social science department. The imperative is that leaders must be trained in the genesis, discourse, and meaning of race and racial inequality. They will not learn it by osmosis and, in fact, by most accounts are actively steered away from such thinking at every turn. Similarly, the standard for leading workshops and seminars at conferences for church leaders should be raised. Simply working in a diverse environment is not enough, and personal biographies, inspiring stories, or similar denominational backgrounds are insufficient. Instead, speakers and consultants should manifest a proven sophistication in the complexities of race, ethnicity, and immigration by their training and credentialing. Specialized programs can mix sensitivity training with deeper insights into the source of our prejudices and more careful instruction on how to anticipate the local-global dynamics of diversity in the near future.

Imagine the difference if evangelical church leaders were, in addition to the strong training in reaching all people and drawing them together, also trained in the thinking encapsulated by this statement of Martin Luther King Jr.: "We will be greatly misled if we feel that the [race] problem will work itself out. Structures of evil do not crumble by passive waiting.... Evil must be attacked by a counteracting persistence, by the day-to-day assault of the battering rams of justice."[40] Such a perspective is currently foreign in most evangelical seminaries, conferences, and workshops and certainly not required learning. But that can and must change if evangelicals are to be true change agents for racial justice. We can expect more from those entrusted with training religious leaders, expecting that they possess sophistication in both macrohistorical patterns as well as the lived experience of race. If knowledge is power, then training is where it must begin. The good news is that a growing number of evangelicals are passionate about diversity. The motivation to learn allows them to be challenged to think more deeply, more analytically, and more comprehensively.

NOTES

1. David Roozen, *Research Report: Faith Communities Today, 2010 Frequencies for Evangelical Protestant Denominations* (2011), accessed March 19, 2012, https://docs.google.com/viewer?url=http://faithcommunitiestoday.org/sites/faith-communitiestoday.org/files/2010EvangelicalFrequenciesV1.pdf.

2. Michael O. Emerson, "A New Day for Multiracial Congregations," *Reflections: A Magazine of Theological and Ethical Inquiry* 100:1 (Spring, 2013): 11–15.

3. Michael O. Emerson and Christian Smith, *Divided by Faith: American Evangelicalism and the Problem of Race in America* (New York: Oxford University Press, 2000); Lisa Sharon Harper, *Evangelical Does Not Equal Republican...or Democrat* (New York: New Press, 2008); Peter Goodwin Heltzel, *Jesus and Justice: Evangelicals, Race, and American Politics* (New Haven, CT: Yale University Press, 2009); Charles Marsh, *The Beloved Community: How Faith Shapes Social Justice, from the Civil Rights Movement to Today* (New York: Basic Books, 2005); Soong-Chan Rah, *The Next Evangelicalism: Releasing the Church from Western Cultural Captivity* (Downers Grove, IL: IVP Books, 2009).

4. George Yancey, "Reconciliation Theology: Results of a Multiracial Evangelical Community" (paper presented at the "Color Lines in the Twenty-First Century" conference, Chicago, 1998).

5. Emerson and Smith, *Divided by Faith.*

6. Cruiss Paul DeYoung, Michael O. Emerson, George Yancey, and Karen Chai Kim, *United by Faith: The Multiracial Congregation as an Answer to the Problem of Race* (New York: Oxford University Press, 2003), 2.

7. These books are written both by scholars examining diverse congregations and by practitioners who focus on the how to or argue why such congregations should exist. For examples of academic works, see Bradley Christerson, Korie L. Edwards, and Michael O. Emerson, *Against All Odds: The Struggle for Racial Integration in Religious Organizations* (New York: New York University Press, 2005); Korie L. Edwards, *The Elusive Dream: The Power of Race in Interracial Churches* (New York: Oxford University Press, 2008); Michael O. Emerson, *People of the Dream:Multiracial Congregations in the United States* (New York: Oxford University Press, 2006); Kathleen Garces-Foley, *Crossing the Ethnic Divide: The Multiethnic Church on a Mission* (New York: Oxford University Press, 2007); Gerardo Marti, *Worship across the Racial Divide: Religious Music and the Multiracial Congregation* (New York: Oxford University Press, 2012); Gerardo Marti, *Hollywood Faith: Holiness, Prosperity, and Ambition in a Los Angeles Church* (New Brunswick, NJ: Rutgers University Press, 2008); Gerardo Marti, *A Mosaic of Believers: Diversity and Innovation in a Multiethnic Church* (Bloomington: Indiana University Press, 2005). For works by practitioners, see David A. Anderson, *Gracism: The Art of Inclusion* (Downers Grove, IL: IVP Press, 2007); David A. Anderson, *Multicultural Ministry* (Grand Rapids, MI: Zondervan, 2004); Mark Lau Branson and Juan F. Martinez, *Churches, Cultures, and Leadership: A Practical Theology of Congregations and Ethnicities* (Downers Grove, IL: IVP Press, 2011); Mark DeYmaz, *Ethnic Blends: Mixing Diversity in Your Local Church* (Grand Rapids, MI: Zondervan, 2010); Mark DeYmaz, *Building a Healthy Multi-Ethnic Church* (San Francisco, CA: Jossy-Bass, 2007); Rodney M. Woo, *The Color of Church: A Biblical and Practical Paradigm for Multiracial Churches* (Nashville, TN: B&H, 2009).

8. Michael O. Emerson, "Managing Racial Diversity: A Movement toward Multiracial Congregations" (paper presented at the annual meeting of the American Sociological Association, San Francisco, CA, 2009).

9. David Van Biema, "The Color of Faith," *Time*, January 11, 2010, 38–41.

10. Gerardo Marti, "The Religious Racial Integration of African Americans into Diverse Churches," *Journal for the Scientific Study of Religion* 49:2 (June 2010): 201–17.

11. Levi Martin, *The Explanation of Social Explanation* (New York: Oxford University Press, 2011).

12. Marti, *Worship across the Racial Divide*.

13. James Cone's articulation of Black Theology is an example of a theological system that includes resources for discussing race. For an older theology, Mormonism includes orientations for discussing racial and ethnic groups.

14. Some may be quick to assert here that there is an important exception in the articulation of understandings of Jewish people descended from Israel. Evangelicalism includes both those who still give significance to physical descendants of Israel, but the majority does not hold literalist views and see all Christians as part of the New Israel. "Neither Jew nor Gentile" is one of many scriptural phrases in the New Testament that indicate a canceling out of racial and ethnic differences.

15. Garces-Foley, *Crossing the Ethnic Divide*.

16. Brenda Salter McNeil and Rick Richardson, *The Heart of Racial Justice: How Soul Change Leads to Social Change* (Downers Grove, IL: InterVarsity Press), 62.

17. Carol Doran and Thomas H. Troeger, *Trouble at the Table: Gathering the Tribes for Worship* (Nashville: Abingdon Press, 1992), 23.

18. Marti, *Worship across the Racial Divide*.

19. George Yancey, *One Body, One Spirit. Principles of Successful Multiracial Churches* (Downers Grove, Illinois: InterVarsity Press, 2003); Pedrito U. Maynard-Reid, *Diverse Worship: African American, Hispanic, and Caribbean Perspectives* (Downers Grove: InterVarsity Press, 2000).

20. For more information on ethnodoxology, see www.worldofworship.org/ Ethnodoxology.php.

21. Marti, *Worship across the Racial Divide*.

22. Curtis Evans, *The Burden of Black Religion* (New York: Oxford University Press, 2008); see also Donald G. Mathews, *Religion in the Old South* (Chicago: University of Chicago Press, 1979).

23. Although race theories and all forms of biological determinism have been largely discredited in the twentieth century, especially through the work of Franz Boas and his influential students Ruth Benedict, Margaret Mead, Jacques Barzun, and Ashley Montague, the popular imagination even in the supposedly most civilized of nations continues to accentuate the belief in racially different traits.

24. Evans, *The Burden of Black Religion*.

25. Evans, *The Burden of Black Religion*.

26. Evans, *The Burden of Black Religion*.

27. Changes in musical education contributed to cultural sensitivity that allowed nonblacks to appreciate and assimilate black gospel into their musical repertoire. See Terese M. Volk, "Folk Musics and Increasing Diversity in American Music Education: 1900–1916," *Journal of Research in Music Education* 42:4 (1994): 285–305; and John A. Davis, "The Influence of Africans on American Culture," *Annals of the American Academy of Political and Social Science* 354:1 (1964): 75–83.

28. Marti, *Worship across the Racial Divide*, chapter 7.

29. Edward Ming Lee, *Case Studies of Multiethnic Churches: Their Motivations and Strategies in Being Multiethnic* (PhD diss., Dallas Theological Seminary, 2011).

30. "The Mosaix Global Network," accessed August 20, 2012, www.mosaix.info/.

31. "Purpose and Vision—ReNew Partnerships," accessed August 20, 2012, http://renewpartnerships.org/about/purpose/.

32. Stephen Cornell and Douglas Hartmann, "Conceptual Confusions and Divides: Race, Ethnicity, and the Study of Immigration," 23–41, in *Not Just Black and White: Historical and Contemporary Perspectives on Immigration, Race, and Ethnicity in the United States*, ed. Nancy Foner and George M. Fredrickson (New York: Russell, 2004).

33. Cornell and Hartmann, "Conceptual Confusions and Divides."

34. Edwards, *The Elusive Dream.*

35. In the context of globalization, an expert system is intended to provide a means of accomplishing things without regard for context. According to Malcolm Waters, "An expert system gives guarantees about what to expect across all contexts."

36. Martin, *The Explanation of Social Explanation*, 57.

37. Charles Tilly, *Durable Inequality* (Berkeley: University of California Press, 1999), 265.

38. Martin, *The Explanation of Social Explanation*, 57.

39. Martin, *The Explanation of Social Explanation*, 57.

40. Martin Luther King Jr., *Where Do We Go from Here: Chaos or Community?* (Boston: Beacon Press, 1968), 128.

9

Prolifers of the Left

PROGRESSIVE EVANGELICALS' CAMPAIGN
AGAINST ABORTION

Daniel K. Williams

PROGRESSIVE EVANGELICALS' NEW social engagement has included action on many issues associated with the political left, including campaigns against poverty, war, nuclear arms buildup, human trafficking, gender discrimination, global warming, racism, and numerous other forms of social injustice. But on one issue, progressive evangelicals and their secular allies on the left have parted company. That issue is abortion.

Progressive evangelicals have embraced the prolife cause, yet their activism against abortion has differed from the policies of both the left and the right. While social conservatives have campaigned for restrictive legislation against abortion and the secular left has embraced abortion rights, progressive evangelicals have pursued an independent course, working for policies that protect life at all levels of development yet eschewing the narrowly defined legislative approach that the right has usually favored. Their political path on this issue has often been a lonely one. Yet it will likely shape the course of evangelical political activism for the foreseeable future. Although evangelicals under thirty are more politically liberal than their parents on many issues, including same-sex marriage, polls show that they are far more strongly opposed to abortion than their secular peers and that they are even more likely to be prolife than evangelicals of their parents' generation are.[1] The particular brand of prolife politics that progressive evangelicals have pioneered will probably shape the political choices of a new generation of socially conscious evangelical youth. So far, most politicians on both the left and the right have turned a deaf ear to the unique form of prolife ideology that progressive evangelicals have fostered. But if they want to win the votes of an emerging group of younger evangelicals, they may be ignoring these ideas at their peril.

The Development of a Progressive Evangelical Prolife Ethic

Progressive evangelicals' particular brand of prolife politics began developing in the 1970s, a decade when the nation's Christian community was becoming increasingly polarized over abortion. Although conservative evangelicals had been mostly silent during the debates over the liberalization of state abortion laws in the late 1960s, the legalization of abortion on demand in the early 1970s and the subsequent rapid rise in the number of legal abortions disturbed them and prompted them to begin speaking out on the issue. Conservative evangelicals saw legal abortion as a product of the feminist movement and the sexual revolution, which they viewed as threats to the family. Liberal Protestants, on the other hand, were generally supportive of the legalization of abortion because many of them viewed the issue as a way to promote women's fundamental human rights and because they did not share conservative evangelicals' concerns about premarital sex. Although a minority of mainline Protestants joined the prolife movement, claiming that the protection of human rights demanded the protection of the right to life for the unborn, the nation's major mainline Protestant denominations, including the American Lutheran Church, the United Presbyterian Church, and the United Methodist Church, passed resolutions endorsing abortion rights at the beginning of the 1970s.[2]

When the progressive evangelical movement began to coalesce in the early 1970s, the young baby boomer evangelicals who forged the movement sided with liberal Protestants rather than conservative evangelicals on most political issues. Like liberal Protestants, progressive evangelicals such as Jim Wallis and Wes Michaelson were strongly supportive of poverty relief efforts and civil rights for African Americans and adamantly opposed to the Vietnam War.[3] Many progressive evangelicals also identified themselves as feminists. Yet on the issue of abortion, they broke with their usual liberal Protestant allies and turned instead to progressive Catholics for inspiration.

Progressive evangelicals rejected prochoice arguments partly because the brand of feminism that shaped their views—which was an evangelical feminism—likewise rejected abortion and heralded a conservative standard of sexual morality as liberating for women. While most secular feminists argued that women could not achieve full liberation until they won legal recognition of their reproductive rights and gained complete control of their own bodies, the evangelical feminists who began to speak out on behalf of women's rights in the middle to late 1960s condemned the sexual revolution as exploitative and therefore did not make reproductive rights a part of their campaign.

Instead, they focused their attention on challenging the patriarchal tradition in evangelical churches that denied ordination to women and that expected submission to a husband's leadership within marriage. They appealed to the gender-egalitarian scriptural promises of Joel 2:28 ("Your sons and your daughters shall prophesy") and Galatians 3:28 ("There is no longer male and female, for all of you are one in Christ Jesus") to argue that God had extended an equal calling to both men and women to serve in ministry. Evangelical feminism was therefore based not on the concept of a right to individual autonomy—including sexual and bodily autonomy—as some forms of secular feminism were, but rather on a belief in God's calling of both men and women for equal roles in service to God. Evangelical feminists were sympathetic to secular feminists' demands for equal roles within secular society—that is, an end to glass ceilings in the workplace and political structures and the realization of equal pay for equal work. They wanted to see men share 50 percent of the housework and child care in the home, and they encouraged married women to pursue fulfilling careers, including careers as pastors if they felt God had called them to that role. But when it came to issues of sex, they parted company with many of their secular feminist compatriots. They believed that the sexual revolution had been harmful to women, so they were just as opposed to premarital sex as other evangelicals were. In the midst of writing articles promoting evangelical feminism, Letha Scanzoni published *Sex and the Single Eye*, a book that advised against premarital sexual relationships. Nancy Hardesty, another early proponent of evangelical feminism, wrote an article against abortion for *Eternity* magazine while promoting egalitarian roles for women in ministry.[4]

Progressive evangelicals' flagship magazine, *Sojourners*, accepted this brand of evangelical feminism. From the moment when Jim Wallis and his staff of progressive evangelical writers launched the magazine in the 1970s, *Sojourners* endorsed an egalitarian view of women in ministry and called for political and societal changes to promote women's rights.[5] Several of its contributing editors unhesitatingly described themselves as feminists. Yet the magazine never accepted the legitimacy of sex outside of marriage. Instead, *Sojourners* published condemnations of the "*Playboy* world" and linked its defense of marriage to an ethic of nonviolence and respect for individual persons. Promiscuous sex, progressive evangelicals argued, contributed to divorce, fatherlessness, and a variety of other "social ills." And it was a direct violation of Jesus' teaching of nonviolence in all relationships. "Sex apart from a committed relationship is violent," Elizabeth McAlister, a regular contributor to *Sojourners*, declared. Sex was also intrinsically linked to the creation of new life, so couples who were unmarried and unprepared to raise children together should abstain from sex. "We as Christians must be willing to limit our sexual activity to those situations in which we would be willing at least to bear a child to term and see it responsibly cared for should a pregnancy result," Shelley Douglass, a self-described feminist, stated in *Sojourners* in 1980.[6]

Progressive evangelicals' views on sexuality precluded them from following liberal Protestants into the prochoice camp, but that did not mean that they were ready to embrace the particular brand of prolife politics that conservative evangelicals were beginning to adopt. Conservative evangelicals' prolife activism was, for the most part, narrowly focused on securing legal prohibitions on abortion, ignoring other "life" issues such as war and capital punishment. For progressive evangelicals such as Wallis, whose political radicalism had been forged in the antiwar movement, this approach was unconscionable. Instead of looking to the early conservative evangelical prolife advocates for inspiration, progressive evangelicals took their guidance from young progressive Catholics who drew a parallel between the fight against abortion and the struggle against war and oppression.

One of the first articles on abortion that *Sojourners* magazine published lauded the approach of the National Youth Pro-Life Coalition (NYPLC), an organization that politically progressive prolife college students in the Midwest had started in 1971.[7] Throughout the late 1970s and 1980s, *Sojourners* regularly asked young politically progressive Catholics who were either associated with the NYPLC or who shared its ideology to write about the abortion issue. Progressive evangelicals were not present at the founding of the NYPLC, but over the next few years, they imbibed the NYPLC's prolife ideology and began framing the abortion issue in terms that were almost indistinguishable from the rhetoric of the original NYPLC members.

Like the evangelical left, the students in the NYPLC were strongly opposed to the Vietnam War, and their prolife commitments grew out of a desire to preserve all human life. They identified themselves with the political left, and indeed, one of their group's national leaders in the early 1970s worked for Senator George McGovern's presidential campaign. "The most liberal cause is protecting other people's lives," Sue Bastyr, a University of Minnesota student who was one of the group's charter members, told a reporter in 1971. She was disturbed when many of her fellow students who joined the peace movement and rallied against the Vietnam War simultaneously supported the right to kill fetuses through abortion, a stance that she viewed as inconsistent. "To be pro-life you have to be for all life," she said.[8]

Unlike most other prolife organizations, the NYPLC did not make the legal prohibition of abortion its principal goal. To be sure, the members of the NYPLC supported legislation to protect the unborn and campaigned for an antiabortion constitutional amendment (commonly referred to as the

"Human Life Amendment") because they saw a parallel between the right to life for fetuses and civil rights for African Americans. Just as it had been right to pass civil rights legislation for African Americans in the 1960s, so it was necessary to pass civil rights legislation for the unborn in the 1970s; both groups were minorities deserving full legal protection of their human rights. But the members of the NYPLC also wanted to go beyond the mere legal protection of the right to life and change societal structures and values in order to produce a culture in which all life was valued. They thought that the power of the state could be used more effectively to provide maternity care for impoverished women who might choose abortion if they were not given the resources to deal with crisis pregnancies. More broadly, they favored the use of direct action strategies, such as music-filled rallies on the Washington Mall, to draw attention to the way in which contemporary American social institutions devalued human life.[9]

The evangelical left's main political representative in Washington, Senator Mark Hatfield, held a view of abortion that was very similar to that of the NYPLC, because like his younger prolife counterparts, he saw a connection between the violence of the Vietnam War and other societal sanctions of violence, including the violence of abortion. Immediately after the Supreme Court issued its ruling in *Roe v. Wade*, Hatfield responded by cosponsoring a Human Life Amendment to extend constitutional protection to all human life from the moment of conception. Yet like the NYPLC, he did not believe that the societal problems that had led to a devaluation of unborn human life could be solved merely by enacting a legal ban on abortion; the Human Life Amendment, while important, was not a sufficient measure to stop abortions from happening. Instead, he thought that society needed to offer help to women facing crisis pregnancies and promote a new social ethic that valued human life at all stages of development. When Hatfield addressed the National Right to Life Committee's annual convention in June 1973, he used the opportunity to advocate for a prolife political ethic that would transcend the abortion issue by confronting a similar societal disrespect for human life in Vietnam, in America's prisons, and on death row. Abortion was merely a symptom of a much larger problem, he argued. "The evidence of how life can be degraded, cheapened, and dehumanized by forces and attitudes in our society is painfully obvious," Hatfield said. "Should it come as any surprise, then, that our society has come to regard abortion as an increasingly permissible and acceptable form of human behavior? . . . Abortion is a form of violence. It is condoned by a society that has become callous and indifferent to the ultimate value of human life. It is undergirded by a whole moral climate that elevates selfish personal convenience to a supreme status in human decision-making."

Echoing the NYPLC, Hatfield suggested that prolifers needed to change cultural attitudes toward life and death not only by passing laws against abortion but also through crisis pregnancy centers, comprehensive sex education, rape treatment centers, and help for "unwanted children" and unwed mothers.[10]

The emerging evangelical left adopted Hatfield's prolife ethic, perhaps partly because some members of the movement had worked closely with the senator and considered his political stances an inspiration. Wes Michaelson, for instance, who was one of the early staff members of *Sojourners* magazine, was one of Hatfield's legislative aides. Hatfield was also a regular contributor to *Sojourners* in its early years. In 1976, he published an article in the magazine about Jesus' nonviolent ethic.[11] It was thus not surprising that the magazine's earliest statements about abortion echoed some of the themes that Hatfield had stressed in his speech to the National Right to Life Committee. Charles Fager's article, "The Abortion Impasse: A Way Out" (December 1976), argued that the right of the fetus to live should be protected in public law, but that instead of imposing criminal sanctions on abortion, the government should offer women facing crisis pregnancies the resources they needed to carry their pregnancies to term. "Many women abort only because they see no other way out," Fager wrote. "The more genuine alternatives women have...the more likely it is that the number opting to abort will decrease." Fager lauded the approach of Burke Balch, vice president of the NYPLC, as a model for how to promote the prolife cause without placing undue weight on legal sanctions as the answer to the problem of abortion. Though the progressive evangelicals who wrote against abortion were not opposed to the Human Life Amendment—indeed, they believed that such an amendment had important symbolic value—they did not believe that law could coerce behavior and end the practice of abortion. Ultimately, to stop abortion, they had to find a way to change societal values and offer help to pregnant women.[12]

Conflict with the Christian Right

The evangelical left's approach to the abortion issue differed from the approach that most conservative evangelicals were beginning to adopt in the 1970s. From the moment that conservative evangelicals first became concerned about abortion in the early 1970s, they viewed the issue primarily in terms of public law because they viewed the removal of legal protections for the unborn child as a sign that the state was abandoning its foundational principle of protection for the right to life. *Christianity Today*, the leading magazine of the mainstream and conservative wings of the evangelical movement, responded to *Roe v. Wade* in 1973 with a warning that evangelicals could no longer count on the government to uphold the basic tenets of its founding principles. "Christians should accustom themselves to the thought that the American state no longer supports, in any meaningful sense, the laws of God, and prepare themselves spiritually for the prospect that it may one day formally repudiate them and turn against those who seek to live by them," the magazine editorialized. Similarly, when the evangelical popular theologian Francis Schaeffer alerted many of his coreligionists to the abortion issue in his film documentary *How Should We Then Live?* he spoke about abortion almost exclusively as a legal problem. The legalization of abortion in the United States, he said, showed that the law had become "arbitrary" in its classification of which lives would be legally protected and which would not. Like many other prolife activists, Schaeffer compared *Roe v. Wade* to *Dred Scott*, a nineteenth-century Supreme Court decision that deprived African American slaves of the right to personhood. *Roe*, too, had deprived a category of people—the unborn—of the right to personhood, and the only way to counteract that was to work through the legal system to restore legal protections for fetal rights.[13]

This view of the abortion issue as a legal problem led conservative evangelicals to identify the prolife cause with the Republican Party. Because the GOP, after the late 1970s, was the party that was officially committed to securing legal restrictions on abortion—while the Democratic Party, by contrast, endorsed abortion rights—prolife conservative evangelicals believed they had a duty to vote Republican. A majority of white evangelical voters cast their ballots for the Republican candidate in every presidential election after 1976, and in several of these elections, including 1984, 1988, 2004, and 2008, white evangelical support for the Republican ticket exceeded 70 percent. The prolife cause was the rallying cry that the Christian Right used to mobilize evangelicals on behalf of the party that promised to appoint Supreme Court judicial nominees who were inclined to overturn *Roe v. Wade*. For many, voting Republican became synonymous with saving unborn babies' lives, especially after the election of President Ronald Reagan in 1980. "There is no doubt that the future of our nation for the rest of this century and into the beginning of the 21st century rides on the outcome of this election," Moral Majority Vice President Cal Thomas told his radio listeners in 1984. "Supreme Court judges will probably be chosen by the next President. Will they keep the abortion floodgates open or start to close them? It's up to you."[14]

Progressive evangelicals saw the issue differently. In contrast to their conservative counterparts, they placed very little value on the status of abortion in public law, partly because, unlike conservatives, they felt that they were outsiders to the nation's legal system, and they had never viewed it as representative of their values. Thus, they were not shocked when the public law was changed to allow abortion; to them, abortion was merely symptomatic of a much larger cultural acceptance of violence, an acceptance that had been especially manifest in the Vietnam War. A society that sentenced its criminals to death, that refused to care for its poor and needy, and that continued to invest in nuclear arms was not a society whose legal code could be expected to respect the life of a helpless minority like the unborn. Instead of working within the system to change the law—a goal that progressive evangelicals thought had limited value—the evangelical left was more sympathetic to prolife campaigns that posed a much more radical challenge to the culture and sought to change social attitudes as well as societal laws.[15]

Progressive evangelicals were particularly sympathetic to campaigns that involved civil disobedience. They revered Martin Luther King Jr. and other civil rights activists who confronted societal injustice by refusing to obey unjust laws. They signaled their approval of Daniel Berrigan's civil disobedience in defiance of the Vietnam War by inviting him to contribute articles to *Sojourners* magazine. When a few prolife activists in the late 1970s adopted nonviolent civil disobedience as a tactic to shut down abortion clinics, some progressive evangelicals were intrigued.

Prolife nonviolent civil disobedience began as an ad hoc effort, but it became an organized political strategy in 1979, when several veterans of the NYPLC, including Burke Balch, joined with other young prolife activists to form the Pro-Life Non-Violent Action Project (PNVAP) to promote the use of nonviolent civil disobedience to stop abortion. Like the NYPLC, the PNVAP was fully committed to protecting human life from destruction at every stage of existence. One of the PNVAP's charter members, John Cavanaugh-O'Keefe, was a young progressive Catholic who had begun his political activism not as an antiabortion activist, but as an antiwar protestor during the last years of the Vietnam War. When he became interested in the abortion issue, shortly after *Roe v. Wade*, he thought it made sense to apply the direct action techniques of the New Left to the prolife cause and begin conducting nonviolent sit-ins in abortion clinics to draw attention to the horrors of abortion. Another charter member of the PNVAP, Juli Loesch, was a member of the progressive Catholic organization Pax Christi. Like several other left-leaning prolife activists, Loesch had gotten her start in direct action politics not through the prolife movement, but through the peace-and-justice politics of the left, which in her case included support for the United Farm Workers in California and the antinuclear movement.[16]

When *Sojourners* published a lengthy series of articles in 1980 in support of the prolife movement, the magazine turned to progressive antiwar Catholics to tell left-leaning evangelicals how to apply a consistent life ethic in a way that would link the issue of abortion to other life issues. Daniel Berrigan wrote one of the articles against abortion, as did Loesch. Both of them linked their opposition to abortion to a broader concern for human life that had led them to become peace activists. *Sojourners* considered these articles so important that it republished them as a booklet, *Abortion: What Does It Mean to Be Pro-Life?* which it continued to distribute for the rest of the decade.[17]

As the mainstream prolife movement moved into closer alliance with the Republican Party, progressive evangelicals stepped up their criticism of this alliance, warning that prolifers who voted for conservative Republican candidates were sacrificing other prolife principles solely for the sake of finding a candidate who shared their view on abortion. In this critique, they were presaged by progressive Catholics. In 1980, for instance, Msgr. George Higgins, a priest known for his strong support of the United Farm Workers, warned that "prolife Catholics" needed to "seriously consider the possibility that in collaborating with the right wing on abortion they risk defeat of the overall social justice agenda." Higgins said that he was firmly opposed to abortion, but he was disturbed that the prolife cause had linked itself to a conservative political agenda that included "a potpourri of other right-wing issues that, almost without exception, contradict the official positions of the church." Why should prolifers tolerate a political program that included capital punishment, nuclear arms buildup, and other policies that disrespected human life solely because those who promoted this agenda paid lip service to prolifers' opposition to abortion?[18]

Many of those who shared Higgins's perspective heralded the Catholic bishops' pastoral proclamation, "The Challenge of Peace: God's Promise and Our Response," which Joseph Cardinal Bernardin helped to create in 1983 in an attempt to connect the prolife cause with opposition to nuclear arms buildup. "In a society where the innocent unborn are killed wantonly, how can we expect people to feel righteous revulsion at the act or threat of killing noncombatants in war?" the bishops' letter asked. Bernardin declared that prolifers must be equally concerned with both abortion and nuclear arms buildup. "Promotion of peace," he said, was integrally linked to "promotion of the life of the unborn," because "all life issues constitute a seamless garment."[19]

Bernardin's slogan, "seamless garment," became a slogan for progressive Catholics and evangelicals who opposed abortion, nuclear arms buildup, and capital punishment and who supported a political agenda that protected human life from all of these threats. In 1985, the liberal Democratic Michigan state senator Stephen Monsma, an evangelical who had taught political science at Calvin College, joined with Juli Loesch in launching JustLife PAC, a political action committee designed to put Bernardin's slogan into action.

JustLife aided political candidates who embraced all aspects of the "seamless garment," opposing abortion, capital punishment, and nuclear arms buildup. In 1987, members of Loesch's Prolifers for Survival founded the Seamless Garment Network, an umbrella organization of organizations that favored the agenda that Bernardin and JustLife had outlined. Progressive evangelical organizations such as Evangelicals for Social Action joined the Seamless Garment Network, and progressive evangelical leaders such as Jim Wallis and Ronald Sider endorsed it. Sider, in fact, published an entire book dedicated to the seamless-garment life ethic. Titled *Completely Pro-Life: Building a Consistent Stance* (1987), Sider's book explained why evangelicals needed to link their opposition to abortion with an equally strong commitment to eradicate poverty and prevent nuclear arms buildup.[20]

Most conservative evangelicals, by contrast, did not heed Bernardin's call for a seamless-garment life ethic. Because of their strong opposition to communism, many evangelicals supported Reagan's strategy of nuclear deterrence. Reagan devoted much of his speech to the National Association of Evangelicals in January 1983 to a call for support of his policy of nuclear arms buildup, using the phrase "evil empire" to appeal to evangelicals' sense of the battle against communism as a spiritual struggle. Jerry Falwell's Moral Majority lobbied against a nuclear freeze and supported Reagan's Strategic Defense Initiative. Public opinion polls likewise indicated strong evangelical support for capital punishment.[21]

Progressive evangelicals criticized politically conservative evangelicals for not being consistently prolife. Throughout the 1980s, *Sojourners* magazine published articles against Reagan's defense policies and denounced the Republican Party on a host of life issues. Ronald Sider issued a similar critique. "Why do the members of the National Right to Life Committee... score far lower on other pro-life issues like opposition to the arms race, handguns and concern for the poor than do the members of the National Abortion Rights Action League?" he asked. "Don't handguns and poverty obliterate precious human beings as surely as abortion?"[22]

Conflict with the Secular Left

The progressive evangelicals who castigated the mainstream prolife movement for ignoring the dangers of nuclear arms buildup were equally upset when their allies on the left stridently defended abortion rights. While they did not expect the Democratic Party to support a legal ban on abortion, they were perturbed when Democratic politicians spoke of abortion as a woman's "right to choose" rather than as a moral problem that the nation needed to address. "To vote for either party in this election is to seriously compromise some aspect of our pro-life stance," one *Sojourners* writer, Bill Weld-Wallis, declared in October 1984. A vote for Ronald Reagan was unthinkable because of his "war on the poor and the Third World." Yet a vote for Democratic presidential candidate Walter Mondale was a vote for "a continuation of the slaughter of innocents." In the end, Weld-Wallis concluded, "We must advocate for the life that is within the womb," "seek God's Spirit for counsel," and "ask for forgiveness for our part in a world that leaves us with choices such as these."[23]

Many politically liberal prolifers, whether evangelical or Catholic, shared Weld-Wallis's disappointment with both parties for abandoning the principles of life. Republicans' support for military buildup and cuts in social welfare programs prevented liberal prolifers from supporting the GOP, but increasingly, the abortion issue was making them feel just as uncomfortable in the Democratic Party. Only a few years earlier, in the mid-1970s, the Democratic Party had still included a number of national leaders who spoke out against abortion. One of the contenders for the 1976 presidential nomination, Sargent Shriver, was a devout prolife Catholic whose wife, Eunice Kennedy Shriver, had been writing articles against abortion since the late 1960s. Reflecting the progressive Catholic and evangelical approach to the abortion issue, Shriver called for the enactment of legislation to assist pregnant teens. Similarly, in 1977 civil rights activist Jesse Jackson wrote an article for the *National Right to Life News* in which he linked his opposition to abortion—including his call for an antiabortion constitutional amendment—with a broader concern for the rights of minorities and the impoverished. Yet by the 1980s, those voices in the Democratic Party had all but disappeared, as the party embraced the abortion rights agenda of the feminist movement and the secular left. When Jackson competed for the Democratic Party's presidential nomination in 1984, he embraced a prochoice platform, calling not only for continued legal protection of abortion rights but also for a restoration of federal funding of abortion through Medicaid. Walter Mondale, the party's nominee for president that year, was unapologetically prochoice, as was his running mate, Geraldine Ferraro.[24]

Prolife Democrats were dismayed in the 1980s that the party was abandoning the values of its prolife contingent, leaving them with nowhere to turn except the Republicans—which for many of these prolife liberals was unimaginable. In an article titled "The Dilemma of an Anti-Abortion Democrat," prolife Democratic state legislator David Carlin lamented that, given that all of the leading Democratic contenders for the 1984 presidential nomination had become outspoken champions of abortion rights, he had no one for whom to vote. Like many progressive evangelicals and left-leaning Catholics, Carlin did not think that a legislative prohibition against abortion was feasible or enforceable. Yet he shrank from the idea of voting for politicians who spoke out in favor of the right to engage in what he considered homicide against the unborn. "If abortion really is the killing of a person, it must weigh very heavily in the balance, so heavily that it is difficult to imagine what collection of agreements with Mondale or any other pro-choice Democrat could outweigh it," Carlin wrote. On the other hand, the "Reagan administration's belligerence abroad" and its "indifference to problems of social justice both at home and abroad" made it impossible for him to imagine supporting the Republicans. "Whatever alliances we are able to work out with conservatives on the abortion question, there must be no generalized cozying up to them," he wrote.[25] Having rejected the views of both the Democratic and Republican presidential candidates, Carlin—along with the prolife progressive evangelicals and Catholics who shared his views—had few political options.

The Intensification of the Progressive Prolifers' Dilemma

Progressive evangelicals' agony over the abortion issue in the mid-1980s was exacerbated by a rapidly increasing commitment on the part of all evangelicals—whether progressive or conservative—to the antiabortion cause. In the mid-1980s, the Southern Baptist Convention and other evangelical churches began an annual observance of Human Life Sunday, a tradition that had begun in the Catholic Church more than a decade earlier. Christian radio, which had not focused on the prolife issue at the beginning of the 1980s, began featuring regular commentary on abortion by the middle of the decade. Contemporary Christian music spread the prolife gospel to evangelical teens. Older evangelicals picked up the same message from their favorite televangelists or their local pastors. All of these sources reiterated a consistent theme—namely, that abortion, which killed more than 1 million unborn children every year, was the nation's most important social justice issue and that evangelical Christians had a responsibility to end it.[26]

The increased attention to abortion in evangelical churches created a dilemma for progressive evangelicals who shared their conservative counterparts' opposition to abortion but disagreed with them about how to frame the issue. Most conservative evangelicals believed that the most effective way to save the unborn was to vote for political candidates who promised to vote for restrictions on abortion and support Supreme Court justices who would overturn *Roe v. Wade*. Progressive evangelicals, on the other hand, were dubious about this approach, believing that legislative changes alone would not reduce the abortion rate. Social welfare provisions for pregnant women, which many conservatives were reluctant to support, would be far more effective in deterring women from abortions, they thought. They also had no intention of voting for so-called prolife political candidates whose policies on nuclear arms buildup and other life issues were diametrically opposed to their values.

For a brief moment in the late 1980s, Randall Terry's Operation Rescue brought these feuding factions of the prolife movement together by uniting conservative and progressive evangelicals, along with many prolife Catholics, in a coalition to stop abortion. Terry himself was a conservative evangelical who took his inspiration from Francis Schaeffer's call for immediate action against abortion. Like most conservative evangelicals, he had little interest in the other issues covered in Bernardin's seamless garment; he connected abortion not to capital punishment or nuclear war, but to homosexuality, sex education, and other culture war issues that interested the Christian Right. Yet in spite of Terry's own culturally conservative views, his organization attracted many progressive evangelicals and Catholics because it employed the technique of civil disobedience that left-leaning prolife Catholics had first used a decade earlier. Some of the veterans of the PNVAP, including Juli Loesch, joined Operation Rescue. *Sojourners* gave Operation Rescue favorable press coverage. For a young generation of evangelicals, Operation Rescue became their primary entrée into the world of civil disobedience and radical political activism—a world that was completely foreign to most conservative evangelical churches. By the end of 1990, more than 40,000 Operation Rescue volunteers, many of whom were college-age evangelicals, had gone to jail because of their nonviolent civil disobedience on behalf of the unborn.[27]

Operation Rescue fell on hard times after a series of lawsuits in the early 1990s nearly bankrupted the organization, but its brief period of activism led conservative evangelicals to view the prolife cause as the civil rights movement of the late twentieth century. Many prolife evangelicals, including Terry, made an explicit comparison between the quest for legal recognition of the human rights of the unborn in the late 1980s and the campaign for legal recognition of African Americans' civil rights in the 1960s.[28] Both campaigns involved civil disobedience. Both campaigns were focused on fundamental human rights. And both campaigns created a new generational consciousness. For evangelicals who came of age in the late 1980s, abortion was a national evil that could not be ignored. Neither progressive nor conservative evangelicals could ignore Operation Rescue's call to action, even after the organization's demise.

Yet in the end, Operation Rescue disappointed progressive evangelicals. As the organization's cultural conservatism, patriarchal organizational structure, and militancy became increasingly obvious, left-leaning prolifers such as Loesch left the organization. After the early 1990s, most progressive evangelicals abandoned their interest in civil disobedience as a tactic to fight abortion, but they remained suspicious of conservatives' proposed method of eliminating abortion through the enactment of legal prohibitions against the procedure. They continued to believe that abortion was a social problem that could be addressed only through structural changes in society and improved social welfare provisions. Neither the left nor the right seemed sensitive to their concerns. "When I'm in a room with progressives from the Left, my stomach knots up as soon as abortion is mentioned," *Sojourners* writer Shelley Douglass stated in 1992. "In the next breath will certainly come the phrase 'Right-wing evangelical fascists.'" Yet Douglass was equally uncomfortable discussing abortion with the political right because she disagreed with the militant rhetoric of organizations such as Operation Rescue, and she had little in common with politically conservative prolifers, despite her belief that "abortion is almost always a moral wrong."[29]

Progressive evangelicals became even more uncomfortable with the mainstream left's stance on abortion after President Bill Clinton vetoed the Partial Birth Abortion Ban Act in the spring of 1996. While Clinton argued that he vetoed the bill only because of his concerns about women's health and only after praying about the issue, even the most left-leaning progressive evangelicals rejected his reasoning. Jim Wallis criticized mainline Protestant clergy for excusing the president's veto, which he considered a moral outrage. *Sojourners* also published a two-page article condemning Clinton's action. "One cannot escape the clarity that it is indeed a human life destroyed in this procedure," the article stated. "From the perspective of a consistent life ethic, Clinton's veto cannot be condoned." The veto was, in fact, "obscene and stupid." The article described partial-birth abortion in graphic detail, using language that was indistinguishable from the descriptions given by more conservative prolifers. On most political issues, *Sojourners* was unlikely to side with the leadership of the Southern Baptist Convention or the National Association of Evangelicals, but on the issue of partial-birth abortion, *Sojourners* echoed the complaints of Republican-leaning social conservatives. "If we can't say no to something as gruesome as this," *Sojourners* writer Julie Polter asked, "then to what will we say no?"[30]

The Current Moment: An Opportunity for Progressive Prolifers?

By the early twenty-first century, evangelicals—whether they were progressive or conservative—were more strongly prolife than ever. A 2008 survey revealed that two-thirds of evangelicals under thirty believed that abortion should be illegal in all or most circumstances. Young evangelicals of the early twenty-first century had grown up immersed in a church youth culture that celebrated the value of fetal life. As rights-conscious citizens, they viewed the prolife cause as a human rights issue. On the issue of gay rights or the environment, they felt free to break with their parents. But on the issue of abortion, they could not escape the belief that terminating a pregnancy meant taking a human life and was therefore wrong.[31]

Progressive evangelicals such as Wallis recognized that abortion had become the biggest impediment in convincing their fellow evangelicals to join the Democratic Party. "Virtually everywhere I go, especially during an election year, I encounter many moderate and progressive Christians who find it painfully difficult or even impossible to vote 'Democrat' given the party's highly ideological and rigid stance on this critical moral issue, a stance that they regard as 'pro-abortion,'" Wallis wrote in 2005. "To be a pro-life Democrat is to be a very lonely political creature in America." Wallis claimed that the Democratic Party was losing "millions of votes" from prolife evangelicals and Catholics because of its refusal to listen to prolife concerns. "Political liberals generally fail to comprehend how deep and fundamental the conviction on 'the sacredness of human life' is for millions of Christians, especially Catholics and evangelicals," he wrote.[32]

Wallis suggested that prolife Christians and prochoice liberals could find common ground in the shared concern of "reducing the abortion rate" and in promoting the entire agenda of the seamless-garment life ethic. He lauded the efforts of Democrats for Life to increase funding for prenatal care and promote adoption reform legislation in order to offer positive alternatives to abortion, measures that some claimed might reduce the abortion rate by 95 percent within the next ten years. This was a continuation of the argument that progressive evangelicals had been making for decades—namely, that reducing the abortion rate was more important than changing the public law on the issue and that liberal social welfare policies that helped the poor offered the best chance to reduce the number of abortions in the nation. The abortion rate remained steady under President Reagan's administration but dropped during President Clinton's term in office, they pointed out.[33] Nevertheless, it was difficult to gain traction for this argument as long as Democratic politicians offended prolifers by publicly championing abortion rights or opposing bans on partial-birth abortion.

For a brief moment, Barack Obama seemed to be sensitive to these concerns, both on the campaign trail and in his early days in the White House. He began cultivating an alliance with progressive evangelicals as early as 2006, when he addressed a Sojourners–Call to Renewal conference and called for a respectful dialogue on abortion. Progressive evangelicals such as Wallis appreciated Obama's openness to their position, even though they knew he was solidly prochoice. When the Democratic Party allowed prolife Senator Bob Casey Jr. (D-PA), to speak at its 2008 convention—a reversal of the perceived slight given to Casey's father, who had been denied the opportunity to present his prolife views to the Democratic national convention sixteen years earlier— Wallis applauded the move. When the Democratic Party adopted a platform statement that coupled an endorsement of *Roe v. Wade* with a pledge to pursue policies that would "reduce the need for abortion," Wallis called the new language "a real step forward." "We've gone from dogmatic positions to practical solutions," he said.[34]

Yet for many evangelicals, including a number of young evangelicals who took left-leaning stances on other political issues, these actions on the part of Democratic Party leaders were insufficient to win their support. A 2007 survey showed that 70 percent of white evangelicals under age thirty wanted to see additional legal restrictions on abortion, something that the Democratic Party was unlikely to deliver.[35] As Wallis recognized, the Democrats' position on abortion deterred many progressive evangelicals and Catholics from joining the party, and even those evangelicals who voted Democratic frequently objected to their party's stance on abortion. Indeed, at the beginning of 2012, *Sojourners* called the Obama administration's mandate for employer-provided contraceptive health insurance "a step backward" in the administration's relationship with religious organizations.[36]

The government mandate for employer-provided contraceptive health insurance—which included a mandate for employers to finance insurance coverage for abortion-inducing drugs—was particularly galling to some progressive evangelical prolifers because even before Obama became president, they had warned him against doing anything that would require Americans to violate their consciences by financing abortions. "If you want to build bridges, you must do more to understand and respect those of us who feel that the present thinking and action on abortion in America is a moral tragedy," a worried Ronald Sider told Obama in 2008, during the senator's presidential campaign. "By all means, do not ask or insist that those who oppose abortion pay for abortions through your health plan."[37] Despite his reservations about Obama's record on abortion, Sider wanted to believe that the senator was sincere in his attempts to find common ground with prolifers. During Obama's presidential campaign of 2008, Sider defended him against attacks from the Christian Right. Yet when the Obama administration issued its controversial mandate regarding insurance coverage of contraceptives, Sider joined with

Christian Right leaders such as the Southern Baptist Convention's Richard Land and Focus on the Family's Tom Minnery in signing a letter of protest to the White House. JustLife PAC cofounder Stephen Monsma also signed.[38] Many prolife liberals who favored a consistent life ethic wanted to be able to support the Obama administration, but they could not do so as long as the White House insisted on forcing some employers to violate their consciences by purchasing insurance coverage for abortion-inducing drugs for their employees. Like the Clinton administration, the Obama White House had given rhetorical support for the concept of reducing the abortion rate through socially conscious legislation—a concept that appealed to progressive prolifers—but had then undermined whatever credibility it had with prolifers on the left by adopting abortion policies that even some of the most liberal prolifers considered egregious. When forced to choose a side, some prolife liberals joined with the Christian Right in protesting the Obama administration's actions, despite their deep disagreements with conservatives on other life issues.

For the past three decades, the politics of abortion have made it difficult for even the most liberal evangelicals to support the Democratic Party. While conservative evangelicals have succeeded in convincing the Republican Party to embrace a platform calling for the reversal of *Roe v. Wade* and the protection of the unborn through a constitutional amendment, prolifers on the left have had much less success in convincing Democratic presidential candidates to embrace their brand of prolife politics. Although a few Democratic politicians have shown an interest in liberal prolifers' call to use generous social welfare policies to discourage abortion and promote an increased respect for all human life, Democratic presidents who have been forced to choose between pleasing their prochoice allies or their potential progressive prolife supporters have usually sided with the prochoice activists, leaving prolife progressive evangelicals without a political home. Yet many progressive evangelicals, including Jim Wallis, remain hopeful that political liberals will eventually change course and realize that they can find common ground with prolifers in the quest to reduce the abortion rate and promote societal respect for human life. Although progressive prolifers have endured years in the political wilderness, feeling equally estranged from both the left and the right, they may be poised to exercise greater political influence than they ever have before. Because younger evangelicals are far more likely than their parents to couple their prolife commitment with support for liberal political positions on the environment and poverty relief, the number of progressive prolife voters is likely to increase markedly as a younger generation of evangelicals reaches political maturity. Whether these younger evangelicals can succeed in translating their movement's consistent life ethic into an electorally viable political program remains to be seen. But if they can, the alternative that their views offer to the long-standing, gridlock-inducing conflict between the Christian Right and the secular left has the potential to transform the nation's politics.

As American politics have become increasingly polarized over abortion, with the two major parties sharply divided on the issue, progressive evangelicals have promoted a third alternative that they hope will bring the two sides together and reduce the abortion rate by using social welfare policies traditionally favored by prochoice liberals. Finding common ground between the two opposing sides on the abortion issue, while simultaneously reducing the abortion rate and fostering societal respect for unborn human life, may seem like an impossible proposition. But progressive evangelical prolifers believe they must strive for no less.

NOTES

1. Robert Wuthnow, *After the Baby Boomers: How Twenty- and Thirty-Somethings Are Shaping the Future of American Religion* (Princeton, NJ: Princeton University Press, 2007), 173–75; Dan Cox, "Young, White Evangelicals: Less Republican, Still Conservative," Pew Forum on Religion and Public Life, September 28, 2007, www.pewforum.org/Politics-and-Elections/Young-White-Evangelicals-L ess-Republican-Still-Conservative.aspx.

2. Lutheran Church of America, Statement on Abortion, July 1970; United Presbyterian Church in the USA, Resolution on Abortion, 1970; United Methodist Church, General Conference, Statement on Abortion, April 1970. Copies of these denominational resolutions are included in the folder "Organizational Positions on Abortion, 1970–1973," carton 8, MC 313, NARAL Records, Schlesinger Library, Harvard University. For differences between mainline and evangelical Protestant understandings of sexuality in the 1960s, compare "The Church and the Sexual Crisis," *Christian Century*, June 29, 1966, 823, with Alma Gilleo, "Standards for Sex Morality," *Christian Life*, February 1965, 51–52. For differences between mainline Protestants and evangelicals over abortion at the beginning of the 1970s, compare John Moore and John Pamperin, "Abortion and the Church," *Christian Century*, May 20, 1970, 629–31 (which argued, from a mainline Protestant perspective, that abortion was acceptable, though tragic), with "The War on the Womb," *Christianity Today*, June 5, 1970, 24–25 (which condemned most abortions).

3. For Wallis's political journey, see Jim Wallis, *Revive Us Again: A Sojourner's Story* (Nashville, TN: Abingdon Press, 1983). For the emergence of a progressive evangelical political movement, see David R. Swartz, *Moral Minority: The*

Evangelical Left in an Age of Conservatism (Philadelphia: University of Pennsylvania Press, 2012).

4. Pamela D. H. Cochran, *Evangelical Feminism: A History* (New York: New York University Press, 2005); Letha Scanzoni, "Women's Place: Silence or Service," *Eternity*, February 1966, 14–16; Letha Scanzoni, "Elevate Marriage to Partnership," *Eternity*, July 1968, 11–14; Letha Scanzoni and Nancy Hardesty, *All We're Meant to Be: A Biblical Approach to Women's Liberation* (Waco, TX: Word Books, 1974); Letha Scanzoni, *Sex and the Single Eye* (Grand Rapids, MI: Zondervan, 1968); Nancy Hardesty, "Should Anyone Who Wants an Abortion Have One?" *Eternity*, June 1967, 32–34.

5. *Sojourners* began publication in 1976 as the successor magazine to *The Post-American*, which Wallis helped to create in 1971.

6. Jackie Sabath, "From Principles to Partnership," *Sojourners*, July 1980, 19–21; Danny Duncan Collum, "It's a Playboy World after All," *Sojourners*, January–February 2000, 52; Elizabeth McAlister, "Is Marriage Obsolete?" *Sojourners*, March–April 1996, 18; Shelley Douglass, "Without Judgment," *Sojourners*, November 1980, 18.

7. Charles Fager, "The Abortion Impasse: A Way Out," *Sojourners*, December 1976, 10.

8. Marion K. Sanders, "Enemies of Abortion," *Harper's*, March 1974, 26-30; Joan Beck, "Collegians Who Campaign for the Unborn," *Chicago Tribune*, September 16, 1971.

9. National Youth Pro-Life Coalition, Direct mail, Re: National Rally for Human Life, September 3, 1972, "Miscellaneous Information and Handouts, 1971–1972" folder, box 5, North Dakota Right to Life Association Records (NDRLA), State Historical Society of North Dakota, Bismarck.

10. Mark O. Hatfield, Address to National Right to Life Convention, Detroit, June 9, 1973, "Correspondence, 1974" folder, box 2, NDRLA.

11. Mark O. Hatfield, "No Limits to Love: The Bible and Violence," *Sojourners*, April 1976, 20–23.

12. Fager, "The Abortion Impasse," 10.

13. "Abortion and the Court," *Christianity Today*, February 16, 1973, 32–33; Francis A. Schaeffer, *How Should We Then Live? The Rise and Decline of Western Thought and Culture* (Old Tappan, NJ: Fleming H. Revell, 1976), 218–23.

14. Lyman Kellstedt et al., "Faith Transformed: Religion and American Politics from FDR to George W. Bush," in *Religion and American Politics: From the Colonial Period to the Present*, 2nd ed., ed. Mark A. Noll and Luke E. Harlow (New York: Oxford University Press, 2007), 273; Cal Thomas, "Moral Majority Radio Report," March 26, 1984, folder 2, MOR 1–3, Liberty University Archives (LUA), Lynchburg, VA.

15. Jim Douglass, "Patriarchy and the Pentagon Make Abortion Inevitable," *Sojourners*, November 1980, 14–15.

16. Paul Galloway, "Pro-Life Strategist," *Chicago Tribune*, August 20, 1986; Juli Loesch to Burke Balch, February 15, 1978, folder 11, box 4, John Cavanaugh-O'Keefe Papers, Wisconsin Historical Society, Madison.

17. Daniel Berrigan, "An Inkling of a Life Being Snuffed Out," *Sojourners*, November 1980, 25; Juli Loesch, "Anti-Abortion, Gospel Peace," *Sojourners*, November 1980, 18–19.

18. George G. Higgins, "The Prolife Movement and the New Right," *America*, September 13, 1980, 108, 110.

19. National Conference of Catholic Bishops, "The Challenge of Peace: God's Promise and Our Response," May 3, 1983, 285, http://old.usccb.org/sdwp/international/TheChallengeofPeace.pdf; Kenneth A. Briggs, "Bishops to Draft Statement on Catholic Women's Role," *New York Times*, November 18, 1983.

20. Peter Steinfels, "Beliefs: The Plight of Voters Whose Views on Abortion Are at Odds with Their Party's," *New York Times*, March 28, 1992; Mary E. Bendyna, "JustLife Action," 195–96, in *Risky Business? PAC Decisionmaking in Congressional Elections*, ed. Robert Biersack et al. (New York: M. E. Sharpe, 1994); Consistent Life, "About Us," www.consistent-life.org/about.html; Swartz, "Left Behind," 588; Ronald J. Sider, *Completely Pro-Life: Building a Consistent Stance* (Downers Grove, IL: Intervarsity Press, 1987).

21. Ronald Reagan, Address to the National Association of Evangelicals, Orlando, Florida, March 8, 1983, www.reagan.utexas.edu/archives/speeches/1983/30883b.htm; Brad Kutrow, "Falwell Takes Aim at Freeze," *Lynchburg News*, March 16, 1983; Jerry Falwell, direct mail, May 3, 1985, "Moral Majority—'Star Wars' Letter, 5/3/85" folder, People for the American Way, Washington, DC; Howard Grasmick et al., "Religion, Punitive Justice, and Support for the Death Penalty," *Justice Quarterly* 10 (1993): 289.

22. Sider, *Completely Pro-Life*, 12–13.

23. Bill Weld-Wallis, "Abortion: The Political Dilemma," *Sojourners*, October 1984, 4–5.

24. Sargent Shriver, Press release in response to President Ford's statement on abortion, February 1976, "Series 8.4.2—1976 Campaign—EKS—Subject Files—Issues: Abortion" folder, box 246, R. Sargent Shriver Personal Papers, John F. Kennedy Presidential Library, Boston; "Ban on Abortion," *Washington Post*, November 27, 1975; Jesse L. Jackson, "How Respect Life Is Over-Riding Moral Issue," *National Right to Life News*, January 1977; Excerpts from Press Conference of Rev. Jesse Jackson, Washington, DC, November 3, 1983, folder 3, box 9, Mildred Jefferson Papers, Schlesinger Library, Harvard University; Sandra Salmans, "Abortion Foes Assail Mondale Ticket," *New York Times*, August 4, 1984.

25. David R. Carlin Jr., "The Dilemma of an Anti-Abortion Democrat," *Commonweal*, November 18, 1983, 626–28.

26. "New CLC Materials Deal with Abortion," *Baptist Standard*, December 25, 1985, 7; Cal Thomas, Moral Majority Radio Report Broadcast transcript, March 26, 1984, folder 2, MOR 1–3, LUA; Eileen Luhr, *Witnessing Suburbia: Conservatives and Christian Youth Culture* (Berkeley: University of California Press, 2009), 137–40.

27. James Risen and Judy L. Thomas, *Wrath of Angels: The American Abortion War* (New York: Basic Books, 1998), 205–377; Randall A. Terry, direct mail on behalf of Operation Rescue, July 16, 1990, folder HH616: "Operation Rescue," box 1–7, MS 76.1, Hall-Hoag Collection, John Hay Library, Brown University, Providence, RI; Operation Rescue brochure, "DC Project II: Repentance and Reformation," November 1990, folder HH616, box 1–7, MS 76.1, Hall-Hoag Collection; Tamar Lewin, "With Thin Staff and Thick Debt, Anti-Abortion Group Faces Struggle," *New York Times*, June 11, 1990.

28. Risen and Thomas, *Wrath of Angels*, 303; Lorri Denise Booker, "250 Protest Falwell Talk on Abortion," *Atlanta Journal-Constitution*, December 10, 1988.

29. Shelley Douglass, "The Abortion Battle: Silencing the Middle," *Sojourners*, July 1992, 4–5.

30. Jim Wallis, "Lift Every Voice," *Sojourners*, July–August 1996, 7; Julie Polter, "Outrage over the Abortion Veto," *Sojourners*, July–August 1996, 9.

31. Pam Chamberlain, "Younger Evangelicals: Where Will They Take the Christian Right?" *Public Eye Magazine*, Spring 2009, www.publiceye.org/magazine/v24n1/younger-evangelicals-where-wil-whey.html.

32. Jim Wallis, *God's Politics: Why the Right Gets It Wrong and the Left Doesn't Get It* (New York: HarperCollins, 2005), 297–99.

33. Jim Wallis with Chuck Gutenson, *Living God's Politics: A Guide to Putting Your Faith into Action* (New York: HarperCollins, 2006), 68–69.

34. Transcript of Barack Obama's keynote address at Sojourners–Call to Renewal Conference, Washington, DC, June 26, 2006, http://sojo.net/blogs/2012/02/21/transcript-obamas-2006-sojournerscall-renewal-address-faith-and-politics; Teddy Davis, "Democrats Soften Edges on Abortion," Sojourners website, August 13, 2008, http://sojo.net/press/democrats-soften-edges-abortion.

35. Cox, "Young, White Evangelicals."

36. *Sojourners*, press release, "*Sojourners*' Statement on Contraception Exemptions," January 25, 2012, http://sojo.net/press/sojourners-statement-contraception-exemptions-0.

37. Rusty Pritchard, "Ron Sider on Obama's Abortion Position," July 2, 2008, http://rustypritchard.com/page/7/.

38. Stephen Ertelt, "Sixty Religious Leaders Unite against Obama Insurance Mandate," LifeNews.com, December 22, 2011, www.lifenews.com/2011/12/22/sixty-religious-leaders-unite-against-obama-insurance-mandate/.

10

Global Reflex

INTERNATIONAL EVANGELICALS, HUMAN RIGHTS,
AND THE NEW SHAPE OF AMERICAN SOCIAL
ENGAGEMENT

David R. Swartz

IN 2001, JUST one month before 9/11, 32,000 evangelical youth invaded Midland, Texas. Drawn to a Christian music festival called "Rock the Desert," they clapped and danced to the rock anthems of Newsboys and dozens of other bands. Festival organizers also highlighted a social and diplomatic crisis in Sudan, then a war zone with one of the worst global records of religious persecution and human rights violations. Over the next several years, as the attendance exceeded 90,000, organizers built a mock slave cell and an authentic Sudanese village and handed out promotional material on the Sudan Peace Act. These activities represented a substantial evangelical campaign for human rights.

Activism surged well beyond the festival grounds. Midland itself, the site of a recent evangelical revival in a city already saturated with churches, hosted the International Day of Prayer for the Persecuted Church, which directed considerable attention to Sudan. Ex-child slave Francis Bok frequently visited local churches, speaking of his desire "to free his people in bondage." Midland activists mobilized in support of the Bachus Amendment to the proposed Sudan Peace Act that would deny access to American stock exchanges for oil companies doing business in Sudan. They rallied against their Republican senator Phil Graham, a free-market purist. They lobbied President Bush and held a series of vigils at the State Department. Bok even traveled to the White House to speak with the president. For the first time since the nineteenth century, observers noted, an American president had met with a former slave. But it was Midland, according to political scientist Allen Hertzke, that became "ground-zero in the grass roots campaign on Sudan...and a strategic player in high-level negotiations leading toward a peace treaty." This activism, documented by Hertzke in *Freeing God's Children*, extended the evangelical efforts that had helped pass the landmark International Religious Freedom Act of 1998.[1]

These actions on behalf of Sudanese human rights contrasted significantly with the lower levels of evangelical activism in the mid-twentieth century. First, the human rights work indicated a significant presence in the nation's capital. Evangelical efforts kept the issue alive at the moment when 9/11 could have swept Sudan off the agenda. "Prayer and hymns," notes Hertzke, "were matched with strategic analysis and pivotal timing." A receptive, just-inaugurated president, himself an evangelical from Midland, greased the political gears. As the new century dawned, it was clear that evangelical politics had matured far beyond its parochial efforts of the mid-twentieth century. Second, the issues involved a social dimension. Midland evangelicals demonstrated attention to the economic and political roots of injustice in ways that the previous generation had not in its focus on personal salvation and evangelism. Third, the activism marked a new ecumenical spirit. At mid-century, *Christianity Today* and significant books contrasted "Catholic power" with "American freedom." But fifty years later, evangelicals in Midland and Washington, D.C., were collaborating with Catholics, Jews, and other religious actors. The evangelical campaign for peace and human rights in Sudan points to growing ecumenical, promotional, and electoral sensibilities.[2]

Recent scholarship explains the rise of public evangelicalism in a variety of ways: reaction to the libertine sixties, the demographic boom of the Sunbelt, racial disruptions in the 1970s, and debates over sex education.[3] But these interpretations, important as they are, fail to attend to the effects of globalization, one of the most significant trends of the twentieth century. In fact, many of the most prominent examples of the new social engagement—HIV/AIDS, human trafficking, Third World poverty, sustainable development, climate change, and peacemaking—include a global dimension. In the first decade of the twenty-first century, U.S. churches spent more than $3.7 billion a year on overseas ministries, a significant jump, even accounting for inflation, over previous decades. Key aspects of the modern globalized order—the self, the nation-state, the notion of human solidarity—contributed to this investment as evangelicals participated in what Roland Robertson calls the "intensification of consciousness of the world." To be sure, those interested in missions had long imagined a global evangelical community that reached beyond the nation. But globalization and its encouragement of efficient bureaucracies and technologies accelerated this consciousness. The rising notion of human solidarity led to what Robert Wuthnow has described as the "disappearing other"—and to a new focus on human rights.[4]

This chapter, using the lens of human rights, tracks the development of a narrowly focused anticommunism to a new and broader internationalism. The new global sensibility stresses social justice in addition to personal evangelism. It emphasizes economic development in addition to disaster relief. It values ecumenism over sectarianism. I contend that the evangelical encounter with the two-thirds world—such as Francis Bok and his advocacy for human rights—critically encouraged this new global sensibility that in turn broadened and intensified evangelical social engagement.

I.

At the turn of the twentieth century, it seemed unlikely that evangelicalism would thereafter significantly shape domestic or international affairs. Evangelicals were retrenching. The formidable foreign missionary movement of the nineteenth century faded in the face of the Great War. Evangelicals generally opposed the international sensibilities of the League of Nations. Fundamentalists ceded mainline ecclesiastical organizations to the liberals. Even the prominent temperance effort to ban alcohol sales receded when the Eighteenth Amendment was repealed in 1933. The "evangelical century," writes Mark Noll, gave way in the twentieth to "cultural pessimism and a fear of governmental encroachment." This separatist posture fueled suspicion of state, mainline, and international activism on human rights, a suspicion that still remains in some evangelical quarters.[5]

World War II, however, reshaped evangelicalism into a less isolationist posture and encouraged attention toward human rights. The rising neo-evangelical movement, led by the National Association of Evangelicals, *Christianity Today*, and Billy Graham, nurtured cultural and social ambitions. Encouraged by their own successful contributions to the Allied defeat of Nazism, evangelicals again saw a place for themselves in an America they viewed as once belonging to them. Building evangelical institutions to compete with secular institutions, locating *Christianity Today* just down the street from the White House, and conducting crusades in the heart of liberal cities such as Los Angeles and New York City reflected the bold aspirations of the neo-evangelical movement.[6]

These ambitions took geopolitical shape as the Nazi threat gave way to the red tide of Marxism. Communist aggression in Southeast Asia, Europe, Africa, and even the Americas also reinvigorated evangelical interest in global affairs. Anticommunist activism often meshed with missionary activity, as evangelicals fanned the world in airplanes that were less expensive and more efficient than nineteenth-century ships. This offense against godless communism, in its evangelistic and political forms, claimed a social dimension to faith. Political and economic systems mattered, even if only to preserve space for conversions. Representative evangelical periodicals—*Moody Monthly*, the *Sunday School Times*, and the *Pentecostal Evangel*—showed considerably more attention to international matters in 1950 than in the preceding decades.[7]

While evangelical standards avoided the language of human rights, screeds against "Marxist materialism" peppered the early years of the postwar era. In *Christianity Today*, read by hundreds of thousands of evangelicals, prominent politicians bemoaned Communist expansion and antidemocratic policies. In the 1950s, Walter Judd, a Republican congressman from Nebraska, and FBI Director J. Edgar Hoover lamented the West's failure of nerve in the Suez crisis. These conservative political leaders worried about Marxist threats within Western Europe as France, Britain, and Italy struggled to recover from a devastating world war. Evangelical publishers advertised countless books with titles such as *Communism: Its Faith and Fallacies* (1962), *How to Fight Communism Today* (1962), and *Know Your Enemy: Communism* (1961). A popular vacation Bible school curriculum produced by Scripture Press in Wheaton, Illinois, boasted that it could make "our youth...strong in the Lord and the power of His might." "Our answer to Khrushchev," the ad copy read, "is Patriots for Christ for '62 VBS."[8]

World Vision, an evangelical relief and missionary agency established in 1950 to stem the expansion of communism in Korea, framed the conflict in apocalyptic terms. "Like a deadly red plague spreading out in all directions," founder Bob Pierce wrote, "the massive force of Communism has spread over the globe until today it claims over one third of the world's population." In between caring for orphans and building hospitals, World Vision staged a huge evangelistic crusade in Seoul. Pierce framed the event dramatically: "With Communist jet bombers poised only twenty seconds from Seoul as these words are written, the Seoul Crusade might well prove to be one of the most strategic evangelistic efforts of our day." For American evangelicals in the immediate postwar era, defeating communism and spreading the gospel were companion efforts. Each utilized a rhetoric of liberty. America would protect the human rights of peoples threatened by the tyranny of communism. Then they would be positioned to receive spiritual liberties offered by Christ.[9]

II.

These twin efforts, at least in the short run, met contrasting fortunes. As U.S. armed forces fought to disconcerting stalemates in Korea and Vietnam, thousands of missionaries exulted about millions of conversions. To the surprise of many American evangelicals, however, not all of these missionaries returned as loyal practitioners of the neo-evangelical nationalist consensus. Nor did their converts turn into Coca-Cola-swilling inerrantists in the suburbs of Nairobi. In fact, turning the tables on the renewed neo-evangelical social emphasis, many spoke back critically in a kind of global reflex. International evangelicals in the 1960s and 1970s critiqued American missionary strategies, imperialism, Southern segregation, and lack of attention to human rights abuses.

Courted and caught between Marxist and capitalist imperialisms in an era of decolonization, non-American Christians felt beholden to neither. On one hand, most denounced Marxist totalitarianism. For example, Alexander Solzhenitsyn, author of *Gulag Archipelago* and *One Day in the Life of Ivan Denisovich*, condemned the Kremlin. But Solzhenitsyn, with a full beard that summoned visions of the Old Testament prophet Jeremiah, also leveled prophetic ire toward the West. In his 1978 commencement address at Harvard, he decried "all this freedom with no purpose" but for the "satisfaction of one's whims." "Destructive and irresponsible freedom has been granted boundless space. Society has turned out to have scarce defense against the abyss of human decadence," he declared. Western culture, driven by relentless capitalism, was defined by "the revolting invasion of commercial advertising, by TV stupor, and by intolerable music." America, he suggested, had lost its soul. Even worse, the West was exporting its obsession with capitalistic materialism. In the 1990s, Solzhenitsyn condemned the West's imperialistic designs on Serbia, Ukraine, and Iraq.[10]

A host of missionaries and evangelicals from the two-thirds world amplified Solzhenitsyn's critiques of both Marxism and capitalism as hindering human flourishing. Festo Kivengere, a Ugandan bishop known as the "Billy Graham of Africa," said, "In Marxism...man is useful for the state and is thrown away when no longer useful. In capitalism, persons are useful as they bring profit to the company or to the society and are put on the shelf when they are no longer profitable." American commitment to unfettered capitalism, others suggested, impeded attention to social justice. International evangelicals were particularly sensitive to American alliances with anticommunist nations guilty of human rights abuses. Andrew Kirk, a longtime missionary in South America, wrote, "Evangelicals have a bad track-record in questioning traditions handed down to them....On a number of occasions, for example, I have heard evangelical Christians defend right-wing, totalitarian governments (like those of South Africa or Paraguay) on the grounds that they allow complete freedom to preach the gospel." Sadly, Kirk concluded, "the gospel that some proclaim is indeed 'good news' to oppressive regimes, for, while speaking of an 'inner' freedom that transcends life in this world, it does not in any way challenge policies that have resulted in the severe loss of civic freedoms for vast sections of the nation."[11]

America's poor record on human rights was evident even within its own borders. Missionaries cited Pakistani evangelicals who perceived "something incongruous and contradictory about churches which send missionaries half-way around the world with the Gospel of Christ while refusing to worship with the colored people of their own community." At a 1966 NAACP meeting at Wheaton College, Kenyan Wilson Okite urged classmates to join the civil rights movement, mentioning that independence from colonial powers in Africa inspired him and many others to agitate for equality in America. At Calvin College, a missionary to Nigeria told students that Africans were closely watching the 1964 presidential election. That Goldwater might win, despite his retrograde views on civil rights, "shocks them," Harry Boer reported. Africans receive American missionaries more openly, he explained, when the United States promotes civil rights. A Fuller Theological Seminary student, urging involvement in civil rights, wrote that the race question "reaches also around the world, where other nations look and ask, 'Is that Christianity?'" Howard Jones, an associate evangelist with Billy Graham, was amazed by Liberians' awareness of racial tension in the American South. "From the modern cities to the underdeveloped bush sections of the country, Africans plagued us with questions concerning Dr. Martin Luther King and the 1955 bus boycott in Montgomery, Alabama," Jones told InterVarsity students. "They quizzed us about the Emmett Till lynching in Mississippi and other racial disturbances." According to Jones, these events, publicized by Radio Moscow and Radio Peking, thwart "the progress of Christian missions in Africa, Asia and other parts of the world." Orlando Costas, a Puerto Rican evangelical, was an influential activist in Milwaukee, where in 1968 he founded a community newspaper *La Guardia*, the Latin American Union for Civil Rights, and the Universidad del Barrio. In 1969, he was named by Wisconsin's governor to the State Commission on Human Rights in the Division of Industry, Work and Human Relations. Missionaries and international evangelicals in the 1960s urged American evangelicals to promote social justice, often framing issues in terms of human rights.[12]

Several globally oriented organizations—especially the World Evangelical Fellowship (WEF) and the Lausanne Congress—were important conduits for these critiques. Populated by many non-Americans, these institutions promoted human rights in an American context that remained skeptical of the Universal Declaration of Human Rights. Fearful that international obligations might infringe on national sovereignty, American evangelicals also reacted to the human rights movement's relative antipathy toward religion as a source of intolerance. Global evangelicals, however, felt these pressures less directly. By the 1970s, many were appealing to the declaration's promises of religious, political, and economic freedoms. D. Richard John of the Evangelical Fellowship of India, for example, rebutted American neo-evangelical objections. Human rights, he declared, "are biblically based." John, echoing the declaration, defined human rights broadly, as having to do with poverty and the unequal distribution of resources, hunger, and the "over-exploitation of energy resources." In fact, the World Evangelical Fellowship, of which John was a member, directly borrowed language from the declaration. So did a series of missives by evangelicals from around the world. The "Madras Declaration on Evangelical Social Action" (1979), the "Lima Letter" (1979), and "An Evangelical Commitment to Simple Lifestyle" (1980) each cited the declaration as an authority and an inspiration.[13]

Most significantly, the Lausanne Covenant invoked the logic of human rights. In 1974, 2,700 evangelical leaders (at least half from the two-thirds world) from 150 nations gathered in Switzerland to discuss methods of global evangelism. In front of conservative American planners skeptical of the United Nations and insistent on the primacy of evangelism, hundreds of global evangelicals insisted that social justice should be inextricably tied to missions. In an ad hoc session, Colombian René Padilla and Peruvian Samuel Escobar led five hundred delegates in charging that Lausanne organizers were ignoring "the social and political implications of radical discipleship today." American conservatives bristled, but the Lausanne Covenant underwent telling revisions in the wake of global dissent. The first draft included only one sentence on social justice; the second draft promoted simple living, international sensitivity, and social justice in a section that was larger than any other in the covenant. The resulting document declared that "the message of salvation implies also a message of judgment upon every form of alienation, oppression and discrimination, and we should not be afraid to denounce evil and injustice wherever they exist." Oppressors included "totalitarian regimes of the extreme left or right" who deny "fundamental human rights." American evangelicals were urged to "call upon [leaders of the nations] to guarantee freedom of thought and conscience, and freedom to practice and propagate religion in accordance with the will of God and as set forth in The Universal Declaration of Human Rights."[14]

As the Lausanne Covenant suggested, the most urgent of these concerns was religious freedom. Defining religious liberty in the context of human rights, the World Evangelical Fellowship (WEF) launched a broad-based initiative in the 1980s. This campaign coincided with the emergence of important international voices within WEF. Jun Vencer, a Filipino and the first non-Western executive of WEF, oversaw the Religious Liberty Commission, which appealed to Article 18 of the Universal Declaration as it lobbied the United Nations and cooperated with a diverse collection of agencies that included Amnesty International, Jubilee Campaign, the Institute on Religion and Democracy, Middle East Concern, and Christian Solidarity International. One of WEF's first important campaigns was on behalf of Mehdi Dibaj, an Assemblies of God pastor in Iran convicted of insulting Muhammad and the Ayatollah Khomeini. International pressure by WEF and others in the early 1990s resulted in his release from prison, though he was stabbed to death three days later.

Dibaj's persecution was narrated widely. And several important exposes, most notably Paul Marshall's *Their Blood Cries Out* (1997), told thousands of other stories, underscoring the sobering global realities for millions of American readers, evangelical and nonevangelical alike. Marshall did not plead especially on behalf of evangelicals. "The persecution of Christians," he wrote, "is a harbinger of the repression of other human rights—of political dissidents, of intellectuals, of unionists, of women, of children, of homosexuals." Significantly, evangelicals with global experience framed religious freedom in terms of human rights as much as Christian solidarity.[15]

These stories from the two-thirds world spurred Americans to action. In the early 1980s, the progressive evangelical publication *Sojourners* reported that "Filipino evangelicals call their sisters and brothers to repentance...for past apathy and to become engaged in nonviolent struggle for justice, human rights, and freedom in the Philippines." Ugandan Bishop Festo Kivengere lobbied Washington to address dictator Idi Amin's many atrocities: the expulsion of Asians in 1972, the expulsion of Jews in 1974, and executions without trials. By 1977, 100,000 Ugandans had had died, 50,000 had fled, and Amin was stealing coffee from farmers to purchase fast cars and fund genocide. An exile himself for denouncing the regime, Kivengere met with representatives of the U.S. State Department's Bureau of Human Rights and key members of the House and Senate Subcommittee on Africa to plead for American help. After hearing Kivengere's story, the evangelical Senator Mark Hatfield of Oregon introduced a Senate bill that embargoed Ugandan coffee. Amin's regime fell less than a year later. These and many other examples demonstrate how pleas for human rights from the two-thirds world encouraged American evangelicals toward social action.[16]

III.

These global voices—and the international experience itself—helped drive a new internationalism that both reflected and shaped a new set of evangelical priorities heading into the twenty-first century. First, American evangelicals, especially those in younger cohorts, began to embrace the logic of human rights. Late to join the movement, evangelicals issued an impressive stream of increasingly sophisticated books and conferences. The evangelical left led the way in the 1970s and 1980s with hundreds of screeds against human rights violations perpetrated by both totalitarian regimes and Western powers. Soon after, an increasingly invested evangelical right, which had been preoccupied with Communist and Muslim violations, joined the ranks. Frank Wolf, a Republican representative from Virginia, became one of Congress's most active advocates of human rights. Into the twenty-first century, he continued to speak out against Iran's "systematic persecution" of the Baha'is, China's persecution of women and Christians, and genocide in Darfur. Pepperdine University School of Law's human rights program blossomed. A bevy of other human rights organizations also emerged: the American Anti-Slavery Group, International Justice Mission, and Evangelicals for Human Rights, which has worked almost exclusively on American torture of Muslim detainees. Many of these groups lobbied to pass the International Religious Freedom Act of 1998, the Trafficking Victims Protection Act of 2000, the Sudan Peace Act of 2002, and the North Korean Human Rights Act of 2004. Out of a context in which many secular groups, seeing religion as an oppressive force, have been blind to the plight of persecuted Christians, some commentators now argue that evangelicals have become the new leaders of the human rights movement.[17]

Second, evangelicalism grew more ecumenical. Emerging out of separatist fundamentalism and hostility toward Catholics and mainline churches, evangelicals began to learn from and work with nonevangelicals. Efforts toward human rights encouraged this ecumenism. *Christianity Today*'s editors, who paid significantly more attention to global affairs and human rights in the 1970s than in the 1950s, frequently cited secular human rights groups in their reports of persecutions of Christians. In 1975 alone, for example, the editors ran articles, based on nonevangelical sources, on the status of churches and rights in Russia, North Vietnam, and China. In the 1980s, WEF persistently quoted ecumenical sources on human rights in their journal. In general, according to historian Mark Noll, evangelical periodicals "were gathering their articles and reports from a wider range of international sources." In more recent years, evangelicals have grounded their commitment to human rights in the concept of *imago dei*, a theological strategy derived from Catholic sources. This emphasis on the image of God and divine transcendence has promoted a more robust sense of universal human solidarity.[18]

Theological cross-fertilization fed new networks of activist co-belligerency. In the 1970s and 1980s, WEF, a global body representing over 150 million evangelicals in 115 countries, worked with Amnesty International, Jubilee Campaign, Middle East Concern, and Christian Solidarity International. WEF's Religious Liberty Commission cited the United Nations and the Universal Declaration of Human Rights as authorities. Paul Marshall, a specialist in religious freedom and human rights, collaborated with Amnesty International, Human Rights Watch, the U.S. Institute of Peace, Catholic University, Open Doors, and the Commission on Security and Cooperation in Europe. In the early 1990s, Michael Horowitz, a Jewish human rights advocate, mobilized huge numbers of evangelicals and Catholics. According to sociologist Michael Lindsay, Horowitz tirelessly faxed and called religious leaders to encourage political activism. By the early 2000s, a coalition of evangelicals, Catholics, Jews, Tibetan Buddhists, feminists, the Congressional Black Caucus, and secularists had driven the passage of the International Religious Freedom Act (IRFA). This legislation established the State Department's Office of International Religious Freedom, which was first headed by World Vision's Mark Seiple.[19]

As this ecumenism suggests, the IRFA was not solely the product of an identity politics meant to protect only evangelicals. Christian activists, Allen Hertzke writes, have "created free spaces for other religious minorities in civil society." As the "mother of many other rights," religious rights have encouraged the free press and freedom of political conscience. In India, for example, the Evangelical Fellowship of India's general secretary Richard Howell participated in the United Christian Forum for Human Rights, working alongside John Dayal, a Catholic known as the voice of the human rights movement in India. In 1998, they launched a National Protest Day for human rights that involved the National Council of Churches in India, the Salvation Army, the Methodist Church in India, the Baptist church, the Evangelical Fellowship of India, CRI, All India Catholic Union, and a variety of Christian nongovernmental organizations and secular human rights groups. These groups marched for religious freedom on behalf of Muslim, Christian, and Dalit minorities. Dayal also has been an ecumenical force in the United States, speaking to millions of *700 Club* viewers. Global evangelicals, in drawing attention to human rights abuses, added a new ecumenical spirit to insular sectors of mid-century American evangelicalism.[20]

Third, the new global attention on human rights helped drive a new evangelical emphasis on social structures. Out of a context that emphasized individual rights, personal evangelism, and local efforts of mercy, evangelicals now more easily engage national and global structures. "Social ethics is back on the table," proclaimed the opening essay in the inaugural 1984 issue of *Transformation*, a new evangelical journal featuring the writings of two-thirds world evangelicals such as Tokunboh Adeyemo of Madagascar, David Gitari of Kenya, Bong Rin Ro of Korea, and Vinay Samuel of India. In 1984, Laura Glynn, a longtime U.S. missionary to South America, described horrific human rights abuses in Ecuador. "It should be understood that these crimes against people are not the result of fortuitous happenings and policies," she wrote. "Rather they are the direct consequence of a long history of the systematic violations of civic, political, economic, social, and cultural rights of the person." Twenty-five-year missionary veteran Waldron Scott, highlighting the important work of the Evangelical Fellowship of India Commission on Relief, argued that "the biblical understanding of mission is rectification, the establishment of justice." Dozens of similar articles reframed religious freedom in terms of human rights, added economic and social components, and demanded that such rights be conferred on all people, not only Christians. A multitude of moderate and progressive organizations—including Evangelicals for Social Action, Sojourners, the Association for Public Justice, and World Vision—argued that politics was an appropriate venue for action. A more prominent and electorally successful Religious Right pursued a similar methodology, though disagreeing profoundly with their counterparts on particular policies.[21]

On human rights, however, these diverse wings of evangelical politics cooperated. In the 1980s, a group of evangelical congresspersons—including Tony Hall (D-Ohio), Frank Wolf (R-VA), and Chris Smith (R-New Jersey)—met for prayer and political action on behalf of Chinese dissidents, imprisoned pastors, Sudanese refugees, and victimized women. Wolf, as cochair of the Congressional Human Rights Caucus, successfully pushed to revoke Romania's Most Favored Nation status because of human rights abuses. Dozens of other Christian politicians—including Dan Coats, Richard Lugar, Don Nickles, Spencer Bachus, and Joseph Pitts—soon joined the trio. By 2000, according to sociologist Michael Lindsay, 70 percent of evangelical elites agreed that "stopping religious persecution should be given top priority in American foreign policy." The National Association of Evangelicals' 1996 "Statement of Conscience" built its foreign policy planks around human rights. By the 2010s, hundreds of evangelical organizations—such as Freedom House, Evangelicals for Human Rights, the New Evangelical Partnership for the Common Good, International Justice Mission, and Compassion International—were tapping a constituency increasingly convinced that human rights should animate evangelical politics and American diplomacy.[22]

International Justice Mission (IJM), though it has a short history dating only to 1997, has made perhaps the biggest footprint. Like so many other evangelical organizations, its focus on human trafficking and human rights is rooted in international experience. In the 1980s, IJM's founder, Gary Haugen, worked for Michael Cassidy, a South African who ran African Enterprise and, along with Desmond Tutu, the National Institute for Reconciliation. During law school at the University of Chicago, Haugen volunteered for the Lawyers Committee for Human Rights in the Philippines, where he documented abuses by the regime of dictator Ferdinand Marcos and discovered that these crimes were not prosecuted. He also noted that his native country's record was not spotless. The United States had worked for decades with abusive and corrupt foreign police to advance anticommunist and then anti-drug-trafficking and antiterrorist efforts. In the early 1990s, Haugen worked for the U.S. Department of Justice and led the United Nations' investigation of genocide in Rwanda. Refined in the fire of global injustice, Haugen launched IJM in 1997 as an explicitly Christian organization dedicated to answering scripture's call for justice. According to Haugen, IJM sought to provide "victim relief, perpetrator accountability, victim aftercare, and structural prevention of violence." The organization's first legal cases—human trafficking in Thailand and bonded labor in India—allowed Haugen to "identify the specific gaps in developing countries' legal systems." Haugen's evangelical use of dualistic language, though he distanced himself from the military adventures of the Bush administration, has frightened secularists. But his use of words like *sin*, *good*, and *evil* are theologically compelling to evangelicals, his primary constituency. "I saw my own faith community as spiritually impoverished," he said of his efforts to spark a global social conscience. Opportunities for global reflex within IJM continue. Ninety percent of the organization's foreign staff are nationals.[23]

The trajectory of international exposure leading to structural sensibilities also can be seen in dozens of other evangelical NGOs. Sociologist Robert Wuthnow describes the advocacy directed toward the State Department by evangelical relief agencies on behalf of ethnic Baptists in Southeast Asia. Others working with the State Department have helped thousands of refugees to immigrate to the United States. One church in the Northwest runs overseas ministries and helps immigrants, including undocumented arrivals. "We tend to everyone—Muslim, Jewish. The commitment is at least ten years—you can't do anything with less," the pastor said. Numerous evangelical NGOs, including World Relief and World Vision, have lobbied to loosen U.S. immigration laws. Evangelical "eyes and ears," according to Wuthnow, exert significant pressure on the policy community.[24]

The new evangelical internationalism problematizes the binary that ties individualist logic to conservatism and structural logic to progressivism. On one hand, progressives violate the old model by continuing to use hero myths and individual agency to assert themselves in the public sphere. On the other hand, neoliberal evangelical conservatives increasingly seek national and global structural change in their policy prescriptions. To offer yet another example, WEF helped launch a campaign called the Micah Challenge that addresses education, poverty, hunger, gender equality, maternal health, HIV and other diseases, environmental sustainability, and economic development—and places them in the context of human rights and shared responsibility for the condition of all peoples. Advocates urge pursuit of the Millennium Development Goals devised by the United Nations in 2000. The Micah Challenge represents the significant activity of younger evangelicals in starting institutions, lobbying Washington and other global capitals, and launching media campaigns. They are often very articulate in describing the structural patterns of inequality that lead to poverty, human trafficking, and human rights violations.[25]

And yet these same evangelicals have retained a passion for individual souls and bodies. They see microenterprise programs not only as critical in correcting social injustices but also desirable because they can maintain a long-term relationship with a local community. The Farmer to Farmer program, which pairs farmers from Iowa to farmers in Nicaragua, reflects this strategy, as does World Vision's support of over 440,000 projects in forty-six two-thirds world countries. According to the new evangelical internationalists, impersonal campaigns to stop injustice are humanized and made better when they attend to particular communities. One southern megachurch pastor explained, "We do not tell a community that we know what their problems are and how to fix them. We try to find out what the perspective of the community is, and we often learn more than they do." Shane Claiborne, a New Monastic who is very attentive to structural sources of injustice, speaks ardently about "when people fall in love with each other across class lines." Evangelicals are consistently driven, as if "by gravitational force," according to Omri Elisha, toward direct influence, relationships, and personal purity. Even if the global pandemic of sex trafficking cannot be stopped through the sanctification of men's lustful minds, those minds still need to be purified. As they increasingly acknowledge structural patterns of inequality, evangelicals retain an individualist sensibility.[26]

Numerous other examples also confound long-standing binaries. In chapter 7, Laurel Kearns describes how even leaders of the antienvironmentalist Cornwall Alliance frame many of their arguments in terms of social justice. The organization has begun to argue that environmentalism is a threat to prosperity and freedom—that it hurts the poor and that the cost of curtailing climate change will undermine economic systems. Similarly, John

Schmalzbauer shows that structural language likewise predominates among conservatives in the Heritage Foundation. Most significantly, a rising group of "new evangelicals," as Marcia Pally calls them, have come to a consensus around a "mix of market and common good." She writes that this cohort upholds "individual initiative and entrepreneurialism in markets, but this does not commit them to just any market action but rather to those that follow an ethics of resource-distribution and opportunity-restructuring for the flourishing of all." The National Association of Evangelicals' 2004 statement "For the Health of the Nation" supports a free-market system and private property but it also features startling structural language having to do with religious freedom, family life and the protection of children, sanctity of life, caring for the poor and vulnerable, human rights, peacemaking, and caring for creation. The old individualist-structuralist categories have been complicated.[27]

It is perhaps these mixed methods of personal and structural activism that have animated the relative sophistication of recent evangelical human rights work. Given the success of IJM and others, many observers now nurture a growing conviction that evangelicals can reinvigorate the declining fortunes of the broader human rights movement. In the wake of the IRFA, Elisabeth Bumiller of the *New York Times* documented how evangelical influence in the Bush administration "resulted in surprising human rights achievements." Nicholas Kristof, also of the *Times*, wrote in 2010 that evangelicals have become the nation's "newest internationalists." A wide range of evangelicals—including David Gushee, Ron Sider, Glen Stassen, Richard Cizik, Rick Warren, and Franklin Graham—now use the language of human rights. Many enjoy direct access to political elites occupying some of the highest offices in American politics. This eagerness to use the language of social justice in ecumenical and political spheres stands in striking contrast to the evangelical parochialism of the 1940s.[28]

* * *

To be sure, many other variables—including rising levels of education, wealth, and social status—sparked American evangelical social awareness. Nor were all international evangelicals progressive, especially on issues of sexuality. Moreover, the emergence of the Religious Right in an era when third-world evangelicals were speaking more critically of American capitalist imperialism demonstrates that considerable numbers of American evangelicals disagreed—or were not listening at all. In fact, some fundamentalist evangelicals, notably Jerry Falwell and Pat Robertson, have denied egregious human rights abuses to protect financial investments in South Africa and Liberia. Many remained enthusiastic celebrators of the nation, and their new interest in development often came with the result, if not intent, of securing the world for free-market capitalism. Evangelical missionaries and development workers, believing that they had spiritual and moral resources to offer the world, some-times inscribed tacit neoliberal strategies on their activities. At the very least, neoliberalism created conditions that made evangelicals' global activism (and, ironically, global critiques of America) possible. At the most, globally mobile evangelicals, who have started microbusinesses, constructed high-speed com-puting networks, and worked to reform foreign governments, could be consid-ered the foot soldiers of late capitalist restructuring in emerging global cities.[29]

There is, however, another compelling global narrative. Jay Case, a histo-rian of evangelical globalization in the nineteenth century, argues that mis-sionaries were often poor cultural imperialists. In fact, the most successful missionaries empowered the local population and adapted to local cultures. And as newer theories of globalization recognize, influence often flowed in multiple directions. People of the two-thirds world exerted agency and influ-ence on the West. Within global evangelicalism, Africans have pushed back on sexuality, Asians on methods of evangelization, and Latin Americans on con-sumerism. That two-thirds world action on human rights has helped to shape some of the most striking and visible changes in American evangelical culture in the twentieth century confirms Case's findings. Francis Bok's compelling voice—heard in Midland and in the Oval Office—signified the culmination of several decades of global Christians encouraging their American counterparts to embrace human rights and social justice. Bok also represented the leading edge of what will become a larger and more intense global reflex. International voices will most certainly swell to a chorus in this century as the global south demographically overwhelms northern and western centers. In a world where 60 percent of all Christians now live outside the North Atlantic region and in a nation increasingly open to nonwhite immigrants since the Immigration Act of 1965, global concerns and influence will only carry more weight.[30]

NOTES

1. Allen D. Hertzke, *Freeing God's Children: The Unlikely Alliance for Global Human Rights* (New York: Rowan & Littlefield, 2004), 264–66, 294. On human rights violations in Sudan, see Paul Marshall, *Their Blood Cries Out: The Worldwide Tragedy of Modern Christians Who Are Dying for Their Faith* (Dallas: Thomas Nelson, 1997), 18; Francis Bok, *Escape from Slavery: The True Story of My Ten Years in Captivity—and My Journey to Freedom in America* (New York: St. Martin's Press, 2003), 219–25.

2. Hertzke, *Freeing God's Children,* 289–92.

3. On the historiography of evangelical politics, see John G. Turner, *Bill Bright and Campus Crusade for Christ: The Renewal of Evangelicalism in Postwar America* (Chapel Hill: University of North Carolina Press, 2008); Steven P. Miller, *Billy Graham and the Rise of the Republican South* (Philadelphia: University of Pennsylvania Press, 2009); Darren Dochuk, *From Bible Belt to Sunbelt: Plain-Folk Religion, Grassroots Politics, and the Rise of Evangelical Conservatism* (New York: W. W. Norton, 2010); Daniel K. Williams, *God's Own Party: The Making of the Christian Right* (Oxford: Oxford University Press, 2010).

4. Roland Robertson, *Globalization: Social Theory and Global Culture* (London: Sage, 1992). On growing evangelical investment in missions and development, see Robert Wuthnow, *Boundless Faith: The Global Outreach of American Churches* (Berkeley: University of California Press, 2009), 23.

5. On the fading missions movement, see Nathan D. Showalter, *The End of a Crusade: The Student Volunteer Movement for Foreign Missions and the Great War* (Lanham, MD: Scarecrow Press, 1997). On the League of Nations, see Markku Ruotsila, *The Origins of Christian Anti-Internationalism: Conservative Evangelicals and the League of Nations* (Washington, DC: Georgetown University Press, 2008). On fundamentalist losses to mainliners, see George Marsden, *Fundamentalism and American Culture* (New York: Oxford University Press, 1980). On cultural pessimism, see Mark Noll, *The Scandal of the Evangelical Mind* (Grand Rapids, MI: Eerdmans, 1994), 165. On continuing evangelical suspicion of human rights rhetoric in some sectors, see Amy Rachel Timmons Stumpf, "A Study of the Relationship between American Evangelicals and Human Rights" (PhD diss., Loma Linda University, 2007); Joel A. Nichols, "Evangelicals and Human Rights: The Continuing Ambivalence of Evangelical Christians' Support for Human Rights," *Journal of Law and Religion* 24 (2009): 629–62.

6. On neo-evangelical cultural ambition, see Joel Carpenter, *Revive Us Again: The Reawakening of American Fundamentalism* (New York: Oxford University Press, 1997).

7. Mark Noll, "The View of World-Wide Christianity from American Evangelical Magazines, 1900–2000," 367–86, in *Making History for God: Essays on Evangelicalism, Revival and Mission in Honour of Stuart Piggin*, ed. Geoffrey R. Treloar and Robert D. Linder (Sydney: Robert Menzies College, 2004).

8. For anticommunist screeds in *Christianity Today*, see J. Edgar Hoover, "Communism: The Bitter Enemy of Religion," *Christianity Today*, 3, June 22, 1959, 3–5; Walter H. Judd, "World Issues and the Christian," *Christianity Today*, 2, June 23, 1958, 6; Hoover, "Storming the Skies: Christianity Encounters Communism," *Christianity Today*, 7, December 21, 1962, 3–5. For VBS curriculum, see "Patriots for Christ," *Christianity Today*, 6, March 2, 1962, 23.

9. *World Vision Magazine,* June 1957, 2; Bob Pierce, "Behind the Scenes with World Vision," *World Vision Magazine,* August–September 1957, 2.

10. On Solzhenitsyn at Harvard, see Chuck Colson, "Jeremiah at Harvard," *Christianity Today,* 52, August 5, 2008, 64. For a similar non-American critique of Western consumerism and Marxist totalitarianism, see in Charles Malik, "A Civilization at Bay," *Christianity Today,* 6, November 24, 1961, 3–5; Festo Kivengere, "Creativity and Transcendence," 38–39, in *At the Edge of Hope: Christian Laity in Paradox* (New York: Seabury Press, 1978). Also see W. Harold Fuller, *People of the Mandate: The Story of the World Evangelical Fellowship* (Grand Rapids, MI: Baker Books, 1996), 112; "The Lima Letter," 16, in *How Evangelicals Endorsed Social Responsibility: Texts on Evangelical Social Ethics, 1974–83,* ed. C. RenéNew Padilla and Chris Sugden (Nottingham: Grove Books, 1985).

11. For "no longer useful," see Kivengere, "Creativity and Transcendence," 39. For "bad track record," see Andrew Kirk, *Good News of the Kingdom Coming: The Marriage of Evangelism and Social Responsibility* (Downers Grove, IL: InterVarsity Press, 1983), 86.

12. For "something incongruous," see Warren and Shirley Webster, "Segregation and World Missions"; Bernard Bancroft, "Color and Missions"; and Dave and Anna Gay Newell, "Letters," in *Freedom Now* 3:1 (January–February 1967): 11–13, 17–18. On Fuller Seminary, see Carol Reiss, "Relationship in Action," *Opinion* 7:2 (November 1967). On international pressure at Wheaton, see "International Student Addresses Claphams," *Wheaton Record* 85:20 (February 14, 1963): 1; "Okite Relates African Strides to U.S. Civil Rights Movement," *Wheaton Record* 88:19 (February 17, 1966): 4; So Yan Pul, "Senior Deprecates Racial Attitudes," *Wheaton Record* 88:18 (February 10, 1966): 4. At Calvin, see John LaGrand, "Christian Political Action?" *Chimes* 59:7 (October 30, 1964): 3. For Howard Jones, see "Missions Prejudice," *HIS* 25:4 (January 1965): 1, 3. For similar statements, see "Day-by-Day Synopsis," *HIS* 25:6 (March 1965): 7–8, Ruben Lores, "Feedback," *HIS* 25:7 (April 1965): 28; Mary Anne Klein, "Feedback," *HIS* 25:7 (April 1965): 29; J. Isamu Yamamoto, "Interracial Marriage," *Right On* 8:3 (November–December 1976): 19; Howard O. Jones, *White Questions to a Black Christian* (Grand Rapids, MI: Zondervan, 1975), 80–81. On Costas, see A. Barro, "Orlando Enrique Costas: Mission Theologian on the Way and at the Crossroads" (PhD diss., Fuller Theological Seminary, 1993), 9–44; Elizabeth Conde-Frazier, "Orlando E. Costas," Biola University website, September 3, 2009.

13. On the drafting of the declaration, see Mary Ann Glendon, *A World Made New: Eleanor Roosevelt and the Universal Declaration of Human Rights* (New York: Random House, 2001). On human rights as "biblically based," see D. Richard John, "Evangelicals and Human Rights," 228-34, in Waldron Scott, ed., *Serving Our Generation: Evangelical Strategies for the Eighties* (Colorado

Springs: World Evangelical Fellowship, 1980). For the "Madras Declaration" and the "Lima Letter," see Padilla and Sugden, *How Evangelicals Endorsed Social Responsibility*

14. J. D. Douglas, *Let the Earth Hear His Voice: Official Reference Volume, Papers and Responses* (Minneapolis, MN: World Wide, 1975).

15. On WEF and Dibaj, see Fuller, *People of the Mandate*, 108–9. For examples of the genre on martyrdom and religious persecution, see Nina Shea, *In the Lion's Den: A Shocking Account of Persecution and Martyrdom of Christians Today & How We Should Respond* (Nashville, TN: Broadman & Holman Publishers, 1997) ; Marshall, *Their Blood Cries Out*, 11.

16. On Filipino calls for human rights, see "A Church Awakened," *Sojourners* 12:10 (November 1983): 21. On Kivengere, see Keith Graber Miller, *Wise as Serpents, Innocent as Doves: American Mennonites Engage Washington* (Knoxville: University of Tennessee Press, 1996), 147–48; Kivengere, *I Love Idi Amin: The Story of Triumph under Fire in the Midst of Suffering and Persecution in Uganda* (Old Tappan, NJ: Revell, 1977), 21–22, 24–26, 29; Kivengere, *Revolutionary Love* (Nairobi: African Evangelistic Enterprise, 1981).

17. For examples of the new evangelical literature on human rights, especially from the evangelical left, see Wes Michaelson, "Human Rights: A Surer Standard," *Sojourners* 6:4 (April 1977): 3–5; Gordon Spykman, "Toward a Biblical View of Human Rights," *Theological Forum* 7:1 (1979): 1–17; James Skillen, *International Politics and the Demand for Global Justice* (Sioux Center, IA: Dordt College Press, 1981), 99–109; René Padilla, *The Theology of Liberation* (Sioux Center, IA: International Conference of Institutions for Christian Higher Education, 1981); Ed Vanderkloet and Paul Marshall, *Foundations of Human Rights* (Rexdale, Ontario: Christian Labour Association of Canada, 1981); Bernard Zylstra, *Religion, Rights and the Constitution* (Toronto: ICS, 1981); "Scholars Address Reagan on Latin American Policy," *Public Justice Report* 5:1 (October 1981): 3–4; Paul Marshall, *Human Rights Theories in Christian Perspective* (Toronto: Institute for Christian Studies, 1983); Jimmy Carter, "Human Rights: Dilemmas and Directions," *Transformation*, October–December 1984, 2–5; Kerry Ptacek, "International Religious Liberty and the Great Commission," 81–99, in *The High Cost of Indifference*, ed. Richard Cizik (Ventura, CA: Regal, 1984); Karen King and Chris Moss, "Human Rights in Nicaragua," *The Other Side* 20:5 (May 1984): 24–27; Jim Wallis, "The Rise of Christian Conscience," *Sojourners* 14:1 (January 1985): 12–16. On the religious blind spots of secularists, see James Finn, "The Cultivation and Protection of Religious Human Rights: The Role of the Media," 161–189, in *Religious Human Rights in Global Perspective: Legal Aspects*, ed. J. D. van der Vyver and J. Witte Jr. (The Hague: Martinus Nijhoff, 1996), 188; Marshall, *Their Blood Cries Out*, 181–209. On Wolf, see Frank Wolf, *Prisoner of*

Conscience: One Man's Crusade for Global Human and Religious Rights (Grand Rapids, MI: Zondervan, 2011).

18. For examples of evangelical fulminations in the 1950s against Catholics and the National Council of Churches, see "NAE Reaffirms Strong Anti-Communist Stand," *Christianity Today*, May 9, 1960, 30. For an example of *Christianity Today*'s treatment of human rights in the 1970s, see "News," *Christianity Today*, April 11, 1975, 31. For "wider range," see Noll, "The View of World-Wide Christianity," 367–86. On ecumenical sources from the World Evangelical Fellowship, see Gordan Spykman, "Human Rights: A Selective Bibliography," *Transformation*, 1, July–September 1984, 17. On evangelical uses of "*imago dei*," see John Gladwin, "Human Rights," 167, in *Essays in Evangelical Social Ethics*, ed. David F. Wright (Exeter: Paternoster Press, 1978); Nichols, "Evangelicals and Human Rights," 652; Charles Colson and Richard John Neuhaus, eds., *Evangelicals and Catholics Together: Toward a Common Mission* (Waco, TX: Word Books, 1995); Mark Noll and Carolyn Nystrom, *Is the Reformation Over? An Evangelical Assessment of Contemporary Roman Catholicism* (Grand Rapids, MI: Baker Academic, 2005); Robert Traer, *Faith in Human Rights: Support in Religious Traditions for a Global Struggle* (Washington, DC: Georgetown University Press, 1991).

19. For WEF, see Fuller, *People of the Mandate*, 109. For Marshall, see Paul Marshall, *Their Blood Cries Out*, xviii, 29–31, 33, 37, 77, 102, 246. On Horowitz, see D. Michael Lindsay, *Faith in the Halls of Power: How Evangelicals Joined the American Elite* (New York: Oxford University Press, (2007), 43.

20. On the IRFA, see Hertzke, *Freeing God's Children*, 68–69; Hertzke, "The Role of Evangelicals in the New Human Rights Movement," speech given at the University of Southern California Annenberg School for Communication, Los Angeles, September 22, 2004. For more calls for ecumenicity on human rights work, see Terry C. Muck, "Interreligious Dialogue and Human Rights," 99–113, in *Christianity and Human Rights*, ed. Frances S. Adeney and Arvind Sharma (Albany: State University of New York Press, 2007), 99–113.

21. For writers in *Transformation* magazine, see "Introducing *Transformation*," *Transformation*, January–March 1984, 1–2. On Ecuador, see Laura Glynn, "Quinchuqui: A Case Study on Human Rights in Ecuador," *Transformation*, 1 April–June 1984, 13–15. For "establishment of justice," see Waldron Scott, *Bring Forth Justice: A Contemporary Perspective on Mission* (Grand Rapids, MI: Eerdmans, 1980), xv. For other two-thirds world critiques, see Adeyemo, Samuel, and Sider, "Beyond Equality," *Transformation*, July–September 1984, 1; David Lim, Bel Magalit, and Jun Vencer, "Responding to Philippine Realities Today," *Transformation*, July–September 1984, 6–10.

22. For "stopping religious persecution," see Hertzke, *Freeing God's Children*, 35.

23. Samantha Power, "The Enforcer: A Christian Lawyer's Global Crusade," *New Yorker*, January 19, 2009; Gary A. Haugen, *Good News about*

Injustice: A Witness of Courage in a Hurting World (Downers Grove, IL: InterVarsity Press, 1999). For more on evangelical efforts against human trafficking, see Wuthnow, *Boundless Faith*, 217.

24. On evangelicals and the State Department, see Wuthnow, *Boundless Faith*, 214. On the congregation from the Northwest working with Karen immigrants from Burma and Thailand, see Marcia Pally, "Theology and Practice of America's New Evangelicals," *Radical Orthodoxy: Theology, Philosophy, Politics* 1:1 (August 2012): 304–5. For more two-thirds world sources on the social implications of faith, see Festo Kivengere, "Creativity and Transcendence," 36.

25. On complicating the individualist-structural binary, see James Bielo's response to "Global Reflex" paper, Indiana University-Purdue University Indianapolis, May 18, 2012.

26. For Farmer to Farmer, World Vision, and "learn more than they do," see Pally, "Theology and Practice," 303–7. On the rise in microenterprise, see Wuthnow, *Boundless Faith*, 83. For "gravitational force," see Omri Elisha, *Moral Ambition: Mobilization and Social Outreach in Evangelical Megachurches* (Berkeley: University of California Press, 2011), 109. Claiborne is quoted in Pally, "Theology and Practice," 301.

27. For "an ethics of resource-distribution," see Pally, "Theology and Practice," 281. For structural language in "For the Health of the Nation," see Pally, "Theology and Practice," 301–3; *For the Health of the Nation: An Evangelical Call to Civic Responsibility* (Washington, DC: National Association of Evangelicals, 2004).

28. Nicholas Kristoff, "Learning from the Sin of Sodom," *New York Times*, February 27, 2010; Elisabeth Bumiller, "Evangelicals Sway White House on Human Rights Issues Abroad," *New York Times*, October 26, 2003. On evangelical elites, see Hertzke, *Freeing God's Children*, 35; Lindsay, *Faith in the Halls of Power*, 43. On evangelical reinvigoration of the human rights movement, see "The United Nations' Disarray," *Christianity Today*, 51, February 2007.

29. On Falwell and Robertson, see Wuthnow, *Boundless Faith*, 83. On evangelicalism's commitment to global neoliberalism, see Bethany E. Moreton, "The Soul of Neoliberalism," *Social Text* 25:3 (Fall 2007): 103–23. On the role of neoliberalism in a heightened evangelical global consciousness, see James Bielo's response to "Global Reflex" paper, IUPUI, May 18, 2012.

30. Jay Case, *An Unpredictable Gospel: American Evangelicals and Global Christianity* (New York: Oxford University Press, 2012). On global evangelicalism, see Paul Freston, ed., *Evangelical Christianity and Democracy in Latin America* (New York: Oxford University Press, 2008), 28; David H. Lumsdaine, ed., *Evangelical Christianity and Democracy in Asia* (New York: Oxford University Press, 2009); Terence O. Ranger, ed., *Evangelical Christianity and Democracy in Africa* (New York: Oxford University Press, 2008). Also see Paul Freston, *Protestant Political Parties: A Global Survey* (Burlington, VT: Ashgate,

2004); Freston, *Evangelicals and Politics in Asia, Africa, and Latin America* (Cambridge: Cambridge University Press, 2001). On the demographic shifts of global Christianity, see Mark A. Noll, "Who Would Have Thought?" *Books & Culture* 7 (November–December 2001): 21; Philip Jenkins, *The Next Christendom: The Coming of Global Christianity* (New York: Oxford University Press, 2002); Soong-Chan Rah, *The Next Evangelicalism: Freeing the Church from Western Cultural Captivity* (Downers Grove, IL: InterVarsity Press, 2009).

Global Poverty and
Evangelical Action

Amy Reynolds and Stephen Offutt

EVANGELICALS IN THE United States are deeply involved in international relief and development efforts, and understanding the nature of that participation—as well as how it has grown and changed over time—is critical to understanding the broader realm of evangelical engagement with poverty. In this chapter we seek to dispel the myth that evangelicals exclusively rely on individual-level solutions to reduce poverty, largely through an examination of the work being done by evangelical nongovernmental organizations (NGOs) working with poverty outside the United States.

International poverty has been the topic of much attention, thought, and action within the evangelical community. In the past seventy years, the evangelical nonprofit sector has blossomed into a central institution within American evangelicalism. We begin by examining the emergence and growth of this sector. Evangelical nonprofits began doing disaster relief in the mid-twentieth century. By the 1980s, they were implementing sophisticated approaches to economic development. More recently, they have also begun to engage in advocacy work alongside development.

In the second section of this chapter, we provide an assessment of the state of the evangelical nonprofit sector today. Highlighting examples of work on the ground, we argue that most contemporary evangelical responses are multifaceted and reflect sustained theological thinking about the nature of poverty and development. Most evangelical advocacy efforts, on the other hand, remain weak, yet evangelical organizations are currently rethinking their development paradigms to better incorporate advocacy work.

We conclude by examining the implications of this sector for the larger population of evangelicals in America. While development professionals largely occupy the nonprofit sector, we contend that this sector is influential (and increasingly so) within the larger evangelical realm. World Vision, Samaritan's Purse, and similar organizations are central to the evangelical community and its identity. Evangelicals now overwhelmingly are committed to attacking international poverty. However, we find that such commitment sometimes lacks a deep understanding of poverty, its causes, and its consequences. While evangelical relief and development organizations are educating the evangelical community on such issues, we contend that there is still much work to be done and we highlight some of the current efforts to this end.

From Emerging Concerns to a Thriving NGO Sector

Starting in the middle of the twentieth century, evangelical relief organizations became an institutionalized vehicle for predominantly white evangelicals to act on their concerns for the poor overseas. In this section, we examine the growth and history of this sector. We highlight three temporal phases: a commitment to the poor and attention to relief, an emphasis on community and transformational development, and an engagement in advocacy efforts.

Founding of a Development Sector

When American evangelicalism distinguished itself from the fundamentalist movement in the mid-twentieth century, its cultural package was compatible with global concern for the poor. A central distinguishing feature of evangelicalism from fundamentalism was its desire for public engagement; poverty alleviation was an obvious place to start, and biblical justification could easily be constructed for initiatives in this area. Over the last seven decades, evangelical involvement with this issue has expanded exponentially. It is shaped by a heightened awareness of international social problems, increased evangelical discourse on social concerns, and the rapid expansion of the U.S. nonprofit and nongovernment industry. Such forces enabled the creation, growth, and evolution of the modern evangelical relief and development sector.

American exposure to global poverty increased steadily at the same time that the evangelical movement was growing. Soldiers, journalists, and others (mostly via the media) witnessed the ill effects of war and poverty overseas[1] and sought ways to mobilize their faith communities to respond. Early evangelical leaders such as Carl F. H. Henry, Charles Fuller, and Harold Ockenga viewed engaging global poverty as a way to "resurrect the temperament and vision" of an eighteenth-century evangelicalism, when evangelicals were "confident and engaged socially, politically, culturally, and intellectually."[2]

World Relief was thus founded in 1944 as the social arm of the National Association of Evangelicals (which itself was founded in 1942). Shortly thereafter, Bob Pierce founded World Vision in 1950 to care for severely disadvantaged children in Asia (and particularly Korea in the early years). Charles Fuller founded Fuller Theological Seminary in 1947; it quickly became the hallmark evangelical seminary and developed very close ties to World Vision. The organizations were so tightly knit that Erica Bornstein reports a World Vision employee recounting in an interview that " 'the idea of World Vision started in conversations in the basement of Fuller Theological Seminary.' "[3] Today, Fuller and World Vision continue to have multiple interlocking relationships.

World Relief and World Vision served as precursors to an increasingly dominant organizational form: the nongovernmental organization, or NGO. They were different from the organizational forms that had been used by many Christians in their earlier international efforts, such as denominational boards and independent mission agencies. The differences are important because they have allowed evangelicals to "focus their attention more on hunger, poverty and disaster relief than on evangelism alone."[4] Many of the earliest NGOs were created by religious groups and were faith-based in orientation.[5] But this religious innovation quickly spread to other parts of society. By the late 1960s, secular actors were creating NGOs to "fill the vacuum in human services left in international relief and development work by both corporations and nation-states."[6]

By the mid-1970s, the evangelical development sector had grown enough that some formal coordination between NGOs made sense. Twelve organizations were invited to an organizational meeting in 1977 in Wheaton, Illinois. The group decided to incorporate the Association of Evangelical Relief and Development Organizations (AERDO)—now Accord—the following year with the intent of sharing information and resources and facilitating collaboration in the field. Most organizations were still primarily concerned with relief work—the provision of basic humanitarian aid after or in the midst of famines, wars, or other calamitous events. In fact, the idea for AERDO may have been birthed when Food for the Hungry founder Larry Ward saw the potential benefits of such a group while responding to a disaster in Bangladesh in 1976.[7]

Moving from Relief to Development

Starting in the 1970s, and gaining popularity in the 1980s, the concept of development emerged that changed the shape and direction of the work of evangelical (and other) NGOs. Development is distinguished from relief work in that it refers to longer term efforts at reducing poverty. It involves strength-ening civil society, energizing local economies, and/or making grassroots political entities more effective.

Debates between modernization and dependency theorists set the intellec-tual context during the time evangelicals were creating new ideas about devel-opment. Walt Rostow, an economic historian at MIT throughout the 1950s and later part of the Kennedy administration, was a primary architect of the mod-ernization theory. In Rostow's paradigm, advanced societies passed through a number of stages of development; traditional or less developed societies could become modern by progressing through these same stages.[8] Economic growth, political democracy, infrastructural improvements, and technological advances all help developing countries in their upward trajectories.[9] In opposi-tion, dependency theory argued that economic development did not occur in one particular way. Western countries represented the core of a global system and were in control of resources. Such resources came from countries in the global South (the periphery of the global system) and were often exploited for profit in the core.[10] These different understandings of development and inter-national relationships created different agendas and ideas about how to help poorer countries succeed.

During this time, many in the NGO sector were shifting from a primary focus on relief work to experimenting with principles of community devel-opment.[11] Thinkers such as David Korten advanced a new theoretical para-digm that placed people at the center of the development agenda.[12] While not neglecting the macrolevel issues on which modernization and dependency theorists focused, this new paradigm emphasized the people embedded in such systems. The NGOs, which were located at the grassroots level and wanted to engage with oppressive social, political, and economic structures in ways that immediately corresponded to felt needs, largely adopted such ideas.

Instigated by changes in the broader NGO world, evangelicals dealing with issues of international poverty recognized that they must engage with struc-tures in a more sophisticated way as well and transitioned from mostly relief efforts to relief and development. Attention to these issues was in part directed by the broader NGO community[13] and in part through sustained partnerships with evangelicals abroad. The Mennonites, for example, developed an evangel-ical precursor to the Fair Trade Movement. In the 1940s, Mennonite women began individualized efforts to sell artisan goods to other Mennonites, and by 1962, this effort had been taken over by the Mennonite Central Committee and turned into SELFHELP CRAFTS, which is now called Ten Thousand Villages. World Vision also made an early transition to community development.[14] In 1974, it incorporated the promotion of self-reliance, which is a basic point of distinction between relief and development work, as part of its organizational objectives.[15]

A movement toward community development among evangelical practitioners spurred innovations in evangelical theology concerning development. Evangelicals needed a deeper theology for thinking about development that included attention to structural concerns.[16] A seminal conference at evangelical Wheaton College in 1983 was a decisive moment in the theology's formation. It was organized by the World Evangelical Fellowship (WEF) and attended by 336 leaders from fifty-nine countries. The conference's achievements included (1) a coalescence of evangelical leaders around the term *transformation*;[17] (2) the founding of a journal called *Transformation: An International Dialogue on Evangelical Social Ethics*; (3) the issuing of the Wheaton '83 Statement, which was published in *Transformation* and continues to be an influential document within evangelical development circles; and (4) the considerable advancement of the creation of transformational development theory. A number of publications immediately preceded the conference formalizing these contributions,[18] and Vinay Samuel, a key leader at Wheaton '83, further refined the theory's central ideas in the ensuing months and years.[19]

Although the relief and development organizations were growing in the 1980s, they were not leading actors in the evangelical community at large. Sherman argues that they were doing more than many noticed.[20] World Vision, World Relief, Food for the Hungry, Transformation International, and World Concern were all involved not only in relief efforts but also in community development projects, microenterprise, and educational and training programs. These organizations generally avoided the dependency theory approaches adopted by liberal and mainline Protestant organizations, but many nonetheless recognized and acted against "structural sin" and problems inherent in the global economic system.[21] Alongside such approaches, corresponding training programs in the evangelical educational world emerged. Eastern University, for example, initiated the first Christian program in economic development in 1984.

The Trend toward Advocacy in Evangelical Social Engagement

A more recent development within evangelical antipoverty efforts has been the move to embrace advocacy. *Advocacy* can be defined as "an organized political process that involves the coordinated efforts of people to change policies, practices, ideas, and values that perpetuate inequality, prejudice and exclusion."[22] Advocacy often requires engagement with people or institutions of power, and faith-based and secular NGOs alike have realized that engaging at the policy level is the only way to solve some of the structural issues.

International antipoverty advocacy work can take numerous approaches. Some involve challenging laws governing economic policies and wealth distribution or work opportunities. Others deal with petitioning governments to increase aid or promote greater economic flows with other countries. Still others deal with some of the larger societal practices that are crucial to understanding the complex nature of poverty.

Evangelicals involved with missions internationally have historically played an important role in advocacy movements. Founding fathers of the modern missionary movement often combined advocacy work with evangelical missions. In India, William Carey (1761–1834) and E. Stanley Jones (1884–1973) both used advocacy to further social agendas that included literacy, political stability, and poverty alleviation. (Jones' work even gained him a nomination for the Nobel Peace Prize.)[23] Religious communities in many ways are well suited for advocacy. The strength of their voluntary organizations, international connections, and cultural resources often place them in position to speak for marginalized communities in the halls of power.[24]

Yet in areas of international relief and development, many white evangelical groups did not begin to consider advocacy until the 1990s. Bread for the World stands out for its focus on advocacy since its founding in 1972, but it is a broader ecumenical Christian organization and not linked solely (or mainly) to evangelicals. World Vision was again doing path breaking work in the area of advocacy among the evangelical community: it adopted a policy prioritizing justice in 1985 and in 1991 added a policy statement on advocacy. Advocacy work is now one of its three primary programming areas (along side of relief and development).[25] World Vision has a $7 million advocacy budget, and Bread for the World spends over $11 million per year.[26]

While some evangelical development groups still shy away from political involvement, a growing number of evangelical groups now have a presence in or near D.C., including Food for the Hungry, the International Justice Mission, the Mennonite Central Committee, World Concern, and World Relief. Bread for the World has made more concerted efforts to work with the evangelical community on issues of advocacy. Working alongside other actors, such advocacy work has helped to close brothels overseas, allowed the vulnerable to gain access to land titles, and pressured governments to commit resources to international aid. Although less successfully, groups have also been involved in protesting aspects of free trade policies and U.S. subsidies that harm farmers overseas.

In 2012, *Christianity Today*, a leading evangelical magazine, ran a two-part series discussing evangelical strategies against international poverty.[27] Responses from relief and development leaders interviewed provide a snapshot of current thinking on advocacy. Food for the Hungry leaders claim they walk with policy leaders. As we do, we are motivated by personal compassion while seeking to influence and improve upon governmental policies that help the poor."[28] A leader from Habitat for Humanity noted, "We agree that individual acts alone cannot solve global poverty. What is required is the fundamental changing of systems to protect the poor. That's something that we can only do together. An effective approach to the issue of poverty is one that encompasses all sectors of society. Any large-scale effort to address the world's housing need, for example, absolutely depends on collaboration."[29] While there are still a number of reservations that some evangelicals in development have about becoming involved in advocacy, these public proclamations indicate a readiness for increased and concerted international antipoverty advocacy efforts among evangelical NGOs. There is also a belief that their constituencies are also ready to support these efforts.

Development Organizations Today: How Are Evangelical Organizations Currently Engaging with Poverty?

In the previous section, we highlighted some of the ways the evangelical relief and development field has evolved since the early days in the 1940s. What does the evangelical relief and development world look like today?

To begin, the field has continued its growth unabated and has manifested itself in various ways. First, individual organizations have experienced exponential growth. Originally, AERDO (now Accord) came together so that small organizations could combine resources and engage in relief efforts more effectively. Several key members are now far larger than the combined size of the twelve initial member organizations in 1977. World Vision alone operates on a budget of $1.02 billion; Compassion International's annual budget has grown to $585 million. Second, the number of evangelical NGOs has also proliferated. More than sixty organizations now belong to Accord, and many more operate independently of any umbrella group. Third, the revenue streams of these organizations has risen dramatically.[30] Giving in 2003 was estimated at $2.3 billion[31] and has continued its rapid growth since then. Some evangelical NGOs use their organizational strength to pursue, procure, and administer large public grants, often from groups like USAID. Others can forgo such funding and rely solely on a private donor base. Those who support them continue to donate larger and larger sums of money.

Current paradigms of transformational development reflect a continued crystallization of the thoughts articulated at the Wheaton '83 conference. Bryant Myers's book on transformational development, *Walking with the Poor: Principles and Practices of Transformational Development*, is easily the most influential book in evangelical relief and development circles. In it, Myers asserts that poverty has to be understood at both an individual and a structural level and that spiritual, material, and social factors are all part of the problem. Poverty is defined as oppressive and broken relationships—of people with themselves and with others, as well as humans' relationships with God and with creation.[32] Development is thus an effort to reorient and restore relational structures. This includes individual-level relationships and the relationships shaped by national and international political, economic, and social structures. Evangelical organizations continue to use this model, and Myers continues to be a thought leader in evangelical relief and development circles. He addressed, for example, the 2011 Accord conference and is a member of Fuller Theological Seminary's faculty.

A corresponding evangelical theory for advocacy does not exist. Davis notes that some evangelical Christians fear that a greater emphasis on advocacy will come at the peril of community development, and so integrating them, or at least balancing them, is important.[33] No resistance to antipoverty advocacy per se has kept evangelical organizations from embracing such practices with full strength, but a more coherent theory explaining why and how advocacy can and should be used remains unarticulated, which limits the range of strategies evangelicals might use.[34] Some are currently engaged in such efforts to create a holistic vision of development that includes advocacy. For example, at the 2011 and 2012 Accord conferences, a track of sessions dedicated to advocacy was newly available to participants. Those sponsoring it hoped to create space for more dialogue among organizations about how to engage in advocacy work.

Evangelical relief and development agencies are increasingly likely to address structural dimensions of poverty in their development efforts. They are doing so even as they remain committed to transformation at the community level. In Central America, for example, World Relief's goal is to improve the lives of impoverished farmers. Whereas a relief-oriented approach might provide homes for farmers or food items to help them survive, the problems that directly contribute to the low wages of farmers include volatile prices in the international coffee market, a lack of business skills valued in the international marketplace, and poor access to market resources (such as loans or financing). Employing ideas of transformational development, World Relief provided economic resources for farmers, including greater access to crop financing. It also strengthened, financially and organizationally, an existing, local export business that could give farmers fairer prices and involve them more directly in the selling of coffee internationally. World Relief emphasized the development of human capital, including agricultural training and business skills, and focused on relationships by prioritizing the formation of a strong farmers association.[35]

Some evangelical actors, albeit a minority, are also engaged in trying to influence global economic policies through political advocacy. Groups like World Vision and the Mennonite Central Committee, for example, consider the impact of free trade policies and economic liberalization on the poor worldwide. They have called for reforming some trade and economic policies, and encouraged discussion over the impacts of increased economic globalization.[36] Some evangelicals have also joined with other religious actors to lobby against such policies. The success of such endeavors has, however, been limited.

Global economic issues intersect with other global justice themes. In a few instances, evangelicals have been willing to engage in ecumenical advocacy efforts to pursue such issues. Jubilee 2000 stands out as an area where religious organizations across the spectrum—both within Christian circles and more broadly—came together to encourage debt relief for poor countries. Perhaps motivated by such a movement, evangelical relief and development groups have rallied around the Micah Network, an evangelically founded network whose principal aim is to advocate for the successful completion of the Millennium Development Goals. Many evangelical development groups, often working alongside local partners, urged national governments to support these goals.[37]

World Vision's child parliaments serve as an example of advocacy work that is indirectly related to international poverty but which is critical for dealing with economic problems. In several countries, World Vision has created child parliaments made up of former child soldiers, sex workers, and at risk children; their goal is to protect children from violence and oppression. In one town in the Democratic Republic of Congo, parliament members have put pressure on local politicians, created preventive measures to stop abuse, and organized sporting and cultural events for children. Through its participation in local legal systems, the child parliament successfully advocated to the local mayor, resulting in the closure of 80 percent of the brothels in this conflict-ridden city.

There is also a relatively new evangelical interest in land rights. Evangelical theologies of land ownership are just beginning to emerge, but evangelical

NGOs are already fully engaged in land-related projects.[38] The International Justice Mission (IJM) works on land rights issues in countries around the world. In Uganda, they have attacked succession-related property grabbing (SPRG), the illegal seizure of property from a surviving spouse or surviving child of a deceased person. The IJM works with the Ugandan government to enact reforms to the administrative, judicial, and clerical procedures that currently create obstacles for the victims of this type of land grabbing. In 2012, they trained 650 local council leaders and 100 police officers to properly respond to SPRG cases.[39] Such programming points to a growing evangelical recognition that engaging with structures is paramount to solving many of the problems plaguing the poor.

These cases reveal that evangelical NGOs are often using a combination of strategies. For some, advocacy may be central; for others, it is nonexistent. Of the many thousands of evangelical development projects on the ground, relatively few focus solely on relief; likewise, few actors are engaged solely in reforming governmental structures. Most are centered in community-based efforts, recognizing that interacting with larger systems is essential to their success.

NGOs and Evangelicals Today

Relief and development organizations have a complex relationship with the rest of the evangelical world. As we discuss later, three points help to bring some clarity to these relationships. First, the growing size of the relief and development sector corresponds to growing support among evangelicals. Many evangelicals, if not most, support NGOs in some way (through individual monetary support, through their churches' financial support, through prayer groups, etc.). Second, such support must be qualified by the fact that it is sometimes provided with only the most basic understanding of what evangelical NGOs actually do. Third, as an evangelical laity travel internationally with greater frequency and NGOs engage in more educational efforts, recognition of the systemic causes of poverty has grown.

Evangelical Concern for the Poor

Many evangelicals support evangelical NGOs in some way. Giving patterns perhaps reflect this most clearly. World Vision alone is financially supported by 4.7 million Americans.[40] Other organizations that provide donors with the opportunity to sponsor children, such as Compassion International, also have millions of individual donors. Groups such as World Relief depend on relationships with churches for their support. Microfinance organizations like Opportunity International and Hope International have also developed effective strategies to attract individual donors. Collectively, these strategies are drawing the evangelical populace into the development agenda. Evangelical relief and development groups receive less government funding—and rely more on private donations—than most other religious and secular groups.[41]

This giving is indicative of the general support such evangelical groups have for addressing poverty. Religious conservatives tend to be more concerned about poverty than other religious actors, and more likely than other individuals to have thought about the problems of poverty; this effect is largely because of their higher levels of religiosity.[42] Many churches feature bulletin board promotions for Operation Christmas Child, a Samaritan's Purse initiative, or a myriad of other NGO programs. For their part, evangelical relief and development organizations have positioned themselves to avoid conflict with the conservative evangelical agenda and to maintain an identity that is distinct from the Christian Right.[43] Thus NGOs enjoy support from across the evangelical spectrum,[44] and it is increasing as congregations become more involved in overseas ministries (with a reported $3.7 billion given annually at the turn of the century).[45] In sum, the rapid expansion of the evangelical relief and development sector has increased its connectivity with the American evangelical populace, including more financial ties between individual evangelicals and development efforts.

Evangelical Attitudes toward Reforming Structures

In spite of such trends, the mainstream evangelical community continues to exhibit more individualistic understandings of poverty than evangelical relief and development actors. This may be in part because a belief in a just and active God can translate into the belief that the world is just.[46] People are rewarded and punished appropriately, which connects with individualistic explanations about poverty and inequality.

But further explanation might be found in the type of relationship that evangelicals have with the relief and development sector. Many evangelicals who donate to organizations like World Vision or Compassion International may have only vague notions about what evangelical NGOs actually do. The popularity of "helping the poor in Christ's name" is surging, but few evangelicals who affirm that notion know anything beyond what appears in a public relations pamphlet. Transformational development theory is not widely known outside professional circles. (To be fair, recent efforts are emerging to change this. For example, the president of World Vision U.S. Richard Stearns's *The Hole in Our Gospel: What Does God Expect of Us? The Answer that Changed My Life and Might Just Change the World* has been widely used and has received a very positive reception among congregations throughout the country, as has *When Helping Hurts: How to Alleviate Poverty without Hurting the Poor and Yourself,* by Steve Corbett and Brian Fikkert. Both books carry the basic message of transformational development and encourage evangelicals to get involved in anti-poverty efforts.) Many lay evangelicals enjoy getting letters from their child sponsor or hearing talks by NGO representatives at church but leave the actual workings of these initiatives to NGO professionals. For their part, evangelical NGOs in the past paid more attention to messages that would garner support than they did real educational content in their donor relations initiatives; they have often framed their work in language of relief (versus development), even when involved in more structural and community-level development.[47] This is why child sponsorship programs still remain one of the central ways that relief and development organizations attract support. Even as such donations are often channeled into community projects such as building better schools or developing sources of clean water, the language of compassion for an individual child is used to appeal to potential donors.

When it comes to advocacy, there appears to be little desire among many evangelicals to engage in efforts to reform political and economic structures. For example, evangelical groups within the United States (with the exception of development organizations) are often less likely than other religious communities to hold critical attitudes toward global economic structures.[48]

Increased megachurch involvement in issues of international poverty proves a case in point. Rick Warren, pastor of Saddleback Church and known in Christian circles for his popular book, *The Purpose Driven Life*, also carries a high political profile, having hosted an Obama-McCain debate and given a prayer at Obama's inauguration. He developed the PEACE program—a plan to promote reconciliation, equip leaders, assist the poor, care for the sick, and educate the next generation. His plan in many ways is indicative of current megachurch efforts to combat poverty. These efforts borrow heavily from ideas of transformational development and holistic mission but lack the structural sophistication (not to mention emphasis on economic advocacy) exhibited by development organizations.[49] These churches are not rejecting the vision of the evangelical industry, but they are piecing together their own responses, often with a higher focus on evangelicalism in the more individualistic sense. They are in some ways engaged in similar projects as development organizations, but with a less developed theological framework concerning the structural and relational forces contributing to poverty.

Even as relief and development organizations enjoy a mostly positive image in the evangelical community, they have had mixed success in more seriously engaging the community. As noted earlier, evangelical discourse still largely remains individualistic. However, there is some evidence that notions of transformational development are starting to permeate the broader evangelical culture. For example, in "For the Health of the Nation," a 2004 document produced by the National Association of Evangelicals and accepted by evangelicals across the political spectrum, there is a commitment to "seek justice and compassion for the poor and vulnerable" and a recognition that this is in part influenced by structures.[50]

Moving Forward toward a More Informed Engagement

Even as individualism is often contrasted with attention to structural realities, research on racism challenges this stark dichotomy. Lawrence Bobo suggests that social responsibility and individualism need not be in opposition.[51] He finds that it is not individualism that is most important in evaluating support for governmental and structural approaches to racism and poverty, but rather a sense of social responsibility. An increased sense of social responsibility and attention to macrolevel systems are not incompatible with the individualistic emphases in which evangelicals remain steeped.

Increasing the evangelical sense of social responsibility for international poverty—in part through providing a strong theological framework for understanding such poverty—is critical for the work of relief and development organizations. We would suggest that participation in international networks and an increasing diversity within US evangelical networks, as well as intentional educational efforts, are both essential toward creating a stronger sense of such responsibility.

Evangelicals are already engaged in strong international networks. More and more people within evangelical congregations are engaged in short-term missions (STM) or otherwise making connections with those involved overseas. An estimated 1.6 million adults–and probably even more youth–go on such trips every year.[52] Many of these trips allow evangelicals in the pews to have hands-on experiences with impoverished communities. When run well, STM trips help hosts and visitors create relationships that are sustained after teams go home. These relationships allow transnational and transcultural flows of people, resources, and communications that can sensitize Americans to international poverty.[53] Such sensitization can lead to changed behavior at home. The STMs increase the likelihood that participants will engage in other forms of charitable and political action, precisely the behavior NGOs would like to encourage.[54]

It is in part *because* of the strength of relief and development organizations that more evangelicals are engaging in these cross-cultural experiences. This is not to say that all evangelicals going abroad are interacting with evangelical development institutions. To be sure, many are not. But some are, and even among those who are not, they are often involved in development initiatives and making connections with local leaders involved in deep poverty-alleviation efforts. These connections are often important in helping to connect international experiences with changed understandings about the nature of poverty.

However, international experiences alone do not lead evangelicals to embrace theologies of transformational development and become aware of structural inequality. A small study of missionaries finds that for many, individualistic understandings of economic life are only reinforced through service, without creating awareness of structural factors shaping poverty.[55] Emerging research seems to suggest that it is the frames through which people interpret these experiences that matter.[56] Educational efforts matter, as do institutional efforts that help people process experiences with people in different contexts.

In this respect, the work being done by educational institutions may be vital. In addition to the work being done at Eastern University (mentioned earlier), a number of Christian colleges have centers committed to development initiatives. The Chalmers Center (Covenant College) has degree programs in community development and economics. Calvin College, Messiah, Westmost, and Wheaton College all have strong development studies programs. Evangelical seminaries, such as Asbury, Denver, and Fuller, also have programs in development. Such efforts by evangelical educational institutions reveal a full-scale support for these endeavors.

Due in part to the growth of evangelical development-related programs, as well as an emerging interest in advocacy, education of the larger evangelical community has become a higher priority. Past antipoverty initiatives by relief and development groups largely required financial support from the church base to be successful; the ability of groups to implement sophisticated development projects was not dependent on the understanding or perspective of donors, as much as it was their dollars. Yet advocacy-oriented efforts are more dependent on individuals' embracing a vision of development that will prompt action in the form of civic and political engagement.

Some sectors of evangelicalism are currently involved in advocacy efforts. While evangelicals as a whole do not engage in debates over economic trade policies, some do.[57] Sojourners has a history of focusing on issues of advocacy when it comes to development issues, such as the Central America Free Trade Agreement (CAFTA) or fair trade.[58] Further, the growing emerging church movement has also been recognized for economic advocacy, with Brian McLaren proposing an international fair trade seal and a global minimum wage.[59] As the predominantly white evangelical church becomes more racially and ethnically diverse, an increasing attention to more structural level issues from such churches is possible. Research reveals that the racial identity of white evangelicals has been connected with their inability to recognize the importance of systemic issues or the need for more structural and macrolevel solutions.[60]

There are numerous ways that development organizations are rallying the troops when it comes to advocacy on economic issues. Many evangelicals are generally open to advocacy, and groups like the International Justice Mission and the Center for Public Justice are evidence of this openness. The importance of advocacy also continues to garner more attention. In chapter 2, John Schmalzbauer notes, for example, that 2009 witnessed the first track of sessions centered on political advocacy for students at the Urbana Missions conference (with around a quarter million student attendees). The Justice Conference is a more contemporary evangelical movement. Begun in 2010, it gathers thousands of young people for a two-day event centered around justice issues, with advocacy as central to their mission.

Asbury Theological Seminary, Bread for the World, and Eastern University have created a web-based curriculum warehouse that is intended to provide easy access to evangelical advocacy resources (evangelicaladvocacy.org). This electronic resource facilitates teaching and learning about advocacy in evangelical educational institutions, and its goals closely align with the efforts of groups like World Vision and Compassion International, whose advocacy budgets include initiatives to educate people within congregations.[61]

Relief and development organizations continue to make deeper inroads in the evangelical community. New initiatives on advocacy provide some unique opportunities in this regard. Evangelicals have largely embraced a priority to care for the poor, even as not all embrace the transformational development efforts and advocacy work. However, both efforts continue to become more accepted. When support for development and advocacy is limited, it seems in part to be due to lack of knowledge as opposed to studied theological dispute.

Conclusion

Concern over issues of international poverty is not a new phenomenon within the evangelical community. Starting largely with relief efforts to help the poor encountered in situations of war, evangelicals have developed strong institutions to combat poverty overseas. The evangelical development industry is a thriving and important aspect of evangelicalism in America. Such organizations have largely served as evangelicals' "primary vehicle of choice for holistic involvement and witness."[62]

Recognizing the ways that the industry has changed since the 1940s, we suggest that these relief and development organizations exhibit increasingly sophisticated approaches—ones that deal with individuals, their communities, and the larger social and political structures—in combating poverty. Instead of just focusing on relief, organizations also prioritize development and advocacy. Within the media and academy today, such contributions are increasingly being recognized and affirmed.[63]

Yet we have also asked in this chapter how such efforts are reflective of the actions and attitudes of the larger evangelical community. Although typical evangelicals both care about international poverty and support these development agencies, this support may be more superficial than desired. Deep understandings of development are lacking. Yet both the growth of transnational networks and an emerging emphasis on advocacy provide the potential for evangelical relief and development organizations to find new ways to promote dialogue and reflection within evangelical communities. In doing so, they may help shape a new evangelical engagement with poverty.

NOTES

1. Robert Wuthnow, *Boundless Faith: The Global Outreach of American Churches* (Berkeley: University of California Press, 2009).

2. Christian Smith, *American Evangelicalism: Embattled and Thriving* (Chicago: University of Chicago Press, 1999), 3.

3. Erica Bornstein, *The Spirit of Development: Protestant NGOs, Morality, and Economics in Zimbabwe* (Stanford, CA: Stanford University Press, 2005), 20.

4. Wuthnow, *Boundless Faith*, 119.

5. Wuthnow, *Boundless Faith*.

6. Marc Lindenberg and Coralie Bryant, *Going Global: Transforming Relief and Development Organizations* (Bloomfield, CT: Kumarian Press, 2001), 3.

7. Chad Hayward, personal correspondence, August 29, 2012. Rachel McClearly, *Global Compassion: Private Voluntary Organizations and U.S. Foreign Policy since 1939* (New York: Oxford University Press, 2009).

8. The stages that countries go through in their economic development are traditional society, preconditions for takeoff, takeoff, drive to maturity, and the age of mass consumption.

9. David Balaam and Bradford Dillman, *Introduction to International Political Economy*, 5th ed. (New York: Longman, 2011).

10. Thomas Lairson and David Skidmore, *International Political Economy: The Struggle for Power and Wealth*, 3rd ed. (Beverly, MA: Wadsworth, 2002).

11. McClearly, *Global Compassion*.

12. David Korten, *The Post-Corporate World: Life after Capitalism* (San Francisco: Berrett-Koehler; West Hartford, CT: Kumarian Press, 1989).

13. Al Tizon, *Transformation after Lausanne: Radical Evangelical Mission in Global-Local Perspective* (Eugene, OR: Wipf & Stock, 2008).

14. Although some have suggested that World Vision has lost some of its evangelical identity and is better conceived of as an ecumenically Christian organization (for example, McCleary, *Global Compassion*), we reject the notion that its evangelical identity is no longer central. They play a leadership role in Accord networks, receive a lot of financial support from evangelical congregations, and are generally recognized by most evangelicals as one of their own. King also highlights the importance of an evangelical identity to this organization. See David King, "World Vision: Religious Identity in the Discourse and Practice of Global Relief and Development," *Faith and International Affairs* 9:3 (2011): 21–28.

15. Graeme Irvine, *Best Things in the Worst Times: An Insider's View of World Vision* (Wilsonville, OR: BookPartners, 1996).

16. Tizon, *Transformation after Lausanne*.

17. Chris Sugden, "Transformational Development: Current State of Understanding and Practice," *Transformation* 20:2 (2003): 70–75.

18. Tizon, *Transformation after Lausanne*, 66.

19. Sugden, "Transformational Development."

20. Amy Sherman, "Christians and Economic Development," *First Things*, March 1990.

21. Sherman, "Christians and Economic Development."

22. Lisa VeneKlasen and Valerie Miller, *A New Weave of Power, People, and Politics: The Action Guide for Advocacy and Citizen Participation* (Bourton-on-Dunsmore, England: Practical Action, 2007), 23.

23. Miriam Adeney, *God's Foreign Policy: Practical Ways to Help the World's Poor* (Vancouver, BC: Regent, 1993).

24. Wuthnow, *Boundless Faith*; Peter Stamatov, "Activist Religion, Empire, and the Emergence of Modern Long-Distance Advocacy Networks," *American Sociological Review* 75:4 (2010): 607–28.

25. King, "World Vision: Religious Identity."

26. Allen Hertzke, Pew Forum, and Pew Research Center, *Lobbying for the Faithful: Religious Advocacy Groups in Washington, D.C.* (Washington, DC: Pew Forum, 2012).

27. Mark Galli, "The Best Ways to Fight Poverty—Really," *Christianity Today*, February 10, 2012, www.christianitytoday.com/ct/2012/february/best-ways-to-fight-poverty.html; Bruce Wydick, "Cost-Effective Compassion: The 10 Most Popular Strategies for the Helping the Poor," *Christianity Today*, February 17, 2012, www.christianitytoday.com/ct/2012/february/popular-strategies-helping-the-poor.html.

28. Greg Forney and Lucas Koach, "Poverty Has Many Enemies," *Christianity Today*, March 8, 2012, www.christianitytoday.com/ct/2012/marchweb-only/fight-poverty-response-fh.html.

29. Jonathan Reckford, "We Can't Do Everything," *Christianity Today*, March 8, 2012, www.christianitytoday.com/ct/2012/marchweb-only/fight-poverty-response-habitat.html.

30. McClearly, *Global Compassion*.

31. Wuthnow, *Boundless Faith*.

32. Evangelical development theorist Bryant Myers states: "Poverty is a result of relationships that do not work, that are not just, that are not for life, that are not harmonious or enjoyable. Poverty is the absence of shalom in all its meanings" (Bryant Myers. *Walking With the Poor: Principles and Practices of Transformational Development*. Maryknoll: Orbis, 1999), 86.

33. Robert Davis, "What about Justice? An Evangelical Perspective on Advocacy in Development," *Transformation* 26:2 (2009): 89–103.

34. David Bronkema, personal conversation, September 18, 2012.

35. Amy Reynolds, "Networks, Ethics, and Economic Values," *Latin American Research Review* 48:1 (2013): 112–132.

36. Amy Reynolds, "Saving the Market: The Role of Values, Authority, and Networks in International Trade Discourse" (PhD diss., Princeton University, 2010).

37. Brian Woolnough. "Christian NGOs in Relief and Development: One of the Church's Arms for Holistic Mission," *Transformation* 28:3 (2011): 195–205.

38. Ryan Juskus, ""The Land is Mine: A Theological Framework of Property Rights and Development."" (MA thesis, Wheaton College. 2013).

39. "Uganda: Five Convictions in One Month – A 'Sea Change' for Vulnerable Communities." Accessed July 16, 2013. http://www.ijm.org/news/uganda-5-convictions-one-month-sea-change-vulnerable-communities.

40. Marcia Pally, *The New Evangelicals: Expanding the Vision of the Common Good* (Grand Rapids, MI: W. B. Eerdmans, 2011).

41. McClearly, *Global Compassion*.

42. Robert Wuthnow, *God and Mammon in America* (New York: Free Press, 1994).

43. David King, "The New Internationalists: World Vision and the Revival of American Evangelical Humanitarianism, 1950–2010," *Religions* 3 (2012).

44. At the same time, it must be recognized that the evangelical left, in many ways, has driven many of the developments and growth in this sector. It is the evangelical left that largely keeps poverty on their faith community's agenda. Progressive evangelicals issued the 1973 Chicago Declaration of Evangelical Concern, successfully lobbied for a clause about Christian social responsibility in the 1974 Lausanne Covenant, and founded socially conscious organizations like Sojourners and Evangelicals for Social Action. See David R. Swartz, *The Moral Minority: The Evangelical Left in an Age of Conservativism* (Philadelphia: University of Pennsylvania Press, 2012).

45. Wuthnow, *Boundless Faith.*

46. Matthew Hunt, "Status, Religion, and the 'Belief in a Just World': Comparing African-Americans, Latinos, and Whites," *Social Science Quarterly* 81:1 (2000): 325–43.

47. Fred Kniss and David Campbell, "The Effect of Religious Orientation on International Relief and Development Organizations," *Journal for the Scientific Study of Religion* 36:1 (1997): 93–103.

48. Reynolds, "Saving the Market."

49. Sharon Gramby-Sobukwe and Tim Hoiland, "The Rise of Mega-Church Efforts in International Development: A Brief Analysis and Areas for Future Research," *Transformation* 26:2 (2009): 104–17.

50. Ronald Sider and Diane Knippers, *Toward an Evangelical Public Policy: Political Strategies for the Health of the Nation* (Grand Rapids, MI: Baker Books, 2005).

51. Lawrence Bobo, "Social-Responsibility, Individualism, and Redistributive Policies," *Sociological Forum* 6:1 (1991): 71–92.

52. Wuthnow, *Boundless Faith.*

53. Stephen Offutt, "The Role of Short-Term Mission Teams in the New Centers of Global Christianity," *Journal for the Scientific Study of Religion* 50:4 (2011): 796–811.

54. Kraig Beyerlein, Jenny Trinitapoli, and Gary Adler, "The Effects of Religious Short-Term Mission Trips on Youth Civic Engagement," *Journal for the Scientific Study of Religion* 50:4 (2011): 780–95.

55. James Wellman and Matthew Keyes, "Portable Politics: Moral Worldviews of American Missionaries," *Sociology of Religion* 68:4 (2007): 383–406.

56. Gary Adler, Kraig Beyerlein, and David Sikkink, "Explaining Differences in Congregational International Travel and Outreach" (paper presented at the annual meeting for the Society for the Scientific Study of Religion, Baltimore, October 29–31, 2010); Brian Howell, *Short-Term Mission: An Ethnography of Christian Travel Narrative and Experience* (Downers Grove, IL: IVP Academic, 2012).

57. Reynolds, "Saving the Market."

58. David Gushee, *The Future of Faith in American Politics: The Public Witness of the Evangelical Center* (Waco, TX: Baylor University Press, 2008); Peter Heltzel, *Jesus and Justice: Evangelicals, Race, and American Politics* (New Haven, CT: Yale University Press, 2009).

59. Kim Hawtrey and John Lunn, "The Emergent Church, Socio-Economics and Christian Mission," *Transformation* 72:2 (2010): 65–74.

60. Michael O. Emerson and Christian Smith, *Divided by Faith: Evangelical Religion and the Problem of Race in America* (New York: Oxford University Press, 2000); Kenneth Wald and Allison Calhoun-Brown, *Religion and Politics in the United States*, 6th edition (Lanham, MD: Rowman and Littlefield Publishers, 2010).

61. Hertzke et al., *Lobbying for the Faithful.*

62. Lindy Backues, "Interfaith Development Efforts as Means to Peace and Witness," *Transformation* 26:2 (2009): 67.

63. Nicholas Kristof, "Evangelicals without Blowhards," *New York Times*, July 30, 2011.

PART THREE

Reflections on Evangelical Social Engagement

12

What's New about the New Evangelical Social Engagement?

Joel Carpenter

OVER THE COURSE of this book, we have been finding out more about dozens of new evangelical movements. They display remarkable variety—from neomonastic inner-city missions to international justice initiatives for combating slavery and sex trafficking, to movements to bring racial reconciliation and to diversify local congregations, to efforts to promote environmentally sustainable daily living. Most of them are sharply critical of the more dominant forms of white American evangelicalism. Some of these groups don't even want to be called evangelical anymore. And some conservative evangelical leaders readily return the favor by reading these dissidents and innovators out of the evangelical camp. While these trends look like new departures, I am convinced that they display important continuities as well, both with evangelical movements in the very recent past and with some classic evangelical traits that surfaced at the very beginning, in eighteenth-century Great Britain and its colonies.

For a historian, the key question to ask for making sense of the new evangelicalism is where did it come from? The first and rather obvious thing to say is that the evangelical tradition is filled with precedents for what we are seeing today. In nearly every generation since the Wesleys and George Whitefield, restless and visionary rebels and innovators have created new ways and means of expressing evangelical commitment. Over nearly three centuries, evangelicalism has seen the rise of many new offshoots, led by ardent young prophets who were discontented with the status quo and who felt called of God to do something new. Quite often that has meant a new churches movement, such as that led by the original evangelicals, the Methodists, or in the early American republic, the Disciples of Christ/Christian Church movement. The most celebrated evangelical social movement was the antislavery campaign, led in the British Parliament by the evangelical Anglican William

Wilberforce and spreading rapidly in the United States during the Second Great Awakening of the 1830s. Early labor movements, in both England and the United States, owed much to Methodism. And contrary to conventional wisdom, the Social Gospel movement to redeem urban America in the late nineteenth and early twentieth centuries probably had deeper roots in the urban revivalist and Wesleyan holiness movements than in liberal Protestant theological seminaries.[1]

The new evangelical social engagement we are examining in this book has not only a continuous line of descent from earlier evangelicals but also roots in the recent past. The new evangelicals of our day have direct ties to two prior waves of new evangelicalism, one arising in the 1940s and 1950s and the other more recently, in the 1970s. We simply cannot understand their thinking and actions today without seeing where they came from, fairly directly. We also should recall some of the classic evangelical traits that they share with their ancestry all the way back—at least to the Wesleys. Whether or not they wish to be called evangelicals, these new movements bear the tradition's genetic stamp in some important ways.

First, the recent history. The term *new evangelicalism* is not new. It was used in the 1940s by a rising generation of intellectual and activist leaders who came from a number of protective Protestant enclaves: fundamentalists, holiness Wesleyans, Pentecostals, and other confessional, pietist, and/or revivalist Protestant groups. These Protestants existed, some more emphatically than others, to the side of mainline Protestantism, that cluster of older Northern denominations that had formed the Federal Council of Churches, accommodated liberal theology, and enjoyed quasi-establishment influence in American business, government, and civic and cultural institutions. The nonestablishment Protestants, by contrast, were a scattered lot, divided by doctrine, polity, ethnicity, and the sectarian stance and outlook that some had developed, which made life on the margins a matter of principle.

Something quite remarkable began to happen along these Protestant spur lines during the 1940s. There was a quickening of evangelical anticipation and initiative that led many to believe that a great spiritual revival could come soon. That prospect encouraged these groups' leaders and led them to consider cooperation. They formed the National Association of Evangelicals (NAE) in 1942, with the challenge, as J. Elwin Wright, the NAE's chief organizer put it, to "renounce the continued fragmentizing of the church," to "heal the wounded spirits" of those who had been battered by sectarian strife, and to engage, with a great cooperative effort, in a national revival campaign that would "sweep across our land like mighty showers of spiritual blessing."[2]

These were days of world war and great social disruption at home, but also of quickening religious interest and a growing sense of challenge. How would America and the West meet the threats of godlessness and totalitarian powers? The answer for evangelicals, of course, was another great awakening, with wholesome social transformations following, and they redoubled their efforts to make this happen. One result was a massive, nationwide "Youth for Christ" movement of evangelistic rally programs that crested during the last year of the war and a restarting of all-city revival campaigns, the likes of which had not been seen since the heyday of Billy Sunday, thirty years prior.

This bracing climate set loose the creative imagination not only of young evangelists such as Billy Graham but also among some younger intellectuals. Perhaps the most influential of these was Carl F. H. Henry, a former journalist from Long Island, New York, who by the late 1940s had earned a doctoral degree from Boston University and who joined the founding faculty of Fuller Theological Seminary in Pasadena, California, in 1947. Henry was converted to Christian faith at age twenty and enrolled first at Wheaton College and then Northern Baptist Theological Seminary with the goal of becoming a theologian. Yet he retained a journalist's interest in public affairs and soon grew impatient with the narrow fundamentalist subculture he had entered. The postwar era was a time for big-picture thinking, Henry was convinced. A number of leading public intellectuals, such as Jacques Barzun, Arnold Toynbee, and Reinhold Niebuhr, were questioning whether Western civilization had the cultural and spiritual resources to survive. Henry tried his hand at this genre as well, publishing his first scholarly book, *Remaking the Modern Mind*, in 1946. Henry argued that the Western world was collapsing and that secular, humanistic faiths could not prop it up. Traditionally orthodox Christians, he believed, had a remarkable opportunity to apply the "Hebrew-Christian world-life view" to the great cultural challenges of the day.

Two years later, Henry issued what became a minor classic for two generations of evangelical critics: *The Uneasy Conscience of Modern Fundamentalism* (1948). Fundamentalists could not meet the challenges facing Western civilization, he charged, because they were too focused on individual sins to address social evils and more interested in charting the details of the Second Coming than working to advance Christ's kingdom now. Fundamentalism, Henry argued, was an ethical and social irrelevancy. It trivialized the power of the gospel and left the field of social reform to the secular humanists and religious liberals. If only fundamentalism could be reformed, Henry sighed, it could mount another Reformation. In a magazine series published the same year, "The Vigor of the New Evangelicalism," he insisted "there is not a problem of human existence but that Christianity... somehow has implications for its solution."[3] A chief organizer of the emerging movement, Harold Ockenga, hoped that a new evangelicalism might gain influence in America with a spirit of "progressive action and of ethical responsibility."[4]

So Henry coined a term, *the new evangelicalism,* and he and Ockenga set an agenda. They would reaffirm the great fundamentals of the faith but avoid the deficiencies of fundamentalism. The new evangelicals would be intellectually engaged, socially aware, balanced and realistic about such themes as biblical prophecy, positive about Christian unity, and offering a fresh and relevant interpretation of the scriptures. To make a long story short, in the postwar American revival of religious interest, this new evangelicalism became an alternative Protestant establishment. It sought to rival mainline Protestantism by forging an alliance between evangelical intellectuals and the innovative postwar revivalists and parachurch agency pioneers, such as Bill Bright, founder of Campus Crusade for Christ; Bob Pierce, founder of World Vision, the evangelical relief and development agency; and most notably, Billy Graham. The new evangelicals built an intellectual network featuring new theological seminaries, such as Fuller; Trinity Evangelical, near Chicago; and Gordon-Conwell, north of Boston. It helped to strengthen and reanimate Christian colleges, notably Wheaton, Gordon, and Calvin, and it featured a variety of thought magazines, such as *Eternity,* published in Philadelphia, and the *Reformed Journal,* published by the William B. Eerdmans Publishing Company in Grand Rapids. Eerdmans also pioneered high-level work in theological and biblical studies. With the support of Graham, the new evangelicals founded *Christianity Today* magazine in 1956 to rival mainline Protestants' *The Christian Century,* as a grand, national voice, and Carl Henry was its first editor. Editorial offices were in Washington, D.C., where, via "leadership prayer breakfasts" and friendships with influential businessmen and other notables, the new evangelicals gained access to governmental leaders as well.

As the new evangelicals encountered the intensifying social conflicts of the 1960s, however, it became evident that their social and political instincts were not at all progressive, as Ockenga put it, in the political sense, but quite conservative. When confronted with the Civil Rights movement, for example, *Christianity Today* counseled patience and the need to keep order. It supported the war in Vietnam and championed individualism and economic freedom over against collectivist views.[5] When Henry even mildly suggested that the United States ought to reconsider its position on Vietnam and that capitalism was not without its weaknesses, a crisis ensued, and he was forced out of the editor's chair.[6] There was no mistaking Billy Graham's orientation when he gave the keynote address at President Nixon and Bob Hope's July 4, 1970, "Honor America" rally.

The stances and alliances of the new evangelicalism made sense to the great majority of white American evangelicals. They formed a core component of Richard Nixon's silent majority, which trusted in the essential goodness of mainstream American government policy and saw the churches' public role, by and large, as shaping the character of citizens. At the height of the Watergate crisis, however, the evangelical establishment's investment in this approach lay in shambles. *Christianity Today* eventually and reluctantly called for Nixon's impeachment. No longer could evangelicals comfortably focus on personal salvation and character formation and entrust the right ordering of society to a benign government.

And what replaced the new evangelical synthesis? By and large, this pro-establishment, moderating conservatism began to give way to sterner stuff. The story of the rise of the Religious Right is well known by now. It had its roots in the fundamentalist-fed anticommunist crusade that sprouted in the Sunbelt in the 1950s. By the late 1970s, it was gaining a national hearing principally from two Virginia-based preachers, the Baptist-turned-charismatic Pat Robertson and the fundamentalist Baptist Jerry Falwell. Francis Schaeffer, an American missionary based in Switzerland who reached out to young intellectuals, came home to persuade evangelical Protestants that legalized abortion, until then largely thought of as a Catholic issue, was the greatest human rights atrocity of the age. Falwell's Moral Majority and Robertson's Christian Coalition were early and fairly successful attempts to mobilize born-again and spirit-filled church people to vote for (Republican) candidates who would support their profamily positions.

In the ensuing culture wars, the Religious Right rallied against the Equal Rights Amendment, abortion, and gay rights. Whatever evangelical sympathies had attached to President Jimmy Carter, the born-again Southern Baptist, shifted dramatically to the longtime champion of Sunbelt conservatism, Ronald Reagan, whose positions were closer to theirs on the issues, and a new era of conservatism emerged in American politics. By the late 1990s, it became abundantly clear that a major partisan realignment had taken place. Nixon's Southern strategy for turning Southern whites away from the Democratic Party and making the Republican Party into the new champion of social conservatism, limited government, and states' rights was an almost complete success, and at its backbone was a supermajority of evangelical voters.

Since then, about 70 percent of evangelicals have consistently backed the Republican Party. Spurred on especially by the abortion issue and increasingly concerned about governmental overreach, America's white evangelicals had become so identified with political conservatism that the original meaning of

their label, as people of the good news, the Christian gospel of God's reconciling love, seemed to be almost buried in the public mind.

But the story of American evangelicals' public engagement since 1945 is
more complicated than that. David Swartz, who writes in this book about the
growing internationalism of evangelicals, has an important new book that
tells an alternative story, also rooted in the late 1960s and the Watergate era.
Ever since that time, there has been a lively evangelical "non-right" that has
sustained a second opinion within evangelicalism.[7] What we call the new
evangelical social engagement is in most cases directly descended from this
late-twentieth-century radical evangelical movement. So it is worth recalling
this movement and gaining a sense of its enduring influence.

Typically, movements cannot be explained via one defining moment or
event, but in the rise of a radical evangelical movement, one occasion stands
out. In November 1973, at the height of the Watergate scandals, a group of
fifty evangelical leaders spent the weekend after Thanksgiving at the YMCA
Hotel on South Wabash Street in Chicago. This was not your typical evangelical weekend conference, and the Y Hotel was no luxury palace. Indeed,
at one point in the meeting, just when a speaker was urging the group to
break evangelicals' silence on the social evils of the day, a shot rang out in
the hotel corridors. And the conferees, for the most part, clearly represented
the more progressive wing of evangelical leaders. Among the conveners were
Ronald Sider, a Messiah College professor living in inner-city Philadelphia
who had been a leader of the Evangelicals for McGovern movement in the
1972 presidential campaign, and Paul Henry, a liberal Republican political scientist at Calvin College who had been organizing annual conferences there on
Christianity and politics. His father, the theologian Carl Henry, was also there,
one of the few delegates of a more conservative stripe. Black evangelicals such
as evangelist Tom Skinner and Fuller professor William Pannell were engaged
in the process, as were pioneering evangelical feminists Sharon Gallagher of
the Jesus movement in Berkeley and Nancy Hardesty, then teaching at Trinity
College in Deerfield, Illinois.

So why were the conferees there? The work at hand was to counteract the
lack of concern for social justice among evangelical Christians and to call them
and the American people more generally to seek "the righteousness that exalts
a nation." The assembled delegates represented varying traditions and view-
points, and they repeatedly confronted each other in their quest to make the
declaration comprehensive and prophetic. Their declaration had to address
the challenges of economic justice, peacemaking, racial justice and reconciliation, and gender equality, all within a biblical framework and in ways congru-
ent with an evangelical passion to spread the good news of salvation in Jesus

Christ. The meeting was turbulent and threatened to unravel at several points, but a rough consensus prevailed in the end, and "The Chicago Declaration of Evangelical Social Concern," dated November 25, 1973, was the result.[8]

Although it attracted scant notice at the time, something important happened in 1973 at the Y Hotel in Chicago. How important? Swartz argues that the evangelical left quickly broke apart along the lines of identity politics and was soon eclipsed as a national political force by the Religious Right. But I doubt that building a game-changing progressive evangelical power base in national politics was what most of the Chicago Declaration signers wanted or hoped for. Even in the exciting early days of their organizing, leaders such as Ron Sider and philosopher Richard Mouw of Calvin College knew full well that they represented a minority perspective among evangelicals, and for the most part, they had no illusions of winning over the preponderance of evangelicals, much less the nation.[9] Even so, in the wake of the Chicago Declaration of 1973, this evangelical nonright movement founded Evangelicals for Social Action (ESA), which Sider led for nearly four decades. Although ESA-type evangelicals never came close to the Religious Right coalitions in size and force, they fostered a variety of emphases that have shaped the new evangelical social engagement that we highlight in this book.

The first of these enduring traits is a broad understanding, now nearly a consensus among evangelicals—right, left, or indeterminate—that Christians have social and political roles and responsibilities. Evangelicals' dominant position on public affairs, even two decades after Carl Henry's *Uneasy Conscience*, was that Christianity's role in social reform was to work at the individual level of conversion and personal transformation, not to emphasize collective political action. In the wake of Watergate, however, two Calvin College professors, Richard Mouw and Paul Henry, wrote primers urging evangelical Christians to do politics. Evangelism and social or political action are not antagonistic, they argued, but are two parts of a larger mandate, which is giving witness to God's kingdom.[10] These ESA-type thought leaders helped evangelicals rediscover rich veins of biblical teaching about God's passionate concern for justice, peace, and the full-orbed flourishing of nature and humanity. *Let Justice Roll Down*, exclaimed the black evangelical community organizer John Perkins, quoting Amos.[11] *God So Loved the Third World*, declaimed Mennonite mission scholar Thomas Hanks, quoting scores of biblical texts.[12] And there were plenty of similar works in the decade following 1973—a torrent of scriptural exposition and exhortation that was impossible for evangelical readers to ignore. In the 1970s, even the conservative *Moody Monthly* magazine carried articles on peacemaking, broader roles for women, and civil rights.[13]

The great irony to this story is that this energetic campaign to raise evangelicals' social concern did not take the directions that the ESA evangelicals were advocating. The great surge of evangelical engagement came from two of the longest holdouts for political quietism and personal transformation, the more militantly separated fundamentalists and the rapidly spreading but largely apolitical Pentecostal and charismatic movements. These "otherworldly" evangelicals, as social scientists liked to label them, began to feel more social responsibility as their movements grew, but the motif for their return to the public arena was culture wars, warfare against secularism and big-government progressivism. The irony has not been lost on the leaders of the ESA. Ron Sider once quipped that "we called for social and political action, [and] we got eight years of Ronald Reagan."[14]

A second enduring influence of ESA-type evangelicals is their ongoing argument against the idea that evangelical equals conservative. Despite very modest resources and the impression sometimes of being marginal to the main lines of public discourse, the ESA-type evangelicals have voiced alternative views and issue positions to the Religious Right and have given these ideas legitimacy and staying power. It may not be clear how much concrete influence they have exerted, but it is clear that they have a large potential audience. A number of studies of American evangelicals in politics over the past fifteen years have shown that a substantial percentage of evangelicals have continued to hold moderate or liberal social and economic views. In a Princeton University survey conducted in 2000, 45 percent of evangelicals said they were ideological moderates, and 19 percent self-identified as liberals.[15] This alternative opinion among evangelicals persists to the present day. In early 2012, the *Economist* published an article claiming that there is a substantial "Non-Right" contingent of evangelicals in America. While 70 percent of white evangelicals consider themselves to be Republican, the article went on, nearly one in four evangelical voters backed Barack Obama in 2008. Among the younger evangelical voters, the ratio was more like one in three. Even though they are overwhelmingly prolife, on other social issues, such as health care and poverty, young evangelicals are more predisposed to seek governmental solutions. The *Economist* argued that this was a new trend, supplied by the rapidly growing nonwhite evangelical ethnic and racial groups and by changing attitudes among the younger generation of evangelicals.[16] Yet nearly fifteen years of opinion polling shows that this is, in fact, a persistent pattern. How much ESA-type evangelicals did to build and sustain that outlook among evangelicals is yet to be proven. But their persistent witness on matters of race, gender, the environment, poverty, economic systems, and peacemaking has kept alternative perspectives in circulation and available to evangelical constituencies.

A third area in which the ESA-type evangelicals have had extraordinary and enduring influence has been in community-based redevelopment and political advocacy. President Obama's background as a community organizer and the very strong ground game that his 2008 and 2012 campaigns put together to get out the vote across America's less-affluent neighborhoods has brought this grassroots phenomenon, sometimes called community populism, to light. Before 1970, there were only a few dozen community development organizations nationwide. By the mid-1990s, there were thousands of them, and they enlisted tens of millions of Americans in neighborhood renewal.[17] Since the early days of this community development movement, faith-based organizations have made up a very large share of these agencies. Among the participants of the Chicago Declaration workshop were Perkins, who had community-building ministries in Mendenhall, Mississippi; Ron and Wyn Potter of the Voice of Calvary Ministries in Jackson, Mississippi; Bill Leslie, the white pastor of the inner-city LaSalle Street Church in Chicago; and Clarence Hilliard, pastor of the interracial Circle Church, also in Chicago. Each of these ministries practiced a holistic gospel, including personal transformation and social justice, for which the ESA would become a consistent national voice.

Through the years, these ministries have been prime exhibits of how to practice what the ESA preaches. These evangelicals have fostered hundreds of community-building organizations, focusing on housing, tutoring and youth ministry, family counseling, legal aid, health care, thrift and food stores, shelter for the homeless, credit unions, banks, job training, and even commercial firms for manufacturing and marketing. Out of these networks rose the Christian Community Development Association (CCDA), founded by Perkins and community ministry leaders in 1989. Currently, the CCDA has more than five hundred institutional and three thousand individual members nationwide. There is probably no better evidence of the vigor that evangelicals have poured into social action than this community ministry movement, which has played an enormous role in urban America since the early 1970s. Community-based economic development and social renewal has become one of those rare regions in public life where political liberals, radicals, and conservatives have found common ground. These programs are prime examples of the faith-based initiatives to which both the Clinton and Bush administrations gave attention via a White House office.

Fourth, ESA-type evangelicals fostered some of the earliest and most enduring ties with evangelical thought leaders from the global South. Slowly but surely, the white Christian subcultures in North America are learning that

Christianity in Africa, Asia, Latin America, and the Pacific is much more than the product of missionaries sent out from here. The ESA-type leaders were some of the first to recognize the emergence of a new world Christianity, a realm of discourse and activity in which the leaders, concerns, ideas, and missions of the churches outside the North Atlantic region are coming to the forefront. Prominent in the Chicago Thanksgiving workshop were two veteran white evangelical leaders, Carl Henry and Paul Rees, who already had important international connections. Henry had been an organizer of the 1966 Berlin Congress on World Evangelization, and Rees represented World Vision, which was becoming one of the world's largest Christian relief and development agencies. Henry and Rees were partners, as was an African American Chicago Declaration delegate, Bill Pannell, with evangelist Leighton Ford, Billy Graham's brother-in-law, in planning a world congress of evangelization, held in 1974 in Lausanne, Switzerland. The historic Lausanne Conference put ESA-type evangelicals in touch with a rising network of global South evangelical mission theologians who both shared and fed ESA-type perspectives. One of these theologians, Samuel Escobar from Peru, was at the Thanksgiving 1973 conference in Chicago.[18]

These international evangelical leaders rocked the Lausanne gathering with their insistence on a holistic gospel and its call for social justice. Out of this network of global South evangelical mission theologians have come such leaders as Samuel Escobar and Rene Padilla of the Latin American Theological Fellowship (LATF); David Gitari, Caesar Molebatsi, and the late Kwame Bediako of the African Theological Fellowship; Melba Maggay of the Philippines; and Vinay Samuel of India. One of the most important organizations for these evangelical leaders has been the International Fellowship of Evangelical Mission Theologians, led for many years by Vinay Samuel. It operates the Oxford Centre for Mission Studies and publishes Regnum Books and *Transformation* magazine. Whenever North Americans have participated in these ventures, ESA-type evangelicals have been in the lead. And via Escobar, who taught for many years alongside Sider at Eastern Baptist (now Palmer) Theological Seminary in Philadelphia, the LATF developed vital links to the rising movement of U.S. Latino evangelicals. The ESA thus anticipated the kinds of partnership that are becoming critical for world Christianity. As we see in chapter 10, the current generation of American evangelicals, both leaders and grassroots activists, are increasingly engaging the international Christian scene. That move was made easier by the connections and networks developed by the prior generation of ESA-type evangelicals.

Indeed, in every area broached by our chapter authors, we see echoes, if not direct connections, to the ideas, issue advocacy, and practical work of the

ESA-type evangelicals. So how new is the new evangelicalism? I do not want to minimize the impressions of this rising generation of evangelical activists and reformers that they are doing a new thing. Yet there is not one trend or emphasis among them that was absent from the Chicago Declaration of 1973 and the ongoing networks that formed in its wake.

There are some important traits among today's new evangelical dissidents and reformers that run much deeper, however—all the way back to evangelicalism's beginnings. One of these traits, said Andrew Walls, is its abiding discontent. "Historic evangelicalism," he says, "is a religion of protest against a Christian society that is not Christian enough."[19] Evangelical concern for restoring a notionally churched society's Christian integrity might become manifest in a political campaign for a season. Yet evangelicals are just as likely, if not more likely, to form new religious movements to restore the faith's spiritual integrity (e.g., the emergent church movement), address a particular social wrong (e.g., abortion), extend mercy to vulnerable people (e.g., World Vision), or occupy and transform distressed neighborhoods (e.g., the Christian Community Development Association). Behind it all is a dissatisfaction with life as it is and a deep desire to find and follow "a more excellent way" (1 Corinthians 12:31).

This ancient evangelical trait resides in the tensions that several of our authors have noticed in the new evangelical movements. Says Will Samson about the New Monastics, their evangelicalism "thrives on an embattled state." Says James Bielo about the emerging church evangelicals, they work with two built-in tensions, between saving themselves and saving society, and between seeking religious and ethical purity and seeking to engage the world in order to save it. Says Adriane Bilous about evangelical women in urban ministry, they chafe under the evangelical label, saying that they are not "*that* kind of evangelical." And while looking at evangelical attempts to address race relations, Gerardo Marti and Michael O. Emerson observe that evangelicals focus almost instinctively on individual relationships. They have trouble seeing racism in larger structural and systemic terms.

In all these ways, the new evangelicals show some dispositions that have been part of evangelicalism since the days of the Wesleys. Mark Noll declares that the original evangelical impulse sought to recover the spiritual electricity of the Reformation, most notably Martin Luther's early excitement about justification by faith, what John Wesley called "a living, daring confidence in God's grace."[20] It came to them via the experience of personal conversion, of being born again. From the start, then, evangelicals cared most deeply about their personal relationship to God and their personal eternal fate. These concerns trump (but do not eliminate) other concerns of this world. But evangelicals were not strictly otherworldly or mystical. They want to convert others, and they care about what they should be doing as converted people. So, says Noll, they have often ended up being more socially engaged than they originally intended.

To understand contemporary evangelicals' social engagement, another old, deep trait is important to note: a tension between two quite different outlooks. On one side is a democratic populism, which echoed the apostle Peter in saying that God is no respecter of persons. Evangelicals are often antiformalists and antielitists who feel very little stake in maintaining ancient institutions. This posture can look like political radicalism, but most evangelical antiformalists have been fairly indifferent to politics. On the other side of the evangelical movement's personality is a middle-class practicality. They frequently have been self-disciplined, self-mobilizing, entrepreneurial religious advocates. Mix the two traits, and what you get is inventiveness. Early on, evangelicals created new, parachurch religious agencies, notably the mission society, out of their desire to spread the evangel. They have been fixers and doers, with no inherent desire to subvert or take away the work of formal church structures, but in finding ways to work around the old structures, that, indeed, is what they have done.

In public affairs, these traits come to the fore also: discontent, egalitarian impulses, willingness to challenge established ways, but ad hoc approaches. Early evangelicals, under Wesley's guidance, engaged public life as advocates in the antislavery movement. But their nonstrategic, nonsystematic, personal, and experiential orientation made it difficult for them to sustain a critique long-term or to bring reform if it meant winning political battles and coercing others to submit. When evangelicals engaged, they did so without a consistent social ethic or body of social thought. It was "fire, ready, aim." They have been susceptible to having their focused passion about a particular issue (e.g., abortion) co-opted by more professional politicos who have other interests more at heart.

When it comes to social engagement, evangelicals—early and lately—are best at personal character formation and inventive resourcefulness. They are weakest on worldviews and principled social and cultural thought. Their focus and priority on personal salvation and holy living remain in tension with and repeatedly have taken away the urgency of thinking about responsible Christian living in this world. At times, evangelicals in their activism have devalued intellectual traditions and deliberative thinking. Their approach to social engagement is to be good people and to do good works but not to develop a sustained, systematic approach to life in society. Thus we see periodic eruptions, such as now, when restive younger visionaries seek to regain social concern.

So even when evangelicals have responded to great social ills, their default method is to seek to change hearts and minds. They can engage in some vigorous advocacy and movement politics for a time, but this is not a sustained approach. It is interesting just now to see this old personalist ethic being worked out in poststructuralist, neo-Anabaptist terms. Even when young evangelical activists such as Shane Claiborne see and critique systemic evils, they seem to prefer to counteract them with a personal act of kindness or a gesture of dramatic protest. "Rage against the machine" seems to work better for them than policy wonking or institution building. So new evangelicals who engage in social reform continue to feel the old tension between their desire to change themselves and the call to change the world.

The heart of evangelicalism, in the end, is not theological, political, commercial, or therapeutic. Evangelicals want true religion, real Christianity—and they want to make it real to ordinary people. If they don't see it, even in evangelicalism itself, they will launch new quests to find it. This makes evangelicalism inherently volatile and unstable, but it also means that the movement has the ability to change and to renew itself. These old traits are forever creating new evangelicalisms.

NOTES

1. Timothy L. Smith and his students see more revivalist continuities than modernist departures in the social gospel movement. T. L. Smith, *Revivalism and Social Reform in Mid-Nineteenth-Century America* (Nashville, TN: Abingdon, 1957); Norris A. Magnuson, *Salvation in the Slums: Evangelical Social Work, 1865–1920* (Metuchen, NJ: Scarecrow Press, 1977); and Gary Scott Smith, *The Search for Social Salvation: Social Christianity and America, 1880–1925* (Lanham, MD: Lexington Books, 2000).
2. J. Elwin Wright, "Report of the Promotional Director," in *United We Stand: A Report of the Constitutional Convention of the National Association of Evangelicals,* La Salle Hotel, Chicago, Illinois, 3–6 May 1943, 5–6.
3. Carl F. H. Henry, "The Vigor of the New Evangelicalism," *Christian Life* 1 (April 1948): 30.
4. Harold J. Ockenga, "Can Fundamentalism Win America?" *Christian Life and Times,* June 1947, 13–15.
5. Robert Booth Fowler, *A New Engagement: Evangelical Political Thought, 1966–1976* (Grand Rapids, MI: Eerdmans, 1982), chapter 2, "*Christianity Today* and the Evangelical Mainstream," 23–41.
6. Carl Henry, *Confessions of a Theologian: An Autobiography* (Waco, TX: Word, 1986), 264–87.

7. David R. Swartz, *Moral Minority: The Evangelical Left in an Age of Conservatism* (Philadelphia: University of Pennsylvania Press, 2012). I think of a somewhat broader assemblage of evangelical views and practices than Swartz's "evangelical left." Perhaps the common denominator for various evangelical liberals, moderates, neo-Calvinists, Anabaptists, and New Left–oriented radicals is Ronald Sider, the gentle Anabaptist church historian who was for many years the director of Evangelicals for Social Action, itself a very broad coalition. What friends of ESA shared in common, in addition to their evangelicalism, was a fundamental regard for the poor and vulnerable (including the unborn), a passion for human rights (including racial and gender justice), commitment to environmental protection, critical views toward consumerist capitalism, and a preference for peace-seeking in international relations.

8. For a complete text of the Chicago Declaration and an eyewitness narrative of the meeting, see Ronald J. Sider, ed., *The Chicago Declaration* (Carol Stream, IL: Creation House, 1974). Swartz, *Moral Minority*, chapter 9, "The Chicago Declaration and a United Progressive Front," draws from multiple eyewitness sources to give a more complete account of the personal dynamics and debates.

9. Jim Wallis of Sojourners may be an exception. One of the most important traits he retained of his evangelical lineage was the belief that another great awakening could come and sweep all before it. See, e.g., Jim Wallis, *Revive Us Again: A Sojourner's Story* (Nashville, TN: Abingdon, 1983).

10. Richard J. Mouw, *Political Evangelism* (Grand Rapids, MI: Eerdmans, 1973); Paul B. Henry, *Politics for Evangelicals* (Elgin, IL: Judson Press, 1974).

11. John Perkins, *Let Justice Roll Down: John Perkins Tells His Own Story* (Glendale, CA: Regal Books, 1976).

12. Thomas D. Hanks, *God So Loved the Third World: The Biblical Vocabulary of Oppression* (Maryknoll, NY: Orbis Books, 1983).

13. Joel Carpenter, "*The Moody Monthly*," 109–110, in *The Conservative Press in Twentieth-Century America*, ed. William Longton and Ronald Lora (Westport, CT: Greenwood Press, 1999).

14. Sider is quoted in Michael Cromartie, "Fixing the World: From Nonplayers to Radicals to New Right Conservatives: The Saga of Evangelicals and Social Action," *Christianity Today*, April 27, 1992, 25.

15. Corwin E. Smidt, "Evangelical and Mainline Protestants at the Turn of the Millennium: Taking Stock and Looking Forward," 29–51, in *From Pews to Polling Places in the American Religious Mosaic*, ed. Matthew Wilson (Washington, DC: Georgetown University Press, 2007).

16. "Evangelical Voters Lift Every Voice," *Economist*, May 5, 2012, www.economist.com/node/21554201, accessed October 24, 2012.

17. Axel R. Schaefer, "Evangelicalism, Social Reform and the U.S. Welfare State, 1970–1996," 256–60, in *Religious and Secular Reform in America: Ideas, Beliefs, and Social Change*, ed. David K. Adams and Cornelis A. van Minnen (New York: New York University Press, 1999).

18. Samuel Escobar, "My Pilgrimage in Mission," *International Bulletin of Missionary Research* 36:4 (October 2012): 206–11.

19. Andrew F. Walls, *The Missionary Movement in Christian History: Studies in the Transmission of Faith* (Maryknoll, NY: Orbis Books, 1996), 81.

20. Quoted in Noll, *The Rise of Evangelicalism: The Age of Edwards, Whitefield and the Wesleys* (Downers Grove, IL: InterVarsity Press, 2003), 97.

13

Evangelicals of the 1970s and 2010s

WHAT'S THE SAME, WHAT'S DIFFERENT, AND WHAT'S URGENT

R. Stephen Warner

I SUSPECT THAT my primary qualification for the task of reflecting on the research reported in this book is my reputation as a sympathetic but not uncritical outside observer of the new evangelical movement in American religion. I earned that reputation through ethnographic field research that I conducted among self-styled new Christians in Mendocino, California, in the 1970s and published, in 1988, as *New Wine in Old Wineskins: Evangelicals and Liberals in a Small-Town Church.*[1] Despite its being my first foray into sociology of religion, the book was well received by my colleagues—and in evangelical circles.

But that was over twenty years ago, and although in the ensuing decades I have energetically kept tabs on American religion in its many changing facets, I have not closely followed evangelicals or stayed on top of the literature about them. At the conference that brought this book's contributors together, I was both enlightened and chagrined to meet for the first time several scholars whose work I should have known. From them, I learned about exciting things going on among today's evangelicals. Because of them, I learned that capable young scholars were tracking these developments. So I am greatly indebted to the organizers for inviting me.

Nonetheless, I think the organizers chose well, for what I can offer from a perspective of nearly forty years is a reflection on why the new evangelical social engagement isn't really so new, that it draws on the deep wellsprings and permeable boundaries of American evangelicalism, which once again have manifested the capacity of the movement to escape both self-imposed limits and externally imposed stereotypes. At the same time, my relatively long-term perspective makes clear to me that the promises of and challenges to evangelicalism in these two moments are different.

First, a comment on the term *evangelical*. I use this term to refer to Christians who stand by three commitments: faith in Jesus Christ as their personal savior, a high view of the scripture from which they draw that faith, and an impulse to testify to and spread that faith. But many of those to whom I apply this label did not use it about themselves (a tiny minority of the new evangelicals I met in the 1970s called themselves by that name), and some would not concede that others to whom I apply the label (e.g., charismatics and fundamentalists) qualify for it. Mine is a big-tent usage.

I. Bringing the Counterculture into Evangelicalism, 1976

The most intensive period of my field research took place in Mendocino from May through December of 1976, which *Newsweek* (then the high-minded liberal competitor to *Time*) dubbed "The Year of the Evangelical." In the most dramatic example of evangelicals coming into widespread public view, born-again Baptist Jimmy Carter was elected president. Some of my new Christian friends were thrilled. My secular friends were astonished. For them, Carter and his religion were profoundly alien.

The rise of evangelicalism nonetheless had deep demographic and religious roots that should have been apparent to sociologists at the time—and were in hindsight. Evangelicals had been moving up the social ladder and out of the South for decades, and, in the founding of the National Association of Evangelicals, their leaders had formally distanced themselves from their fundamentalist predecessors. Despite the biases of liberal and secular observers, evangelicalism hadn't been crushed by the 1925 Scopes trial, and it was not the particular property of backward Southerners. It was widespread, up-to-date, and thoroughly American.[2]

What had caught my attention and motivated my research was the Jesus movement, the mutual opening of evangelicalism and the counterculture, which appeared in the mid-1960s on Southern California beaches and in San Francisco's Haight-Ashbury district before moving further into northern California, following the hippies who were moving in droves back to the land. By 1976, the rural California Presbyterian church on which my research focused was full of self-designated Jesus freaks and hippie Christians. They and others like them brought the long hair and beards, country dress and folk-rock music, and verbal demonstrativeness of the counterculture into the previously straitlaced world of conservative white American Protestantism, along with their personal histories of interrupted college educations, protest politics, drug use, and sexual experimentation. "Praise God!" appeared to be their new way of saying, "Far out!" They experienced radical change in themselves, and they brought far-reaching, although not radical, change to evangelicalism.

Many of those I came to know, as well as those whose trajectories were traced by other social scientists,[3] had embraced evangelicalism in search of a new moral center between the postwar conformity they had rejected in the 1960s and the particular concoction of drugs and transient relationships they had thereafter, however briefly, imbibed. Particularly salient for many of my informants was hurt—and guilt—surrounding mistreatment by, and of, intimate partners, in reaction to which they wholeheartedly embraced norms of fidelity and deference in intimate relationships. They found support and guidance for their conscience-driven change of heart in evangelicalism, where these norms held unchallenged moral high ground.

Yet among Mendocino's new Christians in 1976, a half decade after their conversions, there was still continuity between their former lifestyles in the counterculture and their new one "in the body" (as they put it, i.e., the body of Christ). Using the Bible as a source of inspiration and imagining Jesus to be an intimate were new departures for them. But in the riches of evangelical culture, they found support and meaning for earlier values, and, to an extent, they reinforced these same values, immanent in the prophetic side of evangelical culture, among their newfound cultural partners.

Into their new religious lives they brought the egalitarianism and caring of their personal relationships, their ethic of racial and gender inclusiveness, the creativity and informality of their music and art, and their passion for peace among nations and harmony with nature. What was new was the immediacy and resonance they found for their values in the Bible, as if the events portrayed in the New Testament had happened the day before. (Acts 2:42–47 was perhaps their favorite scripture.) Thus there was much cultural continuity between the 1960s and 1970s. To judge from the portrait of the New Monastics provided by Will Samson in chapter 4, many of these countercultural and biblical themes are alive among engaged evangelicals today.

II. The Multivalence of Evangelicalism

Despite their visible countercultural heritage, already in 1976 I saw my new Christian friends undergoing cultural changes under evangelical tutelage that went well beyond the new norms of family life (no one yet spoke of "family values") that had impelled their conversions. They were told that a family needed a head, who must be the husband. They were admonished that dependence on government (e.g., AFDC) was ungodly. They learned that working too hard to maintain a simple, natural lifestyle could be idolatrous. In October, they were reminded that Halloween verged on worship of Satan. Although they seemed to enjoy reading the Bible mostly for narratives that they could apply to their lives (e.g., Acts 2:42), some nonetheless began to quote proof texts in support of new rules (e.g., Proverbs 31:15). The countercultural spirit they brought to their newly religious life was being visibly disciplined by the more experienced of their evangelical comrades, including some who were lieutenants in the shepherding movement. I worried about my friends getting pushed around by zealots.

Yet most of them spent less time thinking about ideology and politics, whether secular or Christian, than I did. Moreover, as I learned by inspecting public voter rolls in June and November of 1976, the majority of the converts remained registered Democrats. Moreover, a visible, vocal contingent of them had joined the mainline Presbyterian church, bringing the new wine of their religious enthusiasm into the venerable wineskin of one of the oldest Protestant churches on the West Coast. By the end of the 1970s, nearly a third of the church's members had "made Cursillo," becoming alumni of a Roman Catholic–based spiritual renewal movement that impels its initiates into social engagement. Cursillo, along with charismatic renewal, was one channel for the introduction of Catholic sensibilities to evangelicalism that is the subject of Omri Elisha's chapter 3. The evangelicalism I discovered in Mendocino was not sealed off from other religious currents.

Beyond Mendocino, I found that evangelicalism in general was internally diverse. The pastor who drew so many Jesus people into Mendocino's Presbyterian church had been trained at Fuller Seminary, a moderating, albeit forceful, influence in late-twentieth-century conservative American Protestantism. Chicago friends put me in touch with LaSalle Street Church, a youthful evangelical church with an urban mission, and Reba Place Fellowship, a Mennonite Christian commune dedicated to racial reconciliation in my own neighborhood of south Evanston. Inspired by these congregations, I subscribed to *Sojourners* to learn more about the corners of American evangelicalism they inhabited. Eventually, students began inviting me to some of Chicago's black churches, famous ones like Salem Baptist as well as obscure ones, where I encountered what must be called evangelical theology linked to a radically different social teaching than that I encountered in white-led evangelical churches. To the consternation of my evangelical friends, I even encountered palpably evangelical (and Pentecostal) influences in the Metropolitan Community Church, the gay church, to which one of my students invited my class in 1985.[4]

As much as I struggled to capture the internal logic of American evangelicalism, I eventually followed the lead of Martin Marty[5] to understand the coherence of the twentieth-century evangelical movement as more a socio-historical than a theological phenomenon. White American evangelicalism, the movement that I saw Mendocino's Jesus people being tutored by, was a religious party, whose identity and boundaries had to be understood as, in part, reactions to another religious party, sometimes called liberalism, sometimes modernism, that had different, not simply contrary, focal concerns. It was logically quite possible to be both evangelical and liberal. Sociologically, it was very difficult.[6]

I lost touch with most of the Mendocino evangelicals during the 1980s, but along with the broader Jesus movement, they had an enormous impact on American religion. Their informality and their music were adopted by seeker-sensitive evangelical churches and disseminated by means of the sprawling contemporary Christian music industry. Their enthusiasm gave evangelicalism new and powerful ways of appealing to youth. Their energies led to the founding of worldwide protodenominations like Calvary Chapel and the Vineyard. Their numbers and their vitality contributed to the increasingly assertive presence of evangelicalism in American culture.

The book inspired by my research did not appear until late in the second term of Ronald Reagan, to whose landslide reelection in 1984 evangelicals made a significant contribution. Despite my opposition to right-wing politics, I resisted the temptation to demonize and stereotype those I had met ten years earlier. In the years since, I have argued that my fellow political liberals should not reflexively scorn the concerns of religious conservatives, who are often indispensable allies on issues of economic equality and social justice and who number among them proportionately far more people of color than do the mainline Protestant churches with which I am affiliated.[7]

But I must finally face the fact that evangelicals have enabled thirty years of increasing right-wing radicalism in the Republican Party. For decades, evangelicals traded their votes for Republican promises of a culturally conservative agenda, a trade that emergent leader Tony Jones, as quoted in Adriane Bilous's chapter 5, calls "a match made in hell."[8] Meanwhile, by 2012, it had become increasingly clear that the core right-wing agenda is neither conservative nor cultural but the economically radical one of dismantling the New Deal. What liberals (and I would add Christians of all stripes, especially new evangelical activists) ought to be worrying about is not the phantom of theocracy. It is the advance of plutocracy.

III. The Present, 2012

Given my sympathies and fond memories of my evangelical friends of the 1970s, I have been heartened by news of social engagement among American evangelicals, including the analyses in this book. New evangelical activists are staking out progressive positions on global human rights, the environment, and racial reconciliation, to mention three issues. Leaders of so-called emergent communities are calling into deep question hidebound ideas and willful neglect of social reality on the part of the conservative churches they grew up in. At a minimum, this book testifies to the continued internal diversity—and vitality—of American evangelicalism.

Most exciting to me are the broader currents within the new evangelical social engagement documented in chapter 1 by James Bielo (on emerging leaders), chapter 4 by Will Samson (on the New Monasticism), chapter 3 by Omri Elisha (on resonance with Catholic teaching), and chapter 5 by Adriane Bilous (on evangelical women activists). Bielo's empathetic yet critical ethnography of FORMED, the program of spiritual formation developed by certain emergent leaders, brilliantly illuminates the dilemmas they face in their struggles to combine personal and public transformation. In the end, though, I was disappointed—not in Bielo's excellent ethnography, but in FORMED itself. Did they really need to spend so much intellectual effort reinventing the wheel for themselves when they might have joined preexisting communities that were conducive to their aspirations? Might they not have focused less on codifying what struck me as familiar vows and more on very practical impediments to faithful living? (Bielo's illustration of the "handy Midday Prayer...for days when you are on the go" in FORMED's section on the vow of simplicity is priceless.) Having seen a mass movement bringing the age of Aquarius into evangelicalism four decades ago, I am not as convinced as are these emerging leaders of the hegemony of modernity over evangelicalism.

Perhaps because they seem to be more oriented to practice and less to theory, I was more drawn to Samson's New Monastics. The twelve marks of the New Monastics are very similar to the eleven vows of FORMED'S first-year curriculum, but Samson's protagonists seem more willing to commit themselves to building actual human communities around these ideals than in endlessly reforming themselves. Samson's opening vignette of a New Monastic gathering (based on field research done in Kentucky in 2008) reminded me of nothing so much as the Mendocino new Christians' Friday night meetings of thirty-two years earlier.[9] In both places, we see the local chapter of the body of Christ in action.

Samson's endorsement of the rubric of monasticism, as well as several of the twelve marks of that movement (e.g., the parish concept implicit in "geographical proximity to community members who share a common rule of life"), gives additional credence to Elisha's intuition of Roman Catholic resonances within contemporary evangelical social engagement. To be sure, mainstream evangelicalism has buried the anti-Catholic hatchet partly out of common cause over abortion and homosexuality. But that is by no means the whole story.

In the local popularity of the Cursillo movement in Mendocino in the late 1970s, I witnessed an implicit evangelical-Catholic rapprochement well before the polarization on hot-button issues. Moreover, even that partisan realignment seems to have paved the way for mutual influence on less politicized matters. Elisha and Bielo both stress the growing experimentation with liturgical and sensory practices among contemporary evangelical groups, an observation consistent with what I have seen in other evangelical churches.

Despite the continuing evangelical obsession with various forms of separation, or "distinction" from sources of moral pollution, these developments might promise an American Christian church conceived in ever-broader terms. Evangelicals ought to recognize that, however little their moral crusades have done to lower abortion rates or delegitimate homosexuality, their confident assertion of fundamentals of faith (e.g., incarnation, resurrection, grace, biblical witness) has influenced the old-line churches, where Jesus-seminar thinking is no closer to the religious center than was the "death of God" movement of a half century ago. The evangelical-Catholic detente promises also a significant enrichment of the intellectual capital available to emerging leaders, especially on questions of social justice.

Two huge differences between the groups that Bielo and Samson interviewed in the 2000s and those I met in the 1970s are, first, that the recent groups are trying to escape the confines of the evangelical culture that the earlier group was just entering and, second, that, although the new evangelicals in both decades were committed to geographic place, the recent groups have chosen to pursue their vocations in the city. By contrast, Mendocino's new Christians were, as I put it in 1988, "small-town people by choice, elective parochials"; one of the attractions of evangelicalism for them was precisely its small-town mentality.[10] But today's twenty-first-century newly engaged evangelicals have embraced the city as the place to put their lives on the line. In my view, this is the most encouraging news about them.

As I am sure many of the emerging leaders and New Monastics know, it is in the city where they are likely to encounter deeply religious Christians who are not white evangelicals. In the city, they will confront structural injustices more intimately. Chief among structural injustices is the inequality of wealth that has grown to shocking levels since 1980 and is most prevalent in the city. And in the city, evangelicals are far more likely than in the suburbs or small towns to be in the midst of a political culture that will not merely echo the Religious Right ideology that they are said to want to escape. Just as Mendocino's new Christians brought into their newfound faith predominantly liberal, educated, and cosmopolitan sensibilities from the cities whose disorder they were escaping, so today's emerging evangelicals will be well served by the diffuse cultural leaven they are likely to absorb in the city.

IV. Urgent Tasks Ahead

My hope is that the commitment to living in the city—with all its diversity and elbow-rubbing—will facilitate the accomplishment of two tasks I see as necessary for the new evangelical social engagement to have the transformative impact its activists intend. The first is a reconsideration of the Religious Right's campaigns on abortion and homosexuality, which, to judge from the portrayals in this book, those activists would like to distance themselves from.

Dan Williams's chapter 9 shows that the way abortion has been framed has deeply damaged American politics. One reason may be that for the evangelical mainstream, restricting abortion was intended not only to protect life but also to deter nonmarital and teenage sex. Thus, the political expression of prolife became part of a family values platform (including parental notification), which, whatever its merits, gave credence to the opposing view that the prolife label was a cover for worries about unauthorized sexual activity. Insofar as they suggest that innocent women deserve a break, exceptions for rape or incest, as relatively popular as they are among moderates, give credence to the view that restricting abortion rights is part of a war on women. I would add that my party, the Democrats, have compounded the problem by becoming dependent on the votes of suburban prochoice fiscal conservatives, who are not promising allies on the issues of social justice that Williams's progressives are dedicated to.[11]

The issue of abortion bears the mark of tragic conflict, right against right. After forty years of stalemate and increasing partisan polarization, this much is clear. Americans have become ever more ambivalent about abortion, no doubt because of more widespread acknowledgment both of the reality of fetal life (through advances in ultrasound technology and intrauterine surgery) and of the determined persistence of the practice in spite of restrictions. It is entirely likely that more Americans will reject the facile equation that unplanned pregnancies are unwanted. It is equally likely that very few Americans will want to imprison those who undergo or provide abortions.

What seems most promising as a practical response is to minimize the demand for abortion by making it less burdensome for a woman to carry a pregnancy to term and to make reliable contraception readily available for those who are not ready to reproduce. The new engaged evangelicals could help protect life by withdrawing support for abstinence-only programs, which are intended to delay onset of sexual activity, not to protect life. (Ironically, such programs have the opposite effect by making it more likely that first sex will be unprotected sex.) Progressive evangelicals could add their support for such parenting-friendly measures as parental leave, the earned income tax credit, subsidized day care, and open adoption. Otherwise, motherhood threatens to become effectively a privilege of the affluent or, to the extent that abortion provision continues to be curtailed across the U.S. landscape, an undue burden for the poor.

What distorted American politics even more was the sequel to the stalemate over abortion, when the Religious Right turned its attention to the increasingly visible, but at the time socially marginalized, homosexual rights movement. By 2004, opposition to same-sex marriage materially helped reelect President George W. Bush. But it seems clear that, as a consequence of the most rapid and profound shift in public opinion that I have ever witnessed, the issue will soon lose its potency, even among the religious public. As reported by Robert Putnam and David Campbell, by 2008 the *most* religious members of the post-baby-boom generation were as likely to support same-sex marriage (32 percent) as the *least* religious among the preboomer generation.[12] In effect, what had been unthinkable—respectable homosexual couples—became unthreatening when people saw them face to face.

The evangelical-Catholic-Mormon coalition against same-sex marriage is itself a marriage of political convenience. Catholic teaching recognizes that homosexual *orientation* is deep-seated and not in itself sinful. Homosexual *acts* are sinful and must be resisted. But the Catholic Church holds a traditional and honored place for celibates, unlike the dominant, deeply Protestant public culture of the United States, where marriage and parenthood are regarded as among the rights to life, liberty, and happiness to which all Americans are entitled—indeed, not only rights but in many contexts requisites of full cultural citizenship.

In contrast to the case of abortion, no tragic conflict is involved in same-sex marriage, no right against right, only the understandable wish of one group (heterosexuals) to keep to themselves a legally sanctioned and culturally mandated privilege. Such a wish is coming to be seen as one that fair-minded people, on reflection, cannot justify. I suspect that an apprehension of this simple unfairness is one reason behind progressive evangelicals' lack of passion for pursuing the culture wars.

The second, more urgent, and no doubt more difficult task required for the fulfillment of progressive evangelical aspirations is to understand and repudiate evangelical complicity in the right-wing radicalization of the Republican Party and its disastrous consequences for American life. I say more difficult because this task will require of progressive evangelicals more than distancing themselves from the Religious Right and more than a change of heart on same-sex marriage. It will require a change of mind on the nature of the world in which we humans are called to live our lives.

Reading these chapters, it is impossible not to be impressed with the generous social concern expressed by new evangelical activists. Sharing, hospitality, community, and justice are prominent among the eleven vows of FORMED and the twelve marks of the New Monasticism. These are biblical norms. The specter of Mammon as a temptation to be resisted is evident in the scorn for consumerism. Wary respect for what belongs to Caesar and vigilant resistance to Caesar's overstepping his bounds are always in the background of evangelical thinking. But in none of these chapters did I detect an awareness of the parallel danger of concentrated economic power: Walmart, Blue Cross–Blue Shield, Big Pharma, Big Oil, Facebook, Google, and, behind them all, Wall Street. The existence of powerful economic structures between the state and the church is a gigantic evangelical blind spot.

To speak of concentrated economic power is no more to engage in class warfare than warning about the danger of political tyranny is to promote anarchy. Many millions of Americans have a stake in these companies through their pension funds, just as many millions of Americans participate in a deeply flawed political system through their votes. Whether or not we are *of* the world, all of us, evangelical or not, live *in* the real world. One urgent goal must be to reduce the influence of private money in politics.

But to mention politics brings up another aspect of the evangelical mindset, and that is "distinction," which Will Samson characterizes as "the DNA of American evangelicalism." Throughout these chapters, we hear of young activists facing conservative evangelicals' suspicions that they risk coming too close to liberal activists (Elisha's chapter 3) and pantheists (Kearns's chapter 7). Those who have chosen a more liberal stance are similarly concerned with distinction. Bilous's activist women have "a deep desire to separate from older generations," and Samson entertains the possibility that the New Monastics are choosing to express their distinct identity especially through their aesthetics. It is heartening for me to hear that Bielo's engaged leaders distance themselves from the Pharisees of the Religious Right, but what is worrisome is when distinction demands disengagement, as it does for Bilous's women activists. Burned by and subject to scorn for earlier evangelicals' pro-Republican political activism, they intend to avoid political activism altogether. To me, such withdrawal is not responsive to the task of social transformation.

What progressive evangelicals must understand is that the Religious Right not only distorted the gospel in the interest of power, as Tony Jones says. They did damage to the social fabric. The damage I speak of, much of it tracing back to the way the issue of abortion was handled in American politics—the Republicans gaining votes through abortion as a wedge issue and the Democrats tragically playing along[13]—consists especially of the deliberate shrinking of the public sphere through the program of denying revenue to the government ("starve the beast"); the exacerbation of economic inequality through an increasingly regressive tax structure, attacks on union rights, deregulation of banks, and shredding of the social safety net; the polarization of our two parties through the political assassination of moderate Republicans and the discouragement of moderate Democrats; stalemate, because of this polarization, on other issues impacting the most vulnerable people in our society (e.g., immigration, the war on drugs, and assault weapons); and, particularly injurious to evangelicalism, the departure of a third of the newest adult generation from religious identification altogether, as "Christian" has become a bad name, pushing many spiritually inclined people out of religion altogether.[14]

Only the last of these developments is amenable to the sort of winsome, personal, local activism that so many of the newly engaged evangelicals seem willing to undertake. Remedying the others requires political action. Progressive evangelicals must be involved with the political process. Cursing both houses is just another form of distinction.

They need not join my party, the Democrats, who are far from perfect. (My gripes include their excessive deference to trial lawyers and their reflexive tag line of "choice."[15] Readers can add their own. My support for Democrats centers on their vision of a society of shared prosperity and shared risk.) Evangelicals should not need to be admonished not to expect salvation through any human institution. Nonetheless, progressive white evangelicals could learn from African American evangelicals—that is to say, the great majority of African Americans[16]—how to live with such imperfections in order to have any hope of political progress. In the end, to be true to the aspirations we've read about in this book, progressive evangelicals must repudiate the Religious Right and work politically to undo the damage that has been done by thirty years of evangelical-enabled right-wing politics.

NOTES

1. For comments and suggestions on earlier drafts, the author is indebted to Tricia C. Bruce, Anna C. Colaner, Anne Heider, Paul J. Olson, Jerry Z. Park, Brian Steensland, and Jeremy N. Thomas, none of whom bears any responsibility for the views expressed here. R. Stephen Warner, *New Wine in Old Wineskins: Evangelicals and Liberals in a Small-Town Church* (Berkeley: University of California Press, 1988).

2. See Richard Quebedeaux, *The Worldly Evangelicals* (San Francisco: Harper and Row, 1978); and Joel A. Carpenter, *Revive Us Again: The Reawakening of American Fundamentalism* (New York: Oxford University Press, 1997).

3. E.g., Steven M. Tipton, *Getting Saved from the Sixties: Moral Meaning in Conversion and Cultural Change* (Berkeley: University of California Press, 1982).

4. R. Stephen Warner, "The Metropolitan Community Churches and the Gay Agenda: The Power of Pentecostalism and Essentialism," 183–208, in *A Church of Our Own: Disestablishment and Diversity in American Religion* (New Brunswick, NJ: Rutgers University Press 2005).

5. Martin E. Marty, *Righteous Empire: The Protestant Experience in America* (New York: Dial Press, 1970), 177–87.

6. Warner, *New Wine*, 49–60.

7. R. Stephen Warner, "The De-Europeanization of American Christianity," 233–55, in *A Nation of Religions: Pluralism in the American Public Square*, ed. Stephen Prothero (Chapel Hill: University of North Carolina Press, 2006).

8. Tony Jones, *The New Christians: Dispatches from the Emergent Frontier* (San Francisco: Jossey-Bass, 2008), 71.

9. Warner, *New Wine*, 37–44.

10. Warner, *New Wine*, 87, 289–96.

11. William Saletan, *Bearing Right: How Conservatives Won the Abortion War* (Berkeley: University of California Press, 2003).

12. Robert Putnam and David Campbell, *American Grace: How Religion Divides and Unites Us* (New York: Simon and Schuster, 2010), 404.

13. Putnam and Campbell, *American Grace*, 384–418.

14. Michael Hout and Claude S. Fischer, "Why More Americans Have No Religious Preference: Politics and Generations," *American Sociological Review* 67 (2002): 165–90.

15. See Saletan, *Bearing Right*; and Barry Schwartz, *The Paradox of Choice: Why More Is Less* (New York: Harper and Row, 2004).

16. Michael O. Emerson and Christian Smith, *Divided by Faith: Evangelical Religion and the Problem of Race in America* (New York: Oxford University Press, 2000).

14

We Need a New Reformation

Glen Harold Stassen

BRIAN STEENSLAND AND Philip Goff asked me to begin by "reflecting personally on your own evangelical social engagement and what things today look like from your own vantage point as a longtime activist." I will follow their request and, in the process, call attention to an underlying spiritual commitment in the movement, from my perspective and my discipline as a Christian social ethicist.

I come from an evangelical German Baptist church in Minnesota, with an immigrant family's shared loyalties to the American tradition of human rights and a Baptist's loyalties to following Jesus. When I was twelve, we moved to Philadelphia, where I participated in many American Friends Service Committee (AFSC) weekend work camps among the poor of Philadelphia. Friday evenings, we high school students dialogued with an expert in urban problems. On Saturday, we went in teams of two to join with a family in cleaning and painting their apartment with paint AFSC had persuaded the landlord to buy. I experienced children lacking awareness of the world beyond their block, attending poor schools, and being impacted by many dimensions of racial and economic injustice and little encouragement to have hope. Saturday evening, we discussed what we had experienced and learned. Sunday morning, we observed the magistrate's court dealing with adults who were once like those children but now in some trouble with the police, and then we worshiped in a storefront church where the people worshiped. Then lunch, discussion, and home. In AFSC's Week-Long Urban Minorities Close-Up, we studied and experienced the often-unseen structural injustices and also various organizations working to bring some hope and healing. These experiences deeply motivated me to care about racial and economic injustice in the spiritual context of Quaker commitment to peace and justice.

When I did my doctoral studies in Christian ethics at Duke University, the Civil Rights movement was in its prime. Wally Mead, a grad student in political science and a committed Methodist, and I organized the Christian Interfaith Witness Association, Duke's student civil rights organization. We white students joined with black students from Shaw University and many Durham residents in massive civil disobedience and got sweeping results in fair employment practices, school integration, integration of public accommodations, and the election of the progressive candidate for mayor, Nick Galifonikas. We organized two busloads to go to the March on Washington, which climaxed with Martin Luther King Jr. lifting our spirits to soaring heights with his "I Have a Dream" speech. As political scientists Robert Putnam and David Campbell have written, "Martin Luther King, Jr.'s prophetic call for racial justice was persuasive in part because his words and deeds drew on powerful religious symbolism that could not be reduced to base partisanship."[1] King was the spiritual guide, the ethically orienting North Star for our movement. His Baptist, Jesus-following vision resonated deeply for me. The deeply thoughtful pastor of Watts Street Baptist church, Warren Carr, preached profound Christ-centered Barthian sermons that also resonated with my loyalties, but I do not remember his sermons dealing explicitly with racial injustice. Segregationists in the church rallied friends who had not been to church for a long time to vote against my effort—at the request of the chair of the deacons board—to integrate the church membership. Losing the vote demoralized the church. It lost members and also its pastor; deeply disappointed, he moved to pastor another church.

I went to teach in Louisville, Kentucky, where my pastor was John Claypool, who combined Baptist Christ-centeredness with prophetic leadership for racial justice. The most important radio station chose him, along with a thoughtful Catholic priest and a Jewish rabbi, for its weekly *Moral Side of the News*. He recruited me to join the board of the ecumenical Council of Religion and Race. Soon I became the chair of its Action Committee, which coordinated the twenty-seven organizations working together to pass the first open housing law in the South to ban discrimination in housing in the city and then to get a similar law passed in the state legislature, making Kentucky the first state in the South to do so.

Louisville and nearby Bardstown are a historic center for both Catholics and Baptists. I was deeply affected by Sisters of Loretto, Sisters of Charity of Nazareth, and Sisters of Mercy, and I became spiritually half Catholic. I share their deep Christ-centered piety and serious prayer life. I urge our social teaching and engagement to be grounded in deeper practices of listening prayer, in the presence of the living Christ and the Holy Spirit. Practices of the Trappist Abbey of Gethsemane and its best known monk, Thomas Merton, are important for my inner life. It heals some of my loneliness. Without an inner prayer life, our social engagement loses its grounding. Dietrich Bonhoeffer knew that and practiced it. Ji Yong Lee, my PhD student, argues that when some Korean churches turned to social engagement without practices of personal prayer, they lost their deeper strength. He argues for holistic discipleship, both inner and outer, in the tradition of Martin Luther King Jr. and Dietrich Bonhoeffer.

My undergraduate degree and summer employment were in nuclear physics, and like many physicists, I became aware of the growing threat of mutual extinction by nuclear war. And my father developed the Arms Control and Disarmament branch of the U.S. State Department. So I have also been engaged in extensive citizen activism for steps toward nuclear disarmament. In the late 1960s, sociologist Charles Osgood published his *An Alternative to War or Surrender*, with its "independent initiatives" strategy for reducing the threat of nuclear war. At the same time, having been influenced by Baptists Howard Rees, W. W. Adams, Clarence Jordan, and my New Testament professor W. D. Davies, I was working to develop a paradigm shift in interpreting Jesus' Sermon on the Mount as "transforming initiatives." As Gandhi, Jesus, and Rosa Parks had combined to give Martin Luther King Jr. a vision of nonviolent direct action following Jesus' love, Osgood's vision of independent initiatives and my vision of Jesus' transforming initiatives combined to produce a flash of inspiration: we need a new ethic of just peacemaking, with positive initiatives to make peace and prevent war.

In the 1960s and 1970s, I was active in the anti–Vietnam War campaign. What we did in Louisville had a Baptist-Presbyterian-Methodist-Catholic basis, and we won many converts. But the national antiwar campaign lacked the articulate spirituality of a Martin Luther King Jr. and the remarkably well-disciplined practices of nonviolence and love of enemy, and it failed to move the country as effectively.[2]

In 1980, we formed the ecumenical Louisville and Jefferson County Council of Peacemaking and Religion, and Catholic Pat McCullough and I became cochairs of the Executive Committee and the Strategy Committee, respectively, of the national Nuclear Weapons Freeze Campaign. This led to what is probably my biggest social-action contribution, initiating the strategy that eliminated the hugely destabilizing medium-range nuclear missiles in Europe and the Soviet Union totally.[3] It demonstrated the effectiveness of the practices of just peacemaking. The theological ethics of the council were predominantly Catholic and Baptist, and the initial leadership of the freeze campaign included the evangelical Jim Wallis and several committed Christians, but the freeze became predominantly a secular organization. Its successor, Peace Action, is based on local affiliates in many states, but it mostly lacks a strategy for organizing in churches, synagogues, and mosques.[4]

What I think I have learned is what Putnam and Campbell, like many others, have observed: "religion has historically inspired change across the U.S. political spectrum." They write of Martin Luther King Jr.'s "powerful religious symbolism." I want to write more precisely: King's words and deeds were explicitly based on thick exegesis of the way of Jesus in his book *Strength to Love* and on his absolutely clear loyalty to Jesus' way of nonviolence and love. He confronted injustice the way Jesus confronted the authorities in his time. This has been crucial for my own engagement in social change movements and is now crucial for many engaged young adult evangelicals. As Charles Marsh has shown in his The Beloved Community: How Faith Shapes Social Justice, from the Civil Rights Movement to Today, when the Student Nonviolent Coordinating Committee (SNCC) lost King's Jesus-grounded vision, it lost its way.

My social location is Fuller Theological Seminary in Pasadena, California, often spoken of as the flagship evangelical seminary. It is truly centrist evangelical, not the stereotype of the Religious Right. It has about four thousand students, making it probably the largest seminary anywhere. It is also multiethnic and multilingual (including Spanish and Korean) and has many international students and a strong commitment to worldwide Christianity. We have an active student Peace and Justice Advocates group, a Just Peacemaking Initiative organization,⁵ and One Table for healing hateful ideologies about sexual identity. On the last, Fuller's policy is sex only within marriage between male and female, combined with care to provide support for students who, in a seminary this large, have some diversity. I have served as faculty advisor for all three groups, so I do get to know many young adult evangelical activists.

My impression from these students matches well what our book has described. In my elective course on faith and politics this term, students chose the following term paper topics: five on world poverty, economic justice in the United States, and neoliberalism; five on the hijacking of churches by Nixon's Southern strategy and the Religious Right versus a more prophetic posture for churches (Jim Wallis, Shane Claiborne, Greg Boyd); two on immigration justice; two on marriage, sexuality, and Christian political engagement; two on creation care; two on abortion, capital punishment, and a consistent ethic of life; and one on each of American individualism versus community, substance abuse and racism, and Barack Obama's moral formation. Jim Wallis's *God's Politics* received the highest student ratings (actually tied with my *A Thicker Jesus*).

Student interest in creation care is higher than the paper topics indicate; we have a separate elective on creation care, so I did not emphasize it as much in this course. Peace and Justice Advocates have already successfully prodded the seminary to undertake systematic recycling and energy conservation and are now working to persuade the seminary to move into solar energy for electricity, here in sunny Southern California. In my elective on peacemaking and the forums we hold, I find students' strongest peacemaking interest is on Palestine and Israel. Similarly, an impressive group of evangelical young adults engaged in peacemaking organizations who met in a recent conference at Georgetown University, September 14–15, 2012, were more engaged in peacemaking between Palestine and Israel than any other issue.

I want to call attention to the importance of the Sojourners movement, which may be engaging more young adults in social change than any other organization. Sojourners focuses mostly on racial and social justice, but also life and peace, and environmental stewardship, with a strong Christ-centered faith. *Sojourners* magazine continues to win a large number of prestigious awards, and its circulation continues to grow while magazines like *Newsweek* and major newspapers are losing readers. At www.sojo.net, the *Sojourners* website, the number of page views has been steadily increasing each year. It increased 30 percent—by about 1.2 million—in the last twelve months. In the last half year, "Facebook support has grown 12 percent...and Twitter has added 14,000 followers, showing a 70 percent growth." In May, 2012, *Sojourners* was named the best general interest magazine by the Associated Church press, which has bestowed ten other awards on the magazine, and the Evangelical Press Association gave *Sojourners* a dozen awards at its annual convention. Sojourners recently produced *The Line*, a forty-minute documentary on poverty, which immediately had over two thousand screenings and continues to be shown in classes and groups around the nation. The Circle of Protection, with Sojourners leadership, has brought many Christian groups together to persuade the Congress not to try to balance the budget on the backs of the poor—with success at this writing, despite strong pressures in the House of Representatives to cut social programs. Sojourners also led ten organizations in organizing the Evangelical Immigration Table, which influenced the administration to announce they would not kill the dream for young immigrants who came with their parents. "Within the week of launching, the White House announced the opportunity for DREAM students to receive 2-year work permits; both CNN and the White House credited the Table's work for that rule change."[6] The Evangelical Immigration Table prodded both parties, even before the presidential election results had prodded Republicans to change their policy on immigration justice, to become more serious about comprehensive immigration reform.

Sojourners began as a Jesus-following community, with the strong influence of John Howard Yoder's most influential book *The Politics of Jesus*, as well as his *The Christian Witness to the State*, and his emphasis on community.[7] The spirituality of Sojourners is strongly influenced by young evangelicals' loyalty to a deeper understanding of the way of Jesus.

Engagement Rooted in a Thicker Jesus

For theological grounding of the new evangelical social engagement, I see three possibilities: (1) evangelical engagement can emphasize justice and peacemaking but without a deep basis in the way of Jesus and thus drift toward secularism and loss of its spiritual base; (2) evangelical engagement can react against that danger by shunning engagement in justice and peacemaking, and thus be unfaithful to the way of Jesus, who identified with the prophetic tradition and with God's deep caring for justice and peace; (3) evangelical engagement can root its work for justice and peacemaking in a thicker Jesus, richly contextualized in his own Bible, the Old Testament, and in his historical context in first-century Galilee and Israel. Jesus unmasked the injustices of the ruling authorities and repeatedly warned that proclivities toward resentment and rebellion against Rome, and not knowing the practices that make for peace, would lead to the destruction of the temple and Jerusalem. He joined John the Baptist in identifying not with the Pharisees, Sadducees, Essenes, or Zealots, but with the tradition of the prophet Isaiah. Isaiah was the most widely read book in the first century—as both the Dead Sea Scrolls and the Gospels show. Isaiah taught repeatedly that God cares deeply for justice that delivers the poor, the dominated, the marginalized, and the exiles, and for peacemaking. He also taught that God is active in our lives and our history, bringing breakthroughs that we can participate in. He emphasized God's presence as Holy Spirit and as deliverer, and our joy as we can participate in God's healing and delivering presence. These Isaiah themes became central themes for Jesus. God is not an absent monarch or an Aristotelian unmoved mover or a Platonic distant ideal; we have the mustard seeds now of God's coming reign.

Already in the second century, however, Christians were beginning to adopt influences from gnostic and Platonic idealism and thus lose some of their realistic basis in Hebraic tradition. Then came subservience to Constantinianism and loss of the independence of churches from the state. In the Middle Ages, most people could not read, so Christians pictured the Gospels from medieval art. You can see that art in the Cloisters Art Museum in New York City: all the paintings and statues depict either the baby Jesus with Mary or the crucified Jesus on the cross. Not one painting or statue depicts any of Jesus' parables, his actions, or other teachings. It is like the Apostles' Creed and the Nicene Creed: "born of the Virgin Mary, crucified under Pontius

Pilate." All of Jesus' teachings, deeds, and ministry are hidden behind that comma. The magisterial Reformation of Luther, Zwingli, and Calvin reacted against the Anabaptists, defended a state-church establishment, and lacked a full emphasis on the Jesus of the Gospels and the way of discipleship. This is what Dietrich Bonhoeffer criticized in his book *Discipleship* as "cheap grace." He wrote, "People don't want to know what some church leader wants; they want to know what Jesus wants."

In more recent centuries, many evangelical churches were influenced by defense of slavery and segregation, especially in the South; by reaction against the social gospel; and by unholy alliances with economic greed and militarism. They preached from Paul and seldom from the Gospels. Jesus got thinned down to an ideal or two that could fit into the cracks of the reigning ideologies.

Revolt against Accommodating Churches to the Culture

What is happening now among young evangelicals is a revolt against churches that have accommodated too much to a culture of greed, individualism, authoritarianism, militarism, and lack of respect for the sanctity of human life. It is a revolt in favor of a recovery of a thicker Jesus, and it supports the engagement that our book is documenting.

Furthermore, the split between churches of the magisterial Reformation and Anabaptist churches is decreasing, with Anabaptists led by Yoder rejecting disengaged sectarianism and Protestants realizing they need some of Jesus' themes they had formerly labeled Anabaptist. As Omri Elisha (chapter 3) has written, evangelical scholars are also developing stronger support for Catholic social ethics, including the common good and the consistent ethic of life, based in human dignity and human rights of life, liberty, and justice in community. This can be seen in *Toward an Evangelical Public Policy*, edited by Ronald Sider and Diane Knippers, which in summary was endorsed by all forty-three members of the board of the National Association of Evangelicals. A forthcoming book on Catholics and evangelicals for the common good, edited by Ron Sider and John Borelli, further develops the theme of the common good and human rights. As Elisha indicates, this is helping increasing numbers of evangelicals get free of sectarianism and instead develop a thoughtful public ethic without selling their churches out to the ideology of the Religious Right or the left. The theme of the lordship of Christ through all of life runs through *Toward an Evangelical Public Policy* and is central there for overcoming the dualistic split between private and public ethics.

Young adults are right in sensing we need a new Reformation. Look at the research results from the Barna Corporation as reported by Kinnaman and Lyons in *Unchristian*. They write that most Americans outside of Christianity "think Christians no longer represent what Jesus had in mind." In 1996, their poll found that 85 percent of Americans had a favorable attitude toward Christianity's role in society, but only a decade later, the image of the Christian faith had suffered a major setback. "Nearly two out of every five young outsiders (38 percent) claim to have a bad impression of present-day Christianity." And one-third of young outsiders would not want to be associated with Christianity. "Jesus receives outsiders' most favorable feelings, but even the clarity of his image has eroded among young people." Their polls consistently show evidence of what Bonhoeffer called cheap grace—claims to be Christian without following Jesus. "In virtually every study we conduct...born-again Christians fail to display much attitudinal or behavioral evidence of transformed lives."[8]

Political scientists David Campbell and Robert Putnam agree with Kinnaman and Lyons that "this dramatic generational shift is primarily in reaction to the religious right." To those under thirty, "'religion' means 'Republican,' 'intolerant,' and 'homophobic.'" Their data show a dramatic change "as the public visibility of the religious right increased...the last few decades have led directly to an unprecedented turning away from organized religion, especially among younger Americans...20-somethings in 2012 are much more likely to reject all religious affiliation than their parents and grandparents were when they were young—33 percent today, compared with 12 percent in the 1970s."[9] Charles Gutenson and Mike Slaughter, in *Hijacked*, argue similarly.[10]

Numerous evangelical leaders are now expressing sellers' remorse for having sold churches to a partisan political ideology and are backing away from such partisan political involvement. But churches that simply say nothing let the media keep stereotyping us. We are in more than a scandal; we are doing serious damage to the gospel. Theological vacuousness on the left in a social and media context of domination by partisan stereotypes on the right is not serving the gospel well either. Many progressive churches do not seem to be delivering a strongly grounded theological-ethical message that connects life's challenges with a deep gospel message. Many churches are in crisis—either of unfaithfulness to the way of Jesus, of losing members, or both.

Deeper Grounding in a Thicker Jesus

I sense that a significant change is happening toward deeper grounding in a thicker understanding of Jesus and more explicit loyalty to Jesus' way. This can be seen in books by Shane Claiborne and Jonathan Wilson Hartgrove of the New Monasticism, in Scot McBride's *A New Vision for Israel* and his *Jesus Creed*, and in Jim Wallis's recent book, *On God's Side*. Will Samson (chapter 4) identifies twelve practices in the New Monasticism, including "intentional formation in the way of Christ," but Samson does not explain what that means. He does quote Shane Claiborne: "What seems clear to me is that...thirty years ago there was this growing movement of the Moral Majority and the religious right...and that became increasingly a disconnect for a lot of Christians, especially young Christians, that felt like, wow, where did this come from and why is it so specialized in its hot button issues that Jesus spoke very little about." It is symbolized by *Newsweek*'s cover article by Andrew Sullivan on April 2, 2012: "Forget the church. Follow Jesus." "Follow Jesus" was in dramatically large print, was symbolized by an artist's rendering of Jesus, and was the emphasis of the article. "Forget the church" was in much smaller print and was not the theme of the article, but the comments I saw by two evangelical leaders put all their emphasis on defending the church and failed to celebrate the turn to Jesus.

I see the shift to deeper understanding of what it means to follow Jesus happening widely—well beyond the New Monasticism. I think it is deeply important in the new evangelical engagement. Evangelicals had preached Paul much more than the Jesus of the Gospels. This is changing dramatically for young adults now and for the authors they are reading or listening to.

Beyond the examples we see in some of the chapters here, Eddie Gibbs and Ryan Bolger studied over one hundred emerging churches that are attracting mostly young adult evangelicals.[11] These churches share three core practices: First, "identify with the life of Jesus (and embody the kingdom)." Second, "transform secular space rather than accepting the modern split between sacred and secular," and third, "live in community"—both in the church community and the community where we are. These three themes are also in John Howard Yoder, as we saw earlier, and are emphasized by Will Samson. Samson's third theme is "Peacemaking in the midst of violence and conflict resolution within communities along the lines of Matthew 18," which is explicitly identifying with the life of Jesus and embodying the kingdom.

When David Gushee and I began to write our textbook for Christian ethics, *Kingdom Ethics: Following Jesus in Contemporary Context*, our survey of about thirty textbooks across the spectrum from left to right yielded *a total of only six pages* on the ethical implications of Jesus' teaching on discipleship in the Sermon on the Mount. This includes two pages in John Howard Yoder's *Politics of Jesus*, a model for taking the way of Jesus seriously, but even Yoder did not focus on the Sermon on the Mount because of the widespread biases among ethicists against emphasizing the sermon because of its misinterpretation by the long reach of Platonic idealism, rendering it "impossible ideals" or "hard teachings." The Sermon on the Mount is the largest block of Jesus' teaching in the New Testament and the most cited New Testament passage in Christian writings of the first two centuries. Gushee and I decided something is very wrong and worked to remedy that in our textbook, which is enjoying wide use. Things are changing. Now we can count ten Christian ethics textbooks from Catholic and various Protestant denominations that take the way of Jesus seriously.

Significant help is coming from recent scholarship:

1. Greater attention to Jesus' Jewish roots by numerous scholars and greater freedom from the anti-Semitism of early-twentieth-century scholarship are giving us better theology than the old liberal individualist and rationalist biases about Jesus.
2. A spate of studies of the historical Jesus, despite some flaws, are being widely read and giving us a thicker understanding of Jesus' historical context and his interaction with that context.
3. Studies indicating Jesus' more extensive interaction with the prophet Isaiah result in a deeper understanding of the implications of Jesus' teachings and actions.
4. Growing awareness that those Christian leaders who have stood the historical test during the Third Reich, the civil rights movement's struggle against racism, the struggle against economic greed and injustice, and the nonviolent revolution that toppled the Berlin Wall and the East German dictator, Honecker, all had an ethic characterized by a thicker Jesus, opposition to the split between private Christianity and public ethics, and a call for repentance from being hijacked by unfaithful ideologies.
5. Steadily growing attention to the theological ethics of Dietrich Bonhoeffer, with his Christ-centered, holistic, prophetic witness, provides faithful theological grounding for participative grace that includes following Jesus.

This is what I am arguing in my recent book, *A Thicker Jesus: Incarnational Discipleship in a Secular Age* (Westminster John Knox, 2012).

A *Thicker Jesus* Provides the Basis for Engaged Evangelicals

We can see evidence of this new basis for evangelical engagement in many of this book's chapters. David Swartz and John Schmalzbauer both incisively call attention to the increasing emphasis of engaged evangelicals on human rights, with global influence. This connects with a major strand of American tradition—the Preamble of the Constitution and the Bill of Rights, Abraham Lincoln and Martin Luther King Jr. It also connects with Jesus' confrontations of the powerful of his day for their injustices to the poor and marginalized.

Laurel Kearns writes perceptively of the power of symbolic framing in the struggle for caring for the creation and against destroying the earth. When we realize how deeply Jesus' teachings were in dialogue with the prophet Isaiah, we frame care of the creation more deeply in basic Christian loyalties. Again and again, Isaiah emphasized that God the Creator is active in doing new things in our midst. God's present action became central in Jesus' core proclamation of the reign of God. Jesus often taught of God's reign in parables of the growth of seeds, of rocky versus fertile soil, of care for birds and flowers, of the gift of rain and sunshine to the just and unjust alike. Seeing Jesus as dialoguing with Isaiah alerts us to recover a live sense of God's direct and immediate involvement in caring for the creation. When we recover this Jesus, thickly rooted in the prophet Isaiah, Christians have dramatic framing for caring for the creation that God cares deeply about. The creation is an ongoing gift from God and must not be consumed and destroyed in our generation and the next so that future generations have a drastically depleted earth to live on.

Stephen Warner writes of an outcry against economic injustice. Jim Wallis and Sojourners, as well as Ron Sider and Evangelicals for Social Action, are bringing a strong outcry against economic injustice, and they are strongly committed to a thicker Jesus. The chapters by Warner and John Green suggest the value of dropping conservative rhetoric against homosexuality and contraception and instead becoming consistently prolife. In the Gospels, homosexuality was not a theme that Jesus said anything against. But a central theme in his actions and teaching was welcoming the powerless and excluded, women, children, the poor, the lepers, the tax collectors, prostitutes, and even Gentiles and eunuchs into community. In this also he was affirming a theme in the prophet Isaiah. Jesus was consistently prolife, told his disciples that when rumors of war come they should not participate in the war but flee to the hills, wept over Jerusalem because they did not know the practices that make for peace, fed the hungry, and was given the death penalty unjustly, but he never mentioned contraception, homosexuality, or even abortion—though I am consistently prolife on that also. Thus recovering a thicker Jesus fits what Warner and Green are suggesting.

Brian Steensland and Philip Goff, as well as others, point out that many new evangelical activists see the need for structural change, in addition to change in individual practices. As Gushee and I point out, Jesus confronted the structural powers—Sadducees, scribes, Pharisees, the wealthy—thirty-seven times in the synoptic Gospels, and that is why they conspired to get him crucified. In *A Thicker Jesus*, I propose an interpretation of the cross that makes that clear.

Gerardo Marti and Michael Emerson write accurately on overcoming racism as important to many young evangelicals, which fits my experience. And it also finds grounding in Jesus as interpreted thickly in his own Jewish context. Willie Jennings's and J. Cameron Carter's recent books (*Christian Imagination* and *Race*) have both diagnosed the historic roots of racism in anti-Semitism, in interpretations of Jesus devoid of Jesus' own roots in Jewish and prophetic tradition. They are saying that recovering a thicker Jesus deeply rooted in Jewish tradition, who entered incarnationally into the context of diverse others, including Samaritans, lepers, a Roman centurion, and Hellenists in Galilee, is crucial for overcoming racism theologically. If we think of African American and Latino involvement, we need to think of a stronger emphasis on living the way of Jesus. Unlike whites, blacks had no need to thin Jesus down so he could fit into a lifestyle that supported slavery and segregation.

As Dietrich Bonhoeffer testified that he first became an actual Christian in the year that he was engaging deeply in Abyssinian Baptist Church in Harlem, and then wrote his most widely read book, *Discipleship*, on Jesus' ethic in the Sermon on the Mount, I also testify as an evangelical that much of my own impetus to recover a thicker Jesus has come from my experience of African American Baptist churches, including Canaan Baptist Church of Christ in Harlem, where the pastor was Wyatt Tee Walker—Martin Luther King Jr.'s executive director. I am saying that the new Reformation needs to be strongly rooted theologically and ethically in Jesus Christ as Savior and Lord, as revelation of God's action to deliver us. It needs to be characterized by our participation in kingdom breakthroughs—following Jesus, thickly, as Bonhoeffer and King sought to do.

NOTES

1. David E. Campbelland Robert D. Putnam, "God and Caesar in America: Why Mixing Religion and Politics Is Bad for Both," Foreign Affairs 91:2 (March–April 2012): 34–43.
2. Michael Walzer, *Political Action: A Practical Guide to Movement Politics* (Chicago: Quadrangle Books, 1971).
3. Described in "How Just Peacemaking Got Rid of the Missiles in Europe," chapter 5 of my *Just Peacemaking: Transforming Initiatives for Justice and Peace* (Louisville, KY: Westminster John Knox, 1992).

4. Glen Stassen and Lawrence Wittner, *Peace Action: Past, Present, and Future* (Boulder, CO: Paradigms, 1997).

5. See www.justpeacemaking.org.

6. Sojourners Board of Directors Retreat Book (November 15–17, 2012), 23–25.

7. Yoder's influence is seen in Ervin Stutzman's book on the evolution of Mennonite witness, *From Nonresistance to Justice* (Scottdale, PA: Herald Press, 2011).

8. David Kinnaman and Gabe Lyons, *Unchristian: What a New Generation Really Thinks about Christianity—and Why it Matters* (Grand Rapids, MI: Baker, 2007), 15, 24, 27, and 46–47.

9. Campbell and Putnam, "God and Caesar in America," 42, 40.

10. Mike Slaughter and Charles E. Gutenson, *Hijacked: Responding to the Partisan Church Divide* (Nashville, TN: Abingdon, 2012).

11. Eddie Gibbs and Ryan K. Bolger, *Emerging Churches: Creating Christian Community in Postmodern Cultures* (Grand Rapids, MI: Baker, 2005). See also Ryan K. Bolger, ed., *The Gospel after Christendom* (Grand Rapids, MI: Baker, 2012).

Index

Note: Material in figures or tables is indicated by italic page numbers. Endnotes are indicated by n after the page number.

female evangelicals. *See* young
   evangelical women
Fernando, Ajith, 56
Flourish, 158, 170
Food for the Hungry, 246, 247, 248
Ford, Leighton, 274
foreign policy, evangelical public
   opinion, *134*, 135–136
FORMED (emerging evangelical
   curriculum)
  campus ministries and, 35–37, 40
  combined personal and public
   transformation, 38, 40, 41, 42,
   47, 285
  curriculum, 38–42
  house churches and, 35–36, 40, 41,
   43, 44, 45–46
  individualist *vs.* structural logic,
   37–38
  monthly events, 40–42
  monthly prayer book, 40
  monthly vows, 38–40, 285, 289
  Norwood, Ohio, 35, 41, 48n15
  tension with late modern temporality,
   42–45
  See also emerging evangelicalism
For the Health of the Nation: An
   Evangelical Call to Civic
   Responsibility
  environmental concerns, 162
  expanded sociological vision, 11–12
  NAE turn toward the new
   evangelicalism, 3
  references to the common good, 89
  seven areas of public involvement, 10
  statement on social engagement,
   9–10
  structural language in, 12, 234, 254
  suffering as a theological theme, 79
  See also National Association of
   Evangelicals

Fuller, Charles, 243–244
Fuller Theological Seminary, 244, 283,
   295–296

Gallagher, Sally K., 110, 116
Gallagher, Sharon, 270
Generous Justice, 3, 64
global poverty
  advocacy-related education
   programs, 256
  advocacy work by NGOs, 12, 242,
   246–248, 249, 256
  comparison of evangelical and
   fundamentalist movements, 243
  definitions of poverty, 249,
   259n32
  development organization funding
   from donors, 248, 251–252,
   260n44
  development-related education
   programs, 255
  development strategies of NGOs, 12,
   242, 244–246, 248–251
  evangelical attitudes toward
   reforming structures,
   252–254
  individualist *vs.* structural realities,
   252–254
  megachurch efforts to combat
   poverty, 253–254
  ONE Campaign efforts against, 55
  relief efforts by NGOs, 12, 242,
   243–244
  and short-term mission (STM) trips,
   254–255
  and transformational development
   theory, 246, 249–250, 253–254,
   255, 256
  See also international evangelicals;
   nongovernmental organizations
Goff, Philip, 31, 292, 302

YMCA, 57–58
Yoder, John Howard, 57, 101, 298, 300
young evangelicals, general
  disengagement from politics, 117–118
  evangelical millennials, 109–111
  increasing acceptance of gay
    marriage, 16
  intergenerational tensions, 109–110,
    111
  millennials and evangelicalism,
    109–111
  political activism, 109, 111
  and Religious Right, 109, 117,
    118–119
  return to social activism in the 1970s,
    8, 16, 111
  support for Democrats in 2008, 19,
    50, 65n4, 117
  tolerance for gays and lesbians,
    16, 214
  See also campus ministries; New
    Monasticism; Urbana student
    missions conference
young evangelical women

and authenticity, 122
church shopping, 122
disengagement from politics,
  117–118
gender identity negotiations, 110,
  116–117, 119, 125–126
and "ideal Christian woman,"
  115–116, 124
identity construction, 14, 111–117,
  124–126
"I'm evangelical but not *that* type of
  evangelical," 112–114, 275
intergenerational tensions, 109–110,
  112–114, 120–121, 123–124
new spirituality of seeking, 122
and Religious Right, 111, 118–119
second-wave feminist issues,
  114–116
servant-activism in the church in
  New York City, 121–126
servant-activist identities, 117–121
and social justice, 113, 123–124
"woman's submission," 115–117, 202
Youth for Christ movement, 267